PRINTS, POSTERS
& PHOTOGRAPHS
Identification and Price Guide

PRINTS, POSTERS & PHOTOGRAPHS

Identification and Price Guide

FIRST EDITION

SUSAN THERAN

The CONFIDENT COLLECTOR™

AVON BOOKS ◆ NEW YORK

96 8208

Important Notice: The artists' prices in this price guide are based on the Auction Index, Inc., database. All of the information, including valuations, has been compiled from the most reliable sources, and every effort has been made to eliminate errors and questionable data. Nevertheless the possibility of error in a work of such scope always exists. Neither the author nor the publisher will be held responsible for losses which may occur in the purchase, sale, or other transaction of items because of information contained herein. Readers who feel they have discovered errors are invited to *write* the author in care of Avon Books, so the errors may be corrected in subsequent editions.

THE CONFIDENT COLLECTOR: PRINTS, POSTERS & PHOTOGRAPHS (1st edition) is an original publication of Avon Books. This edition has never before appeared in book form.

AVON BOOKS
A division of
The Hearst Corporation
1350 Avenue of the Americas
New York, New York 10019

Copyright © 1993 by Auction Index, Inc.
Front cover photograph by Jasper Johns/VAGA, New York, 1992
Back cover photograph, *In Search of Times Past*, courtesy of Christie's with permission from Mrs. Joella Bayer
The Confident Collector and its logo are trademarked properties of Avon Books.
Published by arrangement with the author
Library of Congress Catalog Card Number: 93-11043
ISBN: 0-380-77161-6

Library of Congress Cataloging in Publication Data:

Theran, Susan.
  Prints, posters and photographs identification and price guide / Susan Theran.
    p. cm.
  1. Art—Prices. 2. Art—Collectors and collecting. I. Title.
N8675. T49   1993   93-11043
760'.075—dc20   CIP

First Avon Books Trade Printing: October 1993

AVON TRADEMARK REG. U.S. PAT. OFF. AND IN OTHER COUNTRIES, MARCA REGISTRADA, HECHO EN U.S.A.

Printed in the U.S.A.

ARC 10 9 8 7 6 5 4 3 2 1

Acknowledgments

There are due many thanks to the people who have helped this book come into being . . .

A thank you to Dorothy Harris, whose genuine professionalism and support has, as always, made the creation of this book a pleasure.

A special thank you to Norma Steinberg for being my "special tutor" to the world of prints and photographs.

and, thank you:

• to the art experts who contributed articles for this book: Robert Braun, Pamela Foster, Tony Fusco, Daile Kaplan, Rona Schneider, Norma Steinberg, and Reba Williams.

• to the many libraries and museums throughout the country who provided their services and information, and most especially to the librarians at the Boston Public Library's Fine Arts Department for their ongoing help and support.

• to Victor Smith of Datatech, without whose programs and expertise this book would not have been possible.

• to my staff, who worked so tirelessly compiling the database and researching artists: Kathryn Acerbo, Joyce Ananian, Fabia Bird, Katherine Dalton, Kristin Dalton, Andrea Des Jardins, Owen Franklin, Paula Jacoff, Christina Lanzel, Keith Larson, Laura Oppenheimer, Jennifer Schafer, Faye Stark, and Trudy Weinstein.

• and most of all, to my daughters, Sally and Rachel, for their patience, love, and support.

Auction House Acknowledgments

Special appreciation and thanks to the many auction houses who provide catalogs and prices in a timely manner for the Auction Index database. All of these are listed in Appendix C.

Thank you to Mary Lou Strahlendorff of Christie's press office and to Elizabeth Wright of Sotheby's publications department for their assistance in gathering together numerous photographs. And a special thank you to all the auction houses who so generously provided the photographs and some of the stories behind the captions. They are James R. Bakker Galleries, Barridoff Galleries, Frank H. Boos Gallery, Butterfield's, Camden House, Christie's New York, Christie's East, Christie's London, William Doyle Galleries, Dunning's Auction Service, Finarte S.A., Freeman/Fine Arts, Morton M. Goldberg Galleries, Grogan & Company, Arthur James Galleries, James D. Julia Galleries, Phillips Son & Neale, Skinner's Inc., C. G. Sloan & Company, Inc., Sotheby New York, Sotheby Japan, Swann Galleries, Adam A. Weschler & Son, Wolf's Auctioneers, and Young Fine Arts Gallery.

Table of Contents

Introduction

Nearly everyone buys art.

Choosing and collecting fine art is a continuous adventure. Like most adventures, it has ups and downs, moments of exhilaration, and times of absolute frustration. Collecting art sounds like such a serious undertaking that, at the beginning, it can seem daunting. Collecting means different things to different people. For some, it is an occasional excursion to a gallery, auction, or flea market, while for others it becomes a life-long passion which absorbs time, space, energy, and money. Whether your interest is intense or casual, creating a collection is a realistic, reachable goal. How you collect depends on you. There are no rules but your own.

The media hype that accompanies record-breaking auction prices for works of art obscures the fact that there are thousands of works by recognized artists that sell for considerably less than $10,000. For the year 1991-1992 auction season statistics drawn from the Auction Index, Inc., database show that 49% of the prints, posters, and photographs sold at auction sold for less than $1,000, and another 35% sold for between $1,000 and $5,000.

The price ranges in this book are extracted from volume #1 of *Leonard's ANNUAL Price Index of Prints, Posters & Photographs*. Volume #1 covers the period from July 1, 1991, through July 30, 1992; for further information on any citation listed in this book refer to *Leonard's Index*, the parent volume.

The art market keeps changing. It has become more sophisticated and competitive at every level. Now, more than ever, the well-informed buyer has the edge. Good luck as you use this book to find and buy the works you are seeking.

Look Before You Leap

You've probably already taken many of the first steps that culminate in collecting. Most of us begin to develop an interest in fine art by visiting museums. There is no better place to start—the phrase "museum quality" denotes the highest standard of workmanship. Museums with extensive collections provide exposure to an encyclopedic variety of styles and artistic media. Smaller museums, especially those with specialized collections, provide an opportunity to study a particular aspect of art in depth.

In every case, museum going will help you develop your own eye for quality. Examine the individual works carefully. Analyze their composition. How does the artist lead you into the work? Are you made to focus on the foreground and then drawn farther back? Are you led immediately to a particular point on the image? What are the primary lines of composition? How are light and shadow achieved? What did the artist set out to accomplish? Does it tell a story? If it is a portrait, does it convey personality? It is the ability of works of art to spark these questions that contributes to their quality. Your ability to respond to them is an indication of your growing understanding of what quality means in art.

At the same time, you will be sharpening your taste and defining your preferences. Is your eye drawn to particular subjects? Do you like still lifes? Landscapes? Animals? Domestic interiors? Abstract shapes? Do you like looking at pictures of activities you enjoy? What kinds of artistic media attract you? Do you like silkscreens? Do you like black and white prints? Do you like photographs? A few leisurely afternoons in a museum will help you make such determinations.

Galleries offer a way of learning about the works of individual artists. Owners are generally knowledgeable and most have chosen to sell art because they love it. Keep in mind, however, that galleries are governed by the realities of the marketplace. Many, but by no means all, are willing to take the time to help educate potential customers and share their often specialized and unique information. Most collectors agree that the very best galleries are the ones that will take the time to educate, confident that their investment in time will ultimately show a return in sales.

Classes, courses, lectures, and workshops offered by museums and historical societies afford additional opportunities to learn. Frequently, individual lectures are planned to coincide with annual or semi-annual exhibits and shows. Since smaller institutions often cannot afford to advertise, you will have to call for information or watch local newspaper "calendars" for announcements.

Above all, you must read—art books, magazines, exhibition catalogs, and auction catalogs. When, after conscientious museum going and gallery visits, you determine you are seriously interested in, for example, WPA artists, and want to begin collecting this 20th-century group, your next stop is the library. What was the Works Progress Administration? Who were the artists who participated in this program? What kinds of art did they create? By doing your own research, you'll pull together the bits of information gleaned from museum labels and dealers and begin to assemble a composite body of data. You don't need to be an expert before you begin to buy art—the learning process is continuous. If you're like most collectors, once you've been drawn into a subject, you'll want to learn more and more.

Thorough knowledge and study lay the groundwork for serious collecting. Anyone who builds a valuable collection has worked hard, studying and learning.

Developing Your Taste

The best way to begin is by buying.

Buy what you can afford. Buy in little shops. Buy in junk shops. Buy in antique shops, flea markets, and at low-priced auctions. But buy!

Nothing else shapes your eye so quickly. Nothing sharpens your taste like making a purchase. In making a financial commitment, you make a statement of your likes and dislikes. It is a process subject to constant refinement.

What catches your eye?

Will the first item in your collection be a scene that you recognize, something that evokes a feeling or memory which you want to preserve? For many people, collecting starts with something very specific that is tied to a strong personal interest and then extends and develops. Many real or armchair sailors collect maritime scenes. Gardeners often are drawn to pictures of flowers. Mountain scenes are popular with many collectors.

Discovering what you really like is akin to stripping paint from a piece of old furniture. As you work through to the essence of your taste, you will reveal successive layers of appreciation for different types of work. In the process, you will refine your taste—and you may end up selling some of your early acquisitions.

But, begin by buying. Don't be afraid to make mistakes.

In the course of building a collection you will develop a consistent eye. That is, over time you will find everything you buy fits together. Buying will enable you to develop a sureness of taste, and the confidence of your own judgments.

Where to Buy Art

Buying art is somewhat less straightforward than buying a washing machine, but it's more absorbing and more fun. The sheer variety of places in which you can look and the process of looking are at once an education and an activity in themselves.

Yard Sales, Garage Sales, and Flea Markets

Yard sales, garage sales, and flea markets are a boon to weekend collectors. Someone we know who has a phenomenal memory for artists' names has been very successful (and very lucky) at turning up pictures that others have cleaned out of their attics. If your personal database is less complete this book is a reliable substitute.

The first rule for getting to any of these sales is *be early.* Most flea markets advertise in the classified section of local newspapers and list their hours. (Some open at dawn.) Often dealers will sell right out of their cars to early arrivals even before they've had a chance to set up their displays. One word of caution—"early birds" aren't always welcome, particularly at garage sales. But it may be worth the risk of a chilly reception on the chance that you'll catch the proverbial worm.

At a flea market you'll find most old prints, posters, and photographs in the antiques or magazine section. Check a map of the field when you arrive, since some markets divide dealers' merchandise into old and new, and you can waste a great deal of time trudging past racks of bubble gum and shoelaces before you find the right area. But don't overlook the "junk" area. Some of the best buys may be in the section reserved for sellers who have just cleaned out their attics or garages and don't know what they have.

Some flea markets are held regularly, even weekly. Others are occasionally sponsored by service groups, churches, or fraternal organizations.

The queen of the flea markets is held three times a year (May, July, and September) in Brimfield, Massachusetts. Thousands of dealers set up their displays on acres of fields for this event that attracts purchasers not only from the Northeast but from the entire nation and abroad. Some European dealers buy a year's stock at Brimfield.

One veteran Brimfield connoisseur recommends arriving before dawn. The show opens at 5:00 A.M. and the line begins to form two hours earlier. "Carry a flashlight," she advises, so you can see what's displayed on the tables, and spot the dealers walking around carrying signs that read, "I buy penknives," or "I buy old cameras." Take the time to savor the unique character of this enormous show, which includes the spectacle of pairs of collectors or dealers who race from one display to the next, using walkie-talkies to announce finds to their partners.

Brimfield runs for a week—you may find the very best buys if you're there before first light, but good quality material is on sale all day long. Brimfield is a joy for collectors, and a good place for dealers as well. Many of them save unique pieces to bring to this market, which attracts thousands of sophisticated purchasers.

Other noteworthy flea markets around the nation include the annual indoor event at the Atlantic City Convention Center conducted each March by the Brimfield Association.

Reminger's #1 Antique Market is a Pennsylvania institution. Held every Sunday year round in Adamstown, this indoor/outdoor spectacular welcomes over 500 dealers each week in its indoor space. In good weather, hundreds more open their stands outdoors. Antiques and collectibles are the mainstay here.

Unbeknownst to most sports fans, the Pasadena Rose Bowl hosts a different sort of competition on the second Sunday of every month. At the Rose Bowl Flea Market and Swap Meet nearly anything is sold and bought by thousands of sellers and shoppers.

Flea markets and garage and yard sales are fun to go to, and great places to buy. They are good sources for paintings, prints, posters, photographs . . . and fakes. Chances are strong that the print you find signed "Picasso" is not an original or was signed by someone other than Pablo. You might, however, find an original of a more obscure artist. Always examine a print with a magnifying glass: a pattern of small dots means that it is a photomechanical reproduction and not an original print.

When you decide to buy at a flea market, yard, or garage sale, examine the condition of the work carefully. Flea market merchandise is sold "as is." Usually it's helpful to ask where the work came from—that is, attic, basement, or Aunt Gertrude. Most sellers know something about what they're selling, and though there won't be a provenance (history) supplied for a picture at a yard sale, there may well be an interesting story attached to it.

The rule of purchase at yard sales and flea markets is *make an offer*. There is usually little science, knowledge, or reason for the price written on the tag. Be ready to negotiate.

One final note.

Don't go to any of these sales expecting to find a lost masterpiece. When you buy, buy because you are drawn to the work, because it appeals to you, because it is consistent with the things you like and own, and because you can afford it.

Second Hand, Junk, and Consignment Stores, and Antique Shops

One step up from garage sales and flea markets (and sometimes a very short step indeed) is browser's paradise—second hand, junk, and consignment shops. With growing numbers of people in the art market, there's more competitive shopping in these stores than before, but there are still finds. Often the owners of these emporia will pick up stray prints, drawings, posters, or photographs in the process of acquiring an estate or cleaning out a garage or attic. Art may be almost hidden in many of these stores. Ask if there are any pictures. Look under tables and behind furniture.

Antique stores are another good source. It's hard to be knowledgeable about everything. Store owners may be expert about furniture but unaware of the value of a picture they have bought. They may have purchased a picture in order to acquire an entire estate and be willing to sell at minimal profit to move it, because they specialize in another field.

Wherever you are, look for frames. Good period frames are hard to find. In fact, there are now auctions just for frames! Even if you don't like the picture, the frame may be just what you need for your picture at home.

Dealing with Dealers

A first trip to a big-city gallery can be intimidating. The imposing front entrance and glacial sales staff can combine to keep beginning collectors at a distance. Yet the same people won't hesitate for a second to get out of the car at a country antiques store and ask if there are any pictures in the back room. It's a mistake to assume that a country dealer in a flannel shirt is any less knowledgeable about value and quality than his Madison Avenue or Newbury Street counterpart, or that his prices will be lower. The overhead will be higher in the city, and that will affect prices, but a higher turnover may enable a city gallery to work on a lower profit margin.

Some collectors who are just starting out may hesitate to visit dealers, for they're convinced this is the most expensive way to purchase, or concerned that they'll be pushed into something they really don't want. Others wouldn't begin to look for a work of art without the guidance of a professional.

The International Fine Print Dealers Association holds their annual show each November in New York City. This is the major U.S. print fair of the year with over 100 exhibition booths. Prices range from $50 to $50,000. Attending the fair is an excellent way to meet dealers from all over the country. In March, The Association of International Photography Art Dealers holds their show; over 90 dealers exhibit every type of photography. The location varies so contact the Association (202-986-0105) for the locale.

If, in fact, you end up developing a very serious interest in collecting, you'll become an expert in the area that interests you. When you walk into a tiny up-country store and spot a small dirty print that looks promising, you'll have the knowledge you need to examine it carefully and decide if you want to add it to your collection.

Should that happen when you're just starting out, and it's a small purchase, go ahead and buy it. As long as the work really appeals to you, there's no such thing as a $50 error. But imagine a different scenario in which the price tag is substantially higher, and you really don't know whether the work is fairly priced, or even authentic. (Of course, you'll have this book in hand, and that will give you confidence and credibility if you decide to negotiate the price.) That's a compelling reason for making major purchases from dealers. Until, and even when, you develop your own store of knowledge, they are the professionals.

A good dealer knows an artist's work and style, can authenticate it, and can recognize the quality of the impression. Experienced dealers know a lot about the process of making art, and the scholarly and technical aspects of art history.

Works completed during certain periods of an artist's life are worth more than others. Martin Lewis is well known for his drypoints of city street scenes but he also did prints of the Holocaust. Lewis's night scenes of city streets will bring a premium price; prints of the Holocaust are relatively inexpensive. There are other nuances to a print or photograph which will change its value. If the artist worked in a realistic style during much of his career, but later became more impressionistic, the pictures from different periods will have differing values. If, in a particular picture, an artist introduced an element which later became characteristic of his work, that image will have special or added value. Printmakers didn't hand-sign their prints until the late 19th century. If an 18th-century print is hand-signed in pencil the signature is a fake. Many photographers chose not to sign their works on the image, but stamped or signed them on the reverse so that they didn't disturb the aesthetic balance of the work. This is the type of specialized information for which you will turn to a dealer.

In addition to being a storehouse of knowledge, a dealer can be extremely helpful in locating the kind of work you find most appealing, particularly if your taste is very specialized. Once you've developed a relationship with a dealer, he or she will buy with you in mind and be able to sell to you with a lower markup because there will be a quicker turnover. An ongoing relationship with a reputable dealer is a good way to assure access to quality work. Every serious collector has a good working relationship with at least a few dealers. It's true that you may pay more when you buy from a dealer than you might at an auction, but you're paying for knowledge and time.

Note, too, that most dealers will generally not sell a print unless it has been cleaned and matted and, if needed, restored by a competent professional restorer. This can save both time and money for a collector.

The key question is, how do you find a dealer with whom you'll be comfortable? There are literally hundreds of galleries, shops, and dealers in most areas. Consult the *Art in America Gallery Guide,* available on newsstands in August and in many libraries. In larger cities you can begin by looking through the yellow pages, the gallery listings in newspapers and magazines, weekly calendar supplements, and even guidebooks. In smaller areas where galleries are dispersed, dealers often form regional associations and publish a listing of members and a map showing their locations. These are available in the stores, or at local, state-sponsored tourist information centers.

Galleries may specialize. Visit as many as you can until you find those dealers whose taste is very much like your own, and begin to cultivate a working relationship. Put your name on their mailing list so that you will be invited to previews and kept informed about publications.

Networking and talking with other collectors is essential. Talk to people at auctions. You may get to discover dealers you'd never meet otherwise because they don't generally sell to the public.

Terms

The term *dealer* covers such a broad range of operations that it will be useful to distinguish among the various types who operate at all different levels of the art market. On the very first rung of the ladder are *pickers*, people with good eyes, developed taste, and eternal optimism. They scour flea markets, yard sales, and country auctions, always on the lookout for the underpriced, unrecognized "find." Pickers have established relationships with lawyers representing estates, dealers, galleries, and individual collectors. They buy and sell to their contacts.

Then there are *door knockers.* The name says it all. Door knockers are a variety of picker who go door to door in search of old paintings, rugs, and furniture to resell to dealers or through auction houses.

Runners are the matchmakers, the link between dealers, or between dealers and collectors. A very few who work the upper end of the market are essentially private dealers who make a handsome commission on costly works of art. Most live a far less glamorous existence, moving individual pieces from one dealer to the next, hoping to make a quick sale and a small profit. *Brokers* are a more elite version of runners, often relying on a large circle of acquaintances to keep up to date about what's for sale and who might be looking. Brokers never actually own any work (although they may take a piece on consignment). They direct their energies instead to bringing buyer and seller together.

Wholesalers don't maintain a retail space, but work directly with galleries rather than individual collectors.

Collector dealers start as collectors, but become so involved with their interest that they sell parts of their collections in order to "feed their habits" and upgrade or diversify their holdings.

Strategies

The term *dealer,* as it is usually used, means an individual who owns and runs a shop or gallery. But the word is so inclusive that it covers everything from an exquisitely decorated world famous gallery which commands instant name recognition to the tiniest, most crowded, backstreet junkstore.

But . . . the range of dealers really runs the gamut from part-time entrepreneurs who do business out of the trunks of their cars, on up. Some limit their activities and participate only in shows. Some will see clients only by appointment.

With this variety, it is clear that no single strategy of dealing with dealers will work in all situations. What follows is the composite of advice from a number of dealers, collectors, and personal experience.

On your first visits to a dealer or gallery, you should make your interests and intentions clear. Establish yourself. Let the owner or salesperson know why you've come in. Are you there to learn or to buy? Do you know what you like? (This can be a particularly important question if you're in a major gallery. Some have enormous inventories, literally hundreds of prints or photographs. It's no time to start trying to define your taste.)

Are you buying for visual and aesthetic pleasure? Are you buying for decoration—a colorful print for your family room? Or, are you buying for investment?

Know what your price range is, and state it, but don't be afraid to look at things you can't afford. Consider it another step in honing your eye and developing your own standards of taste by correlating quality and price.

Authenticity

One of the basic challenges in evaluating a print is the determination of its authenticity. Keen eyes, an 8-10 power magnifying glass, a strong light, a millimeter tape measure, and definitive documentation are essential tools when examining prints. Terms that are important to know are original, copy, restrike, facsimile, and reproductive print.

An original print was produced by or under the direct supervision of the artist. The best way to determine authenticity is by comparing your print to another. Many museums and libraries have print rooms for use by students, scholars, collectors, and members. Make an appointment. Look for watermarks and collector's marks. On an original print you may be able to discern the raised lines of an etching, drypoint, or mezzotint. Examine the quality of the lines. Comparing your print to the museum's will indicate the difference in quality and tell you something about the desirability of your print.

A copy is a replica of the original. These can be hard to differentiate; if possible try to compare two images. Sometimes the copy may have been made by the same artist, usually using the same method.

A restrike is a later printing using the original plate. Rembrandt died in 1669; in the 18th century an etcher named Basan bought a number of Rembrandt's plates. Basan reworked the plates, adding new lines and making deeper grooves in some of the existing lines. Prints from Basan restrikes are available for sale at reasonable prices. But only those prints executed during Rembrandt's lifetime are truly authentic.

A facsimile is a photomechanical reproduction of a print. This process generally produces an image that appears relatively lifeless, crude or grainy. Examining the print with a magnifying glass you may be able to discern a pattern of small dots.

A reproductive print is an original print that is a copy of a painting or drawing. J.M.W. Turner and William Hogarth, 17th- and 18th-century artists, had their paintings popularized by reproductive engravings. After the invention of the camera reproductive prints were rare.

Examine a print closely. Always ask to see it out of the frame and look at the front and back closely with a magnifying glass. With the aid of a lens you can see a watermark, platemark, or collector's mark. Look to see if all the lines on the front are carried through to the back; if not this may be a sign that the image has been retouched. Late impressions of Old Master prints may have been touched with India ink or watercolors to simulate the burr or the rich inking of early impressions. If there is a catalogue raisonné for the artist check the image, edition number and the size. A catalogue raisonné will give the size for a known print. Paper may shrink, but variations in excess of a centimeter are very questionable. It is common for many Old Master prints to be trimmed to the platemark or border. Wide margins became desirable during the last half of the 18th century when, with the availability of cheap glass, prints were often used as wall decoration rather than as scrapbook collections. The best security against fakes is familiarity with the graphic oeuvre of the artist under whose name the print is offered for sale. If you find a watermark or collector's mark there are several standard reference sources. The authoritative source for collector's marks is Lugt's *Les marques de collections de dessins et d'estampes;* Briquet's *Les Filigranes* is a comprehensive listing of watermarks from 1282 until 1600.

Authenticating photographs presents a different set of problems. Witkin's *The Photography Collector's Guide* is an excellent source for researching photographer's signatures and outstanding characteristics. A vintage photograph, or print, is an original; a multiple made directly under the artist's supervision or with his authorization. Many photographs offered for sale are not vintage but printed at a later date; a vintage print is always more valuable. Diane Arbus died at an early age and Neal Selkirk was authorized by the estate to print some of her negatives. An estate printing by Selkirk is identified by the signature of Doon Arbus, her daughter, on the back of the photograph. A vintage print by Arbus, especially a signed print, will sell for considerably more than a later estate print.

The Prints and Photography Division of The Library of Congress has custody of many original negative collections. Modern prints of these negatives can be had for as little as $12; all reprints are stamped on the back "Reproduction from the Collection of the Library of Congress."

Educate yourself by reading. Prints and photographs can be inexpensive and fun to collect. If you find a framed print at a flea market for $40, and you like it and it turns out to be a photomechanical reproduction, enjoy it and learn from your mistake. You haven't broken the bank, you've learned something, and you have a picture that you like.

Provenance

Depending on the level at which you are buying, a print may have a written provenance, a life history from the time it left the artist's workroom to its arrival at the gallery, which includes the names of previous owners and the dates on which it changed hands. Obviously, the better known and more costly the print or photograph the likelier and more necessary the provenance. Not surprisingly, a provenance adds to the value.

You might begin by asking about the picture's history. If the dealer has the estate, he may have the artist's notebook, preliminary sketches for the work (very collectible), or other information. Has the work been in a catalog? Was it included in an exhibit? Has it been awarded any prizes? This may or may not be pertinent to a given work.

A less expensive work may have no written history at all, just the statement of the dealer to the effect that "I bought it from the Smith estate up in Westfield." If you're looking at the work of a relative unknown, this is an acceptable response. The dealer may be able to fill you in on the family that owned the work, the general nature of the estate, and the artist as well.

Negotiating a Price

While the price that a dealer quotes to you is not necessarily the one you'll end up paying, the issue of price negotiations raises questions, eyebrows, and sometimes, tempers.

To negotiate or not to negotiate. Most dealers will insist that they won't. Many buyers will tell you they've tried and sometimes succeeded. If you're embarrassed, don't, but as a general rule of thumb, it's worth a try. Remember that if you can walk away from a potential purchase, there's a far greater chance of getting it at the price you're willing to pay than if you're caught up in the process and dead set on acquiring it.

The possibilities for negotiation depend very much upon the dealer, the gallery, the image, and the realities of the marketplace. Galleries at prestigious addresses in major cities carry enormous overheads which are necessarily reflected in the prices of the art they sell. There is generally a close relationship between the location and prestige of the gallery, the desirability of the print or photograph, and the readiness of the customer to make an offer and the dealer to accept it. This is complicated by the length of time the picture has been in the dealer's possession, and last, but by no means least, by the percentage which it has been marked up.

In other words, if you want to buy a picture which has been in a gallery for only a week, the dealer is not likely to negotiate. If the picture is still on the wall when you come back six months later, it's much more likely that you'll find some flexibility in the price.

Of course, the whole question of negotiation depends upon who you are talking to and where. We know one very genteel lady who successfully bargains at Cartier. While small informal stores which carry a mix of paintings and other things seem to invite bargaining more than others, serious collectors will negotiate anywhere.

Remember, too, that when you question a price, you are at least in part asking why it has been set at a certain level. If it seems especially high, there may be a good reason for it—the work may have some unique quality. Keep in mind as well that some dealers will overprice, expecting to be negotiated down.

Dealers maintain that it is not in their own interest to overprice works of art, since most guarantee that they will take a work back in trade for at least the original price. Most dealers will add that they will not try to outbid an individual collector at auction, since they will later have to resell the piece.

Bear in mind, too, that prices in this *Guide* were achieved at auction, a market that is frequently considered wholesale. It is perfectly reasonable for the dealer who has spent time and money acquiring, and possibly restoring, the work to make a profit on it. Your readiness to make an offer, and the dealer's willingness to be somewhat flexible about pricing, will constitute the negotiation.

Bills of Sale

For major purchases, for purposes of insurance and record keeping, it is important to secure a bill of sale. You can be assured of the authenticity of a work of art if the dealer will write out and *sign* the sales slip to read: "One print, title, *by* Robert Smith, date, size, location of signature, and any other significant details."

If the slip reads: "One print, *signed* Robert Smith" or "One print *inscribed* Robert Smith," or "One print *attributed* to Robert Smith," then the dealer is not liable should the print turn out to be a copy. The terms "bears signature" and "apocryphal signature" are euphemisms for saying the signature is a fake. For prints, the term "lettering" means that there is a printed legend that gives information about the artist, publisher, date, and copyright.

You can be forceful, or you can be innocent and say that your sister the attorney insisted, but always ask for a sales slip that specifically says the work is by the artist. Don't leave the gallery without it.

Methods of Payment

You may find a greater degree of flexibility in price if you can pay cash; however, most people find it more convenient to make major purchases by check.

If you do pay cash, be sure to save your sales slip, since it is the only proof you will have to present to an insurance company in the event of loss.

Some dealers will permit you to pay for a print or photograph in installments, but unless you are a well-established customer, you should not expect to be able to take the work home until it is completely paid for. (However, if you offer to let the dealer keep the print until you finish paying for it, he may let you take it home.)

Auctions

You don't need a course in assertiveness training to bid at an auction. Neither do you need to sit absolutely still while bidding goes on around you, lest an auctioneer mistake some motion as a hidden signal. Auctions are entertaining to attend, and a good way to purchase art.

Terms

As in all specialized fields, there are specific terms used in auctions which you must understand before you begin. The most important, listed alphabetically, are:

Auction. A sale in which the auctioneer, acting as the agent for sellers (called *consignors*), offers a series of objects to prospective buyers who bid incrementally. The highest bidder buys the object. The auctioneer always encourages bidding to try to get the highest price, since his payment is generally a percentage of the sale.

Bought-in (sometimes called passed or unsold). If a lot does not achieve its reserve (see page 13) it is said to be bought-in by the auction house and will be returned to the consignor or be reoffered at a later sale. However, bear in mind that if, on its own momentum, bidding does not reach the reserve, the auction house will bid on behalf of the consignor against bids from the floor. Only if the work still does not reach its reserve is it bought-in. It's not always clear whether there's a reserve on an individual lot. A 1987 New York City law requires the house to announce the disposition of an unsold lot as passed, returned to owner, withdrawn, or bought-in. New York also requires that all lots with a reserve be marked with a black square or dot in the auction catalog.

Buyer's premium. At most auctions, premiums ranging from 10% to 20% of the hammer price are added to the cost of each item. Sales tax and VAT are calculated on the total. An auctioneer who adds a buyer's premium will usually indicate this in advertisements or catalogs.

Catalog sale. An auction for which a printed listing of lots is prepared and distributed in advance. Catalogs can be mimeographed lists with brief descriptions or beautifully illustrated, carefully researched, book-length publications.

Consignor. The individual who has asked the auction house to sell a particular piece or pieces.

Estimate. The price range within which an auction house expects to sell a particular lot. The estimate is included in the printed catalog. Reserve is usually two-thirds of the low estimate. For more expensive lots, reserve is often close to the low estimate. At best, an estimate is the auctioneer's best judgment based on the artist's sales history, and the condition and desirability of the particular piece.

Hammer price (knockdown). The price at which a lot is sold.

Inspection. See "preview."

Left bid (including mail bids). A bid submitted by a prospective buyer who can't attend the auction. These are executed by the auctioneer or a member of his staff during the sale.

Lot. An individual work or group of works offered for sale at one time.

Paddle. A numbered card which may be anything from an imprinted plastic paddle to a paper plate. It is given to bidders when they register and must be held aloft in order to bid.

Passed. If there is no interest from the floor and no bidding on the lot, it is passed over, and the auctioneer goes on to the next.

Preview (exhibition). The period before a sale reserved for the inspection or viewing of items to be auctioned. In larger auction houses, the preview period may be as long as a week. At smaller sales, the preview may be only the day of the sale. Generally, lots cannot be viewed after the sale starts. However, if it is really impossible to schedule a pre-sale inspection, call the auction house in advance and arrange to see the item when you arrive.

Prices realized. A listing of lots sold and the prices achieved. Some auction houses publish these prices and some do not. They may be published with or without the buyer premium.

Reserve. The lowest price which a consignor will accept for a lot. It is ordinarily used only for high-priced works. The reserve is often two-thirds of the low estimate. At the major houses, the reserve for more expensive prints or photographs is frequently close to the low estimate. If reserve is not reached and the lot is bought-in, the piece may be offered again at a later sale. Reserves are rarely set at country sales, so that sparse attendance, or limited interest, may make it possible to pick up a good buy.

The ring (the pool). An informal agreement among dealers that they will not bid against each other for a specific lot. After the sale they adjourn to the parking lot for a "knockout" in which the lot is sold to one of the dealers in the pool. Each writes down the figure that he or she is ready to pay. The highest bidder ends up with the merchandise, while the others split the difference between the actual purchase price at the auction and the price reached in the post-auction action. Most merchandise sold in this manner leaves the parking lot at the price it should have fetched at the sale. The losers, clearly, are the auction house and the consignor. These activities amount to restraint of trade and are illegal in most states. Curiously, some members of the ring never actually deal in merchandise but manage to make a small living simply by participating. While the ring can be a potent force in controlling prices at an auction, an independent purchaser can beat it. Just set your price and stick to it.

Shill. An individual planted in the crowd by the house or by an individual consignor to bid up the price of a lot. Contracts at most houses forbid the consignor or his agent to bid on the lot he has consigned.

Telephone bid. A bid from someone not attending the auction, who makes advance arrangements with the house to bid actively during the auction. Telephone bidding is generally limited to higher priced works, and at important auctions, there may be a bank of telephones in place for long distance participation. (Not all telephone bidding is long distance. Sometimes, bidders use a pay phone in the auction house so they can bid without being identified.)

Underbidder. The losing bidder.

Withdrawn. A lot removed before the sale begins.

Types of Auctions

Auctions vary widely in the selection, type and quality of artwork they offer. At country auctions mixed offerings are the rule, and they will include furniture, paintings and prints, rugs, bric-a-brac, and assorted collectibles. A woodblock sold at a country auction may have been hanging on the same wall for the past 100 years, or it might be the ten-year-old work of a summer artist. That stained work on paper may be an original watercolor, or it may have been clipped from a magazine and hung in a five and dime store frame.

Some auctioneers assemble a collection for a sale by combining lots from many different households or sources. Be aware that some dealers will consign "hard to sell" merchandise at these sales. Such sales are frequently held in halls and lodges, veterans' posts or fraternal organizations, and may include some paintings, prints, and posters.

Some artwork is usually put on the block at estate auctions, where the entire contents of a house are sold on site, often on a weekday. Estate auctions bring fresh, new, and thus desirable material to the market.

Catalogs

One advantage of buying a work of art at a large auction house is that a great deal of your work has already been done for you. By the time something appears in an auction house catalog, it has already filtered through the first levels of professional assessment.

An auction house catalog, a listing of lots to be sold at a particular auction, can be anything from a mimeographed list to a splendidly printed and illustrated volume that looks a great deal like an expensive art book. A catalog can be a source of valuable information, but it should be read in the context in which it is created. An auction house catalog is a sales tool. It can be glamorous and packed with information, but it is compiled to help the house successfully market a product.

Catalogs, while useful art reference tools, are not definitive sources of information. The fact that a work is listed in a catalog does not legitimize it.

Catalogs are not always scholarly works. They may or may not be written by knowledgeable people. They are not infallible and may contain errors in attribution or authentication.

In reading an art auction catalog, it is important to remember that at the major houses, print and photography catalogs are generally arranged alphabetically or chronologically, rather than in order of importance. Color illustrations often draw the reader's attention. Whether a lot is illustrated or not, or in black and white or in color, does not indicate importance. Remember that most auction houses charge consignors for illustrations, and charge more for color than black and white.

Auction houses list the title of the print or photograph, if known. Otherwise they give a descriptive title. Quotes indicate that the title is known from a label or catalogue raisonné.

A typical catalog description will include the artist's name; the title; whether and where the work is signed; the medium; size and condition; and the price estimate. It may also provide information about the provenance of the work, or literature about the artist. (If you buy a picture at an auction, save the catalog, for it becomes part of the provenance.)

Dropping a title or abbreviating a first name to an initial usually implies doubt. If the catalog description says "bears signature" or "apocryphal signature," the signature is false. When you read the description, be aware that state laws vary, as does the buyback policy or guarantee. Terminology and expertise also vary from house to house.

The same cautions apply to the use of such terms as "school," "school of," "studio of," and "circle of," whether in catalogs or anywhere else. "School of," as in "School of Raphael," is generally applied to the work of students or apprentices who studied with a renowned artist. "Circle of" covers a broader area—the connection is more tenuous, but the work of art may still be very valuable. "After" means a copy of the work of an artist— perhaps by an art student sitting in a museum—at least a hundred years after the original was completed. "Attributed to" indicates that a work is *most probably* by a particular artist even though it is not signed.

Auction catalogs are compiled and published by the major houses six weeks to a few days before the actual sale. In the United States and Britain the art auction market is dominated by two huge New York houses, Sotheby's and Christie's. Together they account for 90% of all catalog lots sold annually and dominate the market. Their specialized sales are scheduled in the same seasons each year: major print sales in the U.S. in November and May and in London in December and June. In Europe the major houses are the Hôtel Drouot in Paris, Villa Grisebach and Hauswedell & Nolte in Germany, Finarte in Italy, Fernando Duran in Spain, and Galerie Kornfeld-Bern in Switzerland. Most auction houses offer catalogs by subscription which assure that you are on the auction house mailing list and will receive their newsletter and notices of forthcoming sales. Prices realized are sent to catalog subscribers several weeks after the sale. Appendix C is a list of the major auction houses. All of them offer some art and sell by catalog or flyer.

Read carefully the "Conditions of Sale" at the front of each catalog, which provides important information on absentee bidding, buyer's premium, establishing credit, shipping, insurance, and storage.

Strategy

One basic ground rule covers all purchasing at all auctions:

NEVER BID ON SOMETHING YOU HAVEN'T LOOKED AT FIRST.

Take advantage of the auction preview. Carefully examine the piece you are interested in. Re-examine it just before the sale begins. Sometimes a piece is damaged during the preview.

Inspect carefully. If you've done your reading and research, you'll be aware of the characteristic styles and signatures of the artists you're interested in. Don't be put off by small signs of wear or damage. Don't be afraid to bid on a dirty print—at least a dirty print hasn't been damaged by an amateur restorer. Most prints can be cleaned. Small holes and tears can be repaired. Stains and acid can be removed from paper. Skilled paper conservators can perform near-miracles.

If you've received a catalog in which a piece is described, but not illustrated, ask the auction house to send a fax or mail a black and white photograph for you to examine. After you've looked at the illustration, know that you're interested enough to buy, but can't possibly attend the preview or the sale and don't want to risk a telephone bid on unseen merchandise, there's still hope. You can arrange with a dealer to bid for you. This method provides a built-in advantage—experience. A firsthand examination by a knowledgeable dealer can help a prospective purchaser decide whether or not to bid. The dealer will preview the painting, check its authenticity, examine its condition, assess its value, and look at the frame. The dealer will then call you from the auction house and discuss overall values, and you will be able to decide whether and how much to bid.

Dealer's commissions will vary for this service. Some charge 5% of the purchase price if they bid successfully for you. Some won't charge if they don't get the painting, but other will ask for a flat fee for time and effort. Fees vary and should be negotiated in advance.

Bidding

To bid in an auction you must secure a number by registering and presenting a valid form of identification, usually a driver's license and major credit card, which will enable the auctioneer to accept your check at the end. If you can't establish a line of credit, you will need to leave your merchandise until your check clears.

Bidding strategy is individual. There are as many different strategies as there are bidders. Some people like to be identified as bidders and others do not. Some prefer to get in early and join the action from the opening bid. Others will follow for a while before jumping in. There's no rule that bidding must begin at the auctioneer's opening figure. However, bidding will occasionally start at that level if the work is very desirable, or if an individual bidder has decided to try to bring action on that particular item to a quick close by getting a psychological jump on others who wanted to start much lower.

Before bidding starts on the lot you are interested in, make sure you know what you think the piece is worth. Keep this *Guide* at hand and remember that there are a number of factors that influence prices. Don't be discouraged by high estimates, for they may be wishful thinking. Write your top price for the lot on your catalog or on a pad of paper. Add 10% to give yourself some flexibility and then add another 15% for the buyer's premium. If there's a state sales tax, calculate that as well. Be sure that your opening bid is below what you're finally willing to pay. Be alert for symptoms of "auction fever," a potentially dangerous disease in which a purchaser decides to pay whatever is necessary to own a particular work.

Be prepared to exceed your own limit, but only a little. If you've decided that you'll spend $500 on a print, and your last bid of $450 was followed by someone else's reluctant $500, go ahead to $550—you may get what you're after.

If you've left a bid with the auctioneer, make it an odd figure, such as $375, and consider giving instructions that will enable him to up to the next level on your behalf. In this way you have an advantage, since the bidding goes up in round increments.

Don't be reluctant to bid against dealers. Unless a dealer is bidding on behalf of a client, he will have to resell the painting to make a profit, so he must begin by buying at a price he can mark up.

If you were hesitant, pulled out of the bidding, and the item you wanted was bought-in because it didn't reach its reserve, you may still be able to purchase it after the auction. Most auction house contracts empower the auction house to sell the consigned lot at its reserve price for up to sixty days after the sale. After consulting the consignor, the auction house may sell the lot below the reserve price.

How to Sell

Art collectors share certain fantasies. One of the most common follows this scenario: the much loved Old Master print that hangs in the front hall, but was inherited from a favorite uncle who lived in a gracious, antique-filled home, turns out to be a very valuable Rembrandt print.

That's the fantasy.

The reality is that every age has produced greater and lesser artists, and that our affection for a work does not enhance its value. Art has no absolute financial value. Value is created in the marketplace. Price is influenced by a variety of factors which include the artist's prestige, whether he is currently in vogue or out of fashion, the rarity of his work, state and condition, previous auction records, size, and subject matter.

When reading auction records be aware of the variables. If multiple impressions of the same image are offered in a sale this will usually have a negative impact on the prices realized for this image. Competition between two collectors, the weather, and the date of the sale are other factors that will also affect the prices realized.

While there are many variables that affect art prices, there are still some fundamental guidelines to follow if you want to sell a work of art.

Begin by ascertaining what you're selling. Do you have a provenance (history of ownership) for the work? Does it have collectors' marks? Where was it bought and when? Is it the work of a listed artist? Is there a catalogue raisonné? Is there a sales history? Check Bénézit and *Leonard's ANNUAL Price Index of Prints, Posters & Photographs.*

Review your decision. Are you sure you want to sell? Do you want to keep the work a little longer, or keep it forever to leave to your family?

If you've decided to sell you should consider the next set of options: you can place the piece at auction, sell it directly to a dealer or consign it on a commission basis.

Selling at Auction

Selling at auction assures maximum exposure to the largest possible audience. An experienced auction house will publicize a sale effectively, hoping to draw a large crowd of bidders on sale day. This is the most likely way to achieve fair market value for a piece, and the sales price becomes a matter of public record.

Most auction houses will be happy to help sell an estate, though the largest may sell only the best pieces themselves, and contract out the remainder. Sotheby's and Christie's will conduct an on-site sale only if the proceeds are expected to exceed $2–$3 million.

Make an appointment with a local auction house, and bring your piece to the in-house art specialist. Or you can send a photograph to one of the New York houses. (Before mailing any material, it's a good idea to call ahead and secure the name of the appropriate department head so that you can direct the materials to the right individual. It also provides a name for follow-up.)

If you send a photograph, include information on artist's name, signature, any inscription, edition number, media, whether mounted or matted, and the best provenance you can supply. Working from a photograph, an expert can give you a tentative value but will almost always have to have the print, poster or photograph in hand to give a firm estimate.

Another approach is to bring the work(s) to an appraisal day which all auction houses hold, either on their premises or as benefits for museums or historical societies. On these occasions, experts assess the value of work brought in and provide a verbal appraisal for a minimal fee.

In any event, try to get at least three appraisals to help ascertain the value of a work. This will help you safeguard against any unscrupulous appraiser who might set an artificially low value on a work and offer to buy it, only to resell it at its real worth.

One cautionary note: avoid having any restoration done on a work you are consigning to auction. Most prints sell better before they are restored. If you think restoration is essential, consult the auction house, and ask for a recommendation. One classic restoration horror story concerns a very valuable Old Master print that was permanently mounted to a board, drastically reducing its value.

If you decide to consign to auction, you will be asked to sign a contract with the auction house. There are a number of standard provisions with which you should be familiar.

Auction houses charge the consignor for insurance, shipping, photographs (for catalogs), handling and the seller's commission. There is a charge, a percentage of the reserve, if the work is bought-in. There is also a withdrawal fee if you change your mind.

Standard commission rates prevail: 20% for lots under $2,000, 15% for lots between $2,000 and $7,500, and 10% for lots above $7,500.

If the fees sound high, they must offset the considerable expenses the house carries—rent, staff, storage, catalog, publicity, overhead, and viewing.

A dealer or appraiser who refers a seller to an auction house may be paid a finder's fee, which is paid by the house out of its commission. The need to pay the fee may limit the house's ability to adjust its commission rates.

But, because flexibility and variability are the rule in the auction world, there is often room to negotiate many of these provisions. If, for example, you agree to the reserve the house suggests, the house in turn may agree to waive the buyback commission. The best rule to remember is to ask every question about costs and procedures that comes to mind. After all, the auction house is there to serve you.

Working with a Dealer

Working with a dealer or a gallery presents two additional options—selling the work directly, or placing it on consignment. The fee in the latter option can range up to 25% of the sale price, or it may be a set commission plus the dealer's costs.

There are good reasons to take a work to a dealer, rather than to auction. Going "private" permits exclusivity. The right dealer may know just the right buyer. The right dealer can show only the work you've sold or consigned, and it won't have to compete with other pieces by the same artist. A good dealer is knowledgeable and can act discreetly. The dealer should be willing to agree that the work be shown only to select clients while consigned for an agreed period of time.

If you want to sell a work directly to a dealer, follow the same steps you would take if you wanted to buy. Call your local museum and ask for a reference. Call the Art Dealers Association Headquarters in New York (212-940-8590) and request a list of members; call the Private Art Dealers Association (PADA), a new organization based in New York at 212-573-6113.

Pick a dealer who specializes in the kind of work you want to sell, and check how long the dealer has been in business. Take the time to check the credentials of any source you use. Try to protect yourself from untrained or self-appointed appraisers.

Trust is essential in this relationship. Some prospective sellers are hesitant about contracting for a commission sale, since it can be difficult to ascertain a final price. If you do choose to work with a dealer, be certain that the conditions of the sale are made explicit in writing at the time that you consign. Ask for a status report within two weeks.

Selling a work of art poses some of the same questions as buying—establishing value, creating a working relationship with a sales agent, whether an auction house or dealer, and investigating the various mechanisms that are needed to achieve a sale. By proceeding thoughtfully and cautiously, you are more likely to achieve the result you hope for.

The Impossible Dream

It happens every year—at least once. The lost work reappears; a locked storage closet in a warehouse is opened; a dusty old canvas is brought out of an attic; an Old Master print surfaces at a garage sale. It is the stuff that dreams are made of.

The odds against making a major find are overwhelming. However, there is always the possibility of turning up something undervalued or unrecognized. And if you succeed, what then?

The first step is to do your basic research. If the picture is signed, perhaps the artist is listed in this book. However, the name alone is not enough to authenticate the work; the signature may have been added to a reproduction or the print or photograph may not be a vintage print. Don't believe something just because it's written down.

Next, have the work appraised. Take the picture to an established dealer or auction house. Most auction houses will give a free verbal appraisal. Get a second opinion.

Some museums hold appraisal days. Call for information. On a typical appraisal day, a museum will assemble outside experts, art specialists from auction houses and galleries, who will tell you who, what, and when, but will not set a dollar value. Charges vary from $5–$12 for a verbal opinion.

Every antique hunter, art collector, or heir to an estate has the dream of finding a proverbial lost treasure. When an appraiser from James Julia's gallery in Maine climbed into the attic of an estate, he discovered a pristine pile of advertising posters. Advertising posters are highly collectible, and this early 1881 poster for E & J Ale was particularly desirable because it featured an early New York Yankees team. Estimated at $4,000–$6,000, it sold for $33,000.

(Anonymous, *E & J Ale Paper Sign*, 20 x 26 inches, James Julia, July 25, 1992, $33,000)

Some charitable organizations or schools occasionally sponsor appraisal days.

Auction houses offer free verbal estimates, by appointment, at their main galleries. They will supplement the information provided by the museum by appraising the work for its "auction" value. Sotheby's and Christie's maintain offices around the country, and there are numerous smaller houses listed in Appendix B. If you can't bring the work in, mail a photograph to the appropriate department of your favorite auction house and ask for an unofficial appraisal. Auction houses are responsive to these inquiries, and will follow up immediately if they think you've made a find.

Get a second opinion, for an appraisal is a highly subjective process and linked to the constant vagaries of the art market.

For everyone who cherishes the dream of making a find, hope is fed by stories like the one about the E & J Burke Ale poster found in an attic in Maine.

Restoration

Great art is undaunted by time, but it can certainly be damaged. An old print may have clipped margins, thin spots, hinge stains, or a mat stain. In most cases, a skilled paper conservator can make the print look almost as good as new.

You should bring the same criteria to deciding whether to purchase a slightly damaged work of art as to one in pristine condition. If the print moves you, and you can afford it, buy it. Overlook *small* physical flaws, because they can be repaired. Restorers can fumigate to destroy mold and insects, clean surface dirt and stains, repair minor tears, holes and creases, flatten creases, and remargin.

There are paper problems that are resistant to restoration. Some adhesives used to glue impressions to an album page or backing sheet may be loosened only at the expense of the print itself. (Muslin or cloth backing of fragile lithographic posters by artists such as Toulouse-Lautrec and Mucha is considered acceptable.) Light causes works on paper to fade and restoration cannot reverse the process. Although the process cannot be reversed, a good restorer can lighten the toning (darkening) of a light-struck print. A bad crease will never disappear entirely, and some color prints cannot be bleached. Get the advice of a restorer or knowledgeable dealer before you purchase a work in poor condition.

A word of caution—restoration is a profession, not a hobby. Cleaning works on paper is not a do-it-yourself job. Restoration, or conservation as it is also called, is a delicate procedure. A restorer has an arsenal of materials and techniques, but the same solvents and materials are available to both highly skilled and inept practitioners. The aim of restoration is to put a print into good condition. An incompetent restorer can flatten and whiten paper and completely devitalize it. Poor restoration can do more damage than the ravages of time.

If you buy a blemished print and can't afford a professional cleaning, leave it alone. Proper restoration is time consuming and expensive, but worth it. It is better to leave a print in the condition in which you bought it, than to have the job done poorly.

Common sense and extra care can help avoid many condition problems. Use clean hands or white gloves when handling a print, avoid pressure-sensitive tapes (scotch tape, masking tape), and always mat your print. Use acid-free board for matting and make sure your framer doesn't dry mount or trim your print. Don't expose a print to extremes of light, humidity or temperature; don't hang a print over a radiator or air conditioner and particularly not over a fireplace or wood stove.

Many prints have survived in an excellent state of preservation because they were seldom framed and displayed but stored in portfolios or boxes. It wasn't until the late 18th century that the advent of cheap glass popularized prints as decorative objects. Papers used today for prints are usually durable and stable. Most connoisseurs would not touch a contemporary print with severe damage, but a rare old print is valued more for its rarity and restoration is considered more acceptable.

It must be noted that there is a significant body of opinion that holds that restoration can destroy the value of a work. For clumsy restoration, or restoration that changes the character of the original, that is undoubtedly true. Choosing the right restorer thus becomes vitally important.

Assume that you have purchased a print that seems lovely beneath the accumulated dirt, but has a small tear on the left side. How do you go about finding a restorer who will do the job well, but not charge an exorbitant price?

The cost of restoration varies widely, as does the quality. Probably the best source of referrals is a gallery owner, who will share your interest in paying a fair price for quality work. Major museums maintain their own restoration departments, but they will know of outside restorers, who, perhaps, once worked for the museum.

The price of restoration varies depending on the size of the work and its condition. In 1993, a highly skilled Boston restorer would have charged from $60 to clean and make minor repairs to an 8 x 10 inch print. More elaborate procedures to deal with a large print, a major tear, or improper mounting or mating would increase the price two or three times or more. Most conservators will give you a verbal listing of the work they will do, but will charge for a written one.

Art As Investment

Should you buy art as an investment?

"No!" is the resounding answer of dealers, gallery owners, auction house executives, and investment counselors.

Buy art because it moves you, because it is beautiful, because it appeals to you. Buy quality.

If these are your guidelines, it is quite possible that in ten or twenty years your purchases will be worth substantially more than what you first paid for them. Don't ever buy because you think that a currently underpriced field will come back into demand, or because you've read a glowing review of a talented photographer and you've heard that art is a gilt-edged investment.

Collecting art is an investment in the largest sense. It is an investment in time, in aesthetic pleasure, in developing your own eye and your expertise. If, along the way, your collection appreciates, the increase in value is an added benefit. It should never be a starting point.

Beware of a dealer who suggests a particular work as a good investment. There's a sale pitch in marketing art, sometimes even a hard sell, and the hope that today's modest purchase will both enhance the living room and help send the children to college can be hard to resist.

"But what about those clever connoisseurs who bought Pop Art in the 1960s?" you ask. "Haven't they sat smiling while prices for works by Rauschenberg, Lichtenstein, and Johns increased twenty-five times and more?"

Indeed they have, but those same people who are fortunate enough to own Pop Art paintings or prints that now sell for tens of thousands of dollars were in the forefront of collecting in the 1960s. By the 1970s works by the major Pop Art artists were already selling for thousands of dollars. (Note: An investment of $1,000 in 1970 in an account paying 10% interest would be worth $8,953 in 1993.)

Remember, too, that there are fads in collecting. Many schools of art once popular have now fallen out of favor. During the 1920s works by S. Arlant Edwards and W. Axel Haig were very popular; today works by these artists sell for relatively little.

If, despite all these cautions, you are still intent on assembling your collection as an investment tool, you should bear a number of points in mind.

There is usually a strong correlation between cost and investment. Barring the occasional flukes and finds, investment quality work is expensive. Most works included in museum collections are important examples of an artist's style. A piece in a private collection does not need to be equally representative. In general but not always, a work is more valuable if it is a typical rather than an atypical example. A work that is both decorative and attractive is a safer bet than one that is not. The real trick is to find the museum quality print of the future today.

There are many factors that determine the value of a print or photograph. The name of the artist, condition, quality of the impression, state, edition size, rarity, and authenticity are all key factors. The criteria for determining value will differ for different types of prints. Rarity and the quality of the impression are more important for rare Old Master prints; condition is more important for most contemporary prints.

A listing in a catalogue raisonné or monograph will enhance the value of any print or photograph. Any documentation, especially if the artist has written about it in letters or in a diary, makes the work more valuable. A solid provenance enhances the value of an individual picture. Look for watermarks and also look in the margin or on the back for a collector's mark. A work that has been part of a major collection has accrued value; similarly, a work that has changed hands frequently, or been hawked around from dealer to dealer, may lose value. A work from a "good" period in the artist's career is more valuable than one produced in a less fertile time.

Where a work is sold can greatly affect its value, for art can be geographically chauvinistic. Scenes of the White Mountains of New Hampshire are popular in New England. Cowboy art is popular in the west. And some subjects do better than others—scenes of dead game are generally not sought after in the United States but are popular in Europe.

In general, pleasant subjects are more sought after than troubling ones: country scenes are more appealing than sickbeds; baskets of fresh flowers more attractive than those that are withered.

The size and shape of the work are of great importance. Some modern artists have produced prints or photographs of heroic proportions. (David Hockney's 1982 *Brooklyn Bridge* measures 108 x 58 inches.) Few homes can accommodate such massive works, rendering them difficult to sell. Some dealers consider horizontal pictures easier to sell than vertical ones. The ratio 2 x 3 is thought to be the "ideal" proportion for a painting or print.

Assembling a collection of older art is a challenge, but the highest risks for the investor/collector are in contemporary art, for it hasn't stood the test of time. Chroniclers of the art market note that only about 5% of the artists who have their first one-person shows in major cities in any given year ever have another show. Another concern is that in the curious intersection of art and publicity, some young artists may be heavily promoted by a gallery with a healthy public relations budget and good press contacts. The difference between hype and a consistent display of talent may be difficult to ascertain.

There is, of course, another side to all this caution. Some of today's young artists will be tomorrow's masters, and a collector discerning and lucky enough to find this work will be able to combine aesthetic satisfaction with the pleasure of watching it appreciate.

A collector of contemporary work must be carefully attuned to every turn of the market, attend shows, gallery talks, visit artists' studios, and read the art press. While even the experts make mistakes, if you can buy the artists whom the curators, collectors, gallery owners, and artists themselves are buying, you're closer to the right track, but there are no guarantees. At best, buying contemporary work is a long-term investment, which may take ten years or more to appreciate, if it ever does. Some collectors think that the best time to buy is 30-40 years after an artist dies, when the sales price for his work hits a low.

One of the few characteristics that art and the traditional financial markets have in common is the tendency to run in cycles, with well-publicized periods of solid growth creating a bandwagon effect of purchases, only to be followed by a sharp decline in prices.

In short, you're more likely to find success as an investor by staying with more conventional financial instruments. Your investment in art belongs in a personal portfolio under "A" for aesthetic and "L" for love.

A Brief Guide to Art Research

This chapter will not make you a skilled art researcher. It will, however, provide you with basic approaches to art research, the names of the standard sources, and an overall method of developing your knowledge about a school or a movement in painting, or about an individual artist. A selective bibliography appears at the end of this chapter.*

The Library

General Art Reference Works and Encyclopedias

Where and how you begin to do art research depends very much on what you want to learn. If, fresh from a foray to a museum, you decide to explore a budding interest in flower painting, start at the main branch of your local library.

Inquire at the reference desk for general art sources. The three prime general reference books on the visual arts are *Encyclopedia of World Art*, *McGraw-Hill Dictionary of Art*, and *Praeger Encyclopedia of Art*. Each is well illustrated and geared to the general reader and beginning student. Each contains many articles on artists, periods, styles, terms, museums, and countries. Articles vary in length, from very short ones that define

---

*The approach assumes that you will begin your research in a library. However, it is also advisable to begin to build your own library of art reference books. An inexpensive, pocket-sized handbook, Ralph Mayer's *Dictionary of Art Terms and Techniques*, explains schools, techniques, styles, and art terms. Information is easy to retrieve.

Another very useful book is Lois Swan Jones' *Art Research Methods and Resources: A Guide to Finding Art Information*. This comprehensive guide, geared for more advanced researchers, surveys the basic sources, deals with research methods, and provides practical advice on how to obtain reference material. Of particular value is the inclusion of facsimiles of pages from major reference works and directions for their use. Jones also provides a dictionary of French, German, and Italian art terms.

terms to more substantial pieces on individual artists that include bibli-ographies. The five-volume McGraw-Hill work is especially accessible and readable.

Taking this first step and consulting a general reference book may give you all the information that you need or want to know. Should you require more data, there are various additional sources.

The Card Catalog

The card catalog lists every book in a library's collection. Holdings are indexed by author, subject, and title. If you are checking to see if the library owns a specific work, the author and title listings are the place to turn. If, however, you are pursuing a broader area, track it down in the subject cat-alog, starting with an inclusive topic, such as "print," and then working through the subheadings to the one that will lead you to the pertinent ti-tles. Research an artist by looking under his name. (See Appendix D for a detailed explanation of how artists' names are listed.) Types of books listed in a card catalog include:

Monographs. Books about individual artists that provide historical or biographical material and information about his or her more famous works.

Oeuvre catalogues. Systematic lists of each work of art in an artist's entire creative output, or the works in a specific medium.

Catalogues raisonnés. Similar to *oeuvre catalogues,* but provide a more complete citation for each work. (An auction catalog may try to give a particular lot added cachet by noting that it has been or will be listed in the catalogue raisonné.)

Exhibition catalogs. Document the exhibition of an artist's work at a museum or gallery.

Most public libraries will have some, but not all, of these resources. One time-tested way to find additional titles is to review the bibliography of related books and magazines that is usually found at the end of refer-ence works. Librarians will be able to help you locate the more scholarly materials at an art library or in an adjacent larger city.

General Artist Dictionaries

There are no general dictionaries of artists in English, but there are two outstanding foreign language works that are the basic resources in the field. Many researchers turn first to Emmanuel Bénézit's *Dictionnaire Critique et Documentaire des Peintres, Sculpteurs, Dessinateurs et Graveurs.* Usually called "Bénézit," the ten-volume set, written in French, is an alpha-betical listing of names with life dates and other basic information about in-ternational artists. It may include the names of cities where they studied and worked, and note any honors or awards given to them. Bénézit also provides facsimiles of some artists' signatures and some sales information. Last revised in 1976, the work retains certain idiosyncrasies. The names of some American and English artists, for example, are altered to the French versions—a Henry may be called a Henri; a Mary, Marie. You may occa-sionally hear an auctioneer say that an artist is listed in Bénézit—it's nice to know, but it doesn't really confer any value.

Another general reference, in German, is the highly regarded biographical dictionary compiled by Ulrich Thieme and Felix Becker, *Allgemeines Lexikon der bildenden Künstler von der Antike bis zur Gegenwart*, which runs to thirty-seven volumes. Generally preferred by scholars, it is a specialized, alphabetical index that contains material similar to that in Bénézit. At the end of each entry on an individual artist, there is a bibliography from which the data was drawn, with titles in the original language. Thieme-Becker, as it is usually called, was published from 1907 through 1950. Hans Vollmer's *Allgemeines Lexikon der bildenden Künstler des XX. Jahrhunderts*, which covers artists born after 1870, is a supplement to Thieme-Becker.

Artist Indexes and General Indexes

An index can best be used as a jumping-off point for further research. Brief entries, listed alphabetically by the artist's last name, provide the complete name, nationality, life dates, and abbreviated notations of books or articles from which the information was compiled. The abbreviations used in a particular index are explained in the introduction to the individual work. These short listings direct you to longer articles and books about the artist in whom you are interested.

Patricia Havlice's two-volume *Index to Artistic Biography*, published in 1973, is a survey of sixty-four different biographical dictionaries exclusive of Thieme-Becker and Bénézit, and thus a valuable source of additional information. A supplement including material in seventy additional sources was published in 1981. Daniel Mallett's *Index of Artists*, first published in 1935, and its supplement which appeared in 1940, are other valuable biographical reference tools.

It is especially difficult to find information on little-known 20th-century artists, or on regional or very contemporary artists. The *Biography and Genealogy Master Index* is a guide to more than 725,000 listings in over fifty current editions of *Who's Who*. It includes the names of many individuals who are not listed anywhere else. *The New York Times Index* and *The New York Times Obituaries Index* are excellent sources of information about 20th-century artists. The latter, particularly, includes information about regional artists that may not be found elsewhere.

Major artists, movements, and periods are the subjects of books; less prominent names may become the special subjects of devoted researchers who publish articles in popular or scholarly periodicals. An index of periodical literature provides easy reference to recent articles on both major and minor artists. There are a number of specialized art indexes. Most libraries subscribe to *Art Index*, a quarterly which covers 230 journals and began publishing in 1929. (A selective list of art periodicals, tabloids, and newsletters appears in Appendix B.)

Specialized Artist Dictionaries and Directories

If you already know the basic facts about an artist's nationality and life dates, you may go directly to a specialized dictionary. Mantle Fielding's *Dictionary of American Painters, Sculptors and Engravers* is one of the better known dictionaries, though it is sometimes at variance with other sources and thus less reliable. Peter Falk's *Who Was Who in American Art*, compiled from the original thirty volumes of *American Art Annual, 1898-1933*, and from four volumes of *Who's Who in Art, 1935-1947*, includes biographical data and information about exhibitions, prizes, and membership in artist societies. Chris Pettey's *Dictionary of Women Artists* is international in scope and an excellent source on women artists born before 1900.

Other sources to check are George C. Groce and David H. Wallace's *New York Historical Society's Dictionary of Artists in America, 1564-1860*; William Young's *A Dictionary of American Artists, Sculptors and Engravers*; Peggy and Harold Samuels' *Artists of the American West*; and Eden Hughes' *Artists in California, 1786-1940*.

For information about contemporary American artists, consult *Who's Who in American Art*; the *Art in America Annual Guide to Galleries, Museums and Artists*; Samuels' *Contemporary Western Artists*; Paul Cummings' *A Dictionary of Contemporary American Artists*; and Les Krantz's *American Artists*.

If you are looking for information about a European artist, you will be able to turn to a number of standard texts. The basic biographical references for Italian art are Giulio Bolaffi's *Dizionario Enciclopedico Bolaffi dei Pittori e Degli Incisori Italiani: Dall' XI al XX Sècolo*, published in 1972, and A.M. Comanducci's *Dizionario Illustrato dei Pittori, Disegnatori, e Incisori Italiani Moderni e Contemporanei*, last revised in 1962, which covers the 19th and 20th centuries.

Standard biographical references to British art include Christopher Wood's *Dictionary of Victorian Painters*, originally published in 1971; Grant Waters' *Dictionary of British Artists Working 1900-1950*, 1975; H.L. Mallalieu's *The Dictionary of British Watercolour Artists up to 1920*, 1976; and J. Johnson and A. Greutzner's *Dictionary of British Artists, 1880-1940*, 1976.

Print, Poster and Photography Books

Once you've established that you are interested in an artist who is a printmaker or photographer, or that you are interested in knowing more about the multiples market, there are certain basic books that you may want to have on your reference shelf. There is no one book that will give you all the information you need to know.

Bamber Gascoigne's *How to Identify Prints* and Ivins's *How Prints Look* are two basic texts that walk you though the necessary steps to identify a print. A. Hyatt Mayor's *Prints and People* provides a social history of printmaking. Watrous's *A Century of American Printmaking, 1880-1980* gives a thorough overview of contemporary printmaking. Donson's *Prints and the Print Market* gives a commerical view of the print market and has chapters on conservation and how to detect a fake.

A review of the history of the poster is available in Weill's *The Poster: A Worldwide Survey and History* and Gallo's *The Poster in History*. Patricia Kery's *Art Deco Graphics* and Dawn Ades's *Twentieth Century Poster: Design of the Avant Garde* provide information about specific periods.

Photography is a relatively new field of collecting. John Szarkowski, former curator of photography at the Museum of Modern Art, is credited with introducing photography as an art form to the general public. Gordon Baldwin's handbook *Looking at Photographs: A Guide to Technical Terms* is an excellent reference source that will easily fit into a purse or pocket. Rosenblum's *A World History of Photography* is a basic text book; lavishly illustrated, it gives you the history of photography, biographical information about many photographers, and information on photographic techniques. Witkins's *The Photograph Collector's Guide* provides biographical information about many artists and their techniques and gives a sample of their signature or stamp.

Additional Resources

Additional resources are available to a researcher intent on discovering information about a particular artist. Many are accessible by telephone, greatly easing the research process.

Archives of American Art

The Archives of American Art is a bureau of the Smithsonian Institution which documents the history of the visual arts in America by collecting and preserving original documents, diaries, letters, photographs, oral histories, and other materials.

The main offices of the Archives are in Washington, D.C., and regional offices are located in New York City, Boston, Detroit, San Francisco, and San Marino, California. Records in the Archives include artists' personal papers, letters, diaries, sketches, photographs, exhibition material, financial information, writings, and lectures. The Archives also contains the records of arts organizations and institutions, and the papers of critics, dealers, collectors, and scholars. In addition, the Archives publishes a newsletter which is available by subscription.

The Archives responds to telephone inquiries. If you are interested in a particular artist, call and ask if there is any information on file, and then make an appointment to see the material.

The National Museum of American Art

The Inventory of American Painting Executed Before 1914 was begun as a project to celebrate America's bicentennial in 1976. It is a little-known but invaluable source which now has information on over 22,000 artists and 262,000 paintings, indexed by artist, title, owner/location, and subject matter. The database is an inventory of paintings but the biographical information will be useful for many printmakers. While the information is maintained on computer, and the database is constantly updated, it is not absolutely accurate and may contain errors of date or spelling. However, up to twenty pages of information will be photocopied free of charge, and nominal charges apply to additional pages. Call 202-357-2941 for information.

George Eastman House

The International Museum of Photography at the George Eastman House in Rochester, New York maintains a database which is available for on-line searching. Over 46,000 photographer's biographies and 149,000 images from 565 institutions are catalogued. Users can search by the name of photographer, subject, and image. Contact Andy Eskind at 716-271-4526 for technical information.

Vertical Files

Many libraries maintain files of special material which is not listed in the card catalog, not shelved with books, and may not be otherwise publicized. Generally filed under specific artists' names, these files preserve "casual" information that is quickly lost and almost impossible to replicate, and may include press releases, exhibition reviews, newspaper and magazine clippings, and obituaries. Librarians generally concentrate on artists working in the region. Historical societies also maintain excellent vertical files. If you can locate an artist's home town, call the library or museum there and inquire if they have such information and if they will duplicate these materials. Most will comply and charge only a small fee for the service. These ephemera or vertical files are gold mines of information unavailable anywhere else.

Associations

Many dictionaries will refer to the local or regional associations to which an artist belonged. Many of these groups maintained private archives, another resource of valuable information about individual artists. *The American Art Dictionary* and the *Encyclopedia of Associations* provide the addresses of associations, museums, and art clubs across the nation. The Society of Illustrators may have information on illustrators not found elsewhere. The Guild of Boston Artists, the National Academy of Design in New York, and the National Watercolor Society in Lakewood, California, may all preserve unique resources. Pursue your artist—it's a grown-up treasure hunt.

Price Guides

An artist's sales history is an invaluable record of information. Auction records are frequently the only source of public information about art prices, since those achieved from gallery sales and purchases from estates or personal collections may remain private. More detailed information about the price histories of artists at auction is available in the parent publication of this volume, *Leonard's ANNUAL Price Index of Prints, Posters & Photographs*, published by Auction Index, Inc., Newton, Massachusetts (617-964-2876). *Leonard's Index*, listed alphabetically by artist, includes every print, poster and photograph sold at auction worldwide. Updated annually, it provides the most current information, and can be found in many libraries.

A Selective Bibliography

General Art Reference Works and Encyclopedias

Arts in America: A Bibliography. 4 vols. Edited by Bernard Karpel. Washington, D.C., Smithsonian Institution Press, 1979.

Encyclopedia of American Art. Edited by Milton Rugoff. New York, E.P. Dutton, 1981.

Encyclopedia of World Art. 15 vols. New York, McGraw-Hill Book Co., 1958.

Jones, Lois Swan. *Art Research Methods and Resources.* 2nd ed. Dubuque, Iowa, Kendall/Hunt Publishing Co., 1984.

Mayer, Ralph. *A Dictionary of Art Terms and Techniques.* New York, Harper and Row Publishers, 1981.

McGraw-Hill Dictionary of Art. 5 vols. Edited by Bernard S. and Shirley D. Meyers. New York, McGraw-Hill Book Co., 1969.

Phaidon Dictionary of Twentieth-Century Art. New York, Phaidon Publishers, 1973.

Praeger Encyclopedia of Art. 5 vols. New York, Praeger Publishers, Inc., 1971

General Artist Dictionaries

Bénézit, Emmanuel. *Dictionnaire Critique et Documentaire des Peintres, Sculpteurs, Dessinateurs et Graveurs.* 10 vols. 3rd ed. Paris, Grund, 1976.

Thieme, Ulrich, and Becker, Felix. *Allgemeines Lexikon der Bildenden Künstler von der Antike bis zur Gegenwart; unter Mitwirkung von 300 Fachgelehrten des In-und Auslandes.* 37 vols. Leipzig, E.A. Seemann, 1907-1950; reprint, 37 vols. Leipzig, F. Allmann, 1964.

Vollmer, Hans. *Allgemeines Lexikon der bildenden Künstler des XX. Jahrhunderts.* 6 vols. Leipzig, E.A. Seemann, 1953-1962.

Artist Indexes and General Indexes

Art Index. Edited by Bertrum Deli. New York, H.W. Wilson Co., 1929+.

Biographical Dictionaries Master Index. Detroit, Michigan, Gale Research Co., 1975+.

Havlice, Patricia Pate. *Index to Artistic Biography.* 2 vols. Metuchen, New Jersey, The Scarecrow Press, Inc., 1973. Suppl. 1981.

Mallett, Daniel Trowbridge. *Mallett's Index of Artists.* New York, R.R. Bowker Co., 1935. Suppl. 1940; reprint, 1948.

New York Times Index. Vol. 1, 1913. New York, New York Times Co., 1913+.

New York Times Obituaries Index, 1858-1968. New York, New York Times Co., 1970. Suppl. 1969-1978, 1980.

Specialized Artist Dictionaries and Directories

Art in America Annual Guide to Galleries, Museums, Artists. Edited by Elizabeth C. Baker. New York, Brant Art Publications, 1986.

Baigell, Matthew. *Dictionary of American Art.* New York, Harper and Row Publishers, 1979.

Catley, Bryan. *Art Deco and Other Figures.* Woodbridge, England. Antique Collectors Club, 1978.

Comanducci, Agostino Mario. *Dizionario Illustrato dei Pittori, Disegnatori e Incisori Italiani Moderni e Contemporanei.* Milano, Italy, Luigi Patuzzi Editore, 1970.

A Dictionary of American Artists, Sculptors and Engravers; From the Beginning Through the Turn of the Twentieth Century. Edited by William Young. Cambridge, Massachusetts, William Young and Co., 1968.

Dictionary of Contemporary American Artists. 4th ed. Edited by Paul Cummings. New York, St. Martin's Press, 1982.

Dizionario Enciclopedico Bolaffi dei Pittori e Degli Incisori Italiani: Dall' XI al XX Sècolo. 11 vols. Turin, Italy, Giulio Bolaffi Editore, 1972-1976.

Encyclopedia of New Orleans Artists 1718-1918. New Orleans, The Historic New Orleans Collection, 1987.

Falk, Peter Hastings. *Who Was Who in American Art.* Madison, Connecticut, Sound View Press, 1985.

Fielding, Mantle. *Dictionary of American Painters, Sculptors and Engravers.* Poughkeepsie, New York, Apollo Books, 1983.

Groce, George C., and Wallace, David H. *The New York Historical Society's Dictionary of Artists in America, 1564-1860.* New Haven and London, Yale University Press, 1957.

Harper, J. Russell. *Early Painters and Engravers in Canada.* Toronto, Canada, University of Toronto Press, 1970.

Houfe, Simon. *The Dictionary of British Book Illustrators and Caricaturists.* Baron Publishing, Woodbridge, England, Antique Collectors Club, 1978.

Hughes, Edan Milton. *Artists in California, 1786-1940.* 2nd ed. San Francisco, Hughes Publishing Co., 1989.

Johnson, J., and Greutzner, A. *Dictionary of British Artists, 1880-1940: An Antique Collector's Club Research Project Listing 41,000 Artists.* Baron Publishing, Woodbridge, England, Antique Collectors Club, 1976.

Krantz, Les. *American Artists.* New York, Facts on File Publications, 1985.

Krantz, Les. *American Art Galleries.* New York, Facts on File Publications, 1985.

MacDonald, Colin S. *A Dictionary of Canadian Artists.* Ottawa, Canada, Canadian Paperbacks, 1972.

Mallalieu, H.L. *The Dictionary of British Watercolour Artists up to 1920.* Woodbridge, England, Antique Collectors Club, 1976.

Meyer, George H., ed. *Folk Artists Biographical Index.* Detroit, Gale Research Co., 1987.

Naylor, Colin, and Genesis, P-Orridge. *Contemporary Artists*. New York, St. Martin's Press, 1977; 2nd ed., 1983.

Pettey, Chris. *Dictionary of Women Artists: An International Dictionary of Women Artists Born Before 1900*. Boston, Massachusetts, G.K. Hall Co., 1985.

Samuels, Peggy, and Samuels, Harold. *The Illustrated Biographical Encyclopedia of Artists of the American West*. Garden City, New York, Doubleday, 1976.

Samuels, Peggy, and Samuels, Harold. *Contemporary Western Artists*. New York, Crown Publishing, 1985.

Waters, Grant M. *Dictionary of British Artists Working 1900-1950*. Eastbourne Fine Art, Eastbourne, England, 1975.

Wood, Christopher. *The Dictionary of Victorian Painters*. 2nd edition. Antique Collectors Club, Woodbridge, England, 1971, 1978, 1981.

Print Bibliography

Ackley, Clifford S.; Krens, Thomas; and Menaker, Deborah. *The Modern Art of the Print: Selections from the Collection of Lois and Michael Torf*. Williams College Museum of Art, Museum of Fine Arts, Boston, 1984.

Acton, David. *A Spectrum of Innovation: Color in American Printmaking 1890-1960*. New York, W.W. Norton & Co., 1990.

American Prints in The Library of Congress: A Catalog of the Collection. Compiled by Karn F. Beall, Baltimore, Library of Congress, Johns Hopkins Press, 1970.

Briquet, C.M. *Les Filigranes*. Paris, 1923. Reprint, 4 vols. New York, Hacker Art Books, 1966.

Buchsbaum, Ann. *Practical Guide to Print Collecting*. New York, Van Nostrand Reinhold Co., 1975.

Castleman, Riva. *Prints of the Twentieth Century: A History*. New York, Museum of Modern Art, 1976.

Claasen, Lynda Corey. *Finder's Guide to Prints and Drawings in the Smithsonian Institution*. Washington, D.C., Smithsonian Press, 1981.

Doloff, Francis W., and Perkinson, Roy L. *How to Care for Works of Art on Paper*. Museum of Fine Arts, Boston, 1971.

Donson, Theodore. *Prints and the Print Market*. New York, Thomas Y. Crowell, 1977.

Gascoigne, Bamber. *How to Identify Prints: A Complete Guide to Manual and Mechanical Processes from Woodcut to Ink Jet*. Thames Hudson, 1986.

Hind, Arthur M. *A History of Engraving and Etching: From the 15th Century to the Year 1914*. Boston, 1924. Reprint, New York, Dover Publications, 1963.

Hind, Arthur M. *Introduction to a History of the Woodcut*. 2 vols., Boston, 1935. Reprint, New York, Dover Publications, 1963.

Ivins, William M., Jr. *How Prints Look.* New York, Metropolitan Museum of Art, 1943. Reprint, Boston, Beacon Press, 1968. Revised by Marjorie Cohn, Beacon Press, 1987.

Lugt, Frits. *Les marques de collections de dessins et d'estampes.* Amsterdam, Vereenigde Druckkerijen, 1921. Reprint, San Francisco, Alan Wofsy Fine Arts, 1975. Supplement, The Hague, 1956.

Madigan, Mary Jean, and Cologan, Susan, editors. *Prints and Photographs: Understanding, Appreciating, Collecting.* New York, Art and Antiques Magazine, 1983.

Mayor, A. Hyatt. *Prints & People, A Social History of Prints & Pictures.* Princeton University Press, Princeton, New Jersey, 1971.

Mayor, A. Hyatt, preface. *American Printmaking: The First 150 Years.* Washington, D.C., Museum of Graphic Art, Smithsonian Institution Press, 1972.

Riggs, Timothy A. *Print Council Index to Oeuvre: Catalogues of Prints by European and American Artists.* Millhouse, New York, Krause Publications, 1983.

Smith, Selma. *The Print World Directory.* Bala-Cyndwyd, PA, Print World Inc., 1982+.

Warner, Glen. *Building a Print Collection, A Guide to Buying Original Prints and Photographs.* New York, Van Nostrand Reinhold Lt., 1981.

Watrous. *A Century of American Printmaking, 1880-1980.* University of Wisconsin Press, 1984.

Zigrosser, Carl, and Gaedhe, Christa M. *A Guide to the Collecting and Care of Original Prints.* New York, Crown Publishers, 1965.

Poster Bibliography

Ades, Dawn. *Twentieth Century Poster: Design of the Avant Garde.* New York, Abbeville Press, 1984.

Barnicoat, John. *A Concise History of Posters.* New York, Oxford University Press, 1980.

Circker, Hayward. *Golden Age of the Poster.* New York, Dover Publications, 1971.

Gallo, Max. *The Poster in History.* New York, American Heritage Publishing, 1974.

Keay, Carolyn. *American Posters of the Turn of the Century.* New York, St. Martin's Press, 1975.

Kery, Patricia. *Art Deco Graphics.* New York, Harry N. Abrams, 1986.

Kiehl, David W. *American Art Posters of the 1890s in the Metropolitan Museum of Art.* New York, Harry N. Abrams, 1987.

Margolin, Victor. *American Poster Renaissance.* New York, Watson Guptill Publications, 1975.

Marx, Rodger, preface. *Masters of the Poster, 1896-1900.* New York, Images Graphique, New York, 1977.

Menten, Theodore. *Advertising Art in the Art Deco Style.* New York, Dover Publications, 1975.

Rebello, Stephan, and Allen, Richard. *Reel Art.* New York, Abbeville Press, 1988.

Weill, Alain. *The Poster: A Worldwide Survey and History.* Boston, G.K. Hall & Co., 1985.

Photography Bibliography

Baldwin, Gordon. *Looking at Photographs: A Guide to Technical Terms.* London, J.Paul Getty Museum and the British Museum Press, 1991.

Booth, Mark Haworth. *The Golden Age of British Photography, 1839-1900.* Willerton, New York, Aperture in association with the Philadelphia Museum of Art, Viking Penguin, 1984.

Coke, Van Deren. *Avant-Garde Photography in Germany, 1919-1939.* New York, Pantheon, 1982.

Crawford, William. *The Keepers of Light.* Dobbs Ferry, New York, Morgan and Morgan, 1979.

Daniel, Pete, et al. *Official Images New Deal Photography.* Washington, D.C., Smithsonian Institution Press, 1987.

Freund, Gisele. *Photography and Society.* Boston, David Godine Publisher, 1980.

Greenough, Sarah, et al. *On the Art of Fixing a Shadow: 150 Years of Photography.* National Gallery of Art, Chicago Art Institute, 1989.

Hambourg, Maria Morris. *The New Vision: Photography Between the Wars* MMA, 1989.

Jeffrey, Ian. *Photography, A Concise History.* London, Thames and Hudson, 1989.

Homer, William Innes. *Alfred Stieglitz and the Photo-Secession.* Boston, Little, Brown & Co., 1983.

Jammes, Andre, and Janis, Eugenia Parry. *The Art of French Calotype with a Critical Dictionary of Photographers.* 1845-1870, Princeton University Press, 1983.

Newhall, Beaumont. *The History of Photography from 1839 to the Present Day.* rev. ed. MoMA, 1978 (1964).

Pollack, Peter. *The Picture History of Photography from the Earliest Beginnings to the Present Day.* New York, Harry N. Abrams, 1969, abridged edition 1977.

Reilley, James M. *Care and Identification of 19th-Century Photographic Prints.* Rochester, Eastman Kodak, 1986.

Rosenblum, Naomi. *A World History of Photography.* New York, Abbeville Press, 1984.

Sandweiss, Martha A., ed. *Photography in Nineteenth Century America.* Harry N. Abrams, 1991.

Szarkowski, John. *Mirror and Windows: American Photographs Since 1900.* MoMA, 1978.

Turner, Peter, ed. *American Images: Photographs 1945-1980.* New York, Viking Press, 1985.

Witkin, Lee D., and London, Barbara. *The Photograph Collector's Guide.* Boston, New York Graphic Society, 1979.

Association Directories

American Art Directory. 50th ed. New York, R.R. Bowker Co., 1986.

Encyclopedia of Associations. 21st ed. Detroit, Gale Research Co., 1987.

The Official Museum Directory: United States and Canada. 1st issue. Washington, D.C., American Association of Museums, 1971+.

Price Guides

Gordon, Martin. *Gordon's Print Price Annual.* Naples, Florida, 1991.

Leonard's ANNUAL Price Index of Prints, Posters & Photographs. 1 vol. Edited by Susan Theran. Newton, Massachusetts, Auction Index, Inc., 1992+.

Glossary

The world of collecting works on paper, prints, posters and photographs is composed of specialized terms. These glossaries will provide you with the information you need to start learning and collecting.

General Terms on Condition, Papers, and Collecting

4to. A paper size. See *quarto*.

8vo. A paper size. See *octavo*.

AAA. Abbreviation for the Associated American Artists, a gallery and publisher of fine art prints.

A.P. See *artist's proof*.

after letters. An edition of a print pulled in its final *state* after the addition of the complete text or engraved inscription.

after. When referring to prints *after* has several meanings which convey varying degrees of authenticity. The correct meaning of *after* refers to a *print* based on another artist's painting, drawing, or watercolor. The engraver or lithographer who executed the print may become as well known as the original artist. The first edition of Audubon prints were engraved and colored mainly by Havell, a significant artist in his own right. All of the Audubon prints are *afters*, but they may be catalogued in different ways. *After* is also used incorrectly to mean a *restrike*. *After* is sometimes used as a catch-all term.

annotated. Information handwritten by the artist, someone representing the estate, a collector, or someone else.

artist's proof. An impression of a work different from the stated edition. Pulled during the creative process as an example of a stage in development, it may be called *a trial proof, proof, artist's proof (A.P.), edition proof, bon à tirer, hors commerce (H.C.), or épreuve d'artiste*. There is often a cachet to these prints, which may be numbered with Roman numerals or annotated. See *state*.

as issued. This phrase indicates that the condition of the print, such as mounting to cardboard, which would ordinarily lower the print's value, is one the artist or publisher accepted or authorized.

attributed. When a work is catalogued as attributed to an artist, this means there is a lesser degree of certainty as to its authenticity.

bears date. Has a date which, in the opinion of the auction house, has been *inscribed* or written on the print by someone other than the artist.

bears signature. Has a signature which, in the opinion of the auction house, has been added to the print in a hand other than the artist's.

before letters. That portion of a *run* pulled before the addition of the engraved text, titles, or inscriptions. Sometimes this is designated as *hors texte*.

blindstamp. An embossed stamp without color, outside the image, used to identify the publisher, printer, photographer, printmaking studio, collector, or, less often, the artist. The stamp may be a symbol, initials, or the full name and address. *Drystamp* and *chop* are synonyms.

bon à tirer. See *edition proof, artist's proof*.

canceled. A plate or stone that was defaced after the edition to ensure that no reprinting would be possible. Sometimes the canceled prints are marketed, as with Picasso or Degas, or the marks are removed and the prints sold as if pre-cancellation.

catalogue raisonné. A published, systematic list of prints (or paintings) of an artist with titles, dates, sizes, states, editions, reprintings, and conditions of known prints.

chine-collé. An impression printed on a thin sheet of China or Japan paper that is adhered to a sheet of heavier artist backing paper and printed at the same time. It may be an intaglio or planographic print. *Chine-appliqué* is a synonym.

chop. See *blindstamp*.

collector's mark. A handwritten annotation, ink stamp or *drystamp* by the owner(s) of the work. This mark does not indicate authenticity but a work with a *provenance* from an important collection might indicate high quality.

colophon. When a group of works is presented as a whole (as in a portfolio or book), the colophon is the statement that presents the pertinent information for the work: the artist's signature, the *edition* size and *number*, publisher, and date. The colophon is most often on the last page, but sometimes the frontispiece serves as a colophon.

copyright. An inscription or mark under a print indicating protection by government acts. The *copyright* usually includes the date, since copyrights are in effect for a specific number of years.

counterproof. A counterproof is made by running the print, before the ink has dried, through the press against another sheet. The resulting image is in reverse of the print, but in the same direction as the plate. Artists often make counterproofs during the printmaking process to facilitate corrections. See *offset*.

dated. Printed on that date, either as indicated in the plate or stone, by the hand of the artist, or as annotated or attested to by the *catalogue raisonné*.

deckle edge. The soft, naturally ragged edge of a handmade piece of paper, produced by small amounts of the paper pulp slipping beneath the sides of the frame (deckle) that holds the paper pulp on the screen.

dedicated. An annotation designating the recipient and/or donor of a gift or presentation print.

drystamp. See *blindstamp*.

E.A. See *épreuve d'artiste*.

edition. A limited run of numbered impressions pulled by (or under the supervision of) the artist. This term is relevant only for works printed since about 1880, when artists like Whistler began to limit the number of *impressions* and to cancel the plate. Prints issued in various states are often considered different editions — e.g. *before letters*, *after letters*, or in different colors. See also *limited edition, numbered*.

edition proof. The specific impression used by the artist or designated to the printer as the standard against which every impression in the edition is to be judged. Also *bon à tirer*, literally "good to pull."

épreuve d'artiste. An *artist's proof*. Abbreviated *E.A.*

estate stamp. A stamp affixed to an impression by the family of an artist, or the executor of the artist's estate, which attests to the authenticity of the work. This was usually done when the work was found in the artist's studio after his or her death.

estimate. The price range within which an auction house expects to sell a particular *lot*. The estimate is frequently included in a printed catalogue.

folio. A paper size at least 12 inches in height. When used for books, it refers to a sheet folded in half to make four pages or two leaves. For prints it refers to size only.

foxing. Brown or pale patches of discoloration or stains on a sheet of paper. Foxing is caused either by impurities in the paper or by molds. It can be treated with conservation methods.

full margins. A phrase indicating that the margins have not been trimmed since the print was issued. Some cataloguers will use the phrase to mean only that the margins are wide.

gum arabic. This natural gum of the acacia tree is a main ingredient in lithographic etching materials. It was also used as a glaze on the surface of some hand-colored prints (e.g. Currier and Ives) to produce a darker tone in certain areas.

H.C. See *hors commerce*.

hand-colored. A phrase indicating that watercolor, ink, or other colored medium has been applied to the print after printing.

hinge. The paper or tape used to affix a print to a backing.

hors commerce. A term refering to an *impression* outside the limits of the edition. The phrase originally meant "not for sale." Since these prints have a cachet, artists often produce a large number of H.C. prints. See *artist's proof, proof, bon à tirer*.

hors texte. See *before letters*.

identified. Information supplied by a label or collector's annotations.

impression. A print that is part of the stated edition or artist's proofs. Sometimes the term refers to the quality of the image.

initials. Letters of an artist's name rather than the full signature.

inscribed. The word *inscribed* has different meanings when used for paintings and prints. For prints it refers to the information (title, date, copyright, publisher, etc.) supplied in letterpress or engraving outside the image of the print. When the information is handwritten, the correct term is *annotated*.

laid down. A condition in which a print has been affixed to a mount to give it greater strength, to repair minor tears, or to prepare it for presentation. A paper conservator may be required to remove the backing. "Laid to cardboard as issued" means that the artist or publisher intended the use of a support. See *mounted*.

laid paper. Paper showing the pattern of vertical wire-marks and horizontal chain-lines produced by the papermaker's mold during its manufacture.

light-staining. When a print has been exposed to strong or prolonged light, the discoloration (light or dark) is referred to as light-staining or light-toning.

limited edition. An annotation indicating that the edition is of a specific size without stating the number of prints in the edition.

losses.   A general term for such changes to the pristine condition of a print as tears, skinning, rubbing, punctures, pin holes, and shavings. Remargined and reinforced refer to repairs of losses.

lot.   An individual work or group of works offered for sale at one time.

margins.   See *full margins* and *thread margins.*

mat staining.   Discoloration of a print due to its contact with an acid-bearing mount, support surface or facing.

matrix.   A term used to refer to the image when the printmaking process is uncertain, or to refer to the base on which the image to be printed is prepared, such as wood, linoleum, copper and so on.

mounted.   Attached to a support or backing. Photographs are often affixed to mounts by the artist's studio to give them greater strength. Photography authentication stamps are often on the back of the mount. Both prints and photographs can be mounted. See *laid down* and *as issued.*

multiples.   This refers to any art object that can be reproduced in quantity from a single original matrix. Prints were the first multiples, but many sculptures and pottery are now classed as multiples.

numbered.   When a print is numbered, the numbering is usually hand-written below the image as a fraction. The top number is that of the particular *impression,* and the bottom number is the size of the *edition.* Since there may be *A.P.* prints in addition to the total *edition,* the denominator may be slightly below the number of *impressions* in the complete *run.* The print number is for cataloguing identification only and does not indicate the order of printing. No individual prints were numbered before the beginning of the twentieth century.

octavo.   A sheet of paper about 9 x 6 inches. The size (and thus the term) results when a full sheet of about 18 x 24 inches is folded in eighths. This size is often used for botanical and scientific prints. Abbreviated *8vo.*

offset.   A method of printing in which the inked image is transferred to an intermediary support, such as the rubber cylinders of an offset press, and from that to the sheet of paper. This term most often designates a print reproduced commercially in fairly large runs, or one that is photomechanically reproduced.

plate.   A sheet of metal used for *intaglio* prints. The size of a print is sometimes measured by the area within visible plate marks.

portfolio.   This term refers to both the group of prints presented together and the case that holds and protects the group of prints.

posthumous edition.   The edition printed from the artist's plates after the artist has died. These prints might be authorized by the artist's estate but are not necessarily marked as posthumous printings, e.g. Rembrandt's.

printed later.   *Impressions* printed after the regular edition, with or without the artist's knowledge or supervision.

printer's proof.   A proof retained by the printer, sometimes the same as the *edition proof.*

proof.   See *impression* and *artist's proof.*

provenance.   The ownership history of a work of art. Most often this history is not known for a print, unless there is a *collector's mark.* Ex-collection indicates that the named person was a recent owner.

publisher.   The association responsible for overseeing the printing and distribution of a print or series of prints.

pull.   Each separate print that is placed in the press and removed as a finished print.

quarto.   A sheet of paper about 9 x 12 inches. The size (and thus the term) results when a full sheet of about 18 x 24 inches is folded in fourths. Abbreviated *4to.*

recto.   The side of the paper with the image.

registration.   Prints that use more than one plate, such as multicolor prints, need a way of aligning the paper with the plates. These marks, called the registration, may be pinholes or symbols on the paper or plates, but most are not visible in the finished print.

restrike.   This term has numerous meanings. Most commonly it refers to a reprint of a plate, without a hand signature or numbering, printed without the artist's supervision or knowledge. It may also refer to a reworked plate such as a posthumous edition of Rembrandt's prints. Improperly used, it refers to *photomechanical reproductions.*

run.   The complete *edition,* including the stated edition, *proofs,* and *H.C.* prints.

series.   Prints, in separate editions, that belong together because of related imagery, content, or style, or that the artist or publisher has designated as a series or set.

sheet.   The measurement that records the dimensions of the entire sheet of paper. The image may fill the sheet, or it may be irregular, or the sheet may have been trimmed to the image.

sight.   An approximate measure of the visible image generally recorded through the protective glass of the frame.

signed in pencil.   Has a handwritten signature which, in the opinion of the auction house, is the artist's signature.

sold after sale.   If a lot has been *bought-in* but purchased from the auction house after the sale, it is *sold after sale.*

state.   One stage in the progress toward completion of the plate. Any impression that shows additional work on the plate is another state. Some artists (Rembrandt and Degas, for example) produced numerous states, each of which can stand on its own.

thread margins.   Margins that are so narrow they can only be described as the width of a thread, less than one millimeter.

time staining.   A condition that indicates evidence of dust and handling.

trial proof.   A proof made during the creative process by the artist to check on the progress of the work. *See proof, artist's proof, edition proof.*

trimmed to subject.   A phrase referring to a print with no margin, with not even a thread of paper remaining beyond the image. This is usually considered detrimental to the print, for it cannot be repaired adequately.

verso.   The back of a sheet of paper.

water staining.   Damage to a print from seeping water. It can be treated by a conservator.

watermark.   A translucent identifying mark on a sheet of paper made during its manufacture by variations in pulp thickness. It may be a symbol (e.g., fool's cap or crown), a monogram, or a company name that has been formed in wire on the papermaker's mold. Whatman paper often has the date of manufacture included in the watermark. Watermarks are usually read from the image side of the paper.

wove paper. Paper manufactured on a screen of brass wires all of the same weight that have been woven to produce an even, smooth surface. The paper itself is smooth and free of visible marks from the wires. See *laid paper*.

Print Media and Techniques

aquatint. An *intaglio* process. Particles of powdered resin are adhered to a metal plate with heat, either before or after *etching* the lines. When the plate is treated with acid, the acid corrodes it, leaving tiny depressions around each granule that retain ink when the plate is wiped. Treating *(stopping out)* some areas with varnish may vary the effect. Aquatints have broad tonal values and are thought to resemble ink or watercolor washes.

block print. A phrase used to describe certain woodcuts, particularly Japanese ukiyo-e prints, but sometimes also Provincetown or other Arts and Crafts relief prints. See *woodblock* and *woodcut*.

burin. A steel rod with a sharp beveled point that forms an incised V-shaped line in a metal plate. See *burr*.

burnished aquatint. A method by which the granular surface of an aquatint is partially polished with a scraper and burnisher to produce lighter areas or highlights.

burr. The ridge of metal raised on either side of a line incised by a *burin* or *drypoint* needle. The rough surface on a *mezzotint* is also called a burr. See *steel facing*.

carborundum. An abrasive powdered mixture, primarily silicon carbide, used to produce a dotted or tonal effect when the plate is passed through a press. Similar to a *sandpaper ground*.

chromolithograph. A color lithograph, specifically those of the nineteenth and early twentieth centuries, e.g., Louis Prang. Modern colored lithographs are usually catalogued as "printed in colors." In lithographs, each color requires a separate stone or plate.

cliché verre. See *photographic processes*.

collograph. A relief plate formed by adding materials like found objects or textured materials to a solid base such as cardboard, metal, masonite, or plastic.

collotype. A *photomechanical* process. The preparation of a plate by coating a metal surface with light-sensitive gelatin. A photographic negative is placed on the surface and the two are exposed to light. The gelatin dries and hardens in proportion to the strength of the light transmitted through the negative. Collotypes are primarily lithographs and are especially good for reproducing watercolors, lithographs, drawings, and photographs.

copperplate. See *intaglio*.

crayon manner. An *intaglio* method. When a *roulette*, or other stippling tool, is used to prepare a *ground* plate, the marks have a soft effect that resembles the crumbly look of a chalk, pastel, or crayon drawing. *Pastel-manner* prints use the same methodology, but separate plates are prepared for each color. See *ground*.

drypoint. An *intaglio* process by which the marks are scratched directly into the copper, zinc, or steel plate with a sharp steel point. The *burr* that is thrown up on either side of the line catches and holds extra ink, which produces a rich tone. The plate usually produces only twenty or thirty good impressions, for the *burr* is fragile The printer's skill is an important component in the quality of the print. See *steel facing*.

electrotyping.   An electrolytic casting process used to copy a block or plate into a metal facsimile. Wood engravings made for book illustration in the late nineteenth century were printed mainly from electrotypes rather than the original wood, which might have deteriorated over the run.

embossed print.   A print with an impression in high relief, that is, with all or part of the image higher than the unmarked areas. Some embossed prints have no color other than that of the paper.

engraving.   Metal plates that have been engraved (incised) with a *burin*. The oldest form of *intaglio* prints, the word is sometimes used incorrectly to refer to all *intaglio* prints.

etching.   An *intaglio* method in which the lines are bitten by acid. The plate is coated with an acid-resistant material *(ground)* through which the artist draws lines that expose the metal. The plate is immersed in acid until the lines are bitten into the plate. The ground is removed before the plate is inked for printing. See *ground*.

ground.   The surface applied to an etching plate that is impervious to acid.

half-tone block.   A photomechanical process that reproduces all gradations of black through white on a relief metal plate. The process produces thousands of black and white dots of varying sizes that give the illusion of a range of values. There are procedures for making half-tone blocks in all of the classes of printmaking *(intaglio, relief, planographic, stencil)*. See *photogravure*.

heliogravure.   See *photogravure*.

intaglio.   One of the four major classes of printmaking. After a metal plate has been incised, ink is dabbed into the lines, the surface is cleaned by *wiping,* and dampened paper is placed onto the plate. The two are passed through a roller press, which lifts the ink up onto the paper. *Engraving, etching, aquatint, stipple, drypoint,* and *photogravure* are forms of intaglio prints. Intaglio is sometimes called *copperplate*.

letterpress.   Printing of text from *relief* type, especially of pre-20th-century broadsides and books. Since the advent of laser printing, phototypesetting, and offset lithograpy in the past twenty years, little is printed by letterpress.

lift ground.   See *sugarlift process*.

line-block.   A photomechanical process, similar to electrotyping, that reproduces a line drawing. Modern methods of line block use electronic scanners and automatic etching machines. Line-block facsimiles of woodcuts and wood engravings may be difficult to discern from the originals except that the lines in the reproductions are more consistent in tonality. *Photoengraving* is a synonym.

linocut.   An abbreviation for linoleum cut, a popular relief process due to the soft, pliable nature of linoleum. Multicolor linocuts usually use separate blocks for each color.

lithograph.   The *planographic* method, invented in 1792 by Aloïs Senefelder, based on the natural antipathy of water and grease. Greasy crayon or fluids are applied to a stone (or zinc or linoleum) matrix. Water is washed across the matrix and then ink is applied and adheres to the greasy crayon creating the image. Stone and paper are then passed together through a flat-bed scraper press. See *planography*.

metalcuts. A metal plate made in the fifteenth century by punching designs and dots into the surface of the metal and then printing the relief surfaces. Often called "dotted-manner" prints.

mezzotint. An *intaglio* process. The plate is prepared by completely roughening (grounding) the plate with a spiked tool (rocker) that produces an overall *burr*. The artist develops the image by scraping and burnishing to produce gradations of dark through light. This technique was used widely in 18th-century England for the reproduction of portraits.

monoprint. A unique printmaking technique. The artist paints an image in printing ink on a sheet of metal, Plexiglas, or other flat nonabsorbent surface and then runs it and a piece of paper through a press. Only one good impression can be made. Monotype is a synonym.

monotype. See *monoprint*.

multilevel color intaglio printing. A color print technique first developed by Stanley Hayter in the late 1920s. Various depths of etched lines retain the separate inks based on their individual viscosities. *Simultaneous color printing* and *viscosity printing* are synonyms.

nature print. A color impression from a printing plate based on actual plants. Plants are embossed into a soft lead plate under pressure, and this is transformed into a printing plate by *electrotyping*. The final *intaglio* plate is printed *à la poupée*. This method was popular in the late nineteenth century.

pastel manner. See *crayon manner*.

photoengraving. See *line-block*.

photogravure. A photomechanical process that reproduces all gradations of black through white on an *intaglio* metal plate. The process produces a finer image than *half-tone block* and *photoengraving*. Stieglitz used photogravure to reproduce the facsimile photographs for *Camera Work*. Photogravures are sometimes referred to as heliogravures.

photographic processes. Photographic processes can be used to transfer a positive or negative image to any *matrix* (wood, metal, or silkscreen) that has been light-sensitized beforehand. Words beginning with the prefix "photo" or "process" (photoetching, photolithography, photosilk-screen, or process lithography) and other terms like *line-block, half-tone block, collotype*, and *photogravure* all indicate that a photographic process is involved. When a print has been reproduced with a photographic process *after* a work in another medium, it is not considered an original print. When the photographic process is a part of the artist's working method, then it is authentic. *Cliché verre* (literally "printing from glass") is an example of an original photographic process. E.g., Frenchmen Corot, Millet, Rousseau, and Daubigny, and Americans Thomas Moran and Eastman Johnson.

photomechanical. Any of several processes that combine photographic (rather than an artist's hand methods) with printmaking techniques. See *photographic processes*.

photomontage. A photographic print of a montage or assemblage of disparate images which may be photographs themselves, engravings, collage elements, and so on.

planography.   One of the four major classes of printmaking. Unlike *intaglio* and *relief* matrices, there is no difference in level between the inked surface and the non-inked surface. Planography usually refers to *lithographs*, but it also includes zincographs, aluminographs (algraphs), and *photolithographs.*

plate tone.   The gray or other light tone that may be left on the surface of the plate during the *wiping* process. It is transferred to the paper during printing. It may be an overall tone or differentially wiped, in which parts of the background seem to be brighter than others.

pochoir.   A method of applying color to a print. Color is applied through stencils (pochoirs) after the print has been pulled. Characteristics of this method are crisp edges and flat color. See *à la poupée* for another way to add color.

à la poupée.   A method of adding color to an *intaglio* plate. Tightly rolled cloth (called a dabber or poupée) is dipped into colored ink and applied to the plate. Small areas of mixed color are a sign that this method has been used.

relief.   One of the four major classes of printmaking, a relief print is one in which the printed mark is created by the raised areas of the matrix. Examples are *metalcuts, woodcut, wood engraving, linocut, line-block, half-tone block,* and *cliché verre.* Ink is rolled onto the raised areas, and when paper is pressed against the block, either with a press or various hand tools, the ink is transferred to the paper.

relief etching.   A relief method first used by Blake for producing illuminated books printed in 1788-1820. Text and image were transferred to the metal so that they formed the acid–resistant element and the background was etched away. The prints were either printed in colors or hand-colored after printing, or in some cases both kinds of coloration were used.

remarque.   A scribbled sketch by an artist outside the main design that might serve as a trademark but is often removed before the final edition is pulled.

retroussage.   A technique sometimes used in the final wiping of intaglio plates. A fine muslin is dragged along the inked lines to soften their definition and give a richer, almost *drypoint* effect.

roulette.   A multispiked wheel that produces a series of *intaglio* dots with *burr*. It is used for *crayon–manner* prints and to repair *mezzotint* plates.

sandpaper ground.   A background prepared by running the plate and a sheet of sandpaper together through the press. This produces an overall grey in the final print, for each of the resulting dots holds a small quantity of ink.

screenprint.   A *stencil* process in which the stencil is placed on a screen. Ink is forced through the screen onto paper, fabric, or metal, forming a distinct layer of pigment on the surface. The terms *serigraph*, screenprint, and silkscreen are synonymous.

serigraph.   A term used to indicate a fine art *screenprint.*

silkscreen print.   The original support for stencils in *screenprinting* was fine silk.

simultaneous color printing.   See *multilevel color intaglio printing.*

soft-ground etching.   An *intaglio* method in which the lines are bitten by the acid. The *etching* plate is covered with an acid–resistant material (the soft ground) through which the artist draws lines to expose the metal.

Because the ground is highly sensitive, it can be marked by hand or any tool, such as a pencil. Fabrics and other soft materials may be applied and then removed, leaving a textured surface.

steel facing. Copper plates are commonly used for *engravings* because they are receptive to the artist's touch, but they have a limited run because they wear down easily. Steel facing, a process patented in 1857, lengthens the life of the plate by depositing through electrolysis a fine layer of steel on its surface. Some connoisseurs believe that steel facing decreases the richness of the *burr* in *drypoints*.

stencil. One of the four major classes of printmaking, this method involves the application of ink onto the paper's surface through previously cut stencils. This is the one print-making method which does not reverse the image. Examples are *screenprint* and *pochoir*.

stipple engraving. A method of modeling areas of a plate by using the tip of the *burin* to make dashes rather than full lines where a lighter tone is required. Stipple engraving is often used in conjunction with *crayon manner* or regular *engraving*.

stopping out. The method of protecting with varnish any part of a metal plate that is not to be etched during the biting process. Differential stopping out provides the opportunity for *etching* various parts of the plate to different depths. See *multilevel color intaglio printing*.

sugar lift process. An *intaglio* method. The artist draws on a plate with a fluid saturated with sugar. After drying, *stopping-out* varnish is applied to the whole plate, and the plate is immersed in water. This causes the sugar to lift the stopping-out varnish off the plate and expose the metal. The plate is then etched and printed in the usual way. An *aquatint* base may have been applied first, so that the etched portions carry an aquatint tone. *Lift ground* is a synonym for this process.

viscosity printing. See *multilevel color intaglio printing*.

wiping. A part of the inking process in intaglio printmaking. To remove surface ink, the printer uses several muslin or tarlatan pads. The wiping motion is circular and the printer may accidentally leave scratches or circular deposits of ink on the plate. A final step uses the palm of the hand or a piece of tissue. See *plate tone* and *retroussage*.

woodblock. This term, used interchangeably with *woodcut* but more often for Japanese ukiyo-e prints and the woodcuts of Provincetown or Arts and Crafts printmakers, also refers to the block of wood that forms the basis of this relief process. Soft wood is cut lengthwise along the grain, seasoned to prevent warping, and planed smooth. See *woodcut* and *block print*.

woodcut. A *relief* printmaking method. The design is cut with a knife or V–shaped gouge into plank wood with the grain. Chisels and gouges are used to remove large areas of background and ink is then applied to the raised surfaces. Historically the oldest printmaking method. See *woodblock*, *linocut*, and *block print*.

wood engraving. A *relief* print made from end–grain wood. Boxwood or other hard fruitwoods were usually selected for its fine grain. Since boughs of such wood have a small diameter, small squares of wood are clamped together to make up the block. *Burins* are used for carving into the wood. What distinguishes wood engravings from *woodcuts* is the grain of the wood, the tool used, and the fine details of the image.

Photography Media

albumen print.   A *contact print* on paper usually made from a *collodion* negative. The paper, which has been treated with a solution of albumen (egg white) and salt, is sensitized with silver nitrate. The print is made by placing the paper in contact with the negative and exposing it to the sun. The prints are often brown with gold highlights, but they may be reddish or purple-brown. The most popular kind of print of the 19th century, albumen prints were used mainly from 1850-1890.

ambrotype.   A *collodion* wet-plate negative on glass that appears as a positive image when backed with an opaque coating like black-lacquer. Ambrotypes are sometimes confused with *daguerreotypes* because both are fragile and presented in cases. A good way to differentiate the two is to hold the image at an angle; unlike daguerreotypes, ambrotypes will appear positive no matter what the angle of view. Named after James Ambrose Cutting, they were in vogue from the 1850s to the mid 1860s.

autochrome.   A colored, transparent image on glass meant to be viewed by being held up to the light or projected onto a surface. The process, which was invented in 1904, involves coating a glass plate with grains of starch dyed red, green, and blue-violet, a varnish, and then a bromide emulsion solution that acts as a light filter. The result is a unique positive transparency.

bichromate.   See *gum bichromate print*.

bromoil print.   A print based on a gelatin silver-bromide *contact print* or enlargement that has been treated with a potassium bichromate solution. After the print has been chemically altered, it will selectively accept an oil pigment in proportion to the amount of silver in the original image. Different colored oil pigments may be used. The resulting image may be dried as is or transferred to another matrix while wet under pressure. This process originated in England in 1907 and was popular into the 1930s.

C-print.   See *Type-C print*.

calotype.   The first successful negative to positive process and thus the first to produce multiple photographic images. The paper negative was used to produce a *salt print* positive. Calotypes were popular from their invention in 1841 until the early 1850s; the process was revived about 1900 by the Pictorialist photographers. Characteristics of calotypes are a lack of sharp detail and an overall subtle mottling of tones. They are sometimes called *talbotypes* after their inventor William Henry Fox Talbot.

carbon print.   Significant as the first permanent photographic process, carbon prints were most popular between 1870 and 1910, although they remained in use until the 1940s. Unlike other photographic processes that use silver, which deteriorates over time, carbon prints use a paper that has been treated with potassium bichromate and a pigment (usually carbon black). The print is made by a contact process in daylight; the gelatin hardens in proportion to the light that is exposed through the negative, and the excess gelatin is washed away. Characteristics are visible paper fibers in the lighter areas and sometimes cracks in the thicker layers of gelatin.

carbro print.   A permanently colored (less often monochrome) photographic print popular about 1920-1930. It is produced like the carbon print, but with three bromide transfer prints stacked in registration to produce a single colored image. The color negatives are made by photographing through a red, a green, and a blue filter. About 5 or 6 images may be made from the original negative. The name carbro comes from *car*bon and *bro*-mide. See *dye-transfer print*.

carte-de-visite. A stiff piece of card measuring about $4\frac{1}{2}$ x $2\frac{1}{2}$ inches, the size of a formal visiting card of the 1860s, with an attached photograph, usually a full-length studio portrait, of nearly the same size. Sometimes the subject matter was a tourist attraction or a work of art. Cartes-de-visite were most popular during the 1860s and were often collected in albums.

chromogenic color print. A subtractive color print process developed about 1930. The developer contains dye couplers which compound with silver in three layers of emulsion. Each layer is sensitive to one of the primary colors in light-blue, green, and red. Colors in these prints are not as stable as those in *dye-transfer prints*.

Cibachrome print. A brand name. See *chromogenic color print*.

collodion positive. See *ambrotype*.

collodion process. Collodion (a derivative of gun cotton that has been dissolved in alcohol and ether and then mixed with potassium iodide and potassium bromide) is a viscous fluid that forms a transparent film when the solvents evaporate. The wet-collodion process, in use from about 1851 to 1855, used a glass plate coated with wet collodion and sensitized with silver nitrate. The plate was placed in the camera while still wet and immediately exposed. After being exposed, the plate had to be developed before it dried, generally within the hour. This process was valued for its resolution of detail and because exposure times were shorter than for *daguerreotypes* or *colotypes*. The dry-collodion process, in use from the mid-1850s to the mid-1860s, was a variant of the wet-collodion process, but the exposure time was almost six times as long and dry-collodion plates never became widely popular. Multiple prints could be made from the collodion process.

contact print. A print made by placing light-sensitive paper in direct contact with a negative. Most 19th-century prints were contact prints; most modern-day prints are enlargements.

cyanotype. Cyanotypes are produced by placing a negative, plant specimen, or drawing on a sheet of paper treated with iron salt and potassium ferricyanide. When the sheet is placed in direct sunlight, an impression will form that eventually turns bright blue (cyan) where it has been exposed to light and white where the sunlight was blocked. Although the process was first invented in 1841, most cyanotypes were produced from the late 1880s to 1920. One common use was for architectural drawings in blueprints.

daguerreotype. The first practical photographic process, popular from the early 1840s until the late 1850s. A daguerreotype is a unique image on metal produced by treating a copper plate with a light-sensitized surface coating of silver iodide. A daguerreotype is distinctive for its highly polished silver support and its quality of appearing either as a negative or a positive, depending on the angle and light from which it is viewed. Daguerreotypes are light-sensitive and fragile and are usually stored in cases for protection.

dry-collodion print. See *collodion process*.

dye-transfer print. The most permanent of color prints, this complex method is based on the earliest *carbro print* method. The subject is photographed three times, using a different color filter each time. After several steps, the three, or more, separate gelatin negatives dyed cyan, magenta, and yellow are transferred one at a time in daylight in registration to form a positive color image. Also called a dye imhibition print.

Ektachrome print. A brand name. See *chromogenic color print.*

gelatin silver print. A photograph printed on paper that has been coated with gelatin containing light-sensitive silver halides. First introduced in 1872, gelatin silver prints are the standard black-and-white prints in use today.

gum bichromate print. A photograph printed on paper that has been coated with an emulsion of gum arabic, potassium bichromate, and pigment. The emulsion hardens in relation to the amount of light it receives, and the emulsion is then washed away. Introduced in 1894, popular into the 1920s, and occasionally used today, the gum bichromate process is valued for the artistic control it gives the photographer; gum bichromate prints have broad tones and often resemble crayon or charcoal drawings. Also called a gum print.

half-tone. A photomechanical process to transfer a photographic image to a relief plate that can be printed on the same press as type. The continuous tones of the photograph are converted into a pattern of tiny dots (larger and closer together in the dark areas) that are visible under magnification. In duotone printing, two passes of the press are used. The process was first used commercially in 1880.

heliogravure. See *photogravure.*

jetgraph. The color-print process in which cyan, magenta, yellow, and black are controlled by a computer and a digital scanning system.

orotone print. Using a negative, an image is printed on a glass plate that has been covered with a gelatin silver emulsion. After the image has been developed, the back of the plate is painted gold. Orotones were popularized by Edward S. Curtis in the early 20th century.

palladium print. See *platinum print.*

photogram. A photograph made without a camera by laying objects on a light sensitive surface. The images are negative silhouettes. See *rayograph.*

photogravure. A photomechanical printing process to reproduce photographs. First developed in 1879, the process is based on the traditional printmaking technique of *intaglio.* Most of the reproductions in Steiglitz's *Camera Work* were photogravures, for the process produces prints (gravures) of high quality. Under magnification, the black areas may look like a fine mesh pattern rather than the dots of a *half-tone* reproduction. Also referred to as *heliogravure.*

photomontage. A composite image made by bringing together different photographs or parts of photographs to form a blended whole, which is often photographed.

platinum print. First developed in 1873, platinum coated papers were commercially available until 1937, when the cost of platinum made the process prohibitively expensive. For a short while the platinum was replaced with the less costly palladium. The process is based on the light sensitivity of paper that has been treated with iron salts and a platinum compound and then developed in potassium oxalate. Platinum prints were popular because of their permanency and their wide range of soft gray tonalities. Some modern photographers such as Irving Penn still use this process by hand-sensitizing their own papers.

printing-out paper. A paper treated with sodium chloride and silver nitrate (forming silver chloride) that becomes light-sensitized and darkens when exposed to direct sunlight or daylight. (No chemical treatment is required to make the image visible.)

rayograph. The name the artist Man Ray gave to his *photograms.*

salt print. A *contact print* made from a *calotype* or *collodion* negative. A sheet of paper that has been treated with light-sensitive silver chloride salts is placed into a frame in contact with the negative and exposed to sunlight. Salt prints are reddish-brown with a matte surface. The color may be a purplish-brown if it has been toned or a gold-brown if it has faded. The resolution is not as sharp as in albumen prints. Invented in 1840, salt prints were the earliest form of positive prints; they were in use until about 1860 when they were replaced by the albumen print.

schadograph. The name Christian Schad gave to his *photograms.*

silver print. See *gelatin silver print.*

stereograph. A cardboard mount holding two photographs of the same subject, each from a slightly different point of view. When viewed with binocular vision, a stereoscopic effect, 3-D (depth of field) is achieved.

talbotype. See *calotype.*

Type-C print. Kodak's old designation (before Kodacolor, 1941) for a color print made from a color negative or color transparency. See *chromogenic color print.*

wet-collodion print. See *collodion process.*

How to Use This Book

The Confident Collector: Prints, Posters & Photographs Identification and Price Guide is a compilation of prices from auctions held worldwide from July 1, 1991, through June 29, 1992. The price structure for art is established in the marketplace—at galleries, private sales, and auctions. Only those established at auction are public record (in most cases governed by state regulations). Auction prices are the only prices listed in this *Guide.*

The prices in this book are derived from the database established by *Leonard's ANNUAL Price Index of Prints, Posters & Photographs. Leonard's* includes full citations for the prices realized from the sales of prints, posters, and photographs at 115 auction houses, both domestic and international. Sales are included from the major New York, California, and European houses as well as smaller houses here and abroad. Every effort has been made to cover all sales possible. Some works by contemporary photographers such as Cindy Sherman or Barbara Kruger are offered at auction at contemporary art sales; results from these sales have been included.

By providing data about the actual prices realized at auction for the work of thousands of artists, *The Confident Collector: Prints, Posters &*

Photographs Identification and Price Guide presents a baseline of information about the art market. Auction prices are sometimes considered to be wholesale—sometimes retail, depending on location and date of sale. This *Guide* will help you assess comparative price data for individual artists and will help you determine whether a particular work is fairly priced, overvalued or a bargain. The prices in this book are a range, not a definitive price. For further information and complete citations check *Leonard's*. The final consideration, however, must be the artistic quality of the print, poster, or photograph—condition and other factors being equal.

There are over 13,000 artists listed in this *Guide*. Similar names have not been merged because of the uncertainty as to whether they were the same person. In some instances, artists' first names were not readily available; these entries are listed with last names only. Prints provide a special problem, as the same edition of a print may be listed as "after" by one auction house and directly by the artist by another auction house. John James Audubon painted watercolors and Robert Havell executed the lithographs and etchings after the paintings. Correctly catalogued, all of Audubon's prints should be listed as "after." In this book you will find several separate listings for Audubon. Our listings reflect the manner in which these artists' works have been catalogued by various auction houses.

The price range reflects the low and high prices for a category of work. Identical prices in "low" and "high" reflect that more than one work by the artist has sold at the same price. If only one work by an artist was sold, the price will appear in the high column. Conversions for foreign currencies are based on the *New York Times* exchange rate for the day of the sale.

Price ranges are just that. Prices for an artist's work vary for a tremendous variety of reasons, including rarity, quality of the image, edition, state, and condition. Other factors are the desire of competing bidders, condition, subject matter, framing, provenance, attendance, weather, etc. The price ranges in this book reflect these variables.

For the purpose of this *Guide*, prints are categorized into eight different types. They are *intaglio, relief, stencil, planographic, mixed media, photomechanical reproduction, others*, and *generic*. There are separate listings for posters, photographs and portfolios, and books. Appendix E provides a complete listing by category.

There are approximately 300 artists whose works are listed only under "port/book." Portfolios, books, sets or any multiple offerings fall into this category. An artist with a singular listing under portfolios/books is a printmaker unless otherwise designated as a photographer.

Indexing in this *Guide* conforms to the *Anglo-American Cataloging Rules for Names*, revised in 1979. Appendix D provides a brief summary of the cataloging rules. If there is any doubt, check all the possibilities.

Nationality and life dates are included for all artists where available. When conflicts have arisen as to their validity, we have been diligent in our research and have made informed decisions.

Prices reflect the popularity of a particular artist or style in a certain region, fads, and fashion in art. Above all they reflect the overall strength of the economy, but price is not the only index of value of an individual work. Price will not tell you if a work is authentic. Neither will it tell you the unique characteristics or rarity of a print or photograph. Note, too, that the price a work sells for at auction is not necessarily what you will receive if you want to sell.

Finally, don't be discouraged by high prices. If you desire a work by a famous artist, it may be possible to buy a minor example for a reasonable sum. Smaller or less typical examples may sell well below the price of a major work. The works of lesser known, undiscovered, or undervalued artists provide many good buying opportunities.

For more specific information on the works of a particular artist, refer to *Leonard's ANNUAL Price Index of Prints, Posters & Photographs*, which provides more detailed information on titles of works sold, size, auction house, and date of sale.

SPECIALIZED FIELDS OF COLLECTING

Collecting can take many forms. Its themes can be as diverse as WPA prints, black and white prints, miniatures, photojournalism, boxing, Art Deco, Audubon prints, or the Ash Can School. A memorable collection of paintings was the Prescott Collection, which was sold at Christie's in 1981. Its theme was strawberries: each still-life—Old Master, 19th-century, contemporary—prominently pictured strawberries as its subject.

Some of these niches of collecting are discussed in the following articles by experts, each of whom is recognized by his or her peers as "the" person in the noted field. Their expertise is both academic and commercial.

ART DECO POSTERS

by Tony Fusco

Tony Fusco is a partner in Fusco & Four Associates, a gallery and public relations firm in Brighton, Massachusetts. He is the President of the Art Deco Society of Boston and the author of The Confident Collector: Art Deco Identification and Price Guide, 2nd Edition (1993), *and* The Confident Collector: Posters Identification and Price Guide, 2nd Edition *(to appear in 1994).*

Today the term "Art Deco" is applied to a whole complex of decorative trends in the applied arts and architecture in the period roughly between 1909 and 1939. The term came into use in the late 1960s and was derived from the title of the 1925 Exposition Internationale des Arts Décoratifs et Industriels Modernes in Paris. This exposition marked the culmination of an early French Art Deco style and the emergence of the more geometric, Germanic "Modern" style. The last phase of the style, reflecting the impact of industrial designers on household appliances and furniture in the 1930s, is referred to by many as "Streamline."

French designers were influenced by the opulent sets and costumes of Les Ballets Russes, which arrived in Paris in 1909 and set off an explosion in fashion, illustration, and interior design. It was design movements outside Paris, coupled with a changing society and the economic pressures of urbanization, that would slowly replace the early, flowery French Art Deco style with its more Modern phases.

In America, Art Deco is also closely related to Hollywood of the 1920s through the 1940s, which helped popularize the style. In the end, it was Hollywood's continual exaggeration of the style that would cause Art Deco to fall out of favor with designers. The advent of World War II was the final blow to a style thought of as just "too chic" for wartime.

Graphic design changed during the Art Deco period to attract wider markets to the host of new products being offered. In Europe, posters were an effective way of reaching mass audiences, but earlier Art Nouveau posters were too leisurely in delivering their messages. Modern posters had to be strong enough to be read from passing cars, capturing attention with typography, the image of the product, bold lines and colors, short messages, and interesting angles. The poster's job was to sell a product in a competitive way. It has been argued that had it not been for advertising art, the new style would not have gained acceptance so rapidly.

Typography

The Bauhaus, the German school of architecture and applied arts, revolutionized typography as much as it did architecture. Often elongated and condensed, new German typefaces contributed a new sense of speed that dominated graphic design. Many of the new typefaces were *sans serif*, that is, individual letters were without the short lines at the ends of their strokes. Popular new styles included Paul Renner's Futura (1928), Koch's Kabel (1927), Eric Gill's Gill Sans (1928), and others such as Bifur, Bauhaus, and Broadway, a decidedly American Art Deco type style. In looking at Art Deco posters, notice how much the typography can affect the overall visual appeal.

Adolphe Mouron (1901-1968) was born in Russia and studied at the Academie Julian in Paris. Mouron worked for a printer to earn room and board. He began to design posters and in 1922 began to use the pseudonym A.M. Cassandre. He worked as a painter, posterist, theater designer, and typographer. In 1963, he designed the famous logo YSL for Yves Saint-Laurent. Cassandre is well known for his travel posters; *Nord Express*, designed in 1927, is considered one of his masterpieces. The retail price for this poster ranges from $14,000–$18,000. (A.M. Cassandre, *Nord Express*, courtesy Fusco & Four Associates)

Design Influences

As with other applied arts, Art Deco posters were influenced by many earlier design movements. At the turn of the century, Charles Rennie Mackintosh of Glasgow influenced Josef Hoffmann and other designers of the Vienna Secession and *Wiener Werkstätte* (Vienna Workshop). Mackintosh himself was somewhat influenced by the straight lines and sober style of the English Arts and Crafts Movement.

From the first Vienna Secessionist exhibition poster in 1898, by Gustav Klimt (1862-1918), it was clear that the poster would be used both to advertise products and to make known the Secession's artistic values. Koloman Moser (1868-1918), Egon Schiele (1890-1919), Berthold Löffler (1874-1960), and other artists introduced bold geometric shapes and patterns and the radical use of typography to achieve graphic effects.

These and other artistic movements, like the Dutch De Stijl movement, Cubism, and Futurism had a profound effect on advertising design.

The Bauhaus, with its well-known designers like Ludwig Mies van der Rohe, Walter Gropius, and Marcel Breuer in turn strongly affected French and American designers after 1925. American Art Deco was much more influenced by these Modern movements than by the early French style.

French Posters

The best known and highest priced French Art Deco posterist is Adolphe Mouron Cassandre (1901-1968). His first poster, *LeBoucheron* (1923), set the tone for a whole new style, influencing graphic designers both in France and abroad.

By subject, travel posters are the most highly realized Art Deco designs, and Cassandre was the master of these, designing many for ocean liners and trains: *Étoile du Nord* (1927), *Nord Express* (1927), *L.M.S. Bestway* (1928), *L'Oiseau Bleu* (1929), *Chemin de Fer du Nord* (1931), *L'Atlantique* (1931), *Wagon Bar* (1932), and *Normandie* (1935). Other travel poster artists are inevitably compared to Cassandre.

Cassandre also designed posters for a wide range of companies and products, including cigarettes, radios, liquor, magazines, newspapers, lightbulbs, shoes, and more. It is no wonder that the first advertising agencies were founded by poster artists, such as Cassandre's agency Alliance Graphique.

Other French Art Deco posterists worth finding are Robert Bonfils (1886-1972), Roger Broders (1883-1953), Jean Carlu (b. 1900), Paul Colin (1892-1985), Jean Dupas (1882-1964), Maurice Dufrène (1876-1955), Pierre Fix-Masseau (b. 1905), Charles Gesmar (1900-1928), Georges Lepape (1887-1971), and Charles Loupot (1892-1962).

Fix-Masseau, whose style is similar to Cassandre's, is best known for his train posters. Broders is known for his highly stylized resort posters for the French railways. Bonfils was a fashion illustrator who created the official poster for the 1925 Paris Exposition, with its leaping gazelle and stylized flowers. Another fashion designer, Georges Lepape, is best known for his fashion illustrations for *La Gazette du Bon Ton* and *Vogue* magazine, but he also created several posters for such clients as entertainers, the department store Galéries Lafayette, and the Théâtre des Champs Elysées.

Many great posters were created for stage performers like Josephine Baker, Mistinguett, and others. Charles Gesmar, who designed about fifty posters in his short lifetime, created almost half of them for Mistinguett! Paul Colin's 1925 poster for Josephine Baker's *Revue Nègre* introduced a new style of poster design influenced by the rhythms of jazz. Josephine Baker posters and memorabilia have skyrocketed in value. The very rare *Revue Nègre* poster was recently sold by a dealer for $45,000.

Inspired by the Cubists, Carlu was the creator of neon tube posters, both in three dimensions and as graphic designs. He designed posters for the 1937 Paris Exposition as well as for everyday items like toothpaste. During World War II he created effective wartime Art Deco posters.

Dupas was a fine artist whose distinctive, recognizable style carried over into his advertising graphics. His posters for the Salon des Artistes Décorateurs, English railways, and the department store Arnold Constable are very desirable.

Many other talented though lesser-known French designers created appealing Art Deco posters, which tend to be more affordable to collectors than those by the artists named above.

Belgian and Dutch Posters

The best "Belgian" Art Deco posterist came from Switzerland: Leo Marfurt (1894-1977), who moved to Belgium in 1927 and created an advertising agency, Les Créations Publicitaires, which he ran until 1957. Like

SUMATRA
JAVA
ROTTERDAMSCHE LLOYD

Travel posters have always been highly popular as a nostalgic reminder of places we have been or as tantalizing visions of places we would like to go. After World War I there was a dramatic increase in travel on ocean liners. Many of these ocean liners were palaces of Art Deco design and their posters reflected this image. Johan von Stein (1896-1965) was a painter but mainly a graphic designer and is best known for his posters. *Rotterdamsche Lloyd, 1930* was designed for the Lloyd line; the retail price ranges from $2,400–$2,600. (John von Stein, *Rotterdamsche Lloyd, 1930,* courtesy Fusco & Four Associates)

Cassandre, Marfurt created posters for many clients, such as Belga cigarettes, Chrysler automobiles, resorts, and a host of others.

Some good Belgian poster designs of the period also came from Francis Delamare, Auguste Mambour (1896-1968), Milo Martinet (b. 1904), Lucien de Roeck (b. 1915), and others including the country's leading surrealist painter, René Magritte (1898-1967).

The best Dutch Art Deco posters were for products and travel. One notable designer is Wim ten Broek (b. 1905), whose posters for Holland-America Line ocean liners are reminiscent of A. M. Cassandre. This is not surprising: Cassandre also designed posters for Holland-America and other Dutch companies.

Other Dutch designers include Jan Wijga (1902-1978), notably his posters for KLM (Royal Dutch Airlines), Johann von Stein (1896-1965) for Lloyd Lines, Nicolaas Petrus "N. P." de Koo (1881-1960), Agnes Canta (1888-1964), and Wilhem Gispen (1890-1981).

Swiss Posters

Switzerland is a vacationer's playground, and travel posters in a modern style appeared early on. Emile Cardinaux (1877-1936) and Otto Morach (1877-1973) were the first to make notable contributions in this field.

The Swiss artist Herbert Matter (1907-1984), a pioneer of photomontage, is well known for his designs for the men's clothing store PKZ. Another recognized Swiss artist is Otto Baumberger (1889-1961), in whose posters the product takes center stage. Other Swiss posterists to look for are Donald Brün, Hans Erni (b. 1909), Herbert Leupin (b. 1916), and Nicklaus Stoecklin (1896-1982).

In keeping with their national reputation for tidiness, in 1914 the Swiss established a standard format for posters, which is roughly 35 inches wide by 50 inches high, and with the exception of a very few, all Swiss posters are this size.

English Posters

In England, the finest poster artist was an American, Edward McKnight Kauffer (1890-1954), known for his posters for the London Underground, English Rail, and Shell Oil, the three most important poster "patrons" in England.

Shell Oil produced a series of posters using variations of the slogan "Motorists Prefer Shell" and, along with London Transport and English Rail, gave poster commissions to numerous artists. Many of the best artists worked for more than one of these three clients: Austin Cooper (1890-1964), who emigrated to England from Canada; Charles Pears (1873-1958), Frank Newbould (1887-1950), Tom Purvis (1875-1963), and Fred Taylor (1875-1963).

Almost all British Rail posters were produced in two standard sizes: a vertical one-sheet 25 inches wide by 40 inches high (sometimes called a "double royal") and a large horizontal format 50 inches wide by 40 inches high (sometimes called a "quad royal").

German Posters

Ludwig Hohlwein (1874-1949) was the master of modern design in German posters, creating thousands of posters in his dramatic style and striking color combinations. His posters of animals, especially for the Munich Zoo, are prized, along with his film, travel, and product posters.

Lucien Bernhard (1883-1972) is notable because of his typography, and was the creator of the Bernhard typestyles. He was the first to create something he called the *"Sach Plakat"* or "Object Poster" as early as 1906, where the product being advertised occupied the main field of the illustrated design. He moved to the United States in 1923 and taught design at the Art Students' League in New York City.

Hans Rudi Erdt (1883-1917) produced an enormous number of posters for the theater, cars, and cigarettes, often using a theme of horseriding, race driving, or tennis playing. Walter Schnackenberg (1880-1961) created posters with a darker "cabaret" feel; he is noted also for magazine covers.

Other German artists whose works are sought after today are Edmund Edel (1863-1934), Julius Klinger (1876-1950), Ernst Deutsch (1883-1938), Fritz Rehm (1876-1950), Jupp Wiertz (1881-1939), known for his posters for German travel and cinema, and Hans Koch (1899-1977), who designed in a Hohlwein style. The rise of Hitler put an end to the inventiveness of posters of the era, turning them into little more than propaganda.

Italian Posters

Italian Art Deco posters have been increasing in popularity recently. Many of the best of them were designed for operas and for the music publisher Ricordi by Leopoldo Metlicovitz (1868-1944) and Marcello Dudovitch (1878-1962), both of whom also created posters for other clients.

Another outstanding Italian artist, Severo Pozzati (1895-1983), signed his works "Sepo." His product posters have been compared to those by Cassandre; he did, in fact, work in France after 1920. Other Italian artists whose works are worth finding are Marcello Nizzoli (1887-1960), Giorgio Muggiani (1887-1938), Erberto Carboni (1899-1984), Gino Boccasile (1901-1952), Plinio Codognato (1878-1940), Fortunato Depero (1892-1960), Mario Sironi (1885-1961), and Federico Seneca (1891-1976).

American Posters

One might assume that the popularity of the Modern style in the United States had yielded a wealth of fine posters. But in America, with its vast expanses, posters were a less effective advertising vehicle than magazines. And American advertising used photographic images much earlier than in Europe; and when illustrations were used, often European designers were commissioned to execute them.

One "American" posterist we proudly claim is Joseph Binder (1898-1972), an Austrian who worked extensively in Germany before coming to the U.S. Binder won the design competition for the poster of the New York World's Fair of 1939. Ironically, another great collectible American Art Deco poster for the 1939 World's Fair is by an Englishman, John Atherton.

American train posters from the 1920s and 1930s are hard to find, but some of the best are by Leslie Ragan for the New York Central Railroad, Sascha Maurer for the New Haven Railroad, and Gustave Krollman for Northern Pacific Railways. Little is currently known about these three artists, but as research in this field continues, these and other American Art Deco posterists will undoubtedly become more widely recognized.

PHOTOJOURNALISM

by Daile Kaplan

Daile Kaplan is Director of Photographs at Swann Galleries, Inc., a New York auction house. A former curator, she has written many articles and essays about photography and is the author of Lewis Hine in Europe: The Lost Photographs *(Abbeville Press, 1988). She recently edited* Photo Story: Selected Letters and Photographs of Lewis W. Hine *(Smithsonian Institution Press, 1992).*

One compelling genre within the field of photography is photojournalism. Traditionally the domain of the press media, photojournalism is now displayed in museums and galleries. American photojournalism had its beginning in the government-sponsored geographical survey photographs of the Far West and the Civil War photographs taken mainly by Matthew Brady's studio. Photojournalism is that niche of photography that attempts to record history to tell a story. Today, photojournalism is offered regularly at auction and is an exciting area to study.

Joseph Rosenthal's photo of raising the flag on Iwo Jima is one of the most memorable images of World War II. The image, which was staged, was later used as the basis for a memorial statue in Washington, D.C. Enlargements of the photograph were distributed among participants in the battle. Estimated at $6,000–$8,000, this rare vintage print sold for $13,200. (Joseph Rosenthal, *Old Glory Goes Up on Mount Suribachi, Iwo Jima*, gelatin silver print, $9\frac{3}{8}$ x $7\frac{1}{2}$ inches, Christie's, April 15, 1992, $13,200)

While the market for photographs evolved out of recognition of the medium as an art form, for many practitioners photography is more than a vehicle of self-expression. Lewis Hine, Henri Cartier-Bresson, Walker Evans, and Dorothea Lange, for example, were mainly interested in using photography as a powerful communications tool. They approached their work artistically but saw the printed page as the ultimate venue for their pictures. And rather than emphasizing the form and physical qualities of a photograph, they emphasized content and made human-interest images that eloquently describe places, a people, and cultures. Typically reproduced in books and magazines, these images convey messages. These photographic epiphanies capture what Cartier-Bresson characterized as the "decisive moment." Today, we use the descriptive label "photojournalism."

What kind of photographs fall under the rubric of photojournalism? One of the benefits of the term is that it demonstrates just how versatile photography is. In the United States, it may encompass 19th-century records of the Civil War, straightforward "human documents" produced during the Progressive period (this was the term Lewis Hine coined to describe his photographs of immigrants, child laborers, and industrial workers), social documentary photographs taken during the Depression by Farm Security Administration (FSA) photographers, or news photos of dramatic or humorously banal national and international events. Contemporary photographers, like Susan Meiselas and Lee Friedlander (both recipients of MacArthur Fellowships, the so-called "genius" award), Danny Lyon, and Sebastiao Salgado simultaneously make work for their editors and themselves.

Depending on when the image was produced and which print process was used, the photo may be albumen, platinum, or silver. The photograph might contain authenticating characteristics such as the photographer's signature, the name of the publisher (if it was done as part of a portfolio), or, if it is a "press print" (a photograph reproduced in newspapers or journals), the handstamp of the publication, stock house, or social agency.

During PBS's broadcast of Ken Burns's "The Civil War," hundreds of sepia-toned photographs conveyed the gruesome tragedies of the conflict. While these images are imprinted in our memories, the names of the photographers may not be. Matthew Brady, Alexander Gardner, and Timothy O'Sullivan are photographers synonymous with the Civil War to the Americana aficionado. Gardner and O'Sullivan were in the field chronicling the war for Brady, who later published their prints in an edition titled *Photographic Incidents of the War*. Later on, Gardner struck out on his own and published *Photographic Sketchbook of the Civil War*, which included his images and those of his colleagues. In 1988, Swann Galleries sold the two-volume *Sketchbook* for $28,000. For those in a position to pay top dollar, a complete set is desirable, but individual prints are available today for $400 to $2,500.

By the turn of the century Jacob Riis's photographs of gritty city life and Lewis Hine's photographs of immigrants pioneered the social documentary style. At this time, weekly magazines wooed readers with photographic reproductions of everything from celebrity portraits to depictions of natural disasters. With the appearance of picture magazines like *Life* and *Look* in 1936 and 1937, photojournalism was in full swing. Photographers had a venue for their material and an avid viewing public clamored for more images.

Given the high recognition factor of news photos and even their overexposure in the press or on television, one might assume that the original photograph is not particularly valuable. What a big mistake! One must distinguish between the image that appears on television (which is transmitted on videotape) or in newspapers and magazines (which, technically speaking, is not a photograph but a photomechanical reproduction) and the availability of original prints from auction houses, galleries, or private dealers. Just because we repeatedly see an image, this does not mean that an equivalent number of prints are available or that the original photograph is not highly desirable.

In the spring of 1991, a world record was set for Dorothea Lange's classic photograph *Migrant Mother*. An image etched in our collective consciousness, *Migrant Mother* is perhaps *the* symbol of Depression-era America. It has been reproduced countless times in books and magazines. Ironically, that fact led an uninformed collector to dismiss the image with the comment: "Everyone's seen it already!" Yes, the image has a tremendously

The Farm Security Administration (FSA), a division of the Department of Agriculture, was responsible between 1935-1943 for recording a pictorial history of American life. Photographs by Walker Evans, Gordon Parks, Arthur Rothstein, Ben Shahn, and Dorothea Lange captured some of the anxiety, bitterness, and hope of this period and form our visual memory of the the 1930s depression years.

Dorothea Lange's work is characterized by natural, unposed shots with a focus on people rather than landscapes. Lange empathized with her subjects and frequently recorded their comments. *Migrant Mother* is one of the most familiar of her images. Most FSA photographers turned their film into the FSA lab for processing and printing; Dorothea Lange was one of the exceptions. She developed her own film and made prints for herself before she sent in her negatives. The print of *Migrant Mother* that set a record at Swann's in April 1991 was a unique vintage print. The oversized silver gelatin print was printed, inscribed, and signed by Lange; it set a record for the artist when it realized $44,000. (Dorothea Lange, *Migrant Mother*, gelatin silver print, 11 x 14 inches, Swann, April 1991, $44,000)

---

high recognition factor, but how many original photographs of it are available? It turned out, not many. The photograph was estimated at $5,000 to $8,000; it brought $44,000 in an intense contest between bidders, setting a world record for a photograph by Lange. Why did it realize such an astronomical price?

Lange's description of how she made the photograph is worth quoting in part:

I was on my way and barely saw a crude sign ... PEA-PICKERS CAMP. But out of the corner of my eye I did see it.

I didn't want to stop, and didn't ... I drove on and ignored the summons. Then, accompanied by the rhythmic hum of the windshield wipers, arose an inner argument:

Dorothea, how about that camp back there?
What is that situation back there?
Are you going back?
Nobody could ask this of you, now could they?

Having well convinced myself for twenty miles that I could continue on ... I
*made a U-turn and went back.**

In photography, photographs (also called "prints") are either "vintage" (sometimes referred to as "original") or "modern" (sometimes referred to as "contemporary"); vintage prints are usually preferable to modern ones. Vintage prints are those the photographers themselves would choose to be judged by. Vintage prints are normally produced around the time the negative was made by the photographer or under the photographer's direction; modern prints are also made from the original negatives but may have been printed at any time, from several years later to very recently.

The print of *Migrant Mother* that sold for a record price was a unique vintage print. Unlike other existing prints, it contained both Lange's signature and her inscription, and the rich, silver-gray tones of the photograph were superb. The print was oversized, larger than the standard 8 x 10 inches. In addition, Lange herself made the print—an unusual circumstance given that she, like other FSA photographers, at first relinquished the original negatives to staff printers, although many photographers received access to them later on.

Although *Migrant Mother* is undoubtedly Lange's most famous image, she produced hundreds of other photographs. Many were later sold to newspapers and magazines. And so, in addition to prints created by photographers, original press prints are now highly desirable even though they were not made with resale in mind. Period photographs—the very photographs that were circulated to newspapers, magazines, and television news rooms—are a much sought after commodity today. Photographers fortunate to live long enough to see their work become valuable are both delighted and surprised with this turn of events.

In the photography community, where until recently fine-art photographs tended to fetch higher prices, *Migrant Mother* also symbolizes the coming-of-age of photojournalistic images. The fact that *Mother* appeared in print so many times strengthened its market value, but it is important to remember the difference between a photomechanical copy and an original. In a culture like ours, where virtually every desirable object is reproduced en masse (on television, in books and newspapers, or on postcards or posters), confusion of these two categories may be understandable. But differentiating the two in photography can mean the difference between a $12 modern print and a vintage print worth $44,000.

For those who do not care to own an original print, a modern print of an image can be purchased today from The Library of Congress, where the

---

*Beaumont Newall, *Photography—Essays and Images: Illustrated Readings in the History of Photography*, New York Museum of Modern Art, 1980, pp. 263-264.

Millions of people were watching their televisions in November 1963 and saw Jack Ruby shoot Lee Harvey Oswald in the crowded basement of the Dallas County Jail. Robert Jackson, photographer for the *Dallas Times-Herald*, managed to snap this photograph of Oswald a split second after the gunshot was heard. The photograph records an important moment in history and won the 1964 Pulitzer Prize. (Robert Jackson, *The Shooting of Lee Harvey Oswald*, silver print, 8 x 10 inches, Swann, October 14, 1992, $3,520)

FSA collection is now housed, for as little as $12.* However, the contemporary print will be printed by a technician on glossy RC paper, a resin-coated (or plastic) paper that is believed to have a short life span and has a decidedly different range of tones from that of the paper Lange used. Like artists choosing their materials, photographers have a full range of papers to select from that come in various sizes, are capable of "cold," "medium," or "warm" tones, and are available in glossy or nonglossy surfaces.

Some of the many photojournalist images that have performed well at auctions are Arthur Rothstein's *Dust Storm, Cimarron County*, which sold for $28,600 in 1990; Weegee's *The Critic*, which brought $9,350 in 1992; and Lewis Hine's *New York City from the Empire State Building*, which realized

*Requests for photographs from The Library of Congress can be placed in person or by mail from the Photoduplication Service, Library of Congress, Washington, D.C. 20540 (phone: 202-707-5640 or by fax: 202-707-1771). Photographs are ordered by negative number or image. If you need help in identifying the image you desire, send a xerox of the image to a reference librarian in the photography division, who will assist you.

(Literature from The Library of Congress also suggests other resources.) One excellent source is Arthur Goldsmith's "Bargain Masterpieces," by Arthur Goldsmith. *Popular Photography*, vol. 95, no. 7 (July 1988), pp. 44-49, 78.

$60,500 in 1989. Nevertheless, for the most part photojournalistic images are an undervalued commodity. Vintage FSA photographs by Arthur Rothstein, Walker Evans, Russell Lee, and others start at $300. Lewis Hine's turn-of-the-century street scenes can be found for $600. Walker Evans's prints from the 1930s start at $1,500. And works by contemporary photographers like Robert Frank, Danny Lyon, Arnold Eagle, Lee Friedlander, and Lou Stettner may be purchased for reasonable prices.

For the enthusiast, the reason to collect photojournalism lies in owning a piece of history or an icon of popular culture, for these pictures tell a universal story.

THE AMERICAN PAINTER-ETCHER MOVEMENT
by Rona Schneider

Rona Schneider is a dealer and collector from Brooklyn Heights, New York. She is a member of the International Fine Print Dealers Association and the editor of Imprint, *the journal of the American Historical Print Collectors Society. Ms. Schneider's specialty is the painter-etcher movement of the 19th century, and many works in her collection have been exhibited in museums throughout the country. Ms. Schneider is now at work on a catalogue raisonné of the etchings of Stephen Parrish.*

In the 1880s, dozens of American painters were inspired by European artists to try etching in a new manner, using a spontaneous, personally expressive style rather than the tight, highly finished reproductive engraver-etchings favored by an earlier generation of artists and patrons. Some artists such as J. Alden Weir, Stephen Parrish, John Twachtman, Samuel Colman, Joseph Pennell, and Mary Nimmo Moran loved this "new" medium and produced hundreds of etchings. There was no American artist in the last quarter of the 19th century who was unaware of the enthusiasm for etching.

James David Smillie's dramatic description of the creation of an etching at the first meeting of the New York Etching Club at his studio in May 1877—"the first-born of the New York Etching Club ... (on) thin, silky Japan paper ... being tenderly passed from hand to hand"—indicates that experimentation with this medium was at first done purely for love. Consideration of reputations, sales, shows, dealers, publishers, and other thorny issues of the business side of art came later. The initial impetus was the artists' joy in a revived and aesthetically rewarding medium.

A major attraction was the ideal of "free-hand etching ... directly from nature." Since most of these artists were landscape painters, this theoretically meant being able to draw their subjects outdoors directly on the prepared copper plate. Most of the painter-etchers favored tranquil landscapes expressing quiet contentment in the simple beauty of nature.

New York and Philadelphia were the major centers of etching activity, and the countryside within a 100 mile radius offered subject matter for landscape artists even when travel time or money was limited. Especially favored areas were the eastern end of Long Island, the Hudson River Valley, and the shores of Brooklyn for New Yorkers, and the suburbs of Philadelphia and the New Jersey shore for Philadelphians.

Joseph Pennell was one of the most prolific etchers of the Painter-Etcher movement which spanned the years 1853-1908. The South was a favorite subject because its landscape and the ways of its people seemed exotic to many Northerners. Pennell etched this scene of Lynchburg, Virginia, in 1882. (Joseph Pennell, *At Lynchubrg, Virginia*, etching on laid paper, $4\frac{1}{2} \times 2\frac{15}{16}$ inches, collection of Rona Schneider)

When the painter-etchers depicted a city scene, they approached the subject as artists examining small slices of the city, representing what they could see at a glance and perhaps even draw in one sitting. They rejected the topographical descriptions of earlier printmakers and resisted any engagement with the tougher realities of city life. Buildings, street views, and isolated figures were acceptable subject matter; the dirt, tumult, emotions, and politics of city life were not. Either things were seen from a slight distance or, when viewed close up, there was a cool objectivity towards the subject.

James Abbott McNeill Whistler was a major influence on the American etching movement. Although Whistler was an American, he worked and studied mainly in Europe. His European scenes showed a sentimental realism, new compositional devices, and an evocative mood, all of which inspired the American Etching Revival.

Joseph Pennell was the most prolific of all the American printmakers and an author of many books. He wrote about his own life, Whistler, art, and printmaking. Pennell learned etching in his native Philadelphia in 1879. He depicted many American views before and after his expatriate years of 1884-1904 and was one of the few painter-etchers whose printmaking career extended well into the 20th century.

In late 19th-century America, French art was fashionable among the wealthy, and to be a successful American artist one needed Parisian train-

Mary Moran and her husband, Thomas, were both artists. Thomas is well known for his panoramic paintings; Mary, for her etchings. During the 1880s the Morans summered in East Hampton, Long Island, where the landscape inspired Mary to create dozens of etchings. One of her most popular prints is *'Tween the Gloamin' and the Mirk, When the Kye Come Hame, 1883.* The title comes from an old Scottish song, but the etching is a view of Hook Pond in East Hampton. (Mary Nimmo Moran, *'Tween the Gloamin' and the Mirk, When the Kye Come Hame, 1883*, etching, roulette, and sandpaper on laid Japan paper, $7\frac{3}{4}$ x $11\frac{5}{8}$ inches, signed in pencil, collection of Rona Schneider)

ing. But there was also a desire for an "American art" among many American artists, patrons, and critics. It was accepted that etching could become an American art by depicting the American landscape, just as the French Barbizon etchers had so lovingly delineated the French countryside. That the technique and style of etching were rooted in French and English practices was not disturbing, so long as the method was applied to the American landscape.

The art-collecting public joined in the excitement of American art, and all over the United States etchings were acquired and admired. The very wealthy who had European paintings and old master prints sometimes included a few American paintings and etchings in their collections (A.T. Stewart; Mrs. Mary J. Morgan), but the most enthusiastic collectors, first of European etchings and then of American etchings, were connoisseurs who were not necessarily wealthy. Some etchings were framed and hung, but more often they were accumulated by serious collectors in such large numbers that they were kept in portfolios and print cases, to be taken out and admired only occasionally.

Etchings, which had begun as an intellectual art form to be made and understood by a select group of thoughtful people, soon evolved into an art

Samuel Colman was multi-talented, producing paintings, watercolors, drawings, and etchings of scenes in America, Europe, and North America. This etching is a late trial proof acquired from the Colman estate. There are pencil markings to indicate reduction of the plate for the published state and touches of gray wash to indicate shading to be added. (Samuel Colman, *The Olive Trees of the Riviera, 1884*, etching and drypoint on laid Japan, $10\frac{11}{16}$ x $14\frac{5}{8}$ inches, collection of Rona Schneider)

form for the masses. In the 1870s and early 1880s, most etchings were small, made to be held in the hand and admired, an intimate medium for refined, aristocratic tastes. When some publishers discovered the sales potential of etchings, they began steel-facing plates for large editions and encouraging the creation of overly large etchings suitable for framing. Etchings were seen not only as an art form but also as a means of elevating the general level of education and taste of the masses. This ambivalence between exclusivity and mass appeal was never resolved and was at the heart of the demise of the etching revival. In the 1890s, the etching craze collapsed under the weight of its own bloated market.

Some of the painter-etchers returned to their quiet studios and resumed the creation of small, personal etchings made in limited editions usually pulled by the artists themselves and desired, once more, mainly by connoisseurs. The medium was carried forward into the 20th century by such men as James David Smillie and Charles Mielatz, both teachers of etching at the National Academy of Design. Younger artists like John Sloan became interested, and a new generation of etchers developed. They had the same technical approach to the medium, but the quiet landscape and the cult of gentility were abandoned in favor of grittier urban subjects and the expectation of appealing to a new audience.

For the collector of painter-etcher prints there is a very wide range of prices, from $50 to $7,000. A print on sturdy etching paper, signed in the plate and printed in 1883 by a skilled New York City printer from a steel-faced plate, even if beautiful, will not command anywhere near the price of an early proof printed by the same artist on fine Japanese laid paper and signed in pencil, perhaps even annotated with some information about the print state.

Today, some of the most eagerly collected painter-etchers are Thomas Moran, his wife Mary Nimmo Moran, his brother Peter Moran, Robert Swain Gifford, James David Smillie, Stephen Parrish, Charles Adams Platt, John Henry Hill, Otto Bacher, Garielle de Vaux Clements, Edith Loring Peirce Getchell, Charles Mielatz, Kruseman van Elten, Frank Duveneck, and many others. Artists like Samuel Colman, whose paintings have found a market, and Henry Farrer, whose watercolors command substantial prices, have received little attention for their etchings. Such works, along with beautiful etchings by many now forgotten artists, are the "sleepers" of the print world. Learning to spot these undervalued etchings is a large part of the challenge of collecting.

The Robinson Collection at the U.S. Naval Academy Museum

by Pamela Foster

Pamela Foster is assistant to the curator of the Beverley R. Robinson Collection at the U.S. Naval Academy Museum .

The Beverley R. Robinson Collection of naval prints at the United States Naval Academy Museum is a vast accumulation of carefully chosen pieces that depict events in Western naval history from the age of discovery in the early 1500s to the emergence of steam-powered vessels in the 19th century. As a fine art collection, the prints represent the work of the most talented marine artists of four centuries and offer a standard theme as a basis for comparison of different schools and eras of marine painting and printmaking. Cumulatively, the images create a visual document of historical value for both military and social scholars. Because the collection illustrates naval engagement in the age of sail so thoroughly, a viewer can see the rise and fall of the world's powerful navies and chart political changes in European and American history. The collection is also strong testimony to the popularity of maritime prints in different periods.

Rich as it is, the Robinson Collection remains a low-profile Navy treasure. Housed in a discreet corner of the campus, the collection consists of over 5,000 woodcuts, lithographs, aquatints, mezzotints, line engravings, and a few watercolors. Beverley Randolph Robinson, a wealthy New York attorney, promised his collection of prints to the Academy upon his death. He had purchased his first print while on his annual vacation in London. Although the year this first acquisition was made is unclear, by 1933 his personal collection numbered nearly 200. Beginning in 1939 Robinson loaned the Academy groups of prints with the hope that they would be displayed with the museum's collection in a newly constructed museum building. With display options and a willing beneficiary, Robinson contin-

The Robinson Collection includes a large number of sailing ships engaged in battle. This print of *Rodney's Victory Off Cape St. Vincent, 1780* was engraved by James Fittler after a painting by Thomas Luny. The hand-colored print is 10¾ x 15¾ inches. (Courtesy Beverley R. Robinson Collection, U.S. Naval Academy Museum)

ued to acquire prints. By 1951, when he died, the collection consisted of over 1,000 images. In the years since then, an endowment established to fund the maintenance and growth of the collection has provided for the addition of more than 4,000 more. Beverley Robinson's will states the expectation that his collection would be permanently displayed in its entirety. But its current size prevents the fulfillment of this request, and the collection is completely displayed only on the pages of a three-volume catalogue.*

Robinson was no stranger to the finer things. He was born in New York City on June 24, 1876, into a respected and well-established family. The great-grandson of Edmund Randolph of Virginia (the first attorney general of the United States and the second Secretary of State) and a cousin of the Delaware Du Ponts, Beverley attended Harvard College and Columbia University Law School. He married Gladys Endicott, the grand-niece of Secretary of State W. E. Seward, in 1917. The Robinsons lived in New York City and summered each year in Europe, where Beverley made most of his purchases.

Although impressive in scope and quality, Robinson's acquisitions represented an essentially trendy pastime. Print collecting was not an obscure interest for upper-class individuals in the first three decades of this cen-

---

*Naval Prints from the Beverley R. Robinson Collection, Volume 1: 1514–1791 was published by the Naval Academy Museum in 1991. Volumes 2 and 3 are currently in production.

Maritime prints and paintings have always been popular. This print of the 1797 battle between British and Spanish fleets was after a painting by Nicholas Pocock and engraved by Robert Pollard. The print was published in 1799. *Capture of the "Resistance" and "Constance" by British frigates "San Florenzo" and "La Nymphe"* is a large print, 40 ¾ x 59 ¾ inches. (Courtesy Beverley R. Robinson Collection, U.S. Naval Academy Museum)

---

tury.* Robinson was a member of exclusive clubs, well-known and wealthy families, and a distinguished law firm and was an active and influential political figure. He served on the board of trustees of the Museum of the City of New York and the American Museum of Natural History. For a gentleman of his position, art collecting and philanthropy were *de rigueur* in New York society. His enthusiasm for sailing images was testimony to the particular appeal of marine prints in the early 20th century. As the scholar E. Keble Chatterton noted, "It was not till the sailing ship had almost disappeared from the ocean highway that people began to realize the romantic pedigree which she possessed."** Although the circumstances of Robinson's collection are indicative of the popularity maritime prints enjoyed in his day, its distinction stems from its comprehensive coverage of important naval events.

One of Robinson's fundamental objectives was to create an illustrated history of naval engagement in the age of sail. His collection is not nationally exclusive; it represents all of Western history before the steamships replaced more aesthetically captivating sail-powered vessels and before cameras took over the task of visual scribe. The collection's images effectively

---

*Anthony Griffiths, "A Checklist of Catalogues of British Print Publishers c. 1650-1830." *Print Quarterly* 1:1 (March, 1984), p. 4.
**E. Keble Chatterton. *Old Ship Prints.* (New York: Dodd, Mead and Company, 1927), p. 2.

illustrate the highlights and turning points of occidental naval history from the 16th century to the end of World War II.

Naval operations were central to the shifting political character and composition of the Western world. The scenes painted and later engraved by both contemporary painters and those who recreated the scenes in retrospect represent the most dramatic and most memorable events in the history of nautical conflict. Consequently, a collection as thorough as Robinson's, when arranged chronologically, becomes a slide show illustrating the rise and fall of the world's powerful nations and navies. This collection, for instance, is particularly complete in its presentation of the dominance of the British Royal Navy: from the English victory over the Spanish Armada in 1588 to conflicts with the Netherlands in the 17th century and with France in the 18th century, and the triumphs of Admiral Horatio Nelson in the 19th century. From a glance through the prints, it is evident that United States naval history began in earnest after centuries of naval engagement in Europe. The growth of U.S. naval power across is shown as the collection depicts nautical battles associated with the American War for Independence, naval encounters of the War of 1812, the development of an American navy, and the naval events of the American Civil War.

In a letter to Rear Admiral Thomas Hart in October 1933, Robinson explained some of his intentions in building his collection:

> When purchasing prints I have tried to specialize in what I call single ship action, disregarding those prints which reproduce the fleet actions, and are, to my mind lacking in character. I like a print to show a ship as a ship and a beautiful object quite as much as on [sic] account of the historical interest attached.*

Because many marine artists worked closely with the officers and merchant seamen who commissioned the paintings, prints from their images serve as relatively accurate indications of the technical and tactical specifics of naval operation. Robinson's partiality to single-ship pictures rather than panoramas of whole fleets makes his collection especially rich in detail. He was able to compile such a comprehensive collection because several images of successful naval campaigns were usually available. Victories increased the demand for images of the battle. In England, accolades of the mighty Royal Navy under the legendary leadership of Admirals Hawke, Rodney, and Nelson created a ready market for pictures. The British East India Company's ships were also popular images to display.

As maritime images became more popular, many artists produced images of past events. Accuracy became subordinate to preserving the drama and glory of seafaring conflict. In the early 18th century, English maritime painters were specialists, commissioned by naval officers or merchant seamen to produce memorabilia. In the second half of the century, painters who had accepted commissions for landscapes also began to accept commissions for ships' portraits. Demand for ship portraits also peaked with the shipping industry boom in the 19th century. So, just as naval history is

---

*From Robinson's correspondence, in the archives of the Beverley R. Robinson Collection.

illustrated by Robinson's images, so is the history of the appreciation and market for maritime prints.*

The vast number of images of sailing ships at war is testimony to the appreciation of the glory and tradition attached to the age of sail. These naval prints are a unique historical source, for as indicative as they are of factual information, they are simultaneously artistic expressions. "They are visual gestures, aesthetic formulation of maritime information and Naval History expressed through the medium of the print ... Through organization of line and shape and space and color on the two dimensional surface; . . . these artists and printmakers give particular form to their vision and seek to mold the experience of the viewer ... the prints need to be read in their own visual terms, not merely as ... neutral document."**

In constructing his visual history, Beverley Robinson skillfully balanced the dual-nature of the naval print as image and document. His collection remains a visual experience rich in information for historians, art historians, and any who appreciate the power and mystique of the sailing ship in combat.

Audubon Prints

by Robert Braun

Mr. Braun is past president of the Historical Print Collectors Society and past president of the Connecticut Audubon Society.

Numerous editions of Audubon prints with a wide range of size, technique, and quality have been produced during the last 167 years.

Although Audubon is now a famous name, John James Audubon's beginnings were humble. Born in Haiti and raised in France, he emigrated to the United States in 1806. Although he had studied drawing briefly under David at the French Royal Academy, he was basically self-taught. Audubon struggled to support his family by working as a drawing teacher, naturalist, and taxidermist. In 1820 he indulged his twin passions of art and ornithology and began his epic project, a pictorial history of all the bird species of North America. His main technique was watercolor, but he often combined media and used pencil and pastels. In 1826, unable to find an American publisher, Audubon traveled to England. William Lizars of Edinburgh produced the first ten plates of Audubon's project in 1826-1827, but his colorists went on strike and he was busy with another project (Selby's 221 folio plates for his *Illustrations of British Ornithology*), so Audubon transferred his work to a gifted English engraver, Robert Havell, Jr. A few of the original Lizars prints, numbered 1 to 10, exist; they look noticeably different from those done by Havell. When the project and the first ten copper plates were transferred to Havell, he reworked these plates,

---

*David Cordingly. *Maritime Painting in England 1700-1900.* (New York: Clarkson N. Potter, 1973), pp. 72, 96, 139.

**United States Naval Academy Museum. *American Naval Prints from the Beverley R. Robinson Collection.* (Richmond, VA: W.M. Brown and Son for the International Exhibitions Foundation, 1972), p. 9-10.

Many of Audubon's bird portraits featured elaborate topographical detail. In *Snowy Heron* the bird was painted by Audubon in the spring of 1832. The flowers, foliage, leaves, and flowers were painted by Audubon's assistant George Lehman. The hunter in the background, also painted by Lehman, is believed to be a portrait of Audubon. The print, after the painting, was engraved by Havell in 1835.

During the 1890s, the eminent extinction of the snowy heron saw the beginning of the conservation movement. The male snowy heron, once numerous in the Southern states and Florida, was hunted for the showy "aigrettes" it exhibited during mating season. The conservation group named itself the Audubon Society. In 1902, the public outcry caused New York City, heart of the millinery trade in the U.S., to ban the use of the heron's plumes. (After John James Audubon, *Snowy Heron or White Egret*, hand-colored engraving, etching, and aquatint, Doyle, December 4, 1992, $19,800)

adding aquatint etching to plates I, II, VI, and VII and substituting his name for Lizar.

Audubon's project was published as *The Birds of America* between the years 1827 and 1838; the prints that were issued were designed to be bound in four huge volumes. This first edition, generally called the Havell edition, is on paper of folio size (technically double-elephant folio) measuring $39 \frac{1}{2}$ x $29 \frac{1}{2}$ inches. The prints were engraved and hand-colored by Havell *after* watercolors by Audubon. The sheets of paper are watermarked along one long margin in outline block capital letters either: "J WHATMAN" with a year from "1826" to "1838" on the second line, or "J WHATMAN" with "TURKEY MILL" on the second line and the year on the third line. The edition size for the different images is about 175. The prints were delivered to subscribers in groups or "parts" of five images, but the exact number of prints of each image produced is impossible to determine since new subscribers were added and old ones dropped during the eleven years of production. Sometimes a plate was reprinted to produce additional impressions; many exist in several states. The major difference between the states is evident in the lettering. Audubon's descriptive text appeared in 1839 in five quarto volumes.

Since Audubon insisted on reproducing each bird's image life-size, Havell used three different sizes of copper plates: $12\frac{1}{2} \times 19\frac{1}{2}$ inches for the small images, 37 x 27 inches for the large images, and an intermediate size for those in between. Each "part" of five prints delivered to a subscriber consisted of one large, one intermediate, and three small images.

The prints are numbered within the platemark with a "part" number from 1 to 87 in the upper left corner, a plate number from 1 to 435 in the upper right corner, "Drawn from Nature" and the artist's name, John James Audubon (or J. J. Audubon) and the initials of his scientific affiliations in the lower left corner, the common and Latin name(s) of the bird(s) and plant(s) in the image in the lower center, and the engraver's name, R. Havell, Jr., and sometimes the year in the lower right corner. The plate numbers are usually in Roman but sometimes in Arabic numerals. The bird names are usually in print but at times in script and not always at bottom center.

Robert Havell, Jr., used a combination of printing techniques to achieve the remarkable beauty of these prints. He engraved the basic image on the copper plate, etched additional detail, and then added the shading with aquatint etching. After a perfected black impression was achieved, a team of artists hand-colored the individual prints with brush and transparent watercolors according to Audubon's original paintings and written instructions. These paintings are often incomplete in some details and contain numerous written instructions to the engraver for additions and modifications penciled in by the artist. It was Havell's genius which perfected Audubon's original inspired art. The original paintings may be seen at the New York Historical Society, which purchased them from Audubon's widow for $4,000.

When the publication of the Havell edition was nearly completed, Audubon had thirteen of the printed plates modified to show male, female, and immature specimens on the same plate. Havell did this by overprinting an existing print with the additional image. Only six copies of such "composite" prints were produced, and they are therefore exceedingly rare. The complete copy of *The Birds of America* owned by the Field Museum in Chicago contains all thirteen of these composite plates. Two other complete sets containing these thirteen composites are known, and individual composite prints rarely appear on the market.

Occasionally, uncolored examples of Havell prints may be encountered, and these are of technical interest to the collector.

Complete Havell folio-size prints with medium, and especially small, images show a considerable amount of paper margin outside the platemark. In the past, before the great rise in value of these prints, owners occasionally trimmed more or less of these margins away in order to fit the prints into smaller frames. While this diminishes the monetary value, as long as the platemark is fully present the artistic integrity of the print is maintained, and the collector has the benefit of a lower price and easier framing for display. In the case of a trimmed print, however, the watermark, occurring along the long edge of the portion of the sheet trimmed away, will be partially or completely absent.

Audubon made an exhaustive effort to portray every bird of North America. His paintings, which showed an extraordinary attention to detail, preceded the invention of the camera. Audubon was an early conservationist and warned of the possible extinction of many species, but in order to accurately paint many of his models he used carefully arranged, freshly killed birds.

This engraving of *Raven* was printed by Havell in 1830 on J. Whatman paper. The two papers used for Audubon's engravings were J. Whatman and J. Whatman Turkey Mill; the latter has a tendency to tone with time. (After John James Audubon, *Raven*, acquatint and etching with hand coloring, Christie's, January 17, 1992, $4,620)

Audubon's two sons, Victor Gifford and John Woodhouse Audubon, had apprenticed with their father. In 1840, the Audubons began the publication of the "miniature" octavo edition* of *The Birds of America*. The Havell folio images were reduced in size with an optical device, printed by limestone lithography, and hand-colored by J. T. Bowen of Philadelphia. They were delivered to subscribers over a period of four years in 100 groups of five prints each, 500 in all, together with text and seven title pages and indices suitable for binding. The total edition was 1,250 sets. The part number appears on the upper left and the plate number is upper right; there is no plate mark because they are lithographs.

Due to the success of the first octavo edition, seven more were published, the last in 1871. The later editions can be distinguished from the first by the fact that the background color was applied by tintstone lithography instead of hand-colored as in the first edition. The later editions command a somewhat lower price.

As Audubon's sight began to fail, his two sons took a more active part in assisting their father. Audubon died in 1851 but his sons continued with his work. In 1858, John Woodhouse Audubon began to re-issue the folio edition in full size by using the technique of chromolithography. The color printing by Julius Bien used a transfer process to reproduce the images exactly from the original copper plates onto the limestones. The publication was abandoned in 1860 due to financial problems and the outbreak of the

---

*The sheet size of a print is 10 x 6 $\frac{1}{2}$ inches.

Civil War. Only 105 sheets measuring 40 x 27 inches were published, showing 150 images. The small images were placed two per sheet, one above the other for horizontal ones and side by side for the vertical. The artist's name appears at the lower left and the lithographer's, J. Bien, at the lower right of each sheet. Thus, the small horizontal images placed on the upper half of a sheet do not show these names, while the lower horizontal images show both. The small vertical images from the left half of a sheet show only the artist's, and those from the right half only the lithographer's name. Each image is numbered in both upper corners in a rather confusing sequence, since an attempt was made to have the numbers correspond to the plate numbers of the octavo edition. There is no watermark or plate mark. The number of sets in this edition is unknown, but may be less than 200.

Audubon's other major work was *The Viviparous Quadrupeds of North America.* Published in 1845-1846, it consisted of 150 folio prints of the mammals of North America. The images were painted by John James Audubon and his two sons. John Bowen of Philadelphia produced the prints by means of hand-colored lithography on sheets measuring 22 x 28 inches in an edition of about 300. Subscribers received them in groups of five from 1845 to 1848. Each print shows the part number in Arabic numerals from 1 to 30 in the upper left corner, and the plate number in Roman numerals from I to CL in the upper right. The artist's name appears at the lower left and may be J. J. Audubon or J. W. Audubon. The lithographer's name, J. Bowen, appears at the lower right. The text, by John Bachman, appeared separately in three octavo volumes with six additional plates.

Again, as in the case of the birds, the Audubons published an octavo edition of the mammals in 1849. Bowen was again the lithographer, and 155 different images were produced and hand-colored, in an edition of about 2,000. The sheets measure about 7 x 10 $\frac{1}{2}$ inches, and were distributed to subscribers with text, title pages, and indices for binding. Several subsequent editions were also produced but cannot be readily distinguished. The plate numbering of 1 to 155 corresponds to the folio edition, with the exception of one deletion and the addition of six further mammals.

Most of the original copper plates of the Havell edition were destroyed, but some survive, and restrikes have been produced from them. Those pulled from plates owned by institutions are generally identified as such by an indelible stamp or blind stamp, but others can present a problem in recognition. Generally, a restrike has lost some of the fine line detail of the original, especially in the text letters and, of course, no restrike has the proper watermark.

In 1985, a particularly fine set of restrikes was produced by Alecto Historical Editions of London from six copper plates owned by the American Museum of Natural History. Unlike the original Havell edition, a portion of each plate was inked in color, and then the entire printed image was hand-colored. This procedure gives the images a very rich and clear appearance. It is thought that Audubon had wanted this technique used originally but it proved too expensive. This edition was limited to 125 sets. They are marked indelibly on the verso as restrikes.

In 1984, art students at Princeton University, using some of the school's plates, published a restrike in an edition of 50. They were beautifully hand-colored and are identified by a blind stamp and signature.

Various editions of full-size facsimiles (photomechanical reproductions) of the Havell folio bird prints have been produced in the past fifty years, but none would show the originals' watermarks. Most were produced by a photomechanical process involving a half-tone screen. This technique is readily recognized with a low-power magnifying lens, which shows the tiny dots of color arranged in geometric patterns.

In 1971, using a photomechanical process, the Johnson Reprint Company published an edition of 250 sets of the 435 folio prints. Known as the Amsterdam Edition for the location of its printing, the facsimile prints bear an imitation plate mark and at a long margin of the sheets the watermark "G. SCHUT & ZONEN AUDUBON."

In 1985 Abbeville Press produced a very fine fascimile edition of 350 sets of the 435 prints using as many as 13 color separations to achieve fidelity to the originals owned by the National Audubon Society. No imitation plate mark was impressed, and the sheets bear the watermark "Audubon Society Abbeville Press" in cursive script along a long margin.

Princeton Audubon Limited, a commercial company, has reproduced a number of the most dramatic of the original Havell folio prints by means of a direct-camera reproduction process, with great accuracy and no plate mark or watermark, in editions of 1,500.

In 1943 the Artistic Picture Publishing Company of New York produced a few hand-colored Audubon folio bird print facsimiles showing a plate mark. The company name appears in the legend.

The Leipzig edition of 20 folio Audubon bird print facsimiles appeared in 1972-1973 in an edition of 500 sets. The collotype process of reproduction was used, resulting in very fine color images that do not show a geometric pattern of dots under magnification. The small and medium sizes of images show a false plate mark, and none of these facsimiles bear a watermark.

The recently developed color laser reproduction technology was used by the Tryon Mint of Canada in 1988 to reproduce 10 of the folio bird prints in editions of 1,000 signed and numbered facsimiles. This technique, like collotype, shows uniform color without a pattern of dots but striations of more and less intense color appear under magnification.

The two most useful reference books for the Audubon print collector are *Handbook of Audubon Prints* by Clark and Bannon (Pelican Publishing Co., 1991) and *An Index and Guide to Audubon's Birds of America* by Susanne Low, (Abbeville Press, 1988).

COLLECTING PRINTS ON A BUDGET

by Reba White Williams

Reba Williams is an art historian and print collector.

If funds are unlimited, acquiring prints is as simple as walking into a gallery or auction house, deciding what to buy, and writing a check. No research is necessary and mistakes are unimportant; no limitations need be observed, and no self-discipline is required.

But few collectors have the luxury of unlimited funds, and working within a budget means hard work, since the first rule of acquiring bargains is to be able to recognize them! All too often novice collectors pay too much for their first prints because they have failed to study the market and haven't researched price histories. A naive buyer will pay a premium for a print at auction—more than the price of that same print at a nearby gallery—because the buyer never bothered to check on the print's availability and current price.

But first, before embarking on a discussion of bargains and budgets, let's define some terms. What exactly is a "print"? Since the beginning of the last century, a collector's print—a fine print—has been defined as a print that involves the hand of the artist from the original concept (or the drawing) to the finished product. A print produced from a drawing *without* the artist's involvement is less valuable. The original—the fine, or collector's, print—since the late 19th century has often been signed by the artist, and it will almost always be in a limited edition, with a handwritten number such as "2/25" signifying that there were only 25 impressions, and this is number two in that group.

And what is meant by the word "collection"? Some people may accept the dictionary definition: "an accumulation of objects gathered for study, comparison, or exhibition." But if the collection is just an "accumulation" without a unifying theme, the objects may *look* like an "accumulation" (or mess!) rather than a "collection." The unplanned collection is haphazard, not harmonious, while the true collection—the result of study, hard work, and careful selection—is harmonious. Serious collectors narrow their focus and define a field within which they work and acquire: *then* the objects they select become a collection.

The print collector's fields might be the *subject* of the images chosen, perhaps portraits, or landscapes, or nudes. Or the focus could be on a *style*—impressionism, abstraction, or precisionism. *Process* may be the guideline, with the buyer choosing only etchings, wood engravings, or colored lithographs. Or perhaps the buyer will select prints from certain *periods*—the twenties, thirties, or forties. Whatever the theme, it should frame the collection and give direction and discipline to the collector.

But suppose collectors need to make *price* the governing concept? Suppose they want to be sure they have selected an area of bargains *before* they select a theme? Prints that are truly cheap are, of course, those that are unpopular. In stock-market terms, the collector wants to "bottom-fish," to be a "contrarian," to look for out-of-favor works.

To determine what's unpopular—what's out of favor—the collector has to look at the *opposite of the trendy*. Consider size: contemporary prints are growing larger and larger, as big as eight feet or more in either direction.

Stow Wengenroth (1906-1978) was born in New York and studied at the Art Students League. In his mid-twenties he turned to printmaking. He is best known for his city scenes but is also closely associated with typical New England landscapes of harbors, lighthouses, and forests. (Stow Wengenroth, *Cool Forest, 1953*, Reba and Dave Williams Collection)

So if large is a trend, to find a bargain think small! Tiny prints—cigarette package size or smaller—are almost always bargains, partly because of fashion and partly because people don't know how to display them! But for the imaginative, those who dare to be different, they're wonderful to collect: frame them in little frames and set them on the piano, on end tables, bookshelves, or the mantel; or hang them in groups. Artists from nearly every nationality and period have made small prints, and nearly every dealer can tell you about them! They turn up at auction, too, usually in batches, or group lots, and they typically sell in the hundreds (as opposed to thousands) of dollars—or even less! Sometimes special miniature print contests and exhibitions are held, and the prints exhibited are for sale. That's a great way to get started.

Another trend is *color*. The colored print of a contemporary artist typically sells for more than a similar print in black and white by the same artist. Artists like Frank Stella and Red Grooms sometimes print the same image in both color and black and white, and when they do, the black and white print is usually a bargain, selling for as little as a third or half the price of the colored print. As for older prints, decorators looking for non-controversial works to "finish" a room want color, so colored prints of flowers, still-life, animals, and the like typically sell for more than the same images in black and white. Yet artists and print connoisseurs will tell you that the black and white print is the true challenge or test of the artist's skill! For this reason, some sophisticated collectors buy only black and white prints.

What about bargain *images?* First, certain artists are associated with a *type* of image, and if artists are famous for one kind of representation, their other works will sell for less. The artist Stow Wengenroth is best known for his prints of city images, but he also made prints of rural scenes and seascapes, and they sell for a fraction of the price of the city scenes. Gustave Bauman, who made beautiful color woodcuts, is known for his Santa Fe scenes, and his flower prints typically sell for much less.

The most popular linocuts by Sybil Andrews—fox hunts, horses—sell for significantly more than her religious images, made in the same Vorticist style. They are avoided by some collectors partly because they are *atypical* of Sybil Andrews's work, but also because contemporary 20th-century religious image prints tend to be unpopular. Contemporary religious imagery offers a bargain opportunity!

For those who wish to collect by type of *process*, wood engravings are bargains; they are typically detailed, often small, and even the rare ones sell for bargain prices! Interesting wood engravings by artists like Clare Leighton, Thomas Nason, and Asa Cheffetz can be bought for a few hundred dollars.

In the late 19th century, a group of artists inspired by Whistler made beautiful etchings; they can still be bought for low prices, since they have never become very popular.[*]

Passionate collectors may so admire an individual artist that they choose to own only works by that artist. An intriguing possibility is Arthur B. Davies, who was an avid promoter of the avant-garde in art. In fact, he was a major factor in organizing the Armory Show of 1913. In the early 20th century, he was highly regarded as a modernist painter and printmaker. His art is a combination of classical figures, symbolism, and cubism, and his prints today sell at tremendous discounts. Those of around 1917-1918 sell for a few hundred dollars.

Another bargain category of prints is the realistic prints of the thirties and early forties, with the exception of well-known artists Grant Wood and Thomas Hart Benton. Many American artists of this period worked in a re-alistic figurative tradition, and their prints typically sell at a discount. These bargain prints are available in both color (screenprint) and black and white, and a number of dealers specialize in them.

Prints made in the 1950s offer a great opportunity for collectors! Except for very few artists, fifties prints are today not admired by curators and col-lectors, and the prices reflect their unpopularity. Much of 1950s art is no-table for strong vertical lines; Richard Florsheim, who worked in this style,

---

[*]See Rona Schneider's essay on "The American Painter-Etcher Movement" p. 66.

English artist Sybil Andrews (b. 1898) is best known for her linocuts of fox hunts and horses. This linoleum cut of *Mother and Son,* executed in 1932, is an unusual subject matter for Andrews and would sell for less than her more popular hunting scenes.

(Sybil Andrews, *Mother and Son,* Reba and Dave Williams Collection)

was popular at the time, and his prints are big and striking, but they are quite cheap. They typically sell for $500 to $1,000.

Dean Meeker is another artist whose fifties prints won prizes and today are real bargains. Sister Corita Kent, a nun who made screenprints in the convent and eventually left the convent and became a full-time artist in Boston, was a fifties art celebrity. She was one of the first artists to use words in her art; she may have been the first artist to commercialize the word "love," putting it on a postage stamp. While her work was extremely popular at the time, it has almost vanished.

To sum up: the bargain-seeker should avoid the crowd and identify the unpopular, by first looking for the popular—the prints and artists that are "in" and in the news, setting new highs—and then choosing the opposite! Building a collection on a budget requires searching for those little pockets that trend-followers are ignoring. A "contrarian" can build a stunning collection for the price of just one or two trendy prints by the trendiest artist.

PORTFOLIOS

by Norma S. Steinberg

Norma Steinberg is a printmaker, art historian, print consultant, and appraiser.

In the print world, the word "portfolio" refers to both the folder or case and to the set of prints collected within it. The first part of the word is from the French for "to carry," and "folio" refers to a paper size—a full sheet or folio. Folio sheets vary in size: "Royal" is about 20 x 25 inches, "Imperial" about 22 x 30, and "Antiquarian" 31 x 53 inches. Artists, print publishers, dealers, collectors, and print curators use the words describing a group of prints interchangeably. The term used—portfolio, set, series, suite, volume, *livre d'artiste*, painter's book—is often just a matter of nomenclature. For example, a group of prints presented in a box is usually a portfolio, but if the sheets are stitched together, it is a *livre d'artiste*. Broadly speaking, prints will be designated as a book, volume, or album if they are bound into signatures. The other terms—portfolio, set, suite, series—imply single sheets, and "portfolio" is usually reserved for the larger sheet size or for presentation in a folder or box.

Early presentations of prints in sets, such as Joseph M.W. Turner's *Liber Studiorum* and J.J. Audubon's *Birds of America*, were issued to subscribers in "parts" or in "paper covers." Francisco Goya's *Los Caprichios* were offered as a group, in both bound and unbound forms.* The collector was responsible for the preservation and presentation of the group, and each collector treated his series differently. Most often, such series of prints were bound together at one edge so they could be read as a book, and we do not now think of Turner's, Audubon's, or Goya's series as being portfolios.

The word "book" always implies a bound edge, but, of course, illustrations in books are not necessarily original works of art. They may be prints after another artist's drawings or paintings or, more commonly, photo-reproductions or half-tones. Still there are large numbers of books with original prints, as, for example, Eugene Delacroix's sixteen illustrations for *Hamlet,* designed and drawn on stone by the artist. William Blake's *Songs of Innocence* and *Songs of Experience*, rare illustrated books, were produced in a nontraditional relief etching method in which the text is as much a part of the creative process as the illustrations.

The designations "painter's books," "artists' books" and *"livres d'artiste"* were originally limited to French illustrated books published before World War I, including such early 19th-century works as Delacroix's *Faust* and *Hamlet*, later 19th-century books like Henri de Toulouse-Lautrec's Yvette *Guilbert,* and early 20th-century School of Paris books like Georges Braque's *Théogonie,* all of which contain original works of art. These terms have recently been expanded to include books of all nations with original graphic work by an artist. They do not, however, embrace the illustrated catalogue

---

*Goya's prints had the additional appeal of being titled, the caption providing a sophisticated dialogue with the subtly satirical imagery, which was otherwise intelligible only to those who knew the contemporary mores of court and cloister. Bound and unbound prints from all of Goya's series are housed in the Boston Museum of Fine Arts Print Room and many other institutions.

raisonné even if it includes specially prepared original prints by the artist, such as those published by Fernand Mourlot on Marc Chagall or Joan Miró. Such prints add to the value of the book but have little independent value.

Publishers of artists' books often promote the production of suites of imagery. When Aloïs Senefelder, the inventor of lithography, sought a patent for his invention in London in 1800, he introduced the process in an album of lithographs, *Specimens of Polyautography*, by contemporary artists, of whom Benjamin West is the only one still well known. Ambroise Vollard, the great art dealer and publisher, is remembered as one of the first publishers to commission printed works from artists who had been primarily painters, a marketing idea that contemporary publishers have emulated. Today, the master printmakers at such firms as Universal Limited Artists Editions, Parasol Press, Crown Point Press, and Tyler Graphics collaborate with artists, often those who have not made prints before, to generate exciting projects that result from the creative synergy of two or more minds.

A collaborative project becomes a "portfolio" when the artist or publisher decides to release it in that format. A portfolio may be like a book in every respect, including the presence of text, except that it is composed of loose sheets. Contemporary portfolios often have a separate title page, and a separate colophon page at the end with printing information, edition size, handwritten portfolio number, and the signatures of the master printer and the artist. The presence of the colophon is the collector's guarantee of authenticity for the individual prints are often not separately signed. When the portfolio is a cooperative venture by a number of artists, then each sheet is hand-signed, and some are also individually numbered.

Collectors who can afford the whole portfolio usually prefer to own the complete set in deference to the artist or group of artists, who want the work to be kept as a complete entity. Other collectors will settle for individual pieces and, perhaps catching the collecting bug, later spend many years amassing the remainder of the portfolio. Aware of these paradoxical collecting styles, dealers sometimes acquire a portfolio prepared to sell it either as a whole to a museum or single collector or broken into individual pieces (a "breaker") for many purchasers.

Collectors in the 18th and 19th centuries often placed their prints in albums. An "album" is a group amassed by a collector rather than designated as a portfolio group by the artist or publisher. Famous collectors like Pierre-Jean Mariette, the great 18th-century connoisseur and publisher of prints, very often collected series—the prints of Callot, for instance, or prints on specific subjects such as biblical scenes or bawdy genre scenes— and placed them in albums.* Because of their availability and the range of subject matter, prints lend themselves to this type of collecting. Single prints would often be carefully drum-mounted** to provide uniformity of

---

*Nine volumes of the Mariette collection (the Spencer Albums) are housed at the Fogg Museum of the Harvard University Museums. For a full description of how the Mariettes assembled and bound their collection, see Marjorie B. Cohn, *A Noble Collection: The Spencer Albums of Old Master Prints*, Fogg Art Museum, Harvard University Art Museums, 1992.

**Drum-mounting means that the print has been trimmed to a narrow width (often at the plate mark) and then pasted from behind into a pre-cut opening in a sheet of paper.

presentation, and the sheets bound into albums that might stand vertically on a library shelf, as compared to the contemporary methods of storing prints flat in air-tight boxes or hanging individual prints on the wall. A collector would then entertain his weekend guests with the opportunity to leaf through some of his albums.

Printmakers and print publishers seem to have been aware almost from the beginning of connoisseurs' preferences to collect in sets. When Albrecht Dürer sought to improve on the earlier (about 1478) crude illustrations to the Bible printed at Cologne, he produced the 15 woodcuts of the *Apocalypse* series (1497-1498). He was probably the first artist to design, print, and publish an entire group of prints meant to be collected as a set. They were so popular they were immediately plagiarized by other printmakers. Judging from its elegant, elongated shape and the absence of text, Dürer's later *Engraved Passion* was specifically directed to connoisseurs and was again a group of prints to be collected as a set.* In fact, some 16th-century collectors mounted them on vellum and illuminated them with color heightened with gold and silver to suggest the appearance of precious miniatures.

Certainly biblical themes lend themselves to serial imagery because of their narrative content. Other historical or social themes (e.g., marriage customs), as well as jewelry, embroidery, and engraving designs have all provided the impetus for print series. The Seven Deadly Sins and the Seven Heavenly Virtues were perennial favorites. Saints, the Ten Commandments, and scenes from works by Shakespeare and Goethe and the Odyssey are others. Perhaps the most popular theme of all was the Four Seasons, because of the latitude it permitted the artist. Artists as diverse as Louis Icart (French, 1888-1950) and Jasper Johns (American, b. 1930) have mined this theme intensively.

Scenes of distant peoples and places are also popular with collectors. The wanderlust and marketing instincts of 19th-century photographers and the topographic interests of collectors combined to generate a spate of albums, books, and portfolios illustrated with photographs of landscape views. Francis Frith's photographs of Egyptian monuments were tipped into previously bound blank books by collectors much as we mount our personal photographs today.

From the artist's point of view, the very act of printmaking produces a set of prints on a single theme in a predetermined format. The physical act of proofing—drawing and proofing, redrawing and reproofing—leaves a record of the development of the visual idea. Picasso loved the process of printmaking for this very reason: each state or transformation of the plate was a possible start for a new work, whether in stone, copper, canvas, or iron. The unalterable framework of the plate or stone provided a pattern within which he automatically composed a set. Instead of modifying a plate toward a more finished image, Picasso would often start afresh after a few trials, produce a different but similar one, and move on. Picasso's *Vollard Suite*, which passes through several artist and model themes, is an example of this manner of working. But most artists do not consider vari-

---

*The plates of the *Engraved Passion* are about $4\frac{1}{2} \times 3$ inches as compared to the 5 x 4 inches of the *Small Passion*.

In 1937, the French art dealer and publisher Ambroise Vollard purchased 100 plates from Pablo Picasso. The images dealt primarily with Picasso's preoccupation with the complex relationship between artist and model and between man and woman.

Published with a total edition of 300, there are few remaining complete portfolios. When a complete set was offered at Christie's in December 1992, it fetched a record 660,000 British pounds. *Faune de Voilant une Femme* is part of *The Vollard Suite* and one of its most recognizable images. If sold separately, the aquatint would sell for $50,000–$80,000. (Pablo Picasso, *Le Suite Vollard*, etchings, engravings, drypoints and aquatints, 370 x 300mm and smaller, Christie's London, BP 660,000, $1,007,991)

---

ous print states to be a series because the plate is altered at each stage. Rembrandt's *Ecce Homo* demonstrates this point. The first state establishes a certain distance between the protagonists and the viewer that is removed by the seventh state, where we are offered an intensely personal narrative moment. There was no retreating to the more objective situation of the early state, however, even had Rembrandt wanted to; only the final state remains.

The same restriction is true of artists who use monotyping to produce a series. In monotypes, once an image has been pulled, little remains of the original but a ghost image. When the artist works further into that ghost image, the transformation is instantly recognizable. The first, however, is irretrievably gone.

The appeal for some artists who work in series is the framework that it provides, whether of subject, technique, color, or shape. The unifying theme combined with its specific restrictions provides a structure, like a musical motif with variations, as for instance Wayne Thiebaud's portfolio, *Delights,* which comprises seventeen images of taste-tempting sweets. The controlling format can also be a text. The relationship of text and imagery may be implied as in Dürer's *Engraved Passion,* tangential as in Leonard Baskin's *A Little Book of Natural History,* related as in Edouard Manet's prints for Stéphane Mallarmé's translation of Poe's *The Raven,* or closely integrated as in Blake's *Songs of Innocence.*

Artists sometimes band together in cooperative units to produce print portfolios as a marketing device to appeal to the collector's eye and to raise funds at the same time. The German Expressionists and the Bauhaus artists generated several examples of group portfolios. Artists would contribute the matrix (the woodblock, etching plate, or lithographic stone) or the prints themselves to a joint effort, for which the title page, colophon, and portfolio cover were designed by one or more of the contributors.* Some of these portfolios were broken up, as for instance the *Bauhaus-Drucke Neue Europäische Graphik,*** while others were maintained as a group. Akin to a collection of short stories, these group portfolios presented artists of varying styles around a single unifying theme. In America, group portfolios were produced during the two world wars, the Spanish Civil War, and other troubled times (for example, today's need for AIDS research) to raise money. The artists were right in their marketing idea—collectors appreciate an appeal to their connoisseurship.

In conclusion, I offer some definitions. A series is a number of prints by an artist or a group of artists on a single subject, such as a group of Scottish landscape photographs or Goya's *Caprichos.* A series has a predetermined sequence, so that we might follow a landscape tour or a conceptual pathway. A set or suite is similar to a series but has no specific sequence of viewing. Thiebaud's *Delights* are a suite. Artists' books have the additional feature of being bound (usually) into a recognizable volume. Portfolio is a term applied to a body of work by an artist, a cooperative, or a publisher, and it usually has a unifying element of subject, medium, or size. The factor of size, which should be important in defining portfolios—a full or double sheet—is unpredictable today when we consider Sol LeWitt's portfolios, which often measure less than 12 x 12 inches. All of the components may vary, but if a wrapper or box is provided, then the group of prints is a portfolio.

A print portfolio is more accessible than a similar cycle of oil paintings in its space requirements, economics, and portability. Print portfolios, series, suites, sets, albums, and artists' books all demonstrate both logical progression and imaginative construction, and a collector might wish to own such a series without having to do the work of putting it together. Connoisseurs, however, often select serial imagery for aesthetic rather than practical rea-

---

*These artists also printed independently of their groups. See entries in *Leonard's ANNUAL Price Index of Prints, Posters & Photographs* for Lyonel Feininger, Alexei von Jawlensky, Ernst Kirchner, Wassily Kandinsky, Paul Klee, Emil Nolde, Karl Schmidt-Rottluff, and others.

**Two sheets from this portfolio by Alexander Archipenko were offered this past year at auction.

Most of the subjects for the 58 plates of the *Miserère* date from 1914-1918 but were not published as a unit until 1948. From 1920 to 1927 Rouault obsessively reworked the copper plates, some as many as 15 times. Most are collotypes with aquatint, etching, and roulette on Arches-laid paper watermarked "AMBROISE VOLLARD." The edition consisted of 425 copies plus 25 hors commerce. *Face à Face* is plate 40 from the series. (Georges Rouault, *Face à Face*, etching and aquatint, $25\frac{3}{4} \times 19\frac{7}{8}$ inches, Barridoff, May 6, 1992, $715)

sons, and a print connoisseur wants to be able to hold and examine each sheet of paper. For the print connoisseur, a portfolio may be the record of the development of an image, the pattern of an intelligence at work, or a paradigm of variation within structure, but above all it is a group of prints.

ARTISTS' PRICE RANGES

ABBEMA, Wilhelm von
1812-1889
intaglio: (H) $83

ABBOTT, Berenice
American 1898-1991
photo: (L) $385; (H) $14,300

ABBOTT, Ernest
intaglio: (L) $52; (H) $104

ABBOTT, Lemuel (after)
stencil: (H) $22

ABBOTT, Robert
generic: (L) $154; (H) $242

ABBOTT, Yarnall
American 1870-1938
photo: (H) $440

ABERLI, Johann Ludwig
Swiss 1723-1786
intaglio: (L) $1,538; (H) $6,152

ABERLI, Johann Ludwig and Heinrich RIETER
intaglio: (H) $5,742

ABRAMOFSKY, Israel
Russian/American b. 1888
planographic: (H) $220

ACCONCI, Vito
American b. 1940
stencil: (H) $990

ACKERMAN
intaglio: (H) $55

ACKERMAN and CO., Publisher
intaglio: (H) $275

ACKERMANN
generic: (H) $440

ACKERMANN, Max
1887-1975
planographic: (H) $297

ACKERMANN, Peter
contemporary
port/books: (H) $62

ACKERMANN, Rudolph, Publisher
port/books: (H) $2,860

ACKROYD, Norman
intaglio: (H) $330

ADAMI, Valerio
Italian b. 1935
port/books: (H) $620

ADAMS, Ansel
American 1902-1984
posters: (H) $380
photo: (L) $193; (H) $24,200

ADAMS, Robert
photo: (H) $825

ADAMS, Wayman
American 1883-1959
planographic: (H) $605

ADLER, Jankel
Polish 1895-1949
intaglio: (H) $2,460

AESCHBACHER, Hans
1906-1980
intaglio: (H) $100

AFFLECK, Andrew F.
Scottish ac. 1910-1930
intaglio: (H) $66

AFRO (Afro BASALDELLA)
Italian 1912-1976
intaglio: (L) $1,127; (H) $2,361
planographic: (L) $193; (H) $2,647

AGAM, Yaacov
Israeli b. 1928
stencil: (L) $110; (H) $1,430
planographic: (H) $110
port/books: (L) $880; (H) $1,540

AGLIO, A. (after)
planographic: (H) $101

AGNEW, Thomas and Sons, Publisher
port/books: (H) $1,320

AGOSTINI, Tony
Italian b. 1916
planographic: (H) $110

AIGNER, Lucien
Czech b. 1901
photo: (L) $480; (H) $1,980

AIKEN (after)
planographic: (H) $110

AIZPIRI, Paul
French b. 1919
planographic: (L) $163; (H) $403

AKIN, Gwen and Allan LUDWIG
photo: (H) $950

ALBANI, Francesco (after)
Italian 1578-1660
intaglio: (H) $77

ALBEE, Grace
American 1890-1985
relief: (L) $77; (H) $231

ALBERS, Anni
b. 1899
planographic: (H) $28

ALBERS, Josef
American 1888-1976
stencil: (L) $143; (H) $4,400
planographic: (L) $83; (H) $1,100
port/books: (L) $528; (H) $6,600
others: (H) $440

ALBERTI, Cherubino
intaglio: (H) $378

ALBIN-GUILLOT, Laure
(photographer)
French d. 1962
port/books: (H) $19,800

ALBRIGHT, Ivan Le Lorraine
American 1897-1983
planographic: (L) $330; (H) $1,320

ALBRIGHT (ZSISSLY), Malvin Marr
American b. 1897
planographic: (H) $165

ALBRO, Maxine
planographic: (H) $303

ALDEGREVER, Heinrich
German 1502-1555/61
intaglio: (L) $369; (H) $10,996
port/books: (H) $5,228

ALDIN, Cecil
English 1870-1930
intaglio: (L) $290; (H) $1,099
planographic: (L) $138; (H) $495

ALDIN, Cecil Charles (after)
planographic: (H) $1,157

ALDO, G.R.
photo: (H) $192

ALDORFER, Albrecht
relief: (H) $1,045

ALECHINSKY, Pierre
Belgian b. 1927
intaglio: (L) $414; (H) $3,300
relief: (H) $275
planographic: (L) $143; (H) $468
mixed-media: (L) $215; (H) $546
port/books: (L) $1,210; (H) $4,400

ALECHINSKY, Pierre and Christian
DOTREMONT
planographic: (H) $1,165

ALECHINSKY-FOLON-BAJ
intaglio: (H) $283

ALEXANDER, Jesse
photo: (H) $660

ALEXANIAN, Nubar
photo: (L) $150; (H) $350

ALF, Martha
photo: (H) $440

ALINARI, Fratelli
photo: (H) $1,913

ALIX, Pierre Michel
intaglio: (H) $880

ALKEN, H.
intaglio: (H) $605

ALKEN, H. (after)
generic: (H) $55

ALKEN, Henry (after)
English 1774-1850
intaglio: (H) $193

ALKEN, Henry (after)
British 1785-1851
intaglio: (H) $248

ALKEN, Henry (after)
intaglio: (L) $60; (H) $1,638

ALKEN, Henry (Sr.)
English 1784-1851
intaglio: (H) $105

ALKEN, Henry
British 1785-1851
intaglio: (H) $330

ALKEN, Henry
intaglio: (L) $131; (H) $2,901

ALKEN, Henry Gordon
British 1784-1850
intaglio: (H) $88

ALKEN, Henry Thomas
English 1785-1851
port/books: (H) $138

ALKEN, Henry Thomas (after)
English 1785-1851
port/books: (L) $165; (H) $303

ALKEN, Samuel (after)
intaglio: (H) $80

ALLAIS, Louis Jean
1762-1833
intaglio: (H) $83

ALLAND, Alexander
photo: (H) $1,100

ALLEN, Arlene Lew
planographic: (H) $44

ALLEN, James
1894-1964
intaglio: (L) $1,210; (H) $1,320
planographic: (H) $330

ALLEN, Lewis
American 1873-1957
relief: (H) $28

ALLMEN, Von
posters: (H) $247

ALLOM, T.
intaglio: (H) $55

ALMAREZ, Carlos
American b. Mexico 1951
intaglio: (L) $1,045; (H) $2,090
stencil: (L) $2,475; (H) $4,675
planographic: (H) $2,750

ALPERT, Max
photo: (H) $4,400

ALTDORFER, Albrecht
German c. 1480-1538
intaglio: (L) $451; (H) $6,283
relief: (L) $992; (H) $37,699
port/books: (L) $24,044; (H) $34,558

ALTDORFER, Erhard
German c. 1485-c. 1562
intaglio: (H) $45,116

ALTENBOURG, Gerhard
1926-1989
relief: (L) $213; (H) $1,515
planographic: (L) $312; (H) $1,122
port/books: (L) $615; (H) $4,292

ALTERE, Lukas Cranach der
1472-1553
relief: (L) $1,885; (H) $36,128

ALTERE, Lukas Cranach der
(school of)
relief: (H) $24,347

ALTERE, Pieter Brueghel der
1525-1569
intaglio: (H) $4,415

ALTMAN, Harold
American b. 1924
intaglio: (L) $105; (H) $358
planographic: (L) $55; (H) $660

ALTOON, John
American 1925-1969
planographic: (H) $550

ALVAR, Gunnar
Norwegian 19th cent.
planographic: (H) $77

ALVAR, Sunol
European 20th cent.
stencil: (H) $176
planographic: (H) $440

AMAN-JEAN
planographic: (L) $178; (H) $178

AMAN-JEAN, Edmond Francois
French 1860-1935/36
planographic: (H) $1,540

AMANO, K.
relief: (H) $70

AMBILLE, Paul
French b. 1930
planographic: (H) $55

AMBRAMOVIC, Ulay and Marina
b. 1940's
photo: (H) $165

AMELIN, Albin
planographic: (L) $647; (H) $1,061

AMEN, Irving
American b. 1918
relief: (L) $55; (H) $143

AMENOFF, Gregory
American b. 1948
planographic: (L) $770; (H) $935

**AMERICAN SCHOOL, 19TH
CENTURY**
port/books: (H) $715

AMIET, Cuno
Swiss 1868-1961
planographic: (L) $124; (H) $231

AMMANN, Jost
Swiss 1539-1591
intaglio: (H) $1,230

AMNESTY INTERNATIONAL,
Publisher
port/books: (H) $483

AMORONI, N.
intaglio: (H) $28

AMSTELODAMI and GEILEKEIK
generic: (H) $220

ANASAGASTI, Teodoro
planographic: (H) $91

ANDERLE, Jiri
Czechoslovakian contemp.
intaglio: (H) $440

ANDERSEN, Mogens
planographic: (L) $72; (H) $224
port/books: (H) $143

ANDERSON, Domenico
1854-1939
photo: (L) $522; (H) $1,980

ANDERSON, Janet
American contemporary
planographic: (H) $17

ANDERSON, Stanley
English b. 1884
intaglio: (L) $154; (H) $358

ANDOE, Joe
American
intaglio: (H) $1,760

ANDREANI, Andrea
c. 1546-1623
relief: (L) $1,889; (H) $2,044

ANDREANI, Andrea (attrib.)
c. 1546-1623
relief: (H) $1,025

ANDRESON, Carlos
American 20th cent.
planographic: (H) $165

ANDREWS, James
planographic: (L) $110; (H) $210

ANDREWS, Sybil
b. 1898
intaglio: (L) $166; (H) $439
relief: (L) $464; (H) $1,540

ANGAROLA, Anthony
American 1893-1929
planographic: (H) $220

ANGAS, George French
Australian 1822-1886
planographic: (H) $10,450

ANGEL, Rifka
American 20th cent.
intaglio: (H) $176

ANNAN, James Craig
1864-1946
photo: (L) $287; (H) $918

ANNAN, Thomas
Scottish 1829-1877
photo: (L) $593; (H) $660

ANNAN, Thomas and James Craig
ANNAN
photo: (H) $1,383

ANNIGONI, Pietro
Italian b. 1910
planographic: (H) $110

ANONYMOUS PRINTS
intaglio: (L) $110; (H) $881
relief: (H) $11
planographic: (L) $35; (H) $1,210
posters: (L) $39; (H) $1,100
port/books: (L) $3,080; (H) $26,400
generic: (L) $138; (H) $605

ANQUETIN, Louis
planographic: (H) $613

ANSON
photo: (H) $514

ANTES, Horst
German b. 1936
intaglio: (L) $62; (H) $185
planographic: (L) $41; (H) $851
mixed-media: (L) $82; (H) $123
photo-repro: (L) $57; (H) $851

ANTHONY, Scott
photo-repro: (H) $154

ANTONELLI, Robert
stencil: (H) $3,630

ANTONIO, Dias
planographic: (H) $2,202

ANTRAL, Robert
intaglio: (H) $70

ANUSKIEWICZ, Richard
American b. 1930
intaglio: (H) $192
stencil: (L) $83; (H) $110
port/books: (H) $220

APPEL, Karel
Dutch/American b. 1921
intaglio: (H) $660
stencil: (L) $468; (H) $1,658
relief: (L) $468; (H) $770
planographic: (L) $35; (H) $7,442
posters: (L) $33; (H) $58
port/books: (L) $3,575; (H) $8,800

APPELT, Dieter
German b. 1935
photo: (H) $717

APPENZELLER, Felix
relief: (H) $413

APPIAN, Adolphe
French 1819-1898
intaglio: (L) $28; (H) $140

ARAKAWA, Shusaku
Japanese b. 1936
stencil: (H) $176

ARAKI, Jypo
Japanese 19th/20th cent.
intaglio: (H) $44

ARATI, Mario
Monegasques b. 1921
intaglio: (II) $248

ARBEIT, Mark
photo: (H) $692

ARBUS, Diane
American 1923-1971
photo: (L) $1,650; (H) $35,200

ARBUS, Diane and Neil SELKIRK
photo: (L) $1,760; (H) $3,575

ARCHIPENKO, Alexander
Russian 1887-1964
planographic: (L) $61; (H) $2,420
port/books: (H) $25,847

ARENGELO, A.D.
stencil: (H) $83

ARMAN
French b. 1928
intaglio: (L) $284; (H) $497
stencil: (L) $66; (H) $887
planographic: (L) $284; (H) $1,063
photo-repro: (H) $704

ARMFIELD, M. Morris, W.
port/books: (H) $66

ARMINGTON, Frank
1876-1941
intaglio: (H) $146

ARMS, John Taylor
American 1887-1953
intaglio: (L) $66; (H) $3,850
generic: (H) $330

ARMSTRONG, Neil
photo: (H) $2,860

ARMSTRONG BEERE and HIME
photo: (L) $1,022; (H) $2,161

ARMSTRONG and COMPANY,
Lithographers
American 19th cent.
planographic: (H) $99

ARNOUX, Guy
French d. 1951
stencil: (H) $248
posters: (H) $467

ARP, Jean (or Hans)
French 1887-1966
relief: (L) $523; (H) $1,557
planographic: (L) $154; (H) $3,492
posters: (L) $25; (H) $36
port/books: (L) $1,980; (H) $2,177

ARTSCHWAGER, Richard
American b. 1924
intaglio: (L) $1,100; (H) $1,100

ASCHENBRENNER, Lennart
stencil: (H) $579

ASHEVAK, Kenojuak
b. 1927
relief: (H) $679

ASIATISCHE, Kunst
relief: (H) $33

ASSELIN, Maurice
French 1882-1947
planographic: (L) $61; (H) $70

ASTOR, Josef
photo: (H) $200

ATGET, Eugene
French 1857-1927
photo: (L) $990; (H) $7,700

ATGET, Eugene and Berenice
ABBOTT
photo: (H) $4,400

John Taylor Arms's early training as an architect at M.I.T. is evident in his skilled draftsmanship and the exquisite detail of the architectural elements. *American Filigree* shows the quality of his craftsmanship. (John Taylor Arms, *American Filigree*, etching, 10 $\frac{1}{2}$ x 10 $\frac{3}{4}$ inches, Wolf, October 26, 1991, $3,850)

ATLAN, Jean
French 1913-1960
planographic: (L) $849; (H) $1,882

ATWOOD, George
19th/20th cent.
intaglio: (H) $83

AUBRY, Charles
photo: (H) $1,320

AUDLA, Alasi
stencil: (H) $92

AUDRAN, Jean
French 1667-1756
intaglio: (H) $890

AUDUBON
intaglio: (L) $220; (H) $550
planographic: (H) $100

AUDUBON (after)
intaglio: (H) $770
planographic: (H) $110
generic: (H) $440

AUDUBON, James J.
American 1785-1851
planographic: (L) $110; (H) $1,815

AUDUBON, John J.
American 1785-1851
intaglio: (L) $193; (H) $1,650
planographic: (L) $55; (H) $1,375
photo-repro: (L) $176; (H) $330
port/books: (H) $14,300
generic: (H) $1,540

AUDUBON, John J. (after)
American 1785-1851
intaglio: (L) $55; (H) $27,500
planographic: (L) $7; (H) $6,050
photo-repro: (L) $616; (H) $770
port/books: (H) $29,700

AUDUBON, John J. and John
BACHMAN
port/books: (H) $6,600

AUDUBON, John James and John
BACHMAN (after)
port/books: (H) $8,250

AUERBACH, Arnold
intaglio: (H) $156

AUERBACH, Frank
British b. 1931
intaglio: (H) $11,501

AUERBACH-LEVY, William
Russian/American 1889-1964
intaglio: (L) $61; (H) $468

AUGSBURG, Oberrhein Oder
c. 1470
relief: (H) $12,566

AUGSBURG,
HOLZSCHNEIDEWERKSTATT
port/books: (H) $32,987

AUMALUK, Leah
relief: (H) $156

AURIFABER, Wolfgang
intaglio: (H) $1,885

AURIOL, Georges
planographic: (H) $1,105

AUSTEN, Winifred
intaglio: (H) $232

AVATI, Mario
French b. 1921
intaglio: (L) $215; (H) $1,488

AVEDON, Richard
b. 1923
photo: (L) $1,277; (H) $33,000

AVERY, Milton
American 1893-1965
intaglio: (L) $550; (H) $1,673
stencil: (H) $1,100
relief: (L) $770; (H) $2,620
planographic: (L) $825; (H) $1,650

AVRIL
stencil: (H) $101

AVRUTIS, Newton
b. 1906
photo: (L) $550; (H) $825

AY, O
b. 1931
stencil: (H) $1,178

AYLWARD, W.J.
posters: (H) $1,320

AZOULAY, Guillaume
b. 1949
intaglio: (L) $121; (H) $293

AZUMA, Norio
American b. 1928
stencil: (L) $88; (H) $220

BACHER, Otto H.
Danish/American 1839-1927
intaglio: (H) $138

BACHMANN, Otto
Swiss b. 1915
planographic: (L) $116; (H) $231

BACKHUIZEN, Ludolf
1631-1708
port/books: (H) $6,344

BACON, Francis
Irish 1909-1992
intaglio: (L) $3,025; (H) $3,117
planographic: (L) $1,650; (H) $10,037
posters: (L) $1,870; (H) $4,125
photo-repro: (L) $2,200; (H) $6,050
port/books: (L) $5,500; (H) $8,250

BACON, Francis (after)
planographic: (H) $3,573

BACON, Peggy
American 1895-1987
intaglio: (L) $220; (H) $1,540
planographic: (H) $358

BAECHLER, Donald
American b. 1956
intaglio: (H) $2,420
mixed-media: (H) $4,400

BAER, Howard
planographic: (H) $132

BAER, Morley
photo: (L) $660; (H) $770

BAERTLING, Olle
contemporary
stencil: (L) $554; (H) $791

BAHNSEN, Axel
photo: (H) $935

BAILEY, David
port/books: (H) $574
photo: (H) $884

BAILEY, William
intaglio: (L) $605; (H) $1,320
port/books: (H) $1,320

BAILLIE, Captain William
1723-1810
port/books: (H) $2,200

BAILLIE, J.
planographic: (L) $33; (H) $495

BAILLIO, James
planographic: (H) $11

BAIREI, Kono
Japanese 19th cent.
relief: (H) $165

BAJ, Enrico
Italian b. 1924
intaglio: (L) $121; (H) $1,242
stencil: (L) $88; (H) $828
planographic: (L) $188; (H) $327
mixed-media: (H) $368
port/books: (H) $1,270

BAKST, Leon (after)
Russian 1886-1924
planographic: (H) $110

BALBONI, Margot
photo: (H) $250

BALDACCINI, Cesar
French b. 1921
mixed-media: (H) $334

BALDESSARI, John
American b. 1931
planographic: (H) $1,320
mixed-media: (L) $3,300; (H) $7,150
photo: (H) $38,500

BALDESSIN, George
intaglio: (H) $2,262

BALDRIDGE, Cyrus Leroy
American b. 1889
intaglio: (H) $44

BALDUNG, Hans (called Grien)
German 1480-1545
relief: (H) $891

BALDUS, Edouard Denis
French 1820-1882
port/books: (H) $42,084
photo: (L) $1,581; (H) $7,652

BALES, Jean
planographic: (H) $55

BALESTRIERI, Lionello
Italian b. 1874
intaglio: (L) $56; (H) $303

BALET, Jan
German b. 1913
planographic: (H) $29

BALL, James Presley
American b. 1825
photo: (H) $63,800

BALLE, Mogens
planographic: (L) $148; (H) $269

BALLMER, Theo
Swiss 1902-1964
photo: (H) $466

The isolation and terror of man is a recurring theme of Francis Bacon's (1909-1992) works. Many of his figures are shown as deformed or diseased, with faces taken apart and reconstructed in a way that bears no relation to reality. This lithograph, *Three Studies for a Self-Portrait*, was printed in 1980. (Francis Bacon, *Three Studies for a Self-Portrait*, lithograph in colors on Arches paper, 18 ½ x 40 ¾ inches, Butterfield, October 23, 1991, $6,600)

James P. Ball was a prominent Cincinnati society photographer in the 1850s. His daguerreotype of a Cincinnati street scene, circa 1851, set a record for a daguerreotype when it sold for $63,800 (est. $7,000-$10,000). The handwritten label in the bottom corner reads "Greatgrandfather Myers' store." (James Presley Ball, *Cincinnati Street Scene*, half-plate daguerreotype, sealed in a half case, Swann, April 13, 1992, $63,800)

BALLOU, Anne
stencil: (H) $22

BALTHUS
Polish/French b. 1908
planographic: (H) $538

BALTZ, Lewis
photo: (H) $550

BALUSCHECK, Hans
1870-1935
planographic: (H) $205

BAMBERGER, Tom
photo: (H) $320

BANNINGER, Otto
Swiss 1897-1973
intaglio: (H) $25

BANTING, John
British 1902-1972
relief: (H) $184

BAR-AM, Micha
photo: (H) $1,540

BARBIER (after)
intaglio: (H) $61

BARBIER, Georges
French 1882-1932
relief: (L) $83; (H) $248

BARCLAY, Edgar
intaglio: (H) $69

BARENGER, James (after)
intaglio: (H) $397

BARETTA, F.
intaglio: (H) $1,586

BARGHEER, Eduard
German b. 1901
intaglio: (H) $497
planographic: (L) $184; (H) $297

BARILE, Xavier J.
American b. 1891
planographic: (H) $176

BARKER, Charles A.
intaglio: (L) $17; (H) $44

BARKER, G.
intaglio: (H) $344

BARKER, George
American 1882-1965
photo: (H) $440

BARKER, Jones (after)
intaglio: (H) $176

BARLACH, Ernst
German 1870-1938
relief: (L) $3,147; (H) $12,566
planographic: (L) $144; (H) $11,019
port/books: (H) $13,475

BARNARD, George N.
American 1819-1902
photo: (L) $220; (H) $15,400

BARNES, Christopher
photo: (H) $700

BARNET, Will
American b. 1911
intaglio: (H) $2,750
stencil: (L) $248; (H) $1,100
relief: (H) $248
planographic: (L) $110; (H) $413

BARNEY, Tina
b. 1945
photo: (H) $5,500

BARRAUD, Aurele
French 1903-1969
intaglio: (L) $17; (H) $100
port/books: (L) $476; (H) $11,905

BARRAUD, F.P. (after)
English ac. 1877-1900, d. 1924
intaglio: (H) $229

BARRAUD, Maurice
Swiss 1889-1954
intaglio: (L) $397; (H) $968
planographic: (L) $25; (H) $745
port/books: (H) $675

BARRAUD, William and Henry (after)
British 19th cent.
intaglio: (L) $468; (H) $583

BARRIERE, Dominique
port/books: (H) $1,430

BARROW, Thomas
photo: (H) $150

BARRY, Anne Meredith
mixed-media: (L) $27; (H) $46

BARRY, D.F.
photo: (H) $605

BARRY, Robert
contemporary
port/books: (H) $1,298

BARTELL, B.
posters: (H) $1,430

BARTH, J.S. (after)
intaglio: (H) $464

BARTH, Wolf
Swiss b. 1926
planographic: (H) $83

BARTLETT, Charles W.
English 1860-1940
intaglio: (H) $275
relief: (L) $358; (H) $495

BARTLETT, Jennifer
American b. 1941
planographic: (L) $550; (H) $550
port/books: (H) $3,300

BARTOLINI, Luigi
1892-1963
intaglio: (L) $1,229; (H) $4,159
relief: (H) $709

BARTOLOZZI, F. (after I.G.
CIPRIANI)
intaglio: (H) $235

BARTOLOZZI, Francesco
Italian 1725/27-1815
intaglio: (L) $99; (H) $451
photo-repro: (H) $516

BARYE, Antoine Louis
French 1795-1875
planographic: (H) $440

BAS, Jacques Philippe le
1707-1783
intaglio: (H) $4,398

BASELITZ, Georg
German b. 1938
intaglio: (L) $154; (H) $6,966
relief: (H) $2,640

BASKETT, Charles H.
English 1872-1953
intaglio: (H) $50

BASKIN, Leonard
American b. 1922
intaglio: (L) $55; (H) $358
relief: (L) $28; (H) $1,045
planographic: (L) $44; (H) $165

BASS, Saul
posters: (H) $660

BASS, Tony
intaglio: (H) $117

BASSET (Rue St. Jaques), Publisher
French 18th/19th cent.
intaglio: (H) $358

BATE, Laurie
planographic: (H) $78

BATEMAN, James
British 1893-1959
port/books: (H) $2,420

BATES, Maxwell Bennett
1906-1980
planographic: (L) $366; (H) $1,024

BAUER, Franz Andreas and John LINDLEY
port/books: (H) $4,180

BAUER, John
contemporary
planographic: (H) $591

BAUER, M.
1864-1932
intaglio: (L) $87; (H) $100

BAUGEAN, Jean Jerome (after)
photo-repro: (H) $220

BAUHAUS
photo: (H) $1,980

BAUMANN, Charles Frederic
b. 1826
planographic: (H) $248

BAUMANN, Gustave
German/American 1881-1971
relief: (L) $660; (H) $5,500
mixed-media: (H) $2,860
port/books: (H) $440

BAUMANN, Jean Henri
1801-1858
intaglio: (H) $133

BAUMBERGER, Georg
planographic: (H) $133

BAUMBERGER, Otto
Swiss 1889-1961
planographic: (L) $50; (H) $107
posters: (L) $660; (H) $2,750
port/books: (L) $100; (H) $149

BAUMEISTER, Willi
German 1889-1955
stencil: (L) $2,861; (H) $8,030
planographic: (L) $1,412; (H) $5,775
port/books: (H) $5,225

BAUMGARTEN, Lothar
German b. 1944
photo: (H) $430

BAWDEN, Edward
planographic: (H) $329

BAY, Enrico
planographic: (H) $93

BAYEFSKY, Aba
relief: (H) $183

BAYER, Herbert
Austrian/American b. 1900
photo: (L) $1,100; (H) $121,000

BAYOT
planographic: (H) $367

BAZAINE, Jean
French b. 1904
planographic: (L) $49; (H) $179

BEAL, Gifford
American 1879-1956
intaglio: (L) $77; (H) $165

BEAL, Jack
American b. 1931
planographic: (H) $154

BEAL, Reynolds
American 1867-1951
intaglio: (L) $99; (H) $303

BEALS, Jessie Tarbox
photo: (L) $330; (H) $523

BEARD, Peter
photo: (H) $3,300

BEARDEN, Romare
American 1914-1988
stencil: (L) $357; (H) $12,100
planographic: (L) $220; (H) $715

BEARDY, Jackson
1944-1984
stencil: (H) $230

BEATO, Felix (attrib.)
c. 1830-1906
photo: (H) $770

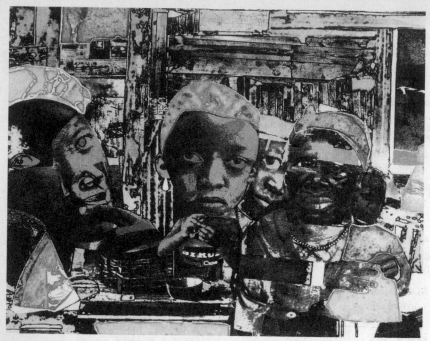

Romare Bearden's vibrant collage-like etchings frequently depict Afro-American street life. (Romare Bearden, *The Train*, 1975, etching and aquatint in colors, 17 ½ x 22 ¼ inches, Weschler, December 12, 1992, $2,820)

BEATON, Cecil
English 1904-1980
photo: (L) $354; (H) $2,750

BEATRIZET, Nicolas
c. 1515-1560
intaglio: (L) $841; (H) $4,241

BEATTY, John William
intaglio: (L) $137; (H) $161

BEAUCORPS, Gustave De
photo: (H) $550

BEAUDIN, Andre
French 1895-1980
planographic: (L) $82; (H) $281

BEAUFORD
British 18th/19th cent.
intaglio: (H) $110

BEAUFRERE, Adolphe
relief: (H) $4,593

BECHER, Bernd and Hilla
Germans b. 1930's
photo-repro: (L) $402; (H) $402
photo: (L) $358; (H) $22,000

BECHTLE, Robert
American b. 1932
planographic: (H) $330

BECK, C.
planographic: (H) $209

BECK, Leonhard
German c. 1480-1542
relief: (H) $10,603

BECKMANN, Hannes
photo: (L) $3,850; (H) $4,400

BECKMANN, Max
American b. Germany 1884, d. 1950
intaglio: (L) $397; (H) $55,453
relief: (L) $1,431; (H) $34,558
planographic: (L) $1,170; (H) $41,800

BEECHEY, William (after)
intaglio: (H) $121

BEGA, Cornelis
Dutch 1620-1664
intaglio: (L) $176; (H) $3,613

BEGG, William (after)
intaglio: (H) $268

BEHAM, Barthel
1502-1540
intaglio: (L) $1,045; (H) $36,128

BEHAM, Hans Sebald
German 1500-1550
intaglio: (L) $70; (H) $30,631
relief: (L) $1,526; (H) $4,398
port/books: (L) $1,980; (H) $2,860

BEHR, Klaus
German b. 1935
photo: (L) $158; (H) $502

BEHRENS, Howard
stencil: (H) $523

BEHRENS, Peter
1868-1940
relief: (L) $826; (H) $4,891

BEHRMANN-BOSSHARD
posters: (H) $215

BEJOT, Eug.
intaglio: (H) $110

BELAMY
intaglio: (H) $66

BELL, Alistair
b. 1913
planographic: (H) $195

BELL, William
photo: (H) $385

BELLA, Stefano della
Italian 1610-1644
intaglio: (L) $171; (H) $713
planographic: (L) $216; (H) $7,069
port/books: (H) $2,718

BELLANGE, Jacques
French c. 1575-c. 1616
intaglio: (L) $7,319; (H) $69,115

BELLEROCHE, Albert
planographic: (L) $189; (H) $2,711

BELLIN, Samuel
English 1799-1894
intaglio: (H) $440

BELLMER, Hans
German/French 1902-1975
intaglio: (L) $116; (H) $409
planographic: (L) $168; (H) $273
port/books: (L) $2,269; (H) $22,000
photo: (L) $3,960; (H) $8,250

BELLOC, Auguste
19th cent.
photo: (H) $7,652

BELLOCQ, E.J.
photo: (L) $514; (H) $660

BELLOTTO, Bernardo
Italian 1720/24-1780
intaglio: (L) $3,778; (H) $7,150

BELLOWS, Albert Fitch
American 1829-1883
intaglio: (II) $88

BELLOWS, George
American 1882-1925
planographic: (L) $495; (H) $13,200

BEN
port/books: (H) $379

BENARD
intaglio: (H) $122

BENDA, Arthur
German 1886-1969
photo: (L) $573; (H) $681

BENDERH, J.D.
posters: (H) $994

BENDIEN, Jacob
contemporary
planographic: (H) $233

BENDINER, Alfred
American b. 1899
planographic: (H) $50

BENEDETTO, G.
intaglio: (H) $44

BENEKER, Gerrit A.
American 1882-1934
posters: (H) $50

BENNETT, William J. (after J.W. HILL)
American
intaglio: (H) $550

Hans Bellmer (1902-1975) was a painter and graphic artist renowned for the disturbing Surrealist quality of his work. In 1934, dolls became his central theme; fabricating jointed dolls in the form of adolescent girls, he drew and photographed them in a variety of erotic positions. *Les Jeux de la Poupee (The Doll's Game)* was a 1949 limited edition text (119 copies) with 17 hand-colored silver prints. This copy sold at Swann's for a record $22,000. (Hans Bellmer, *Les Jeux de la Poupee*, text and 17 hand-colored prints, 4to, Swann, October 8, 1991, $22,000)

BENNETT, William James
Anglo/American 1787-1844
planographic: (H) $550
generic: (H) $193

BENOIS, Alexandre
Russian 1870-1960
port/books: (H) $2,860

BENSON, Frank W.
American 1862-1951
intaglio: (L) $165; (H) $3,025

BENSON, Richard
photo-repro: (L) $320; (H) $380

BENT, Paul
stencil: (H) $87

BENTLEY, Charles
intaglio: (H) $1,586

BENTON, Thomas Hart
American 1889-1975
planographic: (L) $660; (H) $7,700

BERGER, Anthony
photo: (H) $605

BERGES, Werner
b. 1941
port/books: (L) $164; (H) $185

BERGH, Vikke V.D.
posters: (H) $110

BERGMAN, Henry Eric
1893-1958
relief: (H) $74

BERGNER, Yosl Vladimir
stencil: (L) $104; (H) $391

BERIC
posters: (H) $165

BERKE, Hubert
contemporary
mixed-media: (H) $2,597

BERKOWITZ, M.
intaglio: (H) $28

BERMAN, Eugene
Russian/American 1899-1972
intaglio: (H) $66
port/books: (H) $412

BERMAN, Zeke
photo: (H) $770

BERNARD, E.
intaglio: (H) $70

BERNDER, Bernd
German b. 1930
stencil: (H) $50

BERNDT, Jerry
photo: (L) $130; (H) $380

BERNEGGER, Alfred
Swiss 1912-1978
relief: (L) $139; (H) $149

BERNER, Bernd
German b. 1930
stencil: (L) $25; (H) $25

BERNHARD, Ruth
German b. 1905
photo: (L) $550; (H) $4,675

BERNOUD, Alphonse
photo: (H) $770

BERRY, Carroll Thayer
American 1886-1978
relief: (L) $44; (H) $88

BERTAUX, F. Duplessi
late 18th cent.
intaglio: (H) $550
port/books: (H) $550

BERTHON, Paul
French ac. c. 1900
planographic: (L) $138; (H) $523
generic: (H) $110

BERTIN, N. (after)
intaglio: (H) $300
planographic: (H) $120

BERTRAM, Dora
relief: (H) $54

BESNARD, Albert
French 1849-1934
intaglio: (L) $60; (H) $942
planographic: (H) $99

BESSA, P.
port/books: (L) $633; (H) $770

BESSON, L.
planographic: (H) $770

BEURDELEY, Jacques
French b. 1874
intaglio: (H) $33

BEUYS, Joseph
German 1921-1986
intaglio: (L) $1,277; (H) $2,128
stencil: (L) $145; (H) $2,750
relief: (H) $4,421
planographic: (L) $4,125; (H) $8,655
posters: (L) $66; (H) $851
mixed-media: (L) $1,154; (H) $3,246
photo-repro: (L) $74; (H) $2,315
port/books: (H) $2,181
photo: (L) $337; (H) $13,200
others: (L) $362; (H) $627

BEWIDELEY, Jacques
intaglio: (H) $44

BEYNOM and COMPANY, Publishers
planographic: (H) $102

BIANCONI, Giovanni
Swiss 1891-1981
relief: (H) $133

BICKNELL, Wm.
intaglio: (H) $22

BIDDLE, E.C.
planographic: (L) $200; (H) $275

BIDDLE, George
American 1885-1973
planographic: (H) $50

BIEN, J.
planographic: (H) $1,540

BIERENBROODSPOT, Gerti
contemporary
planographic: (L) $177; (H) $272

BIERGE, Roland
planographic: (L) $120; (H) $181

BIGG, William Redmore (after)
intaglio: (L) $310; (H) $738

BIKERE, R.
planographic: (H) $11

BILD-BERICHT, Berliner
photo: (H) $1,100

BILL, G. and F.
planographic: (H) $85

BILL, Henry
planographic: (H) $66

BILL, Max
Swiss b. 1908
stencil: (H) $144
relief: (H) $1,587
planographic: (L) $388; (H) $1,129
posters: (L) $331; (H) $364
port/books: (L) $1,045; (H) $1,650

BILLE, Ejler
planographic: (L) $94; (H) $215
port/books: (L) $448; (H) $1,290

BILLINGS, Lucie L.
American 1907-1935
relief: (H) $33

BINGHAM, George Caleb
1811-1879
intaglio: (L) $605; (H) $1,191

BINGHAM, George Caleb (after)
intaglio: (L) $990; (H) $2,860

BINGHAM, Katherine
photo: (H) $330

BIRCH, Thomas (after)
American 1779-1851
intaglio: (H) $385

BIRCH, William and Son
port/books: (H) $44,000

BIRD, Harington (after)
intaglio: (L) $100; (H) $229

BIRKEMOSE, Jens
planographic: (H) $72

BISAUX, Pierre
planographic: (H) $50

BISCAINO, Bartolommeo
Italian 1632-1657
intaglio: (L) $1,130; (H) $4,869

BISCARETTI, C.
posters: (H) $550

George Caleb Bingham's genre paintings of the West were very popular in the 1800s. This print, after a painting by Bingham, was executed by John Sartain in 1854. (John Sartain [after George Caleb Bingham], *The County Election*, engraving, mezzotint and roulette on wove paper, 22 x 30 inches, Dunnings, October 12, 1991, $2,860)

BISCHOFF, Henry
Swiss 1882-1951
relief: (L) $41; (H) $74

BISHOP, Isabel
American b. 1902
intaglio: (L) $165; (H) $468

BISHOP, Richard E.
American b. 1887
intaglio: (L) $83; (H) $523

BISS
planographic: (L) $66; (H) $99

BISS, Earl
planographic: (H) $385
posters: (L) $11; (H) $55

BISSIER, Julius
German/Swiss 1893-1965
stencil: (H) $451

BISSIERE, Roger
French 1886/88-1964
planographic: (H) $569

BISSON, Paul
intaglio: (H) $22

BISSON-FRERES
photo: (H) $412

BITRAN, Albert
intaglio: (L) $148; (H) $167

BLACHE, Ph. Ch.
planographic: (H) $101

BLACK, Judith
photo: (H) $170

BLACKBURN, Morris
American 1902-1979
stencil: (H) $715

BLACKLEY, A.
planographic: (H) $348

BLACKMAN, Charles
intaglio: (L) $209; (H) $304
stencil: (L) $261; (H) $304
planographic: (L) $157; (H) $174

BLACKWELL, Mr.
generic: (H) $10

BLACKWELL, Tom
stencil: (H) $66

BLACKWOOD, David
b. 1941
intaglio: (L) $732; (H) $3,511
planographic: (H) $1,388

BLAEU, Johannes (after)
intaglio: (H) $181

BLAEUW, Guiljelmo
generic: (H) $385

BLAKE, Leo B.
American b. 1887
relief: (L) $55; (H) $193

BLAKE, Peter
port/books: (L) $1,591; (H) $1,591

BLAKE, William
English 1757-1827
intaglio: (L) $138; (H) $27,466
port/books: (L) $785; (H) $41,250

BLAMPIED, Edmund
English 1886-1966
intaglio: (L) $77; (H) $1,100

BLAUMEISTER, Willi
1889-1955
stencil: (H) $4,649

BLAUSTEIN, Al
American b. 1924
intaglio: (H) $55

BLECKNER, Ross
American b. 1949
planographic: (H) $605

BLEKER, Gerrit Claesz
1610-1656
intaglio: (L) $845; (H) $1,894

BLINKS, Thomas (after)
photo-repro: (H) $99

BLOCH, George
port/books: (H) $357

BLOCH, Julius
American 1888-1966
planographic: (H) $210

BLOCH, M.E.
port/books: (H) $660

BLOEMAERT, Abraham
Dutch c. 1564-1651
intaglio: (L) $138; (H) $248

BLOEMAERT, Abraham (after)
mixed-media: (L) $837; (H) $2,193

BLONDEL, Jacques Francois
port/books: (H) $2,200

BLOTNICK, Elihu
photo: (H) $330

BLUM, Alexander A.
American b. 1888
intaglio: (L) $55; (H) $77

BLUME, Bernhard Johannes
German b. 1937
photo: (L) $502; (H) $1,648

BLUMENFELD, Erwin
1897-1969
photo: (L) $1,540; (H) $1,980

BLUMENTHAL, Hermann
1905-1942
intaglio: (H) $82

BO, Lars
intaglio: (H) $259

BOCCASILE
posters: (H) $660

BOCCIONI, Umberto
Italian 1882-1916
intaglio: (L) $3,317; (H) $11,055

BOCKSTIEGEL, Peter August
1889-1951
intaglio: (H) $945
relief: (L) $1,023; (H) $2,146
planographic: (H) $2,617

BOCOLA, Sandro
Italian b. 1931
posters: (H) $18

BODENEHR, Gabriel
intaglio: (H) $153

BODINE, A. Aubrey
1906-1970
photo: (L) $412; (H) $4,400

Marlene Dietrich's first acting role was in the German movie *The Blue Angel*. American movie posters from before World War II are rare, but German movie posters are even more so. This German poster of *Der Blaue Engel* is thought to be the only existing copy. Estimated at $15,000-$20,000, this poster from the Stanley Caidin Collection of movie posters sold for a record $27,500. (*Der Blaue Engel*, linen-backed poster, 85 x 38 inches, Sotheby-New York, September 12, 1992, $27,500)

BODMER, Charles
1809-1893
planographic: (L) $133; (H) $199

BODMER, Karl (after)
intaglio: (L) $660; (H) $4,125

BODNENEHR, Gabriel
1673-1766
intaglio: (H) $63

BOEHLE, Fritz
1873-1916
intaglio: (H) $134

BOGART, Bram
b. 1921
intaglio: (H) $2,570
planographic: (H) $453
mixed-media: (H) $1,770

BOHDE, G.W.
intaglio: (H) $55

BOHEMAN, K.W.
stencil: (H) $94

BOHEMEN, Kees van
stencil: (H) $285
planographic: (L) $316; (H) $506

BOHROD, Aaron
American b. 1907
planographic: (L) $39; (H) $77

BOILLY, L. (after)
intaglio: (H) $554
planographic: (H) $75

BOITARD, Pierre
port/books: (H) $770

BOL, Ferdinand
Dutch 1616-1680
intaglio: (L) $246; (H) $29,903

BOLDRINI, Niccolo (after Titian)
relief: (H) $462

BOLLEE, Leon
1870-1913
photo: (L) $825; (H) $1,540

BOLLINGEN SERIES
port/books: (H) $880

BOLOTOWSKY, Ilya
Russian/American 1907-1981
stencil: (L) $110; (H) $330
planographic: (H) $110

BOLSWERT, Boetius Adams
1580-1633
intaglio: (H) $791

BOLSWERT, S.A.
intaglio: (H) $55

BOLT, Ronald William
b. 1938
stencil: (H) $170
planographic: (H) $585

BONASONE, Giulio
1498-c. 1580
intaglio: (L) $923; (H) $1,641

BONE, Muirhead
Scottish 1876-1953
intaglio: (H) $193
planographic: (H) $385

BONELLI, Giorgio
intaglio: (H) $8,895

BONFILS, Felix
photo: (L) $344; (H) $660

BONFILS, Felix (attrib.)
photo: (H) $715

BONHEUR, Rosa
French 1822-1899
intaglio: (L) $495; (H) $605
planographic: (H) $110

BONNARD, Pierre
French 1867-1947
intaglio: (L) $60; (H) $1,431
planographic: (L) $440; (H) $29,365
port/books: (L) $141,372; (H) $191,733

BONNET, Louis Marin
French 1736-1793
intaglio: (L) $645; (H) $21,929

BONNETERRE
intaglio: (L) $1,210; (H) $1,540

BOOL, A. and J. and Henry DIXON
port/books: (H) $5,356

BOORMAN, John
intaglio: (H) $248

BOREIN, Edward
American 1872-1943
intaglio: (L) $358; (H) $1,980
port/books: (H) $11,275

BORER, Albert
Swiss 20th cent.
posters: (H) $50

BORGLIND, Stig
contemporary
intaglio: (L) $444; (H) $684

BORIS, Nickolas
photo: (H) $605

BOROFSKY, Jonathan
American b. 1942
stencil: (H) $2,475
port/books: (H) $3,080

BORRELLI, Vincent P.
photo: (H) $180

BORREMIEO, Ghiberto
intaglio: (H) $6

BOS, C.
intaglio: (H) $100

BOSCH, Hieronymous (after)
intaglio: (L) $2,068; (H) $13,035

BOSIO
intaglio: (H) $257

BOSMAN, Richard
American b. 1944
relief: (L) $715; (H) $1,045

BOSSARD, Johann Michael
Swiss 1874-1950
planographic: (H) $116

BOSSCHERE, Jean de
port/books: (H) $100

BOSSE, A.
intaglio: (L) $180; (H) $240

BOSSHARD, Rodolphe Theophile
1889-1960
planographic: (L) $107; (H) $273

BOSWORTH, Barbara
photo: (H) $300

BOTERO, Fernando
Colombian b. 1932
planographic: (L) $4,950; (H) $5,500
posters: (H) $110

BOTKE, Cornelis J.
American 1887-1954
intaglio: (H) $165

BOTT, Francis
German b. 1904
stencil: (L) $78; (H) $78
planographic: (H) $157

BOTTEMA, Tj
1882-1940
posters: (H) $351

BOTTGER, Klaus
German c. 1942
intaglio: (H) $33

BOTTINI, G.
planographic: (H) $2,016

BOUBAT, Edouard
French b. 1923
photo: (L) $1,760; (H) $3,960

BOUCHER, Francois
French 1703-1770
intaglio: (H) $260

BOUCHER, Francois (after)
intaglio: (L) $55; (H) $449
planographic: (L) $55; (H) $220

BOUCHER, Lucien
posters: (H) $110

BOUCHET
posters: (H) $550

BOUDIN, Eug.
intaglio: (H) $693

BOUGHTON, Alice
American 1865-1943
photo: (H) $3,300

BOUGHTON, George Henry
Anglo/American 1833-1905
intaglio: (L) $92; (H) $193

BOUISSET, Firmin (after)
posters: (H) $1,320

BOULONOIS, E. de
intaglio: (H) $120

BOULT, Francis Cecil (after)
planographic: (H) $110

BOULTBEE, John (after)
intaglio: (H) $308

BOUNI, Bruno
American 20th cent.
planographic: (H) $110

BOURDEAU, Robert
photo: (L) $880; (H) $3,300

BOURKE-WHITE, Margaret
American 1904-1971
photo: (L) $138; (H) $28,600

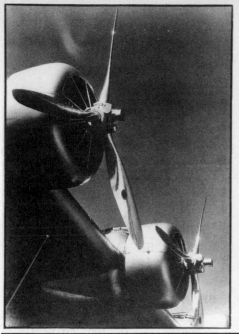

In the late 1920s Margaret Bourke-White (1904-1971) became famous for her photographs of heavy machinery and factories. Her prints from this period, marked by a bold, simplified composition, are printed with a black border. Her photographs were printed by her private printer with her signature or stamp on the verso. During the 1940s Bourke-White specialized in war photos. (Margaret Bourke-White, *Sikovsky S-42*, gelatin silver print, 13 ⅛ x 9 ¼ inches, Butterfield, May 13, 1992, $14,300)

BOUSSINGAULT, Jean Louis
planographic: (H) $416

BOUT, Pieter
Flemish 1658-1719
intaglio: (H) $6,600

BOUTET DE MONVEL, Bernard
French 1884-1949
intaglio: (L) $501; (H) $603

BOVINET
planographic: (H) $138

BOWDEN, Harry
photo: (H) $165

BOWEN, J.T.
American
planographic: (L) $497; (H) $580

BOWEN and CO., Publishers
planographic: (H) $99

BOWLES, Carington
British 18th cent.
intaglio: (H) $275

BOWLES, T.
intaglio: (H) $184

BOWYER, R. (after)
intaglio: (H) $48

BOXER, Stanley
American b. 1926
intaglio: (H) $550

BOYD, Arthur
intaglio: (H) $348
planographic: (H) $304

BOYD, Theodore Penleigh
intaglio: (H) $174

BOYDELL, John
intaglio: (H) $358

BOYDELL, John and Josiah
port/books: (H) $5,754

BOYDELL, Josiah, Publishers (after)
British 1752-1817
photo-repro: (H) $660

BRACK, John
planographic: (H) $522

BRACQUEMOND, F. (after G. MOREAU)
intaglio: (H) $302

BRACQUEMOND, Felix
intaglio: (L) $89; (H) $998

BRADFORD, William (photographer)
American 1823/30-1892
port/books: (H) $13,200

BRADLEY, Cuthbert
planographic: (H) $139

BRADLEY, Helen (after)
photo-repro: (L) $165; (H) $222

BRADLEY, Malcolm
stencil: (H) $114

BRADLEY, Will
posters: (L) $192; (H) $2,640

BRADY, Mathew
American 1823-1896
photo: (L) $880; (H) $6,600

BRADY'S GALLERY
photo: (H) $830

BRADY STUDIO
photo: (H) $1,980

BRAGDON, Claude Fayette
posters: (H) $440

BRAGG, Charles
American 20th cent.
intaglio: (H) $165

BRAMSON, Stern
photo: (L) $495; (H) $825

BRANCUSI, Constantin
Rumanian 1876-1957
photo: (L) $4,950; (H) $30,800

BRANDES, Peter
planographic: (L) $215; (H) $296

BRANDS, Eugene
Dutch b. 1913
stencil: (L) $311; (H) $401

BRANDT, Bill
British 1904-1984
photo: (L) $440; (H) $12,650

BRANGWYN, Frank
British 1867-1956
intaglio: (L) $66; (H) $349
planographic: (H) $229
posters: (H) $110
port/books: (H) $242

Entered according to Act of Congress by M.B.Brady & Co. in the year 1865 in the Clerk's Office of the District Court of the District of Columbia.

During the 1860s, calling cards with a photograph, known as *cartes-de-visite*, were very popular. Collected in albums, those with an autograph were the most desirable. Robert E. Lee autographed this card on the reverse side. In the 1870s many studios began to sell *carte-de-visites* commercially and they fell out of favor. (Mathew Brady, *Robert E. Lee,* 1865, 3 $\frac{1}{2}$ x 2 $\frac{1}{8}$ inches, Christie-New York, April 15, 1992, $6,600)

BRAQUE, Georges
French 1882-1963
intaglio: (L) $138; (H) $49,500
stencil: (H) $110
relief: (L) $1,344; (H) $6,080
planographic: (L) $30; (H) $16,135
posters: (H) $394
mixed-media: (L) $4,400; (H) $6,050
port/books: (L) $1,100; (H) $15,400

BRAQUE, Georges (after)
intaglio: (L) $423; (H) $4,180
planographic: (L) $33; (H) $881
mixed-media: (H) $770
generic: (L) $33; (H) $77

BRAQUEMOND, Felix
photo-repro: (H) $55

BRASHER, Rex
port/books: (H) $5,280

BRASILIER, Andre
French b. 1929
planographic: (L) $423; (H) $2,259

BRASSAI
1899-1984
port/books: (L) $880; (H) $5,500
photo: (L) $786; (H) $4,400

BRATBY, John
intaglio: (H) $315

BRATT, Byron H.
American b. 1952
intaglio: (H) $55

BRAUN, Louis
intaglio: (H) $55

BRAUNIGER, Peter
intaglio: (H) $83

BRAVO, Manuel Alvarez
Mexican b. 1902
port/books: (L) $3,850; (H) $7,700
photo: (L) $747; (H) $2,780

BRAYER, Yves
French b. 1907
intaglio: (H) $110
planographic: (L) $248; (H) $515

BRECHT, George
American b. 1925
stencil: (H) $577

BREITENBACH, Josef
1896-1984
photo: (L) $1,870; (H) $6,050

BREITER, Herbert
planographic: (H) $17

BREMER, Uwe
b. 1940
intaglio: (H) $83

BRENDEL, Karl
German b. 1877
relief: (L) $110; (H) $193

BRESCIA, Giovanni Antonio da (after)
intaglio: (H) $4,510

BRESDIN, Rodolphe
1825-1885
intaglio: (L) $596; (H) $935
planographic: (L) $1,124; (H) $54,978

BRESSANT, Lucien
French 1867-1949
intaglio: (H) $83

BRESSLERN-ROTH, Norbertine von
German b. 1891
relief: (L) $348; (H) $468

BRETON, Jules (after)
French 1827-1906
intaglio: (H) $28

BRETON, Jules Adolphe
French 1827-1906
intaglio: (H) $46

BREWER, Edward P. (after)
planographic: (H) $605

BREWER, Henry Charles
English b. 1866
intaglio: (H) $165

BREWER, J. Alphese
intaglio: (H) $22

BRICHER, A.T.
generic: (H) $250

BRIDGENS, Richard
port/books: (H) $1,100

BRIDGES, Marilyn
photo: (H) $320

BRIERLY, Oswald W.
planographic: (H) $2,262

BRIGNONI, Sergio
Swiss b. 1903
planographic: (H) $294
posters: (H) $41

BRIL, P. (after)
port/books: (H) $770

BRISCOE, Arthur
intaglio: (L) $165; (H) $524

BRISEUX, Charles Etienne
port/books: (H) $1,100

BRISTOL, Horace
photo: (H) $330

BRITTON, John
port/books: (H) $990

BROCAS, S.F. (after)
intaglio: (H) $724

BROCKHURST, Gerald
British b. 1890
intaglio: (L) $198; (H) $9,075
planographic: (H) $247

BROCKMANN, Gottfried
b. 1903
port/books: (H) $887

BRODERS, Roger
posters: (H) $522

BROMLEY, Frederick
1856-1860
intaglio: (H) $457

BROMLEY, Frederick
American 20th cent.
intaglio: (H) $248

BROOD, Herman
contemporary
planographic: (L) $324; (H) $379

BROODTHAERS, Marcel
Belgian 1924-1976
mixed-media: (H) $5,049
photo-repro: (L) $1,836; (H) $5,049

BROOK, Arthur B.
intaglio: (H) $110

BROOKS, Charlotte
photo: (L) $495; (H) $660

BROOKS, Frank Leonard
intaglio: (H) $101

BROOKS and SON, Publishers
British 19th cent.
intaglio: (H) $138

BROOKSHAW, George
British 19th cent.
intaglio: (H) $220

BROSAMER, Hans
c. 1500-1552
intaglio: (H) $3,299

BROUET, Auguste
intaglio: (H) $44

BROUWER, Adriaen
Flemish 1605/06-1638
intaglio: (H) $175

BROWN, Bolton
planographic: (H) $94

BROWN, C. Furlee
photo: (L) $139; (H) $217

BROWN, Daniel P.
b. 1939
stencil: (L) $230; (H) $412

BROWN, Geoffrey
intaglio: (H) $26

BROWN, J. Appleton (after)
1844-1902
planographic: (H) $77

BROWN, James
American
intaglio: (H) $2,200

BROWN, John George
Anglo/American 1831-1913
intaglio: (L) $183; (H) $220

BROWN, L.C.A.
19th/20th cent.
relief: (H) $165

BROWN, Paul
planographic: (H) $22

BROWN, Susan
photo: (H) $380

BROWNE, George Elmer
American 1871-1946
intaglio: (H) $220

BROWNE, Stewart
posters: (H) $66

BROWNLEE, R.W.
generic: (L) $55; (H) $65

BRUEGHEL, Pieter (the elder) (after)
intaglio: (L) $634; (H) $37,640
port/books: (H) $15,400

BRUEGHEL, Pieter (after)
intaglio: (H) $165

BRUEHL, Anton
American 1900-1983
photo: (L) $715; (H) $3,080

BRUEHL, Martin
photo: (L) $522; (H) $1,430

BRUGSAL, Sanders Alexander van
(called Meister S)
intaglio: (H) $1,178

BRUN, Donald
Swiss b. 1909
posters: (L) $50; (H) $220

BRUNEAU, Kittie
Canadian School b. 1929
intaglio: (H) $116

BRUNELLESCHI, Umberto
Italian b. 1879; ac. 1907-1930
stencil: (L) $220; (H) $248

BRUNET, Tan
generic: (H) $55

BRUNI, Bruno
planographic: (L) $246; (H) $246

BRUNING, Peter
1929-1970
intaglio: (L) $308; (H) $603
stencil: (H) $649
planographic: (H) $938

BRUNNING, Walter P.
photo: (H) $412

BRUNSDEN, John
20th cent.
intaglio: (H) $28

BRUS, Johannes
German b. 1942
photo: (L) $394; (H) $1,433

BRUSH, Gloria Defilipps
photo: (H) $100

BRUSTOLINI, Joannes Baptista
intaglio: (H) $1,354

BRY, Theodore de
Flemish 1528-1598
port/books: (H) $9,818

BRYANT, Charles
relief: (H) $87

BRYEN, Camille
20th cent.
intaglio: (H) $102
planographic: (H) $83

BUBLEY, Esther
photo: (H) $1,100

BUCHEL, Emmanuel
1705-1775
intaglio: (H) $124

BUCHER, Carl
Swiss b. 1935
stencil: (H) $36

BUCHER, Etienne
20th cent.
posters: (H) $133

BUCHHEISTER, Carl
1890-1964
port/books: (H) $369

BUCHSER, Fritz
b. 1903
relief: (H) $107

BUEHRMAN, Elizabeth
photo: (H) $550

BUELL, Alice Standish
intaglio: (L) $55; (H) $72

BUFF, Conrad
Swiss/American 1886-1975
planographic: (H) $248

BUFFET, Bernard
French b. 1928
intaglio: (L) $251; (H) $14,405
stencil: (H) $65
planographic: (L) $990; (H) $8,250
posters: (H) $414
port/books: (H) $110,153
generic: (H) $110

BUFFET, Bernard (after)
planographic: (L) $123; (H) $1,268

BUFFON
port/books: (L) $495; (H) $935

BUFFON, Comte De Georges Louis
Marie Le Clerc
1707-1788
intaglio: (H) $44

BUFFORD, John H. (after Benjamin Russell)
American 1837-1871
planographic: (H) $2,310

BUFFORD, John H., Lithographer
American ac. 1835-1871
planographic: (H) $121

BUHOT, Felix
French 1847-1898
intaglio: (L) $110; (H) $3,300
port/books: (H) $2,995

BULL, Clarence Sinclair
port/books: (L) $715; (H) $3,300
photo: (L) $468; (H) $660

BULL HEDLUND, Bertil
contemporary
intaglio: (H) $462

BULLOCK, Edna
photo: (H) $300

BULLOCK, Wynn
American 1902-1972
photo: (L) $275; (H) $3,080

BUNBURY, Henry (after)
intaglio: (H) $283

BURANI, Francesco
ac. 1630
intaglio: (H) $2,324

BURCHFIELD, Charles
American 1893-1967
intaglio: (H) $4,620
planographic: (L) $2,475; (H) $4,125

BURCHFIELD, Jerry
photo: (H) $190

BUREN, Daniel
French b. 1938
port/books: (H) $5,500
photo: (H) $1,218

BURFORD (after)
intaglio: (H) $220

BURFORD, Thomas
British 1710-1774
intaglio: (H) $248

BURGIS, William (after)
1717-1729
intaglio: (H) $2,640

BURGKMAIR, Hans (the younger)
German b. 1500
relief: (L) $7,461; (H) $8,639
port/books: (H) $23,562

BURGUND, Franciscus Perrier
intaglio: (H) $967

BURKHARD, Mangold
planographic: (H) $199

BURNE-JONES, Edward Coley (after)
intaglio: (L) $1,464; (H) $2,509

BURNS, Marsha
photo: (L) $220; (H) $990

BURNS, Michael
photo: (L) $200; (H) $275

BURR, George Elbert
American 1859-1939
intaglio: (L) $110; (H) $935

BURRI
intaglio: (H) $455

BURRI, Alberto
Italian b. 1915
mixed-media: (L) $1,511; (H) $3,117
others: (H) $2,300

BURSON, Nancy
photo: (H) $800

BURTON, Larry
generic: (H) $28

BURY, Thomas Talbot
port/books: (H) $4,986

BUSCHELLE, John
port/books: (H) $715

BUSHMAN, Leo Norman
relief: (H) $122

BUSINCK, Ludolph
c. 1590-1669
relief: (L) $634; (H) $3,573

BUSSCHE, Wolf Von Dem
port/books: (H) $1,320

BUSY, W.
Dutch
intaglio: (H) $39

BUTCHER, F. (after)
intaglio: (H) $222

BUTLER, Henry
intaglio: (H) $220

BUTTRE, J.C.
intaglio: (H) $28

BUTTS, Alfred M.
American b. 1899
relief: (H) $83

BUYTEWECH, Willem
Dutch
intaglio: (H) $8,250

BYRD, David
posters: (H) $330

BYRNE, John L.
intaglio: (H) $243

BYRNE, William
intaglio: (H) $468

BYWATERS, Jerry
planographic: (H) $138

CADDUCK, Kathleen
intaglio: (H) $28

CADMUS, Paul
American b. 1904
intaglio: (L) $358; (H) $4,950
planographic: (L) $220; (H) $633

CAFFERY, Debbie Fleming
photo: (H) $450

CAGLIO, Corrado
Italian b. 1910
intaglio: (H) $91

CAJIGO
planographic: (H) $17

CALAPAI, Letterio
American b. 1904
relief: (L) $66; (H) $105

CALDER, Alexander
American 1898-1976
intaglio: (L) $225; (H) $4,400
stencil: (L) $550; (H) $1,443
planographic: (L) $33; (H) $4,125
port/books: (L) $1,650; (H) $5,500
generic: (H) $425

CALDERARA, Antonio
1903-1978
stencil: (L) $140; (H) $164

CALDWELL
stencil: (H) $605

CALLAHAN, Harry
American b. 1912
photo: (L) $770; (H) $7,700

CALLOT, Jacques
French 1592-1635
intaglio: (L) $33; (H) $15,315
port/books: (L) $1,290; (H) $32,201

CALLOT, Jacques (after)
French 1592-1635
intaglio: (H) $550

CALVERT, Henry (after)
English 1879-1964
intaglio: (H) $358

**CALVERT LITHOGRAPHING
COMPANY,** Publishers (after Seth
Arca Whipple)
American 19th cent.
planographic: (H) $440

CAMARO, Alexander
contemporary
port/books: (H) $287

CAMERON, David Young
British 1865-1945
intaglio: (L) $165; (H) $165

CAMERON, Julia Margaret
British 1815-1879
photo: (L) $593; (H) $3,300

CAMERON, Kate
intaglio: (H) $290

CAMERON, Sir David Young A.
English 1865-1945
intaglio: (L) $110; (H) $165

CAMOIN, Ch.
planographic: (H) $151

CAMPAGNOLA, Giulio
Italian 1481/82-1516
intaglio: (H) $61,261

CAMPAGNOLA, Giulio and
Domenico
c. 1482-c. 1520/1500-1564
intaglio: (H) $11,279

CAMPBELL, Colen, James WOOLFE
and James GANDON
port/books: (H) $4,950

CAMPBELL, Marcus
Swiss 20th cent.
posters: (H) $133

Paul Cadmus (b. 1904), son of two commercial artists, studied etching as a student at the National Academy of Design. He is known for his depictions of muscular nude physiques and human society. Cadmus gained notoriety when *The Fleet's In!*, his print of sailors cavorting with prostitutes, was banned by the Navy. (Paul Cadmus, *Y.M.C.A. Locker Room*, etching, 6 ⅜ x 12 ⅜ inches, Grogan, March 24, 1992, $2,475)

CAMPENDONK, Heinrich
German 1889-1957
relief: (L) $445; (H) $1,757

CAMPIGLI, Massimo
Italian 1895-1971
planographic: (L) $275; (H) $8,312

CANALETTO
Italian 1697-1768
intaglio: (L) $2,530; (H) $14,923

CANE, Luis
planographic: (H) $41

CANEDO (after)
generic: (H) $22

CANOVA, Antonio (after)
intaglio: (H) $1,430

CANTIN, Kathleen
intaglio: (L) $330; (H) $550

CAPA, Robert
Hungarian 1913-1954
photo: (L) $692; (H) $770

CAPOGROSSI, Giuseppe
Italian 1900-1972
planographic: (L) $851; (H) $945

CAPONIGRO, Nervi
relief: (H) $6

CAPONIGRO, Paul
American b. 1932
photo: (L) $660; (H) $4,400

CAPP, Al
American 1909-1979
stencil: (L) $303; (H) $358

CAPPIELLO, Leonetto
1875-1942
posters: (L) $660; (H) $1,210

CAR, Charles Pachter
stencil: (H) $73

CARACCI, Annibale (after)
port/books: (H) $3,094

CARBO, Mariano Fortuny
intaglio: (H) $1,100

CARDENAS, Augustin
planographic: (H) $61

CARDON, A.
Flemish 19th cent.
intaglio: (H) $50

CAREL
planographic: (H) $11

CARIGIET, Alois
1902-1985
planographic: (L) $581; (H) $2,890
posters: (L) $455; (H) $538
photo-repro: (H) $70

CARJAT, Etienne
photo: (H) $880

CARLE (after)
port/books: (H) $3,190

CARLETON, S.L.
photo: (H) $316

CARLU, Jean
posters: (H) $275

CARMICHAEL, Franklin
stencil: (H) $122

CARON
planographic: (H) $165

CARPACCIO, Vittorio (after)
port/books: (H) $1,789

CARPENTER
photo: (L) $440; (H) $770

CARPI, Ugo da
Italian 1480-1520
relief: (L) $1,948; (H) $7,425

CARPI, Ugo da (attrib.)
1480-1520
relief: (H) $3,299

CARRA, Carlo
intaglio: (H) $3,967
planographic: (L) $1,229; (H) $1,700

CARRACCI, Agostino
Italian 1557-1602
intaglio: (L) $779; (H) $3,613

CARRACHE, Aug. (after P.
VERONESE)
intaglio: (H) $277

CARRIERE, Eugene
French 1849-1906
planographic: (L) $139; (H) $495
posters: (H) $36

CARRINGTON, Leonora
English b. 1917
planographic: (L) $880; (H) $3,080

CARRINGTON, Thomas
planographic: (H) $61

CARROLL, John
American 1892-1959
planographic: (H) $77

CARROLL, Lewis
English 1832-1898
photo: (L) $660; (H) $5,500

CARROLL, Patty
photo: (H) $200

CARSMAN, Jon
American 1944-1987
stencil: (H) $121

CARSTAIRS, John Paddy
intaglio: (H) $100

CARTER, C.W.
photo: (H) $44

CARTER, Clarence H.
American b. 1904
intaglio: (L) $303; (H) $1,100
stencil: (H) $11

CARTIER-BRESSON, Henri
French b. 1908
photo: (L) $247; (H) $3,520

CARTON, Jean (after)
photo-repro: (H) $50

CARY, W. de la Montaigne
planographic: (H) $248

CARZOU, Jean
French b. 1907
planographic: (L) $55; (H) $589

CASANAVE, Martha
photo: (H) $750

CASANOVA (after)
intaglio: (H) $338

CASEBERE, James
photo: (H) $700

CASORATI, Felice
planographic: (H) $3,589

CASPAR, Theodor (Baron zu
Furstenberg)
  c. 1600-1675
  intaglio: (H) $13,352

CASSAS, Louis Francois (after)
  French 1756-1827
  planographic: (H) $154

CASSATT, Mary
  American 1844-1926
  intaglio: (L) $467; (H) $104,500
  photo-repro: (H) $7,700

CASSELL
  planographic: (H) $220

CASSENI
  intaglio: (H) $248

CASSIERS, Henri
  Belgian 1858-1944
  posters: (L) $220; (H) $660

CASSIERS, Henri (after)
  Belgian 1858-1944
  planographic: (H) $77

CASSIGNEUL, Jean Pierre
  French b. 1935
  planographic: (L) $443; (H) $18,121

CASSON, Alfred Joseph
  Canadian b. 1898
  stencil: (L) $219; (H) $655
  photo-repro: (H) $269

CASTELLI, Luciano
  Italian/Swiss b. 1951
  stencil: (H) $372

CASTELLON, Feredico
  1914-1971
  planographic: (H) $55

CASTELLON, Heda
  American 20th cent.
  planographic: (H) $33

CASTIGLIONE, Giovanni Benedetto
(called Il Grechetto)
  Italian 1616-1665
  intaglio: (L) $330; (H) $9,228

CASTILLO, Jorge
  Spanish b. 1933
  port/books: (L) $615; (H) $698

CAT, Roland
  planographic: (H) $241

CATESBY, Mark
  British 1679-1749
  port/books: (H) $358

CATHELIN, Bernard
  French b. 1920
  planographic: (L) $184; (H) $935

CATLIN, George
  American 1796-1872
  planographic: (L) $621; (H) $9,350
  port/books: (H) $1,100

CATLIN, George (after)
  planographic: (H) $1,045

CAULFIELD, Patrick
  stencil: (H) $81

CAZALS, Frederic
  planographic: (H) $281

CEHSTOVSKY
  20th cent.
  intaglio: (H) $385

CELMINS, Vija
  American b. Latvia 1939
  planographic: (L) $2,750; (H) $3,850

**CENTURY LITHOGRAPHY
COMPANY**, Publisher
  American 19th/20th cent.
  planographic: (H) $1,650

CESAR
  French b. 1921
  stencil: (H) $307
  planographic: (H) $307

CEZANNE, Paul
  French 1839-1906
  intaglio: (L) $160; (H) $1,394
  planographic: (L) $1,143; (H) $14,300
  port/books: (H) $605

CHABAUD
  intaglio: (H) $22

CHADWICK, Lynn
  English b. 1914
  planographic: (H) $58

CHAFFEE, Ada Gilmore
  American 1893-1955
  relief: (H) $8,525

CHAGALL, Marc
Russian/French 1887-1985
intaglio: (L) $149;   (H) $17,460
relief: (L) $1,984;   (H) $12,698
planographic: (L) $22;   (H) $202,970
posters: (L) $29;   (H) $1,673
photo-repro: (L) $83;   (H) $294
port/books: (L) $168;   (H) $1,463,770

CHAGALL, Marc (after)
intaglio: (L) $3,211; (H) $3,346
planographic: (L) $880;   (H) $16,500
posters: (H) $1,464
generic: (H) $3,211

CHAHINE, Edgar
French 1874-1947
intaglio: (L) $110; (H) $2,604

CHALEE, Pop
stencil: (H) $99

CHALLOT, Jacques
French 1592?-1635
intaglio: (H) $154

CHALRIE
planographic: (H) $22

CHAMBERLAIN, Dean
photo: (H) $500

CHAMBERLAIN, Samuel
American 1895-1975
intaglio: (L) $121; (H) $165
planographic: (H) $110

CHAMBERLAIN, William Gunnison
photo: (H) $176

CHAMBERLIN, J.
intaglio: (H) $193

CHAMBERS, Sir William
port/books: (H) $3,080

CHAMPILLION (after)
intaglio: (H) $50

CHANTEAU, G.
posters: (H) $242

CHAPIN, Francis
American 1899-1965
planographic: (H) $132

CHAPIN, James
American 1887-1975
planographic: (L) $11; (H) $39

CHAPLIN, Prescott
relief: (H) $165

CHAPMAN, C.
American 19th/20th cent.
intaglio: (H) $61

CHAPMAN, M.
English 18th cent.
intaglio: (H) $303

CHAPUY, Jean Baptiste
1760-1802
intaglio: (H) $5,105

CHARBONNEAU, Monique
Canadian School b. 1928
intaglio: (L) $47; (H) $74
planographic: (H) $37

CHARCHOUNE, Serge
Russian 1888-1975
planographic: (H) $124

CHARGESHEIMER (Karl
HARGESHEIMER)
German 1924-1972
photo: (L) $860; (H) $5,017

CHARLESWORTH, Bruce
photo: (H) $300

CHARLET, Nicolas Toussaint
French 1792-1845
planographic: (H) $790

CHARLOT, Jean
French 1898-1979
relief: (H) $330
planographic: (L) $29; (H) $209

CHARPENTIER, Alexandre
planographic: (L) $181; (H) $301

CHASE, Dana
photo: (L) $66; (H) $121

CHASE, William Merritt
American 1849-1916
intaglio: (L) $77; (H) $330

CHATCLAIN (after)
intaglio: (H) $33

CHATHAM, Russel
planographic: (H) $44

CHEESEMAN, J.
intaglio: (H) $140

CHEFFETZ, Asa
American 1896-1965
relief: (L) $77; (H) $198
port/books: (H) $220

CHEMIAKIN, Michel
Russian b. 1940
stencil: (H) $601
planographic: (L) $181; (H) $550

CHENEY, Philip
American b. 1897
planographic: (L) $132; (H) $209

CHERET, Jules
French 1836-1932
posters: (L) $121; (H) $1,430

CHERNIN, Ann
American 20th cent.
planographic: (H) $77

CHEVALIER, Nicholas
planographic: (L) $87; (H) $165

CHEYNE, Ian
relief: (H) $605

CHIA, Sandro
Italian b. 1946
intaglio: (L) $550; (H) $807
planographic: (H) $467
port/books: (H) $4,180

CHIARENZA, Carl
photo: (H) $750

CHILDS, Bernard
American 20th cent.
intaglio: (H) $55

CHILLIDA, Eduardo
Spanish b. 1924
intaglio: (L) $420; (H) $3,606
relief: (H) $482
planographic: (L) $149; (H) $721
port/books: (H) $1,392

CHIMOT, Edouard
intaglio: (H) $170

CHIN, Hsiao
b. 1935
mixed-media: (H) $66

CHIPPENDALE, Thomas
English c. 1709-1779
port/books: (L) $2,200; (H) $5,225

CHIRICO, Giorgio de
Italian 1888-1978
intaglio: (L) $944; (H) $3,300
planographic: (L) $828; (H) $9,410

CHIRICO, Giorgio de (after)
planographic: (H) $482

CHISLETT, John
1856-1938
photo: (L) $412; (H) $2,200

CHOCHOLA, Vaclav
photo: (L) $165; (H) $248

CHODOWIECKI, Daniel
Polish/German 1726-1801
intaglio: (H) $739

CHONG, Fay
relief: (H) $55

CHOPARD, J.F.
French 18th cent.
port/books: (H) $110

CHOUMOFF
photo: (H) $2,678

CHRISTENBERRY, William
photo: (H) $400

CHRISTIANSEN, Hans
Danish 1873-1960
posters: (H) $165

CHRISTO
Bulgarian/American b. 1935
planographic: (L) $565; (H) $2,043
mixed-media: (L) $770; (H) $8,050
photo-repro: (L) $201; (H) $538
port/books: (L) $3,306; (H) $4,950
photo: (L) $1,540; (H) $2,420

CHRISTY, Howard Chandler
American 1873-1952
posters: (L) $88; (H) $880
photo-repro: (H) $33

CHUN, David
planographic: (H) $248

CHURCH, Frederick (after)
American 1842-1927
planographic: (H) $495

CHURCH, Frederick Stuart
American 1842-1924
intaglio: (H) $193

CIPRIANI, Giovanni Battista (after)
intaglio: (H) $735

CIRY, Michel
French b. 1919
intaglio: (L) $82; (H) $277

CITROEN, Paul
German 1896-1983
photo-repro: (H) $186

CITRON, Minna
American b. 1896
intaglio: (H) $77
planographic: (H) $330

CLAASEN, Hermann
German 1899-1987
photo: (H) $645

CLAESSENS, L.A.
intaglio: (H) $180

CLAIRE(?)
stencil: (H) $110

CLARK (after Bradford)
port/books: (H) $358

CLARK, Adam
stencil: (H) $78

CLARK, John Heaviside
intaglio: (L) $335; (H) $598

CLARK, Larry
American b. 1943
port/books: (L) $2,200; (H) $10,450
photo: (H) $505

CLARK, Roland
American 1874-1957
intaglio: (L) $110; (H) $1,175
planographic: (H) $330
port/books: (H) $715

CLARKE, Bob Carlos
photo: (H) $1,081

CLARKE, Graham
intaglio: (H) $226

CLAUDET, Antoine
French 1798-1867
port/books: (H) $1,778
photo: (L) $574; (H) $1,976

CLAUS, Emil
planographic: (H) $298

CLAUS, Hugo
stencil: (H) $108
planographic: (H) $114

CLAUSEN, George
English 1852-1944
intaglio: (H) $97

CLAUSEN, Rosemarie
German 1907-1990
photo: (H) $251

CLAVE, Antoni
French, b. Spain b. 1913
intaglio: (L) $580; (H) $806
planographic: (L) $99; (H) $2,300
mixed-media: (L) $594; (H) $1,298
port/books: (H) $587

CLEIS, Ugo
Swiss 1903-1976
relief: (L) $41; (H) $66

CLEMENS, J.F.
intaglio: (H) $483

CLEMENT, Fon
contemporary
stencil: (H) $227

CLEMENTE, Francesco
Italian b. 1952
intaglio: (L) $1,320; (H) $3,080
relief: (L) $2,200; (H) $5,500
planographic: (H) $9,900
port/books: (H) $16,500
photo: (H) $16,500

CLERGUE, Lucien
photo: (L) $825; (H) $990

CLEVELAND, Walter
port/books: (H) $17

CLEVELEY, James
port/books: (H) $3,914

CLEVELEY, Robert (after)
intaglio: (H) $248
port/books: (H) $815

CLIFT, William
photo: (H) $2,750

CLIME, Winfield Scott
American 1881-1958
intaglio: (H) $77

CLINTON, J.L.
photo: (H) $28

CLOSE, Chuck
American b. 1940
intaglio: (H) $4,400
photo: (H) $4,500

CLOSSON, William Baxter
American 1848-1926
relief: (H) $55

CLYMER, John
American 1907-1989
posters: (H) $77

CLYMER, John and Melvin WARREN
port/books: (H) $110

COBB, Victor
intaglio: (L) $70; (H) $122

COBRA, 1973
port/books: (H) $3,942

COBURN, Alvin Langdon
port/books: (H) $4,208
photo: (H) $3,850

COBURN, John
stencil: (L) $122; (H) $244

COCTEAU, Jean
French 1889-1963
planographic: (L) $471; (H) $1,540

COFFEY, Daniel X.
photo: (H) $275

COHEN, Arthur
American 20th cent.
intaglio: (H) $66

COIGNARD, James
French b. 1925
intaglio: (H) $2,140
planographic: (H) $468
mixed-media: (L) $55; (H) $684
port/books: (H) $1,789

COLEBROOK, Robert H.
port/books: (H) $2,301

COLEMAN, Constance
intaglio: (L) $26; (H) $52

COLEMAN, Glenn O.
American 1884/87-1932
planographic: (L) $660; (H) $3,300

COLEMAN, Michael
port/books: (L) $1,320; (H) $1,430

COLLA, Ettore
1896-1968
stencil: (H) $1,134

COLLEEN, Graham M.
Canadian School b. 1955
intaglio: (H) $388

COLLIER, John
photo: (H) $467

COLQUHOUN, Robert
planographic: (H) $1,199

COLVILLE, Alexander
Canadian b. 1920
stencil: (L) $2,014; (H) $6,295

COMBAS, Robert
French b. 1957
planographic: (H) $163
posters: (H) $33

COMMAROND
posters: (H) $330

CONATANT
intaglio: (H) $267

CONDE, Miguel
contemporary
intaglio: (H) $275

CONDER, Charles
planographic: (H) $370

CONNELL, Will
photo: (H) $715

CONNOR, Linda
mixed-media: (H) $330
photo: (L) $330; (H) $550

CONRAD LODDIGES and SONS
port/books: (L) $110; (H) $160

CONSENTIUS, E.
American 20th cent.
relief: (H) $88

CONSTABLE, John
English 1776-1837
intaglio: (L) $66; (H) $70

CONSTABLE, John (after)
intaglio: (L) $175; (H) $1,320

CONSTANT
b. 1920
intaglio: (L) $267; (H) $538
planographic: (L) $333; (H) $506

CONSTANT-DUVAL
posters: (L) $275; (H) $302

CONTEMPORARY PRINT GROUP
port/books: (H) $2,750

CONTENT, Marjorie
photo: (H) $2,200

COOK, Arthur
planographic: (H) $105

COOK, Beryl
English b. 1926
stencil: (L) $428; (H) $702
planographic: (H) $468

COOK, Captain James
intaglio: (H) $340

COOK, Captain James and John
HAWKESWORTH
British 18th cent.
port/books: (H) $26,850

COOK, Edward William
English 1811-1880
port/books: (H) $384

COOK, Howard
1901-1980
intaglio: (H) $1,045
relief: (L) $605; (H) $4,180
planographic: (L) $28; (H) $1,650

COOK, Joseph
British 20th cent.
intaglio: (H) $28

COOKE, Albert C.
relief: (H) $870

COOKE, George
port/books: (L) $330; (H) $550

COOMANS, Joseph (after)
planographic: (H) $255

COOMBE, William and Thomas
ROWLANDSON
port/books: (H) $425

COOPER, Austin
posters: (L) $412; (H) $825

COPELAND, Lila
port/books: (H) $33

COPLANS, John
photo: (H) $2,200

COPPOCK, Barbara
intaglio: (H) $825

CORINTH, Lovis
German 1858-1925
intaglio: (L) $82; (H) $7,092
relief: (H) $836
planographic: (L) $174; (H) $3,175
port/books: (L) $513; (H) $9,242

CORIOLANO, Bartolomeo
relief: (L) $1,094; (H) $1,100

CORNEILLE
Dutch b. 1922
intaglio: (H) $163
stencil: (L) $222; (H) $2,636
planographic: (L) $88; (H) $675
photo-repro: (L) $185; (H) $226
port/books: (L) $935; (H) $1,210

CORNEILLE and Simon
VINKENOOG
stencil: (L) $316; (H) $414

COROT, Camille Jean Baptiste
French 1796-1875
intaglio: (L) $298; (H) $7,461
relief: (H) $739
generic: (H) $770

CORPORA, Antonio
b. 1909
intaglio: (L) $116; (H) $248

CORRIES
planographic: (H) $121

CORT, Cornelius
1533-1578
intaglio: (L) $390; (H) $2,392

CORTES, Edouard
French b. 1882
planographic: (H) $66

COSGROVE, Stanley Morel
Canadian b. 1911
stencil: (H) $175
planographic: (L) $78; (H) $167

COSINDAS, Marie
photo-repro: (H) $350
photo: (H) $350

COSSIO, Pancho
planographic: (H) $628

COSTER, Gordon
b. 1906
photo: (L) $440; (H) $1,760

COSTER, Howard
1885-1959
photo: (H) $536

COSTIGAN, John E.
American 1888-1972
intaglio: (L) $94; (H) $143

COSWAY, Richard (after)
intaglio: (H) $285

COTNEY, Tom
generic: (H) $149

COTTET, Charles
French 1863-1925
intaglio: (H) $261

COTTINGHAM, Robert
American b. 1935
intaglio: (H) $330
planographic: (H) $440

COUDRAIN
intaglio: (L) $98; (H) $98

COUGHLIN, Jack
American b. 1932
intaglio: (H) $55

COUNIHAN, Noel Jack
relief: (H) $296

COUPON, William
photo: (H) $1,210

COURBOIN, Eugene
posters: (H) $275

COURTIN, Pierre
intaglio: (L) $184; (H) $275

COURTOIS, G.
intaglio: (H) $364

COURVOISIER-VOISIN, Henri
1757-1830
intaglio: (L) $149; (H) $182

COUSSENS, Armand
intaglio: (H) $22

COVARRUBIAS, Miguel
Mexican 1904-1957
planographic: (L) $198; (H) $880

COVIN, Mo
intaglio: (H) $193

COWIN, Eileen
photo: (H) $358

COWIN, Jack L.
b. 1947
planographic: (H) $195

COX, Arthur L.
British exhib. 1934
intaglio: (H) $33

COX, Arthur L. (after)
port/books: (H) $275

COX, Kenyon
American 1856-1917/19
posters: (H) $275

COX, Patrick Douglass
b. 1953
planographic: (L) $183; (H) $276

COX, R.
port/books: (H) $140

COZZENS, Frederick Schiller
American 1846-1928
planographic: (L) $358; (H) $385
port/books: (H) $358
generic: (L) $36; (H) $363

COZZENS, Frederick Schiller (after)
American 1856-1928
planographic: (H) $220

CRADDOCK, J. (photographer)
port/books: (H) $956

CRAGG, Tony
English b. 1949
intaglio: (L) $880; (H) $2,585

CRAIG, Edward Gordon
relief: (H) $676

CRAIG, John
photo: (H) $200

CRAMER, Konrad
German/American 1888-1965
port/books: (H) $1,980
photo: (H) $3,025

CRANACH, Lucas (the elder)
German 1472-1553
relief: (L) $880; (H) $9,350

CRANE, Alan
b. 1901
port/books: (H) $110

CRATSLEY, Bruce
photo: (H) $150

CRAWFORD, Ralston
American 1906-1977
planographic: (L) $1,100; (H) $1,320

CREMER, Jan
stencil: (L) $285; (H) $336
planographic: (L) $240; (H) $727

CRITE, Allan Rohan
American b. 1910
relief: (H) $550

CRONER, Gustav
mixed-media: (H) $752

CROOKE, Ray Austin
intaglio: (H) $174
stencil: (H) $70

CROSBY, Charles H. (and Company)
American 19th cent.
planographic: (H) $303

CROSBY, Charles R. & CO.
American 1819-1896
planographic: (H) $4,675

CROSS, Henri Edmond
French 1856-1910
planographic: (L) $550; (H) $7,700

CROUCH, Steve
planographic: (H) $385

CROWE, Maryjean Viano
photo: (L) $300; (H) $400

CRUIKSHANK, George
English 1792-1878
intaglio: (L) $176; (H) $440

CRUIKSHANK, G. (after)
port/books: (H) $605

CRUMBO, Woody
stencil: (L) $77; (H) $110
generic: (H) $77

CRUMP, William R.
American 20th cent.
port/books: (H) $94

CRUZ-DIEZ, Carlos
Venezuelan b. 1923
port/books: (L) $402; (H) $883

CUCCHI, Enzo
Italian b. 1950
intaglio: (H) $1,210
port/books: (H) $3,191

CUECO, Henri
planographic: (H) $31
port/books: (H) $307

CUEVAS, Jose Luis
Mexican b. 1933/34
planographic: (H) $303
port/books: (L) $660; (H) $3,300

CUIXART, Modesto
planographic: (H) $137

CULLIN, Isaac (after)
photo-repro: (H) $666

CULMANN, Ottfried H.
b. 1949
intaglio: (H) $26

CUNNINGHAM (after)
intaglio: (H) $112

CUNNINGHAM, Imogen
American 1883-1976
photo: (L) $880; (H) $5,225

CUNNINGHAM, Marion
American 1911-1940
port/books: (H) $105

CUNNINGHAM, William Phelps
American 1904-1980
relief: (H) $55

CURRIER (after)
generic: (H) $248

CURRIER, N. (after)
stencil: (H) $17

CURRIER, Nathaniel, Publisher
American 1813-1888
planographic: (L) $11; (H) $14,300
port/books: (H) $1,650
generic: (L) $83; (H) $248

CURRIER and IVES (after)
planographic: (L) $248; (H) $660
photo-repro: (H) $303

CURRIER and IVES, Publisher
American 19th/20th cent.
planographic: (L) $28; (H) $16,500
generic: (L) $33; (H) $853

CURRY, John Steuart
American 1897-1946
planographic: (L) $385; (H) $4,400

CURTIS, Asahel
photo: (H) $1,320

Well-executed prints with a popular subject matter and low cost were the Currier & Ives formula for success. Nathaniel Currier worked in New York selling prints. In 1857 he changed his company name to Currier & Ives when James M. Ives became a partner. They employed a large artistic staff and sold their prints through peddlers and agents. Many of their staff artists remained anonymous, but others such as Fanny Palmer became well known and signed their prints. All of the prints were hand-colored by a staff of women who worked from a model, each specializing in a different part of the image. *American Winter Scenes, Morning* was designed by Fanny Palmer and printed by N. Currier in 1854. At the time they were issued, Currier & Ives prints sold for 20 cents to three dollars. This print, which had some scuffs and discoloration, sold below estimate when it realized $4,125. (N. Currier, Publisher, F.F. Palmer, *American Winter Scenes, Morning*, hand-colored lithograph with touches of gum arabic, 16 ⅝ x 24 inches, Sotheby-New York, January 23, 1992, $4,125)

CURTIS, Edward S.
American 1868-1952
photo-repro: (L) $105; (H) $715
photo: (L) $165; (H) $42,900

CURTIS, Philip C.
mixed-media: (L) $3,080; (H) $4,180

CURTIS, William
1746-1799
port/books: (L) $45; (H) $1,760

CURZ and ALLISON
planographic: (H) $110

CUTHBERTSON, Arch
stencil: (H) $122

CUVIER
port/books: (L) $1,045; (H) $1,430

CZESCHKA, Carl Otto
b. 1878
posters: (H) $987

D'ALESI, Hugo
Italian 19th cent.
posters: (H) $38

D'AMATO, Paul
photo: (H) $200

D'ERCOLE, Paolo
Italian 20th cent.
intaglio: (L) $35; (H) $50

DAGU, A.
posters: (H) $275

DAHL, Barbara
relief: (H) $52

DAHL, Peter
b. 1934
planographic: (L) $924; (H) $3,696
port/books: (L) $4,475; (H) $74,750

DAHL-WOLFE, Louise
port/books: (H) $3,300
photo: (L) $770; (H) $4,180

DAHLBERG, Count Eric Jonsen
Swedish 1625-1703
port/books: (H) $7,150

DAHM, Helen
Swiss 1878-1968
planographic: (H) $294

DAHMEN, Karl Fred
1917-1981
mixed-media: (H) $246
port/books: (H) $2,597

DALI, Salvador
Spanish 1904-1989
intaglio: (L) $165; (H) $7,150
planographic: (L) $100; (H) $2,750
mixed-media: (L) $265; (H) $605
photo-repro: (H) $347
port/books: (L) $358; (H) $16,500

DALI, Salvador (after)
intaglio: (L) $220; (H) $330
planographic: (L) $115; (H) $138

DALI, Salvador (attrib.)
Spanish 1904-1989
intaglio: (H) $77
planographic: (H) $275

DALSTROM, Gustave
intaglio: (H) $138

DALVIT, Oskar
1911-1975
relief: (H) $116

DANCE, Nathaniel
intaglio: (H) $61

DANCHIN, Leon
French d. 1939
intaglio: (H) $193

DANIELL, Thomas
intaglio: (L) $247; (H) $425
port/books: (H) $3,300

DANIELL, William and Richard
AYTON
port/books: (H) $16,302

DANIELS
port/books: (L) $275; (H) $523

DANSON, Leon
generic: (H) $330

DARLEY, F.O.C.
planographic: (H) $165

DARTON, W.
port/books: (L) $330; (H) $440

DASSELBORNE
intaglio: (H) $33

DASSONVILLE, William
photo: (L) $660; (H) $1,320

DATER, Judy
American b. 1941
photo: (L) $275; (H) $2,420

DAUBIGNY, C.F.
intaglio: (L) $220; (H) $330

DAUBIGNY, Charles Francois
French 1817-1878
intaglio: (L) $55; (H) $2,356
photo-repro: (L) $342; (H) $428

DAUDE, Andre
French 1897-1979
posters: (H) $770

DAULLE, J. (after Joseph Vernet)
intaglio: (H) $358

DAUMIER, Honore
French 1808-1879
intaglio: (L) $66; (H) $260
planographic: (L) $22; (H) $19,048

An 1899 expedition to Alaska was the beginning of Edward S. Curtis's (1868-1952) odyssey to record the life of the North American Indian. Financed by J. Pierpont Morgan and endorsed by Teddy Roosevelt, he set out to document the customs, ceremonies, songs, and costumes of many tribes before their ways and memories were destroyed by contact with the white man. He published the first of 20 volumes in 1907. The complete set was priced at $3,000 and sold primarily to institutions. After the last book was published in 1930, his work faded into obscurity. In the 1970s the ecology movement and concern for Native American culture brought a new awareness of Curtis's work. (Edward S. Curtis, *The North American Indian, A Series of 20 Volumes*, Christie-New York, October 13, 1992, $396,000)

DAUTREY, Lucien
  French 1851-1926
  intaglio: (H) $55
  port/books: (L) $165; (H) $468

DAVID, Jean
  posters: (H) $357

DAVID, Richard Barrett (after)
  port/books: (H) $234

DAVIDSEN, Trygve M.
  posters: (H) $330

DAVIDSON (after)
  intaglio: (H) $688

DAVIDSON, Bruce
  port/books: (H) $4,400
  photo: (L) $880; (H) $982

DAVIDSON, David
  American 20th cent.
  mixed-media: (H) $303

DAVIDSON, Julian O. (after)
  American 1853-1893
  relief: (H) $220

DAVIES, Arthur B.
  American 1862-1928
  intaglio: (L) $121; (H) $385
  planographic: (L) $127; (H) $275

DAVIES, G. Christopher
  port/books: (H) $257
  photo: (H) $257

DAVIES, J.W.
photo: (H) $5,720

DAVIES, L. Roy
relief: (H) $35

DAVIS, Gene
American b. 1920
stencil: (L) $220; (H) $440

DAVIS, Johann
planographic: (H) $220

DAVIS, Lynn
photo: (H) $850

DAVIS, R.
20th cent.
intaglio: (H) $11
relief: (H) $28
mixed-media: (H) $303
generic: (H) $11

DAVIS, Stuart
American 1894-1964
stencil: (H) $220
planographic: (L) $880; (H) $16,500

DAVIS, Warren
American 1865-1928
intaglio: (L) $83; (H) $220

DAVISON, George
1856-1930
photo-repro: (H) $383

DAWE, Henry
port/books: (H) $387

DAWE, Philip (attrib.)
1750-1785
intaglio: (H) $4,400

DAWKINS, Henry (after William
TENNANT)
American 18th cent.
intaglio: (H) $22,000

DAWSON, Montague
English 1895-1973
planographic: (L) $220; (H) $385
generic: (L) $212; (H) $242

DAWSON, Montague (after)
photo-repro: (H) $111

DAWSON, Robert
photo: (H) $440

DAY, F. Holland
photo: (H) $5,280

DAYES, Edward (after)
intaglio: (H) $541

DE FEURE, Georges
French 1868-1943
posters: (H) $358

DE KOONING, Willem
American b. 1904
planographic: (L) $341; (H) $7,150
port/books: (L) $6,820; (H) $13,200

DE LATENAY, Gaston
planographic: (H) $1,045

DE LOWENFELD, Heger
mixed-media: (H) $93

DE NEUFFORGE
port/books: (H) $1,870

DE PIETRI, Alberto
planographic: (H) $275

DE WIT, Frederik
intaglio: (H) $478

DEAN, Grace Rhodes
relief: (H) $83

DEBOUT
French
generic: (H) $50

DEBRE, O.
planographic: (H) $240

DEBSCHITZ-KUNOWSKI, Wanda
von
German 1870-1935
photo: (H) $251

DEBUCOURT (after)
port/books: (H) $248

DEBUCOURT, Philibert Louis
French 1755-1832
intaglio: (L) $770; (H) $6,676

DEBUFFET, Jean
stencil: (H) $872

DECANEAS, Tony
photo: (H) $120

DEFOREST, Roy
American b. 1930
planographic: (L) $440; (H) $605

DEGAS, Edgar
French 1834-1917
intaglio: (L) $693; (H) $11,000
planographic: (L) $3,994; (H) $67,488
generic: (H) $592

DEHN, Adolf
American 1895-1968
planographic: (L) $55; (H) $440

DEHNER, Dorothy
b. 1901
intaglio: (H) $1,650

DELACROIX, Eugene
French 1798-1863
intaglio: (H) $281
relief: (H) $1,964
planographic: (L) $221; (H) $7,425

DELACROIX, Michel
b. 1933
planographic: (L) $440; (H) $990
photo-repro: (H) $1,210

DELAFOSSE, Jean Charles
French 18th cent.
port/books: (H) $550

DELAMOTTE, Philip H. and Joseph
CUNDALL
port/books: (H) $4,208

DELANO, Jack
photo: (L) $220; (H) $380

DELARDI, Alfred A.
photo: (H) $550

DELAROCHE
intaglio: (H) $80

DELATRE, Eugene
intaglio: (H) $1,265

DELAUNAY, M.
port/books: (H) $55

DELAUNAY, Robert
French 1885-1941
planographic: (H) $25,471
port/books: (H) $42,982

DELAUNAY, Sonia
Russian/French 1885/86-1979
intaglio: (L) $503; (H) $3,025
stencil: (H) $825
planographic: (L) $245; (H) $1,813
port/books: (L) $880; (H) $4,603

DELAVALLEE, Henri
intaglio: (H) $301

DELBLANC, Sven
contemporary
planographic: (L) $554; (H) $554
port/books: (H) $739

DELECROIX, Eugene
planographic: (H) $1,885

DELPECH, F.
contemporary
intaglio: (H) $961

DELSTANCHE, Albert
port/books: (H) $29

DELVAL
posters: (L) $385; (H) $412

DELVAUX, F. and P. HELLENS
planographic: (H) $299

DELVAUX, Paul
Belgian b. 1897
intaglio: (L) $550; (H) $5,508
planographic: (L) $1,650; (H) $19,800
photo-repro: (H) $2,043
port/books: (H) $5,101

DEMARTEAU, G.
intaglio: (H) $584
port/books: (H) $3,292

DEMARTEAU, G. (after Le PRINCE)
intaglio: (H) $752

DEMARTEAU, G. (after F. Boucher)
intaglio: (H) $299

DEMARTEAU, Gilles (after Francois
Boucher)
port/books: (H) $315

DEMARTEAU, Gilles (l'aine)
1722-1776
intaglio: (H) $1,571
port/books: (H) $4,398

DEMARTEAU, Gilles Antoine (le
jeune)
Flemish 1750-1802
intaglio: (H) $5,341
port/books: (L) $3,927; (H) $11,781

DEMARTELLY, John
planographic: (H) $385

DEMAZIERES, Eric
intaglio: (H) $1,984

DEMEYER, Baron Adolph
1868-1946
port/books: (H) $4,400
photo: (H) $1,320

DEMONNIER, Henri
posters: (H) $385

DENIS, Maurice
French 1870-1943
planographic: (L) $211; (H) $13,709

DENNY, Robyn
port/books: (L) $1,882; (H) $2,196

DENT, John
intaglio: (H) $217

DENTE, Marco (da Ravenna)
ac. 1515-1527
intaglio: (L) $3,176; (H) $4,922

DENTON
port/books: (L) $66; (H) $1,760

DEPATIE, P.
European School 20th cent.
intaglio: (H) $74

DERAIN, Andre
French 1880-1954
intaglio: (H) $1,663
stencil: (H) $550
relief: (L) $2,090; (H) $3,968
planographic: (L) $770; (H) $2,910
port/books: (H) $55

DEROUIN, Rene
Canadian School 20th cent.
intaglio: (H) $299
relief: (H) $187

DESBOUTIN, M.
intaglio: (H) $141

DESBOUTIN, Marcellin (after
FRAGONARD)
intaglio: (H) $245

DESCHAMPS, H.
posters: (H) $55

DESCOURTILZ, J. Th.
port/books: (H) $50

DESCOURTIS, Charles Melchior
French 1753-1820
intaglio: (L) $1,980; (H) $1,980
port/books: (L) $3,579; (H) $29,845

DESGODETZ, Antoine
port/books: (H) $2,200

DESNOYER, F.
intaglio: (H) $100

DESPIAU, Charles
French 1874-1946
planographic: (H) $88

DETMOLD, Charles Maurice
intaglio: (H) $81

DETMOLD, Edward Julius
English 1883-1957
intaglio: (L) $91; (H) $221

DEVELDE, Jan Van
intaglio: (H) $55

DEWASNE, Jean
stencil: (H) $143

DEWS, Edwin, Publisher
American 19th cent.
relief: (H) $110

DEXEL, Walter
1890-1973
relief: (H) $154

DEYROLLE, Jean
intaglio: (H) $148

DEZAYAS, Marius
intaglio: (H) $110

DIAS, Antonio
Brazilian b. 1944
planographic: (H) $10,321

DICKENMANN, Rudolf
1832-1888
intaglio: (H) $414

DICKENS, Charles
English 19th cent.
intaglio: (H) $242

DICKENSON, R.
New Zealand School 20th cent.
intaglio: (H) $186

DICKERSON, Robert Henry
intaglio: (H) $70
stencil: (H) $157
planographic: (H) $61

DICKSEE, Herbert Thomas
British 1862-1942
intaglio: (H) $77

DIDEROT, Denis
1713-1784
port/books: (H) $132

DIEBENKORN, Richard
American b. 1922
intaglio: (L) $715; (H) $38,500
relief: (L) $9,350; (H) $14,300
planographic: (L) $1,540; (H) $30,250
port/books: (L) $1,540; (H) $4,950

DIEDEREN, Jef
relief: (H) $222
port/books: (H) $348

DIETRICH, C.W.E.
intaglio: (H) $121

DIETZ, C.W.
intaglio: (H) $412

DIEUZAIDE, Jean
b. 1921
photo: (H) $593

DIGGELMANN, Alex Walter
Swiss b. 1902
posters: (H) $314

DILL, Laddie John
American b. 1943
intaglio: (H) $330

DILLON, Henri Patrice
planographic: (H) $291

DIMITROV, Slobodan
photo: (H) $160

DINE, Jim
American b. 1935
intaglio: (L) $990; (H) $5,106
stencil: (L) $440; (H) $4,675
relief: (L) $4,600; (H) $18,700
planographic: (L) $193; (H) $14,300
mixed-media: (L) $1,980; (H) $12,100
photo-repro: (L) $836; (H) $2,640
port/books: (L) $1,320; (H) $13,200

DINE, Jim and Lee FRIEDLANDER
port/books: (H) $3,901

DINGUS, Rick
photo: (H) $495

DIRADO, Stephen
photo: (H) $120

DISDERI, Andre Adolphe Eugene
1819-1889
photo: (L) $593; (H) $1,430

DISFARMER, Mike
photo: (H) $468

DISTURNELL and BUFFORD,
Publishers
ac. 1835-1871
planographic: (H) $165

DIX, Otto
German 1891-1969
intaglio: (L) $2,482; (H) $4,067
planographic: (L) $496; (H) $26,964

DIXON, Joseph K.
American 19th/20th cent.
photo: (H) $880

DOBKIN, Alexander
Italian/American 1908-1975
planographic: (H) $110

DODD, C.T. (after)
planographic: (H) $375

DODD, Francis
Scottish 1874-1949
intaglio: (L) $185; (H) $671
planographic: (H) $81

DODD, J.
intaglio: (H) $261

DODWELL, Edward
English 1767-1832
port/books: (H) $13,425

DOHANOS, Stevan
American b. 1907
relief: (L) $385; (H) $385
planographic: (L) $105; (H) $165

DOHMEN, Leo (photographer)
port/books: (H) $2,750

DOISNEAU, Robert
French b. 1912
photo: (L) $632; (H) $4,322

DOLA, G.
posters: (L) $247; (H) $358

DOLICE, Leon Louis
American 1892-1960
intaglio: (L) $83; (H) $132

DOMELA, Cesar
Dutch b. 1900
mixed-media: (H) $164

DOMERGUE, Jean Gabriel
French 1889-1962
posters: (H) $1,760

DON
posters: (H) $770

DONALDSON, Publisher
posters: (H) $165

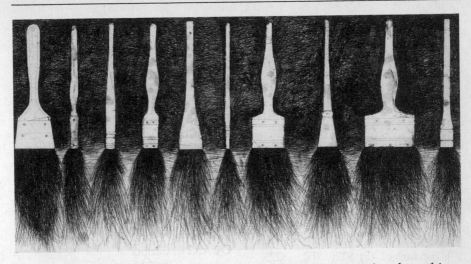

The plate, block, or stone used to make a print is a continual working surface; at any time it can be altered. The artist may want to add new information or change the feeling or meaning. Any alteration to the working surface, whether the addition or deletion of a single line of text or the reworking of an entire area, results in a new state. This print of *Five Paintbrushes*, by Jim Dine (b. 1935), is the sixth state of this image. (Jim Dine, *Five Paintbrushes 1973*, etching in green-black on Murillo sheet, 27 ½ x 39 ½ inches, Christie-New York, November 9, 1992, $10,450)

DONATI, Enrico
  Italian/American b. 1909
  planographic: (H) $303
  port/books: (H) $88

DONAVAN, Edward
  port/books: (H) $550

DONGEN, Kees van
  Dutch/French 1877-1968
  intaglio: (H) $825
  planographic: (L) $83; (H) $3,181
  port/books: (H) $11,550

DONON, Julio and Jose VALLEJO
  planographic: (L) $241; (H) $262

DONOVAN, Edward
  1768-1837
  port/books: (L) $83; (H) $330

DOOLITTLE, Harold Lukens
  American 1883-1974
  intaglio: (H) $165

DORAZIO, Piero
  Italian b. 1927
  intaglio: (L) $248; (H) $982
  planographic: (L) $166; (H) $414

DORE, Ben
  port/books: (H) $193

DORE, Gustave
  French 1832-1883
  intaglio: (H) $205
  planographic: (H) $33

DORFMAN, Elsa
  photo-repro: (H) $450

DORNIER, Marcel
  Swiss b. 1893
  intaglio: (H) $41

DORNY, Bertrand
  French b. 1931
  intaglio: (H) $28
  mixed-media: (H) $21

DOSKOW
intaglio: (H) $20

DOTREMONT
planographic: (H) $204

DOU, Be
photo: (H) $44

DOUGLAS, E.A.S. (after)
port/books: (H) $145

DOUGLAS, Edwin (after)
English b. 1848
intaglio: (H) $165

DOW, Arthur Wesley
American 1857-1922
relief: (L) $220; (H) $2,970
planographic: (L) $220; (H) $275
posters: (H) $275
port/books: (L) $275; (H) $1,760

DOWDESWELL and DOWDESWELL
LTD., Publishers
intaglio: (H) $39

DOWELL, John
American contemporary
planographic: (H) $28

DREIER, Katherine S.
American 1877-1952
port/books: (H) $4,950

DREVET, Pierre
1663-1778
intaglio: (L) $19; (H) $1,728

DREWES, Werner
German/American b. 1899
intaglio: (L) $66; (H) $220
relief: (L) $193; (H) $550

DRIESBACH, David
American b. 1922
intaglio: (H) $110

DRIFFIELD, Lance W.
relief: (H) $43

DROESE, Felix
b. 1950
intaglio: (H) $284
relief: (H) $721
mixed-media: (H) $289
photo-repro: (H) $156
port/books: (H) $649

DROUART, R.
intaglio: (H) $89
relief: (H) $59
planographic: (H) $139

DROZ, L.
planographic: (H) $248

DRTIKOL, Frantisek
1888-1961
photo: (L) $573; (H) $6,600

DRUMMOND, William and Charles J.
BASEBE (after)
intaglio: (H) $898

DRURY, Paul
intaglio: (H) $420

DUARTE, Carlota
photo: (H) $220

DUBAURG, M.
port/books: (H) $17

DUBOURG, Matthew
port/books: (H) $1,547

DUBREUIL, Pierre
1872-1944
photo: (L) $2,420; (H) $28,600

DUBUFFET, Jean
French 1901-1985
stencil: (L) $872; (H) $4,620
planographic: (L) $176; (H) $55,000
mixed-media: (H) $4,675
port/books: (L) $2,475; (H) $22,000

DUCERCEAU, Jacques Androuet
1510/12(?)-1584
port/books: (H) $8,639

DUCHAMP, Marcel
French 1887-1968
intaglio: (L) $4,400; (H) $8,250
stencil: (H) $6,050
planographic: (H) $4,675
photo-repro: (H) $1,430
port/books: (L) $4,675; (H) $41,250

DUDOVITCH, M.
posters: (H) $770

DUEZ, Ernest Ange
intaglio: (H) $291

DUFF, John Robert Keitley
English b. 1862
intaglio: (H) $110

DUFF, Walter
19th/20th cent.
intaglio: (L) $28; (H) $37

DUFRESNE, Charles
intaglio: (L) $685; (H) $3,694
mixed-media: (H) $2,910

DUFY (school of)
relief: (H) $105

DUFY, Jean
French 1888-1964
planographic: (H) $462

DUFY, Raoul
French 1877-1953
intaglio: (H) $110
stencil: (H) $145
relief: (L) $2,200; (H) $4,400
planographic: (L) $28; (H) $5,138

DUFY, Raoul (after)
planographic: (H) $302

DUJARDIN, Karel
Dutch c. 1622-1678
intaglio: (H) $193

DUMARESO, Armand
port/books: (H) $330

DUMAS, Antoine
Canadian School b. 1934
planographic: (H) $111

DUNCAN, Edward (Fores, London, Publishers)
British 1803-1882
intaglio: (H) $440

DUNHAM, Carroll
American b. 1949
planographic: (H) $1,320
port/books: (L) $3,300; (H) $3,520

DUNN, Arthur
photo: (L) $268; (H) $589

DUNOYER DE SEGONZAC, Andre
French 1884-1974
intaglio: (L) $198; (H) $3,095

DUNTON, Herbert
planographic: (L) $605; (H) $880

DUPAIN, Max
photo: (H) $884

DUPAS, Jean
French 1882-1964
intaglio: (H) $3,300

DUPIN, Leon
posters: (H) $165

DUPONT, P.
1870-1911
intaglio: (L) $250; (H) $417

DUPRE, Louis
French 1789-1837
port/books: (H) $53,700

DUPUIS, L.A.
intaglio: (H) $143

DURANT, Andre
photo: (H) $660

DURER
relief: (L) $138; (H) $440

DÜRER, Albrecht
German 1471-1528
intaglio: (L) $77; (H) $99,300
relief: (L) $220; (H) $26,659
port/books: (L) $3,235; (H) $52,250

DÜRER, Albrecht (after)
relief: (H) $468

DURIEU, Eugen
French 1800-1874
photo: (H) $2,150

DUSART, Cornelis
1660-1704
intaglio: (L) $717; (H) $10,603

DUTCH SCHOOL, 19TH CENTURY
port/books: (H) $228

DUTTON, Thomas Goldsworth, Lithographer
British d. 1891
planographic: (L) $77; (H) $1,411

DUVAL and SONS, Lithographers
planographic: (H) $550

DUVENECK
generic: (H) $1,650

DUVENECK, Frank
American 1848-1919
intaglio: (L) $990; (H) $1,100

DUVET, Jean
1485-1570
intaglio: (L) $23,562; (H) $109,956

DWIGHT, Mabel
American b. 1876
planographic: (L) $248; (H) $770

Albrecht Dürer executed a great many paintings and drawings, but it is his large output of engravings, woodcuts, and etchings that is truly extraordinary in both quality and quantity. His 1504 engraving of *Adam and Eve* preceded his 1507 paintings of the same subject. The print, which sold at Christie's in London, had a watermark but was trimmed inside the platemark and had some folds, staining, and repaired tears. (Albrecht Dürer, *Adam and Eve*, engraving, 9 $\frac{13}{16}$ x 7 $\frac{5}{8}$ inches, Christie-London, June 18, 1992, BP 16,500, $30,761)

DYCK, Anthony van
intaglio: (H) $495

DYCK, Anthony van (after)
Dutch 1599-1641
intaglio: (H) $88

DYCK, Sir Anthony van
Flemish 1599-1641
intaglio: (L) $248; (H) $40,841

EAGLE, Arnold
photo: (L) $330; (H) $330

EALTER, John
posters: (H) $132

EAMES, Charles
photo: (H) $1,760

EARLOM, A.
intaglio: (H) $76

EARLOM, Richard
British 1743-1822
intaglio: (L) $236; (H) $1,464
port/books: (L) $303; (H) $6,283

EARLOM, Richard (after Claude LORRAIN)
English 1743-1822
intaglio: (L) $55; (H) $1,650

EASTMAN, Michael
photo: (H) $1,210

EATON, John
photo: (H) $87

EBERZ, Josef
1880-1942
port/books: (L) $2,195; (H) $2,706

EBY, Kerr
American 1889-1946
intaglio: (L) $330; (H) $2,750
port/books: (H) $77

ECHAURREN, Pablo
Italian contemporary
planographic: (H) $33

ECKSTEIN
early 20th cent.
port/books: (H) $94

EDDINS, Homer
20th cent.
planographic: (H) $105

EDGERTON, Harold
1903-1990
port/books: (H) $8,250
photo: (H) $330

EDWARDS, George
1694-1773
port/books: (L) $110; (H) $385

EDWARDS, John Paul
photo: (L) $715; (H) $1,760

EDWARDS, Lionel
English 1877/78-1966
photo-repro: (H) $298

EDWARDS, S. Arlent
English b. 1861
intaglio: (H) $55
port/books: (H) $550

EDWARDS, Samuel Arlent (after)
English b. 1861
port/books: (H) $105

EDWARDS, Sydenham
English 1768-1819
port/books: (L) $176; (H) $2,420

EGGELER, Stefan
port/books: (H) $550

EGGENHOFER, Nick
American 1897-1985
stencil: (H) $1,540

EGGENSCHWILER, Franz
Swiss b. 1930
intaglio: (H) $231
relief: (H) $91

EGGLESTON, William
photo: (L) $550; (H) $1,045

EGLIN, Karl Martin
1787-1850
planographic: (H) $497

EHM, Josef
1909-1989
photo: (L) $880; (H) $1,430

EHRENWORTH, Jan
intaglio: (H) $303

EHRET (after)
port/books: (H) $358

EHRHARDT, Alfred
photo: (H) $1,980

EHRLICH, Georg
Viennese b. 1897
intaglio: (H) $55

EICKEMEYER, Rudolf (Jr.)
photo: (L) $990; (H) $4,400

EIDENBENZ, Atelier
posters: (H) $74

EIDENERGER, Josef
Austrian b. 1899
intaglio: (H) $330

EISEN
Japanese 1790-1848
relief: (H) $110

EISENMANN, Charles (photographer)
German/American b. 1850
port/books: (H) $26,400

EISENSTAEDT, Alfred
b. 1898
photo: (H) $550

ELDRED, L.D.
American 1848-1921
intaglio: (L) $157; (H) $194

ELIAS, Etienne
stencil: (H) $190

ELIASBERG, Paul
1907-1983
intaglio: (H) $62

ELINSON, H.
planographic: (H) $22

ELIOT, Maurice
planographic: (H) $495

ELLIOT (after)
generic: (H) $9

ELLIOT, D.G.
planographic: (H) $248

ELLIS-GOULD
planographic: (H) $880

ELY
planographic: (H) $138

ELZAN (Kikukawa Toshinoba)
Japanese School 1787-1867
relief: (H) $280

EMANUEL, Cedric
intaglio: (H) $157

EMERSON, Peter Henry
English 1856-1936
port/books: (L) $2,869; (H) $5,225
photo: (L) $385; (H) $1,430

EMKA
posters: (L) $110; (H) $247

EMMONS, Chansonetta
(photographer)
port/books: (H) $302

ENDICOTT and COMPANY,
Lithographers
American 1852-1886
planographic: (H) $1,045
port/books: (L) $523; (H) $715

ENDICOTT and COMPANY,
Lithographers (after Jonathan Badger
Balchelder)
American 1852-1886
planographic: (H) $715

ENDICOTT, Publisher
planographic: (L) $440; (H) $545

ENGEL, Morris
photo: (H) $880

ENGEL, Nissan
American
planographic: (H) $314

ENGLISH, Gail
stencil: (H) $122

ENGSTROM, Albert
mixed-media: (H) $1,157

ENNS, Maureen
relief: (H) $58

ENOS, Chris
photo: (L) $380; (H) $600

ENRIGHT, M. Wright
posters: (H) $55

ENSOR, James
Belgian 1860-1949
intaglio: (L) $261; (H) $14,789
port/books: (L) $7,192; (H) $9,544

EPPER, Ignaz
Swiss 1892-1969
relief: (L) $364; (H) $455

ERFURTH, Hugo
German 1874-1948
port/books: (L) $1,720; (H) $1,863
photo: (H) $323

ERHARDT, Alfred
German 1901-1984
photo: (H) $1,147

ERIXSON, Sven
contemporary
planographic: (L) $444; (H) $1,478

ERLER, Fritz
posters: (H) $247

ERNI, Hans
Swiss b. 1909
intaglio: (H) $541
planographic: (L) $83; (H) $1,605
port/books: (H) $275

ERNST, Jimmy
German/American b. 1921
port/books: (H) $330

ERNST, Max
French 1891-1976
intaglio: (L) $678; (H) $6,362
stencil: (L) $440; (H) $1,402
planographic: (L) $364; (H) $3,651
mixed-media: (H) $718
photo-repro: (L) $336; (H) $441
port/books: (L) $1,210; (H) $23,859
photo: (H) $12,100

ERNST, Max (after)
stencil: (H) $2,381
planographic: (L) $192; (H) $385

ERTE (Romain de TIRTOFF)
Russian/French 1892-1990
stencil: (L) $220; (H) $3,630
planographic: (L) $568; (H) $1,320
posters: (H) $220
port/books: (L) $1,870; (H) $16,500
generic: (H) $77

ERWITT, Elliot
b. 1928
photo: (L) $192; (H) $1,186

ESCHER, Maurits Cornelis
Dutch 1898-1972
intaglio: (H) $3,300
relief: (L) $113; (H) $14,300
planographic: (L) $1,812; (H) $29,700
port/books: (L) $506; (H) $4,146

ESCOBADO, Jesus
20th cent.
planographic: (L) $154; (H) $154

ESHERICK, Wharton H.
American 1887-1970
relief: (L) $165; (H) $413

ESLER, John Kenneth
b. 1933
intaglio: (L) $92; (H) $110

ESPLEGHEM, Frans Crabbe van
(Meister Mit Dem Krebs)
1480-1552
intaglio: (H) $40,841

ESSENHIGH-CORKE, H.
photo: (H) $230

ESTELA
posters: (H) $165

ESTES, Richard
American b. 1936
stencil: (L) $550; (H) $8,800
port/books: (L) $2,090; (H) $9,350

ESTEVE, Maurice
French b. 1904
intaglio: (H) $489
planographic: (L) $259; (H) $3,389
posters: (H) $132

ESTEVE, Maurice (after)
b. 1904
planographic: (H) $1,946

ETCHING CLUB
port/books: (H) $835

ETROG, Sorel
American b. 1933
others: (H) $165

ETTINGER, Churchill
American b. 1903
intaglio: (L) $70; (H) $275
port/books: (H) $55

EUSTON, Jacob Howard
American b. 1892
intaglio: (H) $55

EVANS, Floyd B.
1890-1966
photo: (L) $495; (H) $1,980

EVANS, Frederick H.
1853-1943
photo-repro: (L) $220; (H) $990
photo: (L) $550; (H) $2,678

EVANS, Walker
American 1903-1975
port/books: (L) $1,320; (H) $6,600
photo: (L) $413; (II) $7,700

Photorealism, a movement of the 1960s, focuses on the urban landscape: cars, shop fronts, buildings, and faces. The city is a visual spectacle; colors and forms combine to make an almost abstract composition. Artists associated with the movement are Richard Estes, Chuck Close, and Robert Cottingham. (Richard Estes, *D Train, 1988,* screenprint in colors on museum board, 35 $\frac{7}{16}$ x 71 inches, Christie-New York, May 11, 1992, $7,700)

Frederick Evans (1853-1943) is best known for his architectural interiors. More than simply making a record, he created luminous portraits of light, form, and space that emphasized architectural detail. In the 1920s, when commercially made platinum paper became scarce, he found the newer silver paper to lack the richness he desired, and he stopped printing his images. This portrait of Aubrey Beardsley is a photogravure. Although classified as a photographic technique, a photogravure is technically a printing process. Photogravures are becoming more popular as the price of some photographs become prohibitively expensive. (Frederick H. Evans, *Portrait of Aubrey Beardsley*, photogravure, 5 x 4 inches, Swann, October 8, 1991, $990)

EVANS, William (after)
  intaglio: (H) $180

EVENEPOEL, Henri Joseph Edouard
  Belgian 1872-1899
  posters: (H) $715

EVERDINGEN, Allaert van
  Dutch baptized 1621,buried 1675
  intaglio: (H) $88
  port/books: (H) $779

EVERGOOD, Philip
  American 1901-1973
  intaglio: (H) $99
  planographic: (L) $138; (H) $275

EVERGOOD, Philip (after)
  photo-repro: (H) $165

EVITT, E.
  American 1912-1973
  port/books: (H) $110

FABER, Conrad (attrib.)
  German 1500-1553
  relief: (H) $55

FABER, Will
  German 1901-1987
  planographic: (H) $58

FAIRBAIRN, Thomas
  port/books: (H) $383

FALCONER, John M. (after)
  1820-1903
  planographic: (H) $248

FALK, Hans
  b. 1918
  planographic: (L) $139; (H) $579
  posters: (L) $83; (H) $579
  mixed-media: (H) $241
  port/books: (H) $621

FANCH
  planographic: (H) $33

FANTIN-LATOUR, Henri
  French 1836-1904
  planographic: (L) $22; (H) $770

FARINATI, Paolo
  Italian 1524-1606
  intaglio: (L) $1,649; (H) $3,850

FARNY, H.F.
American 1847-1916
generic: (H) $60

FARRAR, Henry
1843-1906
intaglio: (H) $61

FARRE, H.
intaglio: (L) $220; (H) $275

FARRER, Henry
American 1843-1903
intaglio: (H) $66

FARRINGTON, Joseph (after)
port/books: (H) $413

FASSIANOS, Alecos
Italian 20th cent.
planographic: (H) $28

FASSIANOS, Alexandre
planographic: (H) $204

FASSIONOS, Alexos
Greek
planographic: (H) $364

FAUCH
planographic: (H) $358

FAURE
posters: (H) $385

FAUTRIER, Jean
French 1898-1964
intaglio: (L) $1,789; (H) $3,977
planographic: (H) $2,187

FAWCETT, B. (after)
British 19th cent.
relief: (H) $110

FAY, Clark
British 20th cent.
port/books: (H) $330

FEARNLEY, Alan
photo-repro: (H) $550

FECHIN, Nicolai
Russian/American 1881-1955
planographic: (H) $110

FEELAND, Jan
intaglio: (H) $220

FEHR, Gertrude
photo: (H) $1,980

FEININGER, Andreas
b. 1906
photo: (L) $450; (H) $2,475

FEININGER, Lyonel
German/American 1871-1956
intaglio: (L) $6,599; (H) $8,800
relief: (L) $220; (H) $15,996
planographic: (L) $1,980; (H) $5,866
port/books: (H) $385

FEININGER, T. Lux
b. 1910
photo: (L) $1,430; (H) $2,750

FELIXMULLER, Conrad
German 1897-1977
intaglio: (L) $1,683; (H) $4,400
relief: (L) $154; (H) $5,558
planographic: (H) $1,902

FELLMAN, Sandi
photo: (H) $900

FENTON, Roger
1819-1869
port/books: (H) $49,115
photo: (L) $395; (H) $2,358

FERLOW, Sonja
planographic: (H) $282

FERRARA
c. 1465
port/books: (L) $23,562; (H) $23,562

FETTING, Rainer
German/American b. 1949
stencil: (H) $866

FEURE, Georges de
French 1868-1943
planographic: (H) $770

FICHTER, Robert W.
photo: (H) $200

FIELDING, Jed
photo: (H) $110

FIELDING, Thomas, Publisher
intaglio: (H) $164

FIENE, Ernest
German/American 1894-1965
intaglio: (H) $440
planographic: (L) $55; (H) $193

FIGURA, Hans
American b. Hungary 1898
intaglio: (L) $110; (H) $303
port/books: (L) $110; (H) $220

FILLIOU, Robert
contemporary
photo-repro: (H) $161

FINI, Leonor
Italian b. 1908
intaglio: (L) $51; (H) $660
stencil: (L) $139; (H) $225
planographic: (L) $82; (H) $945
port/books: (L) $266; (H) $3,388

FINKELSTEIN, Nat (photographer)
port/books: (H) $1,650

FINLAY, John, Publisher
English 19th cent.
port/books: (H) $44

FINSLER, Hans
Swiss 1891-1972
photo: (H) $287

FIS (Hans FISCHER)
Swiss 1909-1958
intaglio: (L) $54; (H) $124
planographic: (L) $62; (H) $298

FISCHER, Joseph
intaglio: (H) $1,673

FISCHL, Eric
American b. 1948
intaglio: (L) $1,540; (H) $38,500
relief: (L) $1,650; (H) $2,200
port/books: (L) $3,300; (H) $5,500

FISHBEIN, Johann Heinrich (after)
German 1751-1829
photo-repro: (H) $61

FISHER, Al
photo: (H) $480

FISHER, Jonathon
English School 19th cent.
port/books: (H) $358

FISHER, Sir Major General George
Bulteel (after)
intaglio: (H) $1,190

FITZ, Grancel
1894-1963
photo: (L) $247; (H) $3,960

FITZGIBBON, John H. (attrib.)
photo: (H) $4,400

FJAESTAD, Gustaf
contemporary
relief: (H) $702

FLAGG, James Montgomery
American 1877-1960
posters: (L) $275; (H) $440

FLAHERTY, Robert
photo: (H) $825

FLAMENG, Francois
posters: (L) $193; (H) $412

FLEISCHMANN, Adolf
German 1892-1969
stencil: (L) $193; (H) $496

FLEISCHMANN, Trude
b. 1895
photo: (L) $1,100; (H) $1,320

FLEISHER, Pat
intaglio: (H) $58

FLEMING, Ian
intaglio: (H) $462

FLETCHER, H.
port/books: (H) $110

FLINT, Sir William Russell
British 1880-1969
intaglio: (L) $263; (H) $485
photo-repro: (L) $298; (H) $1,676
generic: (L) $157; (H) $971

FLINT, Sir William Russell (after)
photo-repro: (L) $1,003; (H) $1,132

FLINT, Susan
American 1902-1984
relief: (H) $220

FLINT, William Russell (after)
photo-repro: (L) $154; (H) $2,730
port/books: (H) $2,225

FLORENTINE SCHOOL
(Fine Manner)
intaglio: (H) $5,225

FLORENZ (attrib.)
c. 1470-1490
intaglio: (H) $2,985

FLORSHEIM, Richard A.
American 1916-1976/79
planographic: (L) $8; (H) $110

FODOR, Larry
planographic: (L) $33; (H) $99
generic: (H) $165

FOERSTER
planographic: (H) $50

FOLBERG, Neil
photo: (H) $1,650

FOLINSBEE, John
American 1892-1972
intaglio: (H) $250

FOLON, Jean Michel
intaglio: (H) $204

FONSSAGRIVES, Ferdinand
photo: (H) $660

FONTANA, Lucio
Italian 1899-1968
intaglio: (L) $1,162; (H) $1,323
stencil: (L) $543; (H) $1,430
planographic: (L) $1,133; (H) $2,269
mixed-media: (L) $2,823; (H) $4,950
port/books: (H) $1,591
others: (L) $1,591; (H) $1,988

FOOTE, Jim
American b. 1925
planographic: (H) $193
photo-repro: (H) $330

FORAIN, Jean Louis
French 1852-1931
intaglio: (L) $66; (H) $112
posters: (H) $660

FORBES, Edwin (after)
intaglio: (II) $44

FORG, Gunther
German b. 1952
port/books: (L) $788; (H) $2,150
photo: (L) $788; (H) $12,100

FORSS, George
photo: (H) $385

FORTIN, E. (after)
generic: (H) $88

FORTIN, Marc Aurele
Canadian 1888-1970
planographic: (H) $231
port/books: (L) $234; (H) $293

FORTIN, Robert Emile
Canadian School b. 1945
stencil: (H) $37

FOSTER, William
planographic: (H) $440

FOUJITA, Tsuguharu
Japanese 1886-1968
intaglio: (L) $330; (H) $19,933
relief: (L) $662; (H) $2,750
planographic: (L) $220; (H) $3,300
mixed-media: (H) $990
port/books: (L) $330; (H) $2,718

FOUJITA, Tsuguharu (attrib.)
Japanese 1886-1968
relief: (H) $660

FOUQUERAY, Charles Dominique
French 1872-1956
planographic: (H) $110

FOUQUERAY, D. Charles
planographic: (H) $770

FOX, H. Atkinson
generic: (H) $33

FRAGONARD, Jean Honore
French 1732-1806
intaglio: (L) $199; (H) $3,850
port/books: (H) $3,300

FRAGONARD (after) (by J.
MATHIEU)
port/books: (H) $275

FRAGONARD, J.H. (after)
intaglio: (L) $139; (H) $614

FRAILEY, Stephen
photo: (H) $550

FRANCIS, Sam
American b. 1923
intaglio: (L) $1,259; (H) $9,092
stencil: (L) $1,650; (H) $6,454
relief: (L) $17,600; (H) $22,000
planographic: (L) $93; (H) $17,600
posters: (H) $66
mixed-media: (H) $13,200
photo-repro: (L) $647; (H) $1,360
port/books: (H) $4,180

FRANEK-KOCH, Sabine
b. 1939
port/books: (H) $82

FRANK, Howard
photo: (L) $330; (H) $495

FRANK, Robert
b. 1924
photo: (L) $880; (H) $7,073

FRANKE, Rosemarie
American 20th cent.
intaglio: (H) $187

FRANKENSTEIN, Curt
planographic: (H) $33

FRANKENSTEIN, Kurt
American 20th cent.
port/books: (H) $154

FRANKENTHALER, Helen
American b. 1928
intaglio: (L) $1,650; (H) $5,390
stencil: (L) $990; (H) $2,750
relief: (H) $19,800
planographic: (L) $1,320; (H) $4,675
mixed-media: (H) $4,400
photo-repro: (H) $1,760
port/books: (L) $20,900; (H) $24,200

FRANKLIN, W.H. and R. FISHER
photo: (H) $306

FRANZEN, John Erik
planographic: (H) $617

FRATREL, Joseph
1730-1783
intaglio: (H) $984

FREDDIE, Vilhelm
planographic: (H) $282

FREEMAN, Don
American 1908-1978
planographic: (L) $440; (H) $715

FREIJMUTH, Alfons
stencil: (H) $126

FREILICHER, Jane
American 20th cent.
planographic: (H) $55

FRELAUT, Jean
intaglio: (L) $222; (H) $1,122
port/books: (H) $3,118

FRENCH, Leonard
planographic: (H) $87

FRENCH, Russell Lawrence
photo: (L) $440; (H) $770

FRENCH SCHOOL
posters: (H) $220

FRERES, Manuel (photographer)
port/books: (H) $2,200

FREUD, Lucien
British b. 1922
intaglio: (L) $1,658; (H) $57,676

FREUDENBERGER, Sigmund
Swiss 1745-1801
intaglio: (H) $911

FREUND, Gisele
photo: (L) $303; (H) $1,650

FREY
20th cent.
posters: (H) $41

FREYMAN, E.
American
planographic: (H) $83

FRIDELL, Axel
intaglio: (H) $386

FRIEDENSEN, Thomas
intaglio: (H) $174

FRIEDLAENDER, Johnny
French b. 1912
intaglio: (L) $138; (H) $715
planographic: (L) $110; (H) $138
port/books: (L) $825; (H) $1,430

FRIEDLANDER, Isaac
Latvian/American 1890-1968
intaglio: (L) $275; (H) $317
relief: (H) $138

FRIEDLANDER, Lee
port/books: (H) $1,980
photo: (L) $880; (H) $2,860

FRIEDLANDER, Lee & Jim DINE
American b. 1934
photo: (H) $1,505

FRIEND, Donald Stuart Leslie
planographic: (L) $174; (H) $174

FRIESZ, Emile-Othon
planographic: (L) $100; (H) $110

FRIIS, Frederick Trap
port/books: (H) $220

FRINK, Elizabeth
British b. 1930
planographic: (L) $132; (H) $357

FRISCH, A.
port/books: (H) $967

FRISIUS, Simon Wynouts
intaglio: (H) $2,193

FRITH, Francis
1822-1898
port/books: (L) $988; (H) $2,174
photo: (H) $2,750

FRITH, William Powell (after)
intaglio: (H) $250

FRITSCH, Ernst
1892-1965
intaglio: (H) $25

FROMANGER, W.P.
relief: (H) $218

FROST, A.B.
intaglio: (H) $132
planographic: (H) $66
generic: (H) $175

FROST, Joseph
generic: (H) $87

FROST, Terry
port/books: (L) $678; (H) $814

FROST, W.E. (after)
intaglio: (H) $54

FROST and REED, Publishers
photo-repro: (H) $776

FROST and REED, Publishers (after
Montague Dawson)
photo-repro: (L) $193; (H) $413

FRUHTRUNK, Gunther
contemporary
stencil: (L) $161; (H) $161

FRUTH, Rowena
photo: (H) $2,420

FRY, W. Ellerton (photographer)
port/books: (H) $765

FRYE, Thomas
1710-1762
intaglio: (H) $942

FUCHS, Ernst
Austrian b. 1930
intaglio: (L) $112; (H) $4,207
port/books: (L) $2,694; (H) $3,025

FUGUET, Dallet
1868-1933
photo: (H) $1,540

FUHRMANN, Ernst
photo: (H) $385

FUJITA, A.
relief: (H) $55

FULLER, Edmund G.
British 20th cent.
port/books: (H) $55

FULLWOOD, Albert H.
intaglio: (H) $348

FUNK, John
1895-1964
photo: (L) $660; (H) $1,320

FURBER, Robert (after)
port/books: (H) $1,650

FURLAN, L.
20th cent.
posters: (H) $199

FURST, Peter H.
Austrian b. 1939
photo: (H) $788

FUSSLI, Johann Heinrich (after)
Swiss 1741-1825
stencil: (H) $83

FUSSMANN, Klaus
b. 1938
intaglio: (H) $113

GABO, Naum
American 1890-1977
relief: (H) $8,156
mixed-media: (H) $6,050

GAFGEN, W.
intaglio: (H) $24

GAG, Wanda
American 1893-1946
planographic: (L) $83; (H) $385

GAGNON, Clarence Alphonse
Canadian School 1881-1942
intaglio: (H) $2,426

GAINSBOROUGH, Thomas (after)
English 1727-1788
intaglio: (H) $112

GALANIS, Demetrius
intaglio: (H) $191
relief: (L) $624; (H) $624
planographic: (L) $191; (H) $478

GALERIE MAEGHT, Publisher
port/books: (H) $420

GALL, Sally
photo: (H) $650

GALLAGHER, Sears
American 1869-1955
intaglio: (L) $28; (H) $220

GALLE, C.
intaglio: (H) $118

GALLE, Jan
1600-1676
port/books: (H) $487

GALLE, Philip
1537-1612
intaglio: (H) $2,256

GALLE, Theodore
intaglio: (H) $1,046

GALLEN-KALLELA, Akseli
Continental
generic: (H) $3,565

GALVAN, Jose Maria
intaglio: (H) $381

GAMY
planographic: (H) $242

GANSO, Emil
German/American 1895-1941
intaglio: (L) $110; (H) $143
relief: (L) $110; (H) $330
planographic: (L) $165; (H) $660

GARBER, Daniel
American 1880-1958
intaglio: (L) $1,210; (H) $1,430

GARCIA OCHOA, Luis
port/books: (H) $2,676

GARDINER, Eliza
American 1871-1955
relief: (L) $121; (H) $1,320

GARDNER, Alexander
American 1821-1882
photo: (L) $192; (H) $23,100

GARDNER, Alexander and Moses P.
RICE
photo: (H) $3,850

GARDUNO, Flor
photo: (H) $700

GARNERAY, Ambroise Louis
French 1783-1857
intaglio: (H) $990

GARNETT, William
b. 1916
photo: (L) $550; (H) $5,500

GASKELL, Percival
English 1868-1934
planographic: (H) $55

GASSEL, Lucas (after)
c. 1500-1570
intaglio: (H) $1,430

GASSET, Eugene
planographic: (H) $660

GATINE
intaglio: (H) $541

GAUGENGIGL, Ignaz Marcel
German/American 1855/56-1932
intaglio: (L) $77; (H) $275
generic: (H) $110

GAUGUIN, Paul
French 1848-1903
intaglio: (H) $2,475
relief: (L) $1,193; (H) $23,859
planographic: (L) $88; (H) $139,293

GAUGUIN, Paul (after)
French 1848-1903
planographic: (H) $88

GAUGUIN, Paul and Armand
SEGUIN
intaglio: (H) $6,959

GAUL, Winfried
German b. 1928
stencil: (L) $25; (H) $66

GAUTHIER, Michele
port/books: (H) $22

GAYMARD, Antoine
intaglio: (H) $70

GAZAY, R.
posters: (H) $440

GEARHART, Frances H.
American 1869-1958
relief: (L) $110; (H) $1,650

GEARHART, May
American 1872-1951
intaglio: (H) $165

Mathew Brady is one of the best known 19th-century photographers. Opening up a daguerreotype portrait studio in New York in 1844, he soon became one of the nation's foremost portrait photographers. His portrait of Lincoln became so well known that the president ascribed his election to this likeness. When the Civil War began, Brady received permission for his staff to accompany the troops. Extensive photos were taken of every part of the war effort. The many photographers employed in this massive effort worked anonymously, each photo was printed with the Brady name. After the war was over, unable to sell his war photos and pay his debts, Brady went into bankruptcy. Shortly before he died, the U.S. government awarded him $25,000 for the historical services he had performed. This portrait of U.S. Grant was taken by staff photographer Alexander Gardener and signed by Mathew Brady. Signed photos by Brady are very rare. (Mathew Brady photo, *U.S. Grant*, Swann, April 15, 1991, $11,000)

GEARHARTS, The
  relief: (H) $303
GEHR, Herbert
  photo: (L) $660; (H) $1,320
GEIGER, Rupprecht
  German b. 1908
  stencil: (L) $157; (H) $312
  relief: (H) $361
  planographic: (L) $166; (H) $390
GEISER, Karl
  Swiss 1898-1957
  intaglio: (L) $149; (H) $497
GEISSLER, Paul
  French b. 1891
  intaglio: (L) $44; (H) $220
GEKKO, Ogata (called Tai Masanosuke)
  Japanese School 1867-1920
  relief: (L) $93; (H) $234

GELPKE, Andre
  German b. 1947
  photo: (L) $215; (H) $215
GEN PAUL
  French 1895-1975
  intaglio: (H) $86
  planographic: (L) $123; (H) $495
GENERALIC, Joseph
  Italian 20th cent.
  planographic: (H) $44
GENEREUX, Arline
  Canadian School b. 1897
  intaglio: (H) $97
GENN, Robert
  b. 1936
  stencil: (H) $195
GENTHE, Arnold
  1856-1915
  photo: (L) $440; (H) $1,100

GENTILINI, Franco
Italian b. 1909
intaglio: (H) $709

GEOFFRAY, Stephane
photo: (H) $6,600

GEORG, Edward
intaglio: (H) $165

GERARD, Marguerite
French 1761-1837
intaglio: (H) $1,210

GERBER, Theo
Swiss b. 1928
planographic: (H) $25

GERBIG, Richard
Swiss b. 1914
posters: (H) $50

GERICAULT, Theodore
French 1791-1824
planographic: (L) $248; (H) $90,321

GERITZ, Franz
American 1895-1945
relief: (L) $55; (H) $358

**GERMAN SCHOOL, 15TH
CENTURY**
relief: (H) $36,300

GEROME, Jean Leon (after)
French 1824-1904
intaglio: (H) $220

GERSTER, Albert
Swiss b. 1929
relief: (H) $17
port/books: (H) $41

GERTSCH, Franz
Swiss b. 1930
stencil: (H) $993
relief: (L) $91; (H) $182

GERZ, Jochen
German b. 1940
photo-repro: (H) $78
photo: (L) $1,290; (H) $1,290

GESSNER, Salomon
1730-1788
generic: (H) $2,356

GESTEL, L. van
1881-1941
planographic: (H) $184

GHEYN, Jacob de (III)
Dutch 1596-1641
intaglio: (H) $4,367

GHIRLANDIO
intaglio: (H) $110

GHISI, Giorgio
1520-1582
intaglio: (L) $676; (H) $37,699

GIACOMELLI, Mario
b. 1925
photo: (L) $553; (H) $4,400

GIACOMETTI, Alberto
Swiss 1901-1966
intaglio: (L) $920; (H) $3,300
planographic: (L) $111; (H) $6,600
posters: (L) $41; (H) $41

GIACOMETTI, Alberto (after)
Swiss 1901-1966
planographic: (H) $121

GIACOMETTI, Giovanni
1868-1933
relief: (L) $1,049; (H) $6,857

GIBBS, Len
b. 1929
mixed-media: (H) $129

GIBSON, Ralph
photo: (L) $715; (H) $2,200

GIDAL, Tim
German b. 1909
photo: (L) $430; (H) $717

GIEBE, Hubertus
intaglio: (H) $1,976

GIFFORD, Robert Swain
American 1840-1905
intaglio: (L) $55; (H) $143

GIGUERE, Roland
Canadian School b. 1929
planographic: (H) $112

GILBERT, Al
generic: (H) $100

GILBERT and GEORGE
b. 1940s
stencil: (H) $303

GILES, Geoffrey Douglas (after)
photo-repro: (H) $220

GILFILLAN, Tom (after)
posters: (H) $383

GILIOLI, Emile
French b. 1911
planographic: (L) $102; (H) $321

GILL, Eric
relief: (H) $671

GILLBANK, H. (after F. Wheatley)
intaglio: (H) $3,080

GILPIN, Henry
photo: (H) $660

GILPIN, Laura
photo: (L) $1,100; (H) $3,300

GINSBERG, Allen
photo: (H) $200

GINZBURG, Yankel
b. 1945
stencil: (H) $358
planographic: (H) $28

GIORDANO, Luca
Italian 1632-1705
intaglio: (H) $1,193

GIORITO, Michael
Canadian School 20th cent.
intaglio: (H) $78

GIOVANARDI'S
photo: (H) $70

GIR, Ch.
posters: (H) $220

GIRARDET, Charles Samuel
1780-1863
intaglio: (H) $149

GIRAUD, Giuseppe, Publisher
intaglio: (H) $861

GIRBAL, Gaston
posters: (L) $247; (H) $990

GIRONES, Ramon Antonio Pichot
posters: (H) $132

GIVATI, Moshe
stencil: (H) $11

GLACKENS, William
American 1870-1938
intaglio: (H) $20

GLARNER, Fritz
American 1899-1972
planographic: (L) $880; (H) $2,259

GLEASON, F., Publisher
American 19th cent.
planographic: (H) $275

GLEIZES, Albert
French 1881-1953
intaglio: (H) $14,912
stencil: (H) $143
planographic: (H) $1,135

GLESS, Nicolas
port/books: (H) $525

GLOEDEN, Wilhelm von
German 1856-1931
photo: (L) $215; (H) $1,650

GODBY, James
intaglio: (H) $251

GODWIN, Fay
photo: (H) $358

GODWIN, Ted
relief: (H) $73

GOENEUTTE, Norbert
French 1854-1894
intaglio: (L) $100; (H) $1,109

GOERG, Edouard
French, b Australia 1893-1968/69
intaglio: (L) $82; (H) $1,871
planographic: (H) $160
port/books: (H) $727

GOETSCH, Gustaf F.
American 1877-1969
intaglio: (H) $165

GOETZ, Henri
intaglio: (L) $61; (H) $102

GOGOL, Nicolas
intaglio: (H) $36,662

GOISSAUD
posters: (H) $220

GOLDBERG, Jim
photo: (H) $400

GOLDEN, Judith
photo: (H) $400

GOLDHAMMER, Charles
planographic: (H) $170

GOLDIN, Nan
photo: (H) $450

GOLDRING, Nancy
photo: (H) $280

GOLDSMITH, Wallace
American 1873-1945
intaglio: (H) $110

GOLINKIN, Joseph
American b. 1896
planographic: (L) $302; (H) $770

GOLTZIUS, Hendrik
Dutch 1558-1617
intaglio: (L) $110; (H) $31,896
relief: (L) $755; (H) $69,774
port/books: (H) $12,174

GOLUB, Leon
American b. 1922
planographic: (H) $660

GONZOLEZ-TORERO, Sergio
others: (H) $330

GOODCHILD, John C.
intaglio: (L) $130; (H) $209

GOODNOUGH, Peter
American b. 1917
stencil: (L) $33; (H) $33

GOODNOUGH, Robert
American b. 1917
stencil: (H) $99

GORIN, Jean
planographic: (H) $82

GORMAN, Greg
photo: (H) $1,339

GORMAN, R.C.
American b. 1933
stencil: (L) $1,540; (H) $2,090
planographic: (L) $358; (H) $1,760
photo-repro: (H) $66
generic: (H) $121

GORNIK, April
American b. 1953
intaglio: (L) $1,100; (H) $1,100
relief: (L) $715; (H) $3,575

GORSLINE, Douglas
American 1913-1985
intaglio: (H) $17

GORTITZ, Fr.
20th cent.
intaglio: (H) $82

GOSSAERT, Jan (called Mabuse)
Flemish c. 1478-c. 1536
intaglio: (H) $13,352

GOT, Moshe
Israeli 20th c.
planographic: (H) $66

GOTTLIEB, Adolph
American 1903-1974
stencil: (L) $660; (H) $1,210
planographic: (H) $853

GOTTSCHO, Samuel
1875-1971
photo: (H) $394

GOTZ, Karl Otto
b. 1914
relief: (H) $1,443
planographic: (H) $419

GOUDT, Hendrik
Dutch 1585-1630
intaglio: (L) $157; (H) $23,922

GOULD, E.
planographic: (H) $110

GOULD, J. and E.
planographic: (L) $99; (H) $440

GOULD, J. and H.C. RICHTER
planographic: (L) $39; (H) $1,315

GOULD, J. and H.C. RICHTER (after)
planographic: (H) $660

GOULD, J.J.
American
planographic: (L) $83; (H) $660

GOULD, John (after)
planographic: (H) $176

GOULD, John
British 1804-1881
planographic: (L) $138; (H) $715

GOUPIL and CO., Publishers
planographic: (L) $208; (H) $874

GOUPIL et CIE
photo-repro: (H) $154

GOWIN, Emmet
photo: (H) $1,540

GOYA Y LUCIENTES, Francisco de
Spanish 1746-1828
intaglio: (L) $55; (H) $184,569
planographic: (L) $98,175; (H) $341,000
port/books: (L) $2,381; (H) $184,569

GOYO, Hashiguchi
Japanese c. 1880/88-1921
relief: (H) $3,410
generic: (H) $413

GRAESER, Camille
1892-1980
stencil: (H) $397

GRAEVENITZ, Gerhard von
1934-1983
stencil: (H) $57

GRAF, Carl B.
20th cent.
posters: (H) $116

GRAF, Urs
intaglio: (H) $2,750

GRAMBART and CO., Publisher
intaglio: (H) $963

GRANT, Allan
photo: (L) $825; (H) $880

GRANT, Duncan
American 1885-1978
planographic: (H) $72

GRANT, Gordon Hope
American 1875-1962
intaglio: (L) $77; (H) $99
planographic: (L) $55; (H) $248

GRANT, Sir Francis (after)
intaglio: (H) $449

GRANT, Sir Francis
intaglio: (H) $92

GRASSET, Eugene
Swiss 1841-1917
planographic: (H) $13,200

GRAU-SALA, Emile
Spanish 1911-1975
planographic: (L) $82; (H) $275

GRAVEL, Francine
b. 1944
intaglio: (H) $138

GRAVES, Nancy
American b. 1940
stencil: (H) $770

GRAY, Cleve
American b. 1918
planographic: (H) $77

GRAY, Joseph
English 1890-1962
intaglio: (H) $99

GRECO, Emilio
Italian b. 1913
intaglio: (H) $545
planographic: (H) $62

GREEN, Elizabeth S. and Jessie
Willcox SMITH
American 19th/20th cent.
port/books: (H) $495

GREEN, Roland
English 1896-1971
generic: (H) $54

GREEN, V.G.
intaglio: (H) $11

GREENAWAY, Kate (after)
port/books: (H) $8,250

GREENE, Melanie
American b. 1947
planographic: (H) $66

GREENE, Milton H.
American 20th cent.
planographic: (L) $550; (H) $550
photo: (L) $707; (H) $1,218

GREENFIELD-SANDERS, Timothy
photo: (H) $900

GREENLAW, Col. Alexander John
1818-1870
photo: (H) $727

GREENOUGH, F.W.
generic: (L) $66; (H) $77

GREENWOOD, Marion
American 1909-1970
planographic: (L) $33; (H) $400

GREUZE, J.B. (after)
intaglio: (L) $26; (H) $120

GRIDLEY, Enoch G. (after John
COLES, Jr.)
ac. 1803-18
intaglio: (H) $2,860

GRIESHABER, H.A.P.
German b. 1909
relief: (L) $123; (H) $7,552
port/books: (L) $5,444; (H) $8,631

GRIFFIN, Brian
b. 1948
photo: (H) $574

GRIFFIN, N.
stencil: (H) $87

GRIFFIN, Vaughan Murray
relief: (L) $70; (H) $739
planographic: (H) $739

GRIGGS, Francis Landseer Maur
intaglio: (L) $294; (H) $522

GRIGNANI, Franco
photo: (L) $982; (H) $982

GRIMSHAW, Gary
posters: (L) $550; (H) $880

GRIS, Juan
Spanish 1887-1927
stencil: (H) $4,127

GROENEWEGEN, G.
1754-1826
port/books: (H) $1,937

GROMAIRE, Marcel
French 1892-1971
intaglio: (L) $100; (H) $4,493

GROOMS, Red
American b. 1937
intaglio: (H) $1,760
stencil: (H) $880
planographic: (L) $99; (H) $12,100
mixed-media: (L) $825; (H) $4,125
photo-repro: (L) $743; (H) $743
port/books: (H) $6,050
others: (H) $3,300

GROOT, Annemarie de
stencil: (H) $126

GROOVER, Jan
b. 1943
photo: (L) $990; (H) $4,180

GROPPER, William
American 1897-1977
intaglio: (H) $110
planographic: (L) $44; (H) $605
port/books: (H) $132

GROS, Lucien Alphonse
French School 1845-1913
intaglio: (H) $237

GROSECLONE, Mark
photo-repro: (H) $165

GROSMAN, Rose
American 20th cent.
intaglio: (H) $6

GROSS, Chaim
Austrian/American 1904-1990
planographic: (L) $50; (H) $715

GROSSMAN, Rose
American 20th cent.
intaglio: (H) $44

GROSSMANN, Rudolf
1882-1959
intaglio: (L) $41; (H) $45
planographic: (H) $82

GROSZ, Georg
German/American 1893-1959
intaglio: (L) $302; (H) $1,540
planographic: (L) $110; (H) $1,553
photo-repro: (L) $369; (H) $16,865
port/books: (H) $1,980

GROTH, John
intaglio: (H) $88

GROVE, Muriel Annie Florence
relief: (H) $92

GROVE, Stanley Morel
b. 1911
intaglio: (H) $293

GROZER, J.
American 20th cent.
planographic: (H) $193

GRUAN
posters: (H) $302

GRUEL, C.B.
20th cent.
relief: (H) $88

GRUEN, John
photo: (H) $2,750

GRUNEWALD, Isaac
planographic: (H) $471

GRUPPE, Emile Albert
American 1896-1978
planographic: (H) $138

GRUSCHNER, Henry
Continental 20th cent.
relief: (H) $83

GRUTZKE, Johannes
b. 1937
port/books: (L) $185; (H) $205

GUARDI, Francesco (after)
intaglio: (H) $6,273

GUBBELS, Klaas
planographic: (H) $152

GUBCEVSKY, A.
photo: (H) $175

GUDERNA, Ladislav
intaglio: (H) $59

GUERARD, Eugene von
planographic: (L) $279; (H) $609

GUERARD, Henri
intaglio: (H) $281

GUERRERO, Pedro E.
photo: (L) $385; (H) $770

GUIDALEVITCH, Victor
photo: (H) $550

GUIGOU, P.
intaglio: (H) $464

GUILLAUME, Albert
French 1873-1942
posters: (H) $1,077

GUILLAUMIN, Armand
French 1841-1927
planographic: (L) $80; (H) $1,975

GUILLOUX, Charles
planographic: (H) $2,410

GUIRAMAND, Paul
planographic: (H) $191

GUIZZARO, Innocente
intaglio: (H) $440

GURNY, A. Priscilla
intaglio: (H) $28

GURSKY, Andreas
b. 1955
photo: (H) $1,760

GUSTON, Philip
Canadian/American 1913-1980
planographic: (L) $1,320; (H) $3,575

GUTSCHOW, Arvid
German 1900-1984
photo: (L) $143; (H) $466

GWATHMEY, Robert
American b. 1903
stencil: (L) $522; (H) $1,540

GYGAX
Swiss 20th cent.
posters: (H) $50

HAAS, Aad de
port/books: (H) $3,161

HAAS, J.
intaglio: (H) $247

HAAS, Richard
intaglio: (H) $468

HAAS BROTHERS
photo: (H) $11

HABER, Sandy
photo: (H) $220

HADEN, Sir Francis Seymour
English 1818-1910
intaglio: (L) $50; (H) $1,210
port/books: (H) $8,800

HAEN, Anthony de
1640-c. 1675
intaglio: (H) $923

HAGAN, Frederick
planographic: (L) $146; (H) $170

HAGEMEYER, Johan
photo: (H) $5,720

HAGERMAN, Kurt
American 20th cent.
intaglio: (H) $88

HAGERMAN, William Kent
intaglio: (L) $138; (H) $248

HAGHE, Louis
Belgian b. 1806, d. London 1885
planographic: (H) $232

HAGN, Charles
relief: (H) $94

HAHN, Betty
photo: (H) $330

HAHN, Joseph
stencil: (H) $70

HAIG, Axel
b.Sweden, ac. London 1835-1921
intaglio: (L) $61; (H) $385

HAINES, Frederick Stanley
intaglio: (L) $115; (H) $291

HAJEK-HALKE, Heinz
German 1898-1983
photo: (L) $466; (H) $2,222

HALD, Smith
generic: (H) $244

HALL, Harry (after)
intaglio: (H) $229

HALL, Norma Bassett
relief: (H) $275

HALL, Norman
planographic: (H) $11

HALLOWELL, George H.
American 1871-1926
posters: (H) $248

HALSMAN, Philippe
1906-1979
photo: (L) $412; (H) $5,225

HAM, Thomas
intaglio: (L) $174; (H) $196

HAMAGUCHI, Yozo
b. 1909
intaglio: (L) $1,653; (H) $25,093

HAMBLE, J.R.
intaglio: (H) $130

HAMBOURG, Andre
French b. 1909
planographic: (H) $374

HAMILTON, (after)
intaglio: (H) $33

HAMILTON, Richard
b. 1922
intaglio: (H) $2,200
stencil: (L) $433; (H) $3,137
planographic: (H) $1,226
mixed-media: (L) $990; (H) $1,320
photo-repro: (L) $1,210; (H) $1,226
photo: (H) $2,300

HAMILTON, Sir William
English 1751-1807
port/books: (H) $44,000

HAMILTON, Sir William and Pierre
Francois H. HANCARVILLE
18th cent.
port/books: (H) $44,000

HAMMITT, Howard
photo: (H) $247

HANCHER, Madeleine
American 20th cent.
intaglio: (H) $33

HANFSTANGL, Franz Seraph
intaglio: (H) $77

HANICOTTE
planographic: (H) $60

HANKEY, William Lee
English 1869-1952
intaglio: (L) $33; (H) $503

HANKINS, A.E.
planographic: (H) $45

HANSEN, Armin Carl
American 1886-1957
intaglio: (L) $358; (H) $2,090
relief: (H) $358

HANSEN-BAHIA, Karl Heinz
1915-1978
port/books: (H) $1,122

HANSON, Raymond
photo: (H) $450

HANSPERS, Olle
b. 1923
intaglio: (H) $2,432

HARDY, Bert
b. 1913
photo: (H) $765

HARDY, Heywood
English 1843-1932
photo-repro: (H) $330

HARDY, Thomas Bush
English 1842-1897
intaglio: (H) $193

HARE, James H.
1856-1946
photo: (L) $770; (H) $1,980

HARING, Keith
American 1958-1990
stencil: (L) $715; (H) $5,500
planographic: (L) $5,500; (H) $12,128
posters: (L) $50; (H) $74
photo-repro: (H) $1,766
port/books: (L) $5,374; (H) $9,900

HARLAN, Stephanie
planographic: (H) $11

HARM, Ray
planographic: (H) $11
generic: (H) $55

HARNETT, William (after)
planographic: (L) $550; (H) $2,475

HARNETT, William Michael
American 1848/51-1892
planographic: (H) $550

HARRIS, J.
planographic: (H) $495

HARRIS, J. (after H. Hall)
intaglio: (H) $440

HARRIS, J. (after R.B. Davis)
intaglio: (H) $413

HARRIS, J. (after J.F. Herring)
planographic: (H) $495

HARRIS, J. (after W.A. Knell)
planographic: (H) $330

HARRIS, John
intaglio: (H) $404

HARRIS, John (III)
intaglio: (H) $251

HARRIS, Lawren Stewart
Canadian 1885-1970
stencil: (H) $161

HARRISON, Agnes
posters: (H) $193

HARRISON, John Cyril
generic: (H) $212

HARRISON, Joseph, Editor
planographic: (H) $120

HART, George Overbury (called Pop)
American 1868-1933
intaglio: (H) $660
planographic: (L) $88; (H) $138

HART, Pro
planographic: (L) $87; (H) $157

HARTING, D.H.
1884-1970
intaglio: (H) $140

HARTUNG, Hans
German b. 1904
intaglio: (L) $1,443; (H) $2,706
planographic: (L) $351; (H) $3,318
port/books: (L) $1,600; (H) $2,475

HARTWELL, Marianne
American 20th cent.
intaglio: (H) $6

HARUNOBU, Suzuki
Japanese School 1725-1770
relief: (H) $93

The Impressionist painter Childe Hassam (1859-1935) apprenticed as a young boy to a Boston wood engraver. His natural aptitude led him into a career as an illustrator for several periodicals including *Scribner's* and *Harper's*. In the late 1880s he studied in Paris and began to paint watercolors in an Impressionist style. (F. Childe Hassam, *Church Tower, Portsmouth*, etching, 8 x 6 inches, Young, July 13, 1991, $2,100)

HARVEY, Donald
contemporary
intaglio: (H) $193

HARVEY, Harold Leroy
American 1899-1971
photo: (L) $330; (H) $2,420

HASEGAWA, K.
intaglio: (L) $1,803; (H) $2,103

HASEGAWA, Kiyoshi
1891-1980
intaglio: (L) $3,346; (H) $9,967
planographic: (H) $4,182

HASEGAWA, Konobu
Japanese
planographic: (L) $33; (H) $33

HASEGAWA, Sadanou
Japanese 19th cent.
relief: (H) $83

HASKELL and ALLEN, Publishers
planographic: (L) $55; (H) $715

HASSAM, Childe
American 1859-1935
intaglio: (L) $495; (H) $16,500
planographic: (H) $880

HASSELL, J. (after)
planographic: (H) $795

HASUI, Kawase Bunjiro
Japanese 1883-1957
relief: (L) $193; (H) $330

HAUGEN-SORENSEN, Arne
planographic: (H) $93

HAUGH, Graeme
relief: (H) $52

HAUSMANN, Raoul
Austrian 1886-1971
planographic: (H) $358
photo: (L) $287; (H) $1,430

HAVARD, James
American b. 1937
photo-repro: (H) $248

HAVELL, (after)
intaglio: (H) $1,540

HAVELL, Daniel
intaglio: (H) $3,287

HAVELL, R. (after John J.
AUDUBON)
intaglio: (H) $4,180

HAVELL, Robert
English 1793-1878
intaglio: (H) $6,600

HAVILAND, Paul Burty
1880-1950
photo: (H) $1,980

HAVINDEN, John
b. 1909
photo: (H) $990

HAYDEN, Seymour
intaglio: (L) $165; (H) $248

HAYES, William
ac. 1794
intaglio: (H) $121

HAYTER, Stanley William
English 1901-1988
intaglio: (L) $183; (H) $9,350
stencil: (H) $1,479
mixed-media: (H) $1,092
port/books: (L) $1,870; (H) $6,390

HEALEY, The Rt. Hon. Denis
b. 1917
photo: (H) $153

HEATH, David
photo: (L) $330; (H) $330

HECKEL, Erich
German 1883-1970
intaglio: (L) $423; (H) $2,837
relief: (L) $319; (H) $65,808
planographic: (L) $340; (H) $2,766
port/books: (L) $64,525; (H) $212,762

HECKENBLEICKWER, Lorin
German 1867-1948
relief: (L) $83; (H) $83

HECKER, Franz
1870-1944
intaglio: (H) $2,477

HECKMAN, Albert W.
American b. 1893
planographic: (H) $413

HEERUP, Henry
relief: (H) $148
planographic: (L) $151; (H) $555
port/books: (L) $222; (H) $527

Erich Heckel (1883-1970) was a founding member of *Die Brücke*, a German Expressionist group founded in 1905. Harsh angular distortions and pessimistic expressions are characteristic of his portraits. In 1937 Heckel's work was proscribed as degenerate by the Hitler regime. (Erich Heckel, *Bildnis E.H. 1917*, woodcut on laid paper, 14 $\frac{5}{6}$ x 11 $\frac{1}{2}$ inches, Christie-London, July 2, 1992, $3,169)

HEFFERNAN, Edward
relief: (H) $87

HEGE, Walter
German 1893-1955
photo: (L) $394; (H) $1,577

HEGI, Franz
1774-1850
intaglio: (L) $124; (H) $1,064

HEICK, William
photo: (L) $605; (H) $715

HEINDORFF, Michael
port/books: (H) $1,464

HEINECKEN, Robert
b. 1931
photo: (H) $2,200

HEINTZELMAN, Arthur W.
American 1890-1965
intaglio: (L) $33; (H) $303

HEISE, Wilhelm
relief: (H) $89

HELCK, Peter
American b. 1893/97
planographic: (H) $22

HELD, Al
American b. 1928
intaglio: (L) $3,520; (II) $4,620
relief: (L) $1,100; (H) $3,850

HELDT, Werner
1904-1954
planographic: (H) $993

HELION, Jean
French b. 1904
relief: (H) $330
planographic: (L) $163; (H) $225

HELLER, Ben
b. 1913
photo: (H) $1,045

HELLER, Frank J.
photo: (H) $1,760

HELLEU, Paul Cesar
French 1859-1927
intaglio: (L) $55; (H) $7,940
posters: (H) $715

HENDEE, A.
posters: (H) $55

Frenchman Paul Cesar Helleu (1859-1927) was well known in his native country for his paintings of churches and architectural detail. During the Edwardian period in England and the United States, he gained recognition for his sensitive and charming etchings of society beauties. (Paul Cesar Helleu, *Young Woman Wearing a Black Hat*, drypoint, 11 $\frac{5}{8}$ x 10 $\frac{1}{16}$ inches, Boos, July 16, 1992, $1,100)

HENDERSON, Alexander
  photo: (H) $1,913
HENDERSON, Charles Cooper (after)
  intaglio: (L) $275; (H) $619
HENDRIKSE, Jan
  port/books: (H) $822
HENLE, Fritz
  b. 1909
  photo: (L) $192; (H) $192
HENNEMAN, Jeroen
  contemporary
  planographic: (H) $181
HENNEMAN, Nicolaas
  photo: (H) $3,536
HENRI, Florence
  b. 1893
  photo: (L) $550; (H) $1,980
HENS, Frans
  intaglio: (H) $48
HERBERT, Edward
  intaglio: (H) $385
HERBERT, Harold Brocklebank
  intaglio: (H) $130

HERBIN, Auguste
  French 1882-1960
  planographic: (H) $388
HERBINIER, A.
  posters: (H) $165
HERKENRATH, Peter
  b. 1900
  intaglio: (H) $128
HERLINE and HENZEL
  American mid-19th cent.
  planographic: (H) $715
HERMAN
  photo: (H) $1,530
HERMANN, Paul
  German b. 1864
  intaglio: (H) $110
  port/books: (L) $138; (H) $221
HERMES, Gertrude
  relief: (H) $283
HERMINE DAVID
  intaglio: (H) $90
HERMS, George
  contemporary
  port/books: (H) $110

HERNANDEZ MOMPO, Manuel
planographic: (H) $625
port/books: (H) $1,484

HERNANDEZ PIJOAN, Juan
planographic: (H) $357

HERREROS, Enrique
intaglio: (H) $51

HERRING, Ben (after)
intaglio: (H) $39

HERRING, J. (Sr.) (after)
generic: (H) $825

HERRING, J.F. (after)
intaglio: (L) $65; (H) $109

HERRING, J.F.
intaglio: (H) $605

HERRING, John Frederick (after)
intaglio: (H) $360

HERRING, John Frederick (Sr.) (after)
intaglio: (H) $458

HERRING, John Frederick (Sr.)
British 1795-1865
intaglio: (L) $380; (H) $551
planographic: (L) $220; (H) $1,045

HESLER, Alexander
photo: (L) $440; (H) $1,650

HESLER, Alexander and George
AYRES
photo: (H) $4,840

HESS, Allen
photo: (H) $380

HEYBOER, Anton
contemporary
intaglio: (L) $202; (H) $569

HEYDECKER, Joe
b. 1916
photo: (H) $1,148

HEYDEN (after BRUEGHEL)
generic: (H) $330

HEYMAN, Abigail
photo: (H) $200

HIBEL, Edna
American b. 1917
planographic: (L) $303; (H) $413
mixed-media: (L) $165; (H) $1,155

HICKEN, Philip Burnham
American b. 1910
stencil: (H) $132

HIGGINS, Eugene
American 1874-1958
intaglio: (H) $22

HIGHMORE, Anthony (after)
intaglio: (H) $7,998

HILL, David Octavius and Robert
ADAMSON
photo: (L) $1,100; (H) $2,750

HILL, Henry
intaglio: (L) $88; (H) $88

HILL, J.W. (after)
intaglio: (H) $770
planographic: (H) $468
port/books: (H) $1,760

HILL, James T. (after)
American 19th/20th cent.
planographic: (H) $55

HILL, John (after William G. WALL)
American
intaglio: (H) $3,300

HILL, John Henry
American 1839-1922
intaglio: (H) $1,045

HILL, Polly Knip
American b. 1900
intaglio: (H) $55

HILL and CO. and GRAY
LITHOGRAPHY CO.
planographic: (H) $110

HILLERS, John K. (attrib.)
photo: (H) $385

HILSDORF, Jacob
German 1872-1916
photo: (H) $2,150

HILTON, Hedley
British 20th cent.
intaglio: (H) $275

HILTON, Roger
planographic: (H) $147

HINCKS, William
Irish 18th cent.
intaglio: (H) $825

HINE, Lewis
American 1874-1940
photo: (L) $880; (H) $24,200

HIRO
photo: (H) $1,000

HIROSHI, Yoshida
Japanese 1876-1950
relief: (H) $330

HIROSHIGE
relief: (L) $110; (H) $303

HIROSHIGE
Japanese 1797-1858
relief: (L) $22; (H) $28

HIROSHIGE, (II)
relief: (H) $55

HIROSHIGE, Ando (after)
relief: (H) $94

HIROSHIGE, Ichiryusai
Japanese School 1797-1858
relief: (L) $243; (H) $243

HIROSHIGE, Utagawa (Ando)
Japanese 1797-1858
relief: (L) $147; (H) $990

HIROSIGE, (after)
relief: (H) $17

HIRSCH, Joseph
American 1910-1981
planographic: (L) $154; (H) $825

HIRSCH, Stefan
1899-1964
planographic: (H) $66

HIRSCHFELD, Al
American b. 1903
intaglio: (H) $247
planographic: (L) $83; (H) $209
port/books: (H) $1,045

HIRSCHVOGEL, Augustin
1503-1553
intaglio: (L) $1,846; (H) $15,708

HIRTZ and PAUL-MARTIAL
posters: (H) $220

HISCOCKS AND CO., F.E.
planographic: (L) $122; (H) $478

HITCHCOCK, Harold
English b. 1914
planographic: (H) $220

HOBBS, Morris Henry
American b. 1892
intaglio: (H) $66

HOCKNEY, David
English b. 1937
intaglio: (L) $545; (H) $29,579
stencil: (H) $4,125
planographic: (L) $239; (H) $88,000
mixed-media: (L) $1,359; (H) $110,000
photo-repro: (L) $220; (H) $629
port/books: (L) $2,750; (H) $8,250
photo: (L) $385; (H) $5,500
others: (L) $1,392; (H) $7,150
generic: (L) $1,650; (H) $7,150

HODAKA, Yoshida
Japanese 20th cent.
stencil: (H) $165

HODGES, W.P. (after)
intaglio: (H) $99

HODGKIN, Howard
English b. 1932
intaglio: (L) $770; (H) $4,226
stencil: (L) $2,300; (H) $2,475
planographic: (L) $770; (H) $4,971
mixed-media: (L) $770; (H) $2,750
port/books: (H) $4,367

HODGKINS, Frances
planographic: (H) $1,914

HODLER, Ferdinand
Swiss 1853-1918
planographic: (H) $199
photo-repro: (L) $233; (H) $907

HOEHME, Gerhard
1920-1989
intaglio: (L) $319; (H) $1,587
stencil: (H) $269
posters: (L) $128; (H) $128

HOESEN, Beth van
intaglio: (L) $165; (H) $220

HOFER, Karl
German 1878-1956
intaglio: (H) $993
planographic: (L) $426; (H) $1,135
port/books: (H) $6,737

HOFFMAN, Irwin D.
American b. 1901
intaglio: (L) $50; (H) $55
planographic: (H) $88

HOFFMASTER, Maud Miller
American 1829-1886
intaglio: (H) $88

HOFKUNST, Alfred
intaglio: (H) $1,043

HOGALUND, Andrew
American 20th cent.
stencil: (H) $17

HOGARTH, William
English 1697-1764
intaglio: (L) $55; (H) $4,320

HOGARTH, William (after)
intaglio: (L) $83; (H) $176

HOGGARD, Paul
stencil: (H) $87

HOHLWEIN, Ludwig
1874-1949
posters: (L) $1,023; (H) $2,090
port/books: (H) $3,947

HOKUSAI
relief: (L) $72; (H) $138

HOKUSAI, Katsushika
Japanese 1760-1849
relief: (L) $103; (H) $1,705

HOLBEIN, Hans (the younger)
1497/98-1543
relief: (H) $4,400
port/books: (H) $3,520

HOLBEIN, Hans (after)
German 1497-1543
intaglio: (L) $28; (H) $110

HOLGATE, Edwin Headley
Canadian 1892-1977
stencil: (H) $170
relief: (H) $2,379

HOLLAND, Harold
photo: (H) $66

HOLLAR, Wenzel
1607-1677
intaglio: (L) $165; (H) $4,144
port/books: (H) $1,430

HOLLENBERG, Felix
1868-1945
intaglio: (H) $107

HOLLICK, Ruth
photo: (H) $217

HOLMES, James (after)
intaglio: (H) $139

HOLMES, Silas A.
photo: (H) $1,100

HOLTZ, Karl
1899-1978
planographic: (L) $922; (H) $1,135

HOMANN, Johann Baptist
1664-1724
intaglio: (L) $223; (H) $260

HOMER, Winslow
American 1836-1910
intaglio: (L) $3,850; (H) $29,700
relief: (H) $77
planographic: (H) $28,600

HONDA, Kazuhisa
Japanese b. 1948
intaglio: (L) $110; (H) $385
port/books: (L) $358; (H) $880

HONE, John Ramsey McGregor (Mac)
b. 1920
relief: (H) $267

HOOGHE, Romeyn de
1645-1708
intaglio: (H) $3,072
port/books: (H) $245

HOOKER, William
intaglio: (H) $165

HOOVER, Joseph, Publisher
American ac. 1870-1900
planographic: (H) $83

HOPFER, Daniel
German c. 1470-1536
intaglio: (L) $550; (H) $12,174

HOPFER, Hieronymus
c. 1500-c. 1563
intaglio: (H) $4,555

HOPFER, Lambert
ac. early 16th cent.
intaglio: (H) $97

HOPKINS, Edna Boies
American 1872-1937
relief: (L) $605; (H) $1,650

HOPKINS, Thurston
b. 1913
photo: (H) $115

HOPPER, Edward
American 1882-1967
intaglio: (L) $4,400; (H) $38,500

HOPPNER, John (after)
intaglio: (H) $112

HORENSTEIN, Henry
photo: (H) $280

HORNBY, Lester George
American 1882-1956
intaglio: (L) $66; (H) $110

HORNYANSKY, Nicholas
intaglio: (L) $161; (H) $534

HORSBURGH, James, Publisher
British 19th cent.
intaglio: (H) $39

HORST, Horst P.
American b. 1906
photo: (L) $550; (H) $14,300

HORVAT, Frank
photo: (H) $605

HOSOE, Eikoh
photo: (L) $330; (H) $1,650

HOST, Oluf
planographic: (L) $185; (H) $320

HOUBRAKEN, Jacobus
Dutch 1698-1780
intaglio: (L) $121; (H) $198

HOUBRAKENIS
intaglio: (H) $72

HOUSTON, James
planographic: (H) $54

HOWARTH, Albany E.
British 20th cent.
intaglio: (L) $28; (H) $110

HOWE, Graham
photo: (H) $170

HOWEN, David R.
planographic: (H) $66

HOWITT, Samuel (after)
port/books: (H) $566

HOWLETT, Robert
1831-1858
photo: (L) $536; (H) $5,304

HOYNINGEN-HUENE, George
1900-1968
photo: (L) $612; (H) $13,359

HRDLICKA, Alfred
b. 1928
intaglio: (H) $261
photo-repro: (H) $213
port/books: (L) $327; (H) $1,277

HUBBUCH, Hilde
photo: (H) $629

HUBBUCH, Karl
1891-1979
intaglio: (H) $2,340

HUBER, Rudolf C.
photo: (H) $1,147

HUBER, Wolf
German 1490-1553
relief: (L) $21,206; (H) $40,841

HUDSON, Thomas (after)
English 1701-1779
intaglio: (H) $88

HUET, Jean Baptiste (after)
intaglio: (L) $33; (H) $445
planographic: (H) $248

HUET, Paul
French 1803-1869
intaglio: (H) $582

HUFFAM, T.W.
English School 19th cent.
intaglio: (H) $99

HUFFMAN, L.A.
photo: (H) $275

HUGGINS, William J.
English 1781-1845
planographic: (H) $468

HUGNET, Georges
photo: (H) $4,180

HUGO, Charles
French 1826-1871
photo: (L) $1,760; (H) $6,808

HUGO, Leopold
photo: (L) $275; (H) $660

HUGO, Valentine
intaglio: (H) $1,022

HUGON, Roland
posters: (H) $247

HUGUENIN-LASSAUGUETTE, Fritz
1842-1926
planographic: (H) $232

HULL, Edward
port/books: (H) $132

HULLMANDEL, C.
planographic: (H) $193

HUMPSTEAD, Joseph H.
intaglio: (H) $11

HUNDERTWASSER, Friedensreich
Austrian b. 1928
intaglio: (L) $2,467; (H) $4,648
stencil: (L) $555; (H) $21,834
relief: (L) $550; (H) $5,493
planographic: (L) $1,881; (H) $8,337
mixed-media: (L) $1,399; (H) $3,303
port/books: (H) $13,397
generic: (H) $1,484

HUNSIC, R.
posters: (H) $412

HUNT, Bryan
American b. 1947
port/books: (H) $3,300

HUNT, Charles (after Ben Herring)
planographic: (H) $1,650

HUNT, Charles
intaglio: (H) $580
port/books: (H) $353

HUNTER, F. Leo
intaglio: (H) $55

HUNTER, William
intaglio: (H) $87

HUNTINGTON, E.
intaglio: (H) $385

HUNTLEY, Victoria Hudson
American b. 1900
planographic: (H) $6

HURD, Peter
American 1904-1984
stencil: (H) $275
planographic: (L) $28; (H) $303

HURLEY, Frank
photo: (H) $6,050

HURLIMAN, J.
intaglio: (H) $425

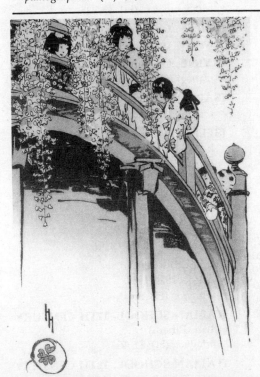

Helen Hyde (1868-1919) spent most of her artistic life in Japan, where she studied the intricate printmaking methods of the Japanese. *Moon Bridge at Kameido* was printed in 1914 shortly before she returned permanently to the United States. Its cherry blossoms and graceful bridge are typical of her work. (Helen H. Hyde, *Moon Bridge at Kameido*, woodcut printed in colors on tissue, 13 $\frac{3}{8}$ x 8 $\frac{7}{8}$ inches, Skinner, March 13, 1992, $660)

HURRAY, Alfred Heber
American 1877-1954
intaglio: (H) $110

HURRELL, George
b. 1904
port/books: (L) $2,420; (H) $6,050
photo: (L) $247; (H) $3,300

HURST and ROBINSON, Publisher
planographic: (H) $812

HUTCHINSON, H.S., Publisher (after Benjamin Russell)
American 19th/20th cent.
photo-repro: (H) $165

HUTTER, Wolfgang
b. 1928
port/books: (H) $962

HUTTY, Alfred H.
American 1877/78-1954
intaglio: (H) $110

HYDE, Helen
American 1868-1919
intaglio: (L) $330; (H) $358
relief: (L) $193; (H) $880
planographic: (H) $495

IACURTO, Francisco
Canadian School b. 1908
stencil: (L) $186; (H) $6,496

IANELLI, Alfonso
Italian 1888-1965
stencil: (L) $110; (H) $330

IBELS, Henri Gabriel
intaglio: (H) $221

IBELS, L.
intaglio: (H) $54
planographic: (H) $96

ICART, Louis
French 1888-1950
intaglio: (L) $220; (H) $7,920
planographic: (H) $1,250
photo-repro: (L) $154; (H) $220
port/books: (H) $1,980
generic: (L) $1,800; (H) $1,900

ICART, Louis (after)
intaglio: (H) $83

ICHIRO, Takushima
intaglio: (H) $11

ICKOVIC, Paul
photo: (H) $950

IGNATOVICH, Boris
photo: (H) $2,420

ILSTED, Peter
1861-1933
intaglio: (L) $37; (H) $4,362

IMHOFF, Joseph
planographic: (H) $165

IMMENDORF, Jorg
German b. 1945
relief: (H) $3,246
planographic: (L) $148; (H) $482

INDIANA, Robert
American b. 1928
stencil: (L) $165; (H) $4,180
relief: (H) $935
planographic: (L) $370; (H) $444
posters: (H) $220
port/books: (L) $3,300; (H) $7,700

INGRES, Jean Auguste Dominique
French 1780-1867
planographic: (H) $5,225

INNESS, George (after)
generic: (H) $17

IRVINE, Gregory
planographic: (H) $122

ISABEY, E. (after)
intaglio: (H) $257

ISELI, Rolf
b. 1934
planographic: (H) $562
photo-repro: (H) $497
port/books: (H) $3,762

ISHULUTAQ, Eleeseepee
Continental b. 1925
mixed-media: (H) $146

ISRAELS, Josef
Dutch 1824-1911
intaglio: (H) $660

ITALIAN SCHOOL, 17TH CENTURY
(attrib. Ribera)
intaglio: (H) $1,464

ITALIAN SCHOOL, 18TH CENTURY
intaglio: (H) $697

Louis Icart's polished prints of American and French beauties were wildly popular in the U.S. from 1920 to 1940. Entirely self-taught, he experimented with printing methods and frequently used a combination of hand-colored drypoint and etchings. During his lifetime he created more than 1,000 subjects. Each image was printed in an edition of 500. (Louis Icart, *Miss America*, oval hand-colored etching, 21 ½ x 17 ½ inches, Goldberg, May 9, 1992, $1,650)

ITALIAN SCHOOL, 19TH CENTURY
intaglio: (L) $171; (H) $320

ITALIENISCHER MEISTER
c. 1550
intaglio: (H) $1,514

ITIER, Jules
photo: (H) $884

ITTEN, Johannes
1888-1967
stencil: (H) $1,049

ITURBIDE, Graciela
photo: (L) $660; (H) $825

IZIS
1911-1980
photo: (L) $1,052; (H) $1,980

JAAR, Alfredo
b. 1956
photo: (H) $5,500

JACHNA, Josef
photo: (H) $250

JACK, Kenneth William
stencil: (L) $87; (H) $157
planographic: (L) $174; (H) $174

JACKSON, A.Y.
planographic: (H) $303

JACKSON, Bob (Robert H.)
photo: (H) $4,125

JACKSON, J. (after)
intaglio: (H) $160

JACKSON, John (after)
planographic: (H) $101

JACKSON, John Baptist
1701-1780
relief: (L) $707; (H) $3,300

JACKSON, William Henry
1843-1942
photo: (L) $440; (H) $3,520

JACKSON, William Henry, and Co.
photo: (H) $1,210

JACOABE, Johann
1733-1797
intaglio: (H) $1,806

JACOB, Walter
1893-1964
relief: (H) $2,995

JACOBE, Johann
1733-1797
intaglio: (H) $785

JACOBI, Lotte
b. Germany, d.U.S. 1896-1990
port/books: (L) $825; (H) $3,300
photo: (L) $990; (H) $1,540

JACOBSEN, Egill
planographic: (H) $130

JACOBSEN, Georg
planographic: (H) $151

JACOBSEN, Robert
intaglio: (L) $833; (H) $847
relief: (H) $190
port/books: (L) $555; (H) $1,035

JACOTTET, Jean
b. 1806
planographic: (L) $100; (H) $133

JACOULET, Paul
b. Japan, French 1902-1960
relief: (L) $193; (H) $1,045

JACQUE, Charles
French 1813-1894
intaglio: (L) $44; (H) $220

JACQUE, Frederic
French 20th cent.
intaglio: (H) $66

JACQUE
intaglio: (H) $155

JACQUEMIN, Andre
intaglio: (L) $82; (H) $342

JACQUETTE, Yvonne
American b. 1934
relief: (H) $2,420

JAFFEE, N. Jay
photo: (L) $192; (H) $220

JAHAN, Pierre
photo: (H) $4,125

JAILLOT, Alexis Hubert
1632-1712
intaglio: (H) $4,370

JAMES, Christopher
photo: (H) $600

JAMES, Clifford Boucher
English d. 1913
intaglio: (H) $193

JAMES, Stewart Ross
American 20th cent.
relief: (L) $55; (H) $303

JANCO, Marcel
Israeli b. 1895
planographic: (H) $110

JANINET, Jean Francois
1752-1814
intaglio: (L) $303; (H) $13,352
planographic: (H) $413

JANSEM, Jean
b. Armenia, French b. 1920
planographic: (L) $110; (H) $1,359

JANSEN, Arno
German b. 1938
photo: (L) $287; (H) $1,075

JANSEN, Franz Maria
1885-1958
port/books: (H) $1,756

JANSONS, Ivars
generic: (L) $87; (H) $122

JANSSEN, Horst
b. 1929
intaglio: (L) $213; (H) $2,553
relief: (L) $2,482; (H) $16,038
planographic: (L) $851; (H) $1,277
port/books: (H) $233

JANTHUR, Richard
1883-1956
port/books: (H) $2,695

JAQUES, Bertha E.
American 1863-1941
relief: (L) $138; (H) $165

JARDIN, Karel du
Dutch 1622-1675
intaglio: (L) $55; (H) $328

JARDINE
intaglio: (H) $220

JARDINE, Sir William and Prideaux
John SELBY
19th cent.
port/books: (H) $165

JARDINE, Sir William, Editor
19th cent.
intaglio: (L) $44; (H) $660
port/books: (H) $204

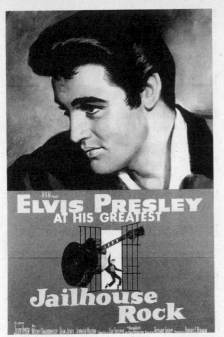

ELVIS PRESLEY
AT HIS GREATEST

Jailhouse
Rock

There are many subcategories of movie poster collecting. The most desirable posters for the general public are *Casablanca*, *The Wizard of Oz*, *Gone With the Wind*, and *Citizen Kane*. For science fiction buffs, the most sought-after posters are *Forbidden Planet* and *The Day the Earth Stood Still*. For many baby-boomers, posters of Elvis Presley are considered highly desirable. There are 200-300 copies in existence of *Jailhouse Rock*, and the poster can sell from $500 to $1,200. This copy sold for a high $2,200. (*Jailhouse Rock*, one-sheet poster, A condition, 41 x 27 inches, Camden House, June 7, 1992, $2,200)

JAVACHEFF, Christo
b. 1935
stencil: (H) $677

JAWLENSKY, Alexej von
German 1864-1941
port/books: (H) $29,150

JAY, William, Charles BEDENBERG, and William EMERSON (pub.)
late 19th cent.
intaglio: (H) $193

JAZET, (after Montpazet)
generic: (H) $220

JEBOULT, Edward
port/books: (H) $99

JEFFRIES, Kathleen G.
intaglio: (H) $28

JEGHER, Christoffel
1596-1653
relief: (L) $365; (H) $11,781

JENKINS, Paul
American b. 1923
planographic: (H) $25,672
photo-repro: (H) $193

JENNINGS, Payne
photo: (H) $589

JENSEN, Alfred
American 1903-1981
port/books: (H) $18,651

JENSEN, Bill
American b. 1945
port/books: (H) $2,200

JEREMENKO, Ted
American b. Yugoslavia 1938
stencil: (L) $605; (H) $1,045

JERZY, Richard
planographic: (H) $39

JINGKIND, J.B.
intaglio: (H) $899

JIRLOW, Lennart
b. 1936
planographic: (L) $675; (H) $2,919

JOCASCIO, Semanick
mixed-media: (H) $25

JOHN, Augustus
British 1878-1961
intaglio: (L) $385; (H) $671

JOHN, Augustus (after)
British 1878-1961
planographic: (H) $66

JOHNNY, J.
stencil: (H) $88

JOHNS, Jasper
American b. 1930
intaglio:	(L)	$3,575;	(H) $165,000
stencil:	(L)	$1,980;	(H) $49,500
relief:			(H) $15,400
planographic:	(L)	$192;	(H) $46,200
photo-repro:	(L)	$315;	(H) $3,850
port/books:	(L)	$2,750;	(H) $33,000
others:	(L)	$15,400;	(H) $20,336

JOHNSON
intaglio: (H) $174

JOHNSON, E. Bourrough
planographic: (H) $41

JOHNSON, Edwin G.
American 19th/20th cent.
port/books: (H) $220

JOHNSON, George Howard
American c. 1823-1879
photo: (H) $10,450

JOHNSON, J.
port/books: (L) $330; (H) $605

JOHNSON, Margaret Kennard
intaglio: (L) $110; (H) $165

JOHNSTON, Alfred Cheney
1884-1971
photo: (L) $660; (H) $3,080

JOHONNOT, Ralph Helm
relief: (H) $110

JOLIN, Einar
1890-1976
planographic: (L) $591; (H) $2,724

JONES, Adrian (after)
photo-repro: (H) $248

JONES, Allen
British b. 1937
stencil:		(H) $545
planographic:	(L) $472;	(H) $674
mixed-media:		(H) $780
port/books:		(H) $1,650

JONES, Bradley
American 1944-1989
planographic: (H) $193

JONES, Charles
photo: (L) $1,375; (H) $2,947

JONES, Inigo
port/books: (H) $4,603

JONES, John
intaglio: (H) $550

JONES, Lawrence
American 20th cent.
planographic: (H) $165

JONES, Myron
stencil: (H) $83

JONES, Pirkle (photographer)
port/books: (H) $2,090

JONES, Rev. Calvert R.
ac. 1840s
photo: (L) $393; (H) $7,858

JONGKIND, Johan Barthold
Dutch 1819-1891
intaglio: (L) $321; (H) $2,381

JONSON, Jim
American 20th cent.
planographic: (H) $110

JONSSON, Lars
planographic: (H) $945

JOPLING, Frederick Waistell
intaglio: (H) $316
port/books: (H) $437

JORDAN, Jack
American b. 1925
relief: (H) $220

JORN, Asger
Danish 1914-1973
intaglio:	(L) $296;	(H)	$1,889
relief:	(L) $111;	(H)	$1,988
planographic:	(L) $377;	(H)	$8,748
posters:	(L) $339;	(H)	$527
port/books:	(L) $709;	(H)	$17,894

JOSSET, Lawrence
intaglio: (H) $132

JOURDAIN, Francis
intaglio: (H) $80

JOUVE, Paul
French 1880-1973
intaglio: (H) $4,125

JUANISIALUK
relief: (H) $156

JUDD, Donald
American b. 1928
intaglio: (L) $330; (H) $715
port/books: (L) $2,860; (H) $3,300

JUDSON, Jane Berry
American 20th cent.
relief: (H) $605

JUKES, Francis
intaglio: (L) $142; (H) $2,417

JULES, Mervin
American b. 1912
relief: (H) $88

JUNG, Moriz
German b. 1865
planographic: (L) $220; (H) $220

JUNGERE, Hans Holbein der
1497/1498-1543
relief: (L) $2,513; (H) $4,084

JUNKER, Leo Helmholz
American 1882-1974
intaglio: (L) $11; (H) $55
planographic: (H) $11

KAEMPF
posters: (H) $302

KAHLER, Carl
Austrian/American b. 1855
photo-repro: (L) $348; (H) $391

KAHLO, Frida
Mexican 1910-1954
planographic: (H) $44,000

KAHN, Max
American b. 1903
planographic: (H) $33

KAIGETSUDO
relief: (H) $165

KAINEN, Jacob
American b. 1909
planographic: (L) $450; (H) $500

KAISER, H.G.
photo: (H) $77

KAISER, Raffi
Israeli contemporary
planographic: (H) $110
port/books: (L) $132; (H) $330

KAKS, Olle
planographic: (H) $598

KALES, Arthur F.
photo: (L) $990; (H) $1,100

KALINOWSKI, Horst Egon
b. 1924
intaglio: (H) $227

KALISCHER
posters: (H) $132

KALMAN, Bela
photo: (H) $200

KALVAK, Helen
b. 1901
relief: (L) $161; (H) $184

KANAGA, Consuelo
photo: (H) $990

KANANGINAK, Pootoogook
b. 1935
intaglio: (L) $184; (H) $184
relief: (L) $230; (H) $345

KANDINSKY, Wassily (after)
planographic: (H) $110

KANDINSKY, Wassily
Russian 1866-1944
intaglio: (H) $4,959
relief: (L) $715; (H) $1,430
planographic: (L) $248; (H) $12,710

KANOLDT, Alexander
1881-1939
planographic: (H) $1,188

KAPLAN, Anatoli L.
1902-1979
port/books: (H) $2,408

KAPLAN, Jerome E.
American b. 1920
planographic: (H) $88

KAPPEL, Philip
American b. 1901
intaglio: (H) $121

KAR, Ida
English 1909-1974
photo: (H) $2,860

KAR-MI
posters: (L) $110; (H) $165

KARLSSON, C.
stencil: (H) $675

KARPIK, Solomon
b. 1947
relief: (H) $129

KARSCH, Joachim
1897-1945
generic: (H) $340

KARSH, Yousuf
b. 1908
photo: (L) $660; (H) $4,675

KART, E.R.
intaglio: (L) $11; (H) $33

KASEBIER, Gertrude
1852-1934
photo: (L) $605; (H) $4,620

KASIMAKIS, N.A.
American 20th cent.
planographic: (H) $28

KASIMIR, Hoernes Tanna
Austrian b. 1887
intaglio: (H) $523

KASIMIR, Luigi
Aus./American 1881-1962
intaglio: (L) $33; (H) $1,210
port/books: (H) $1,732

KASIMIR, Robert
b. Vienna 1914
intaglio: (L) $28; (H) $330

KASIMIR-HOERNES, Tanna
American 20th cent.
intaglio: (L) $165; (H) $220

KASTEN, Barbara
photo: (L) $1,320; (H) $1,760

KATSUKAWA, Shunsho
relief: (H) $61

KATZ, Alex
American b. 1927
intaglio: (H) $8,250
stencil: (L) $358; (H) $9,680
planographic: (L) $825; (H) $4,400

KAUFFMAN, Angelica
Swiss 1740-1807
intaglio: (H) $1,386

KAUFFMANN, Angelica (after)
intaglio: (H) $445

KAUFFMANN, John
1864-1942
photo: (L) $174; (H) $609

KAUFMAN, Edwin
planographic: (H) $11

KAUPFERMAN, Moshe
American contemporary
planographic: (H) $28

KAUS, Max
1891-1977
stencil: (H) $426

KAWANO, K.
relief: (H) $33

KEATS
intaglio: (H) $165

KEEL, T. Nova
Continental b. 1911
stencil: (H) $170

KEENAN, Larry (Jr.)
photo: (L) $193; (H) $550

KEETMAN, Peter
German b. 1916
photo: (L) $287; (H) $2,150

KEIFF, Linda de
stencil: (H) $61

KEIL, Hugo
photo: (H) $104

KEILEY, Joseph
1869-1914
photo: (H) $1,100

KEITH, Elizabeth
English 1887-1956
relief: (L) $110; (H) $468

KELLER, Ernst
Swiss b. 1891
posters: (H) $166

KELLER, Henry
American 1870-1949
intaglio: (L) $22; (H) $220
planographic: (L) $33; (H) $165

KELLEY, Tom
photo: (H) $1,375

KELLOGG
planographic: (H) $88

KELLOGG, E.B. and E.C., Publishers
planographic: (H) $550
port/books: (H) $143

KELLOGG and COMSTOCK,
Publishers
planographic: (L) $17; (H) $95

KELLOGG and WHITING
generic: (H) $193

KELLY, Ellsworth
American b. 1923
intaglio: (H) $3,850
stencil: (L) $770; (H) $2,200
planographic: (L) $990; (H) $8,800
port/books: (H) $147
others: (H) $9,350

KELLY, John
intaglio: (H) $413

KELLY, Thomas
generic: (H) $77

KELLY and SONS, Publishers
planographic: (H) $660

KELLY, Publisher, Thomas (Charles
Severin, Lithographer)
planographic: (H) $385

KEMPF, Franz
planographic: (H) $70

KENNA, Michael
photo: (L) $330; (H) $2,090

KENNEDY, David Michael
photo: (H) $300

KENNINGTON, Eric H.
relief: (H) $387

KENOJUAK, Ashevak
b. 1927
stencil: (H) $368

KENT, Melanie Taylor
American b.c. 1950
planographic: (H) $2,310

KENT, Norman
American 1903-1972
relief: (H) $161

KENT, Rockwell
American 1882-1971
intaglio: (L) $330; (H) $3,300
relief: (L) $55; (H) $2,420
planographic: (L) $165; (H) $1,100
mixed-media: (H) $1,430

KENT, Thomas (photographer)
1863-1936
port/books: (H) $1,186

KEPES, Gyorgy
American b. Hungary 1906
photo: (L) $323; (H) $660

KEPETS, Hugh
American b. 1946
intaglio: (H) $50

KERG, Theo
Luxembourger b. 1909
planographic: (H) $33

KERN, Haim
German b. 1930
planographic: (H) $33

KERR, Illingworth
1905-1989
relief: (L) $92; (H) $293
planographic: (H) $184

KERTESZ, Andre
Hungarian 1894-1985
photo: (L) $751; (H) $53,044

KESSELS, Willy
1898-1974
photo: (H) $495

KESTING, Edmund
German 1892-1970
photo: (L) $645; (H) $6,808

KETCHUM, Robert Glenn
photo: (II) $300

KIDDER, Harvey
American 20th cent.
intaglio: (H) $55

KIECOL, Hubert
b. 1950
relief: (H) $532
port/books: (H) $213

KIFFER, Charles
b. 1902
planographic: (H) $2,937

KILBOURNE, S.A.
planographic: (L) $55; (H) $418
generic: (H) $330

KIMBEI, Kusakabe (photographer)
port/books: (H) $1,148

KIMFF, Linda Le
planographic: (H) $61

KING, Charles Benjamin
American 1785-1862
planographic: (L) $455; (H) $704

Andre Kertesz (b. 1894) photographed this dramatic shot of Mondrian's studio in 1926 shortly after his arrival in Paris. The play between pattern and deep space is typical of his photos. In 1992 a small, *carte-postale* size, vintage 1926 print of *Chez Mondrian* reportedly sold in a private deal for $250,000. Collectors estimate that there are only six of these vintage postcard-size prints. This same image, in a larger format and printed at a later date, sold at Christie's for $3,530. (Andre Kertesz, *Chez Mondrian*, gelatin silver print, 9 ¾ x 7 ¼ inches, Christie-New York, October 10, 1991, $3,520)

KING, Charles Bird (after)
planographic: (H) $2,310

KING, Samuel, Publisher
generic: (H) $83

KING, Sir George and Robert
PANTLING
port/books: (H) $7,700

KINGMAN, Dong
American b. 1911
planographic: (H) $220

KINGSBURY, John
photo: (H) $825

KINGSTON, Peter
stencil: (L) $217; (H) $261

KINGSTON, Rodger
photo: (H) $300

KINNEY, Troy
American 1871-1938
intaglio: (L) $66; (H) $165

KIP, Johannes and John HARRIS
intaglio: (H) $1,160

KIPNISS, Robert
American b. 1931
planographic: (L) $99; (H) $412

KIRA, Hiromu
photo: (H) $880

KIRCHNER, Ernst Ludwig
German 1880-1938
intaglio: (L) $3,333; (H) $121,601
relief: (L) $15,079; (H) $501,455
planographic: (L) $20,028; (H) $310,424
port/books: (H) $205,669
photo: (H) $1,863

KIRKEBY, Per
Danish b. 1938
relief: (H) $1,157
planographic: (L) $264; (H) $301

KIRMSE, Marguerite
Anglo/American 1885-1954
intaglio: (L) $11; (H) $1,430

KISLING, Jean
intaglio: (H) $2,065

KITAJ, R. B.
American b. 1932
intaglio: (H) $143

KITAOKA, Fumio
planographic: (H) $248

KIYOKATA
  relief: (H) $165

KLAPHECK, Konrad
  b. 1935
  planographic: (L) $355; (H) $851

KLAUKE, Jurgen
  German b. 1943
  photo: (L) $430; (H) $8,242

KLEE, Paul
  Swiss 1879-1940
  intaglio: (L) $4,962; (H) $36,438
  planographic: (L) $248; (H) $62,085

KLEIBER, Hans
  American 1887-1967
  intaglio: (L) $66; (H) $825

KLEIN, Astrid
  German b. 1951
  photo: (L) $573; (H) $1,290

KLEIN, Deborah
  mixed-media: (L) $109; (H) $157

KLEIN, William
  b. 1928
  photo: (L) $990; (H) $2,161

KLEINSCHMIDT, Johann Jacob
  b. 1772
  intaglio: (H) $155

KLEINSCHMIDT, Paul
  German b. 1883
  intaglio: (L) $532; (H) $1,064

KLEMENT, Fon
  mixed-media: (H) $152

KLEMM, Walther
  1883-1957
  port/books: (H) $1,244

KLETT, Mark
  photo: (L) $660; (H) $850

KLIEMANN, Carl-Heinz
  b. 1924
  relief: (H) $213

KLIMT, Gustav
  Austrian 1862-1918
  port/books: (H) $3,300

KLINGER, Max
  German 1857-1920
  intaglio: (L) $220; (H) $27,489
  port/books: (L) $1,262; (H) $63,624

KLINKER, Orpha
  intaglio: (H) $110

KLOSS, Gene
  American b. 1903
  intaglio: (L) $193; (H) $1,430

KLOTZ, Lenz
  Swiss b. 1925
  intaglio: (H) $202

KNATHS, Karl
  American 1891-1971
  planographic: (H) $110

KNEE, Ernest
  photo: (H) $523

KNEFF, Thomas
  generic: (H) $28

KNELLER, G.
  intaglio: (L) $138; (H) $138

KNIE, Rolf
  planographic: (H) $1,766

KNIGHT, Laura
  intaglio: (H) $340

KNILLE, Otto (after)
  photo-repro: (H) $275

KNYFF, Leonard
  Dutch 1650-1721
  intaglio: (H) $770

KOBAYSHI, Kiyoko
  planographic: (L) $138; (H) $165

KOBKE, Christen
  intaglio: (H) $6,670

KOCOL, Mary
  photo: (H) $140

KOENIG, Franz Niklaus
  1765-1832
  intaglio: (L) $133; (H) $538

KOGAN, Moissej
  1879-1930
  relief: (H) $1,032

KOKOSCHKA, Oskar
  Austrian 1886-1980
  planographic: (L) $233; (H) $6,517
  port/books: (L) $2,530; (H) $3,764

KOLAR, Jiri
  Czechoslovakian b. 1919
  mixed-media: (H) $649

KOLBE, Carl Wilhelm
1759-1835
intaglio: (L) $1,205; (H) $2,928

KOLBE, Georg
German 1877-1947
intaglio: (H) $794

KOLLAR, Francois
photo: (H) $1,980

KOLLWITZ, Kathe
German 1867-1945

intaglio:	(L)	$55;	(H)	$57,193
relief:	(L)	$302;	(H)	$14,665
planographic:	(L)	$99;	(H)	$81,682
mixed-media:			(H)	$54,260
port/books:	(L)	$1,988;	(H)	$2,386

KOONS, Jeff
American b. 1955
planographic: (H) $6,050
photo: (H) $20,900

KOPPITZ, Prof. Rudolf
photo: (H) $522

KORAB, Karl
German b. 1937
stencil: (H) $48

KORLING, Torkel
photo: (H) $440

KORZULEWICZ, Monica
planographic: (H) $43

KOSA, E.J.
French
intaglio: (H) $165

KOSTYNIUK, Larry
intaglio: (H) $69

KOTHMAR, Hans
posters: (H) $110

KOUDELKA, Josef
b. 1938
photo: (L) $770; (H) $1,430

KOUNELLIS, Iannis
b. 1936
photo-repro: (H) $541

KOWALSKI, (after)
planographic: (H) $199

KRAGH-JACOBSEN, Bamse
planographic: (L) $93; (H) $93

Movie posters are a relatively new area of collecting. During the last five years, specialized sales of just movie posters have been held in New York and Los Angeles. Posters from the horror movies *Dracula, Frankenstein, Mummy, Bride of Frankenstein,* and *King Kong* are considered particularly desirable. One-sheet posters (27 x 41 inches) were used in the interior of theaters. Three-sheet posters (81 x 41 inches) and six-sheet posters (162 x 41 inches) were used outside the theater and are rare and seldom in good condition. In December 1992, a three-sheet *King Kong* poster from the collection of Bruce Hershenson set a record for a movie poster when it sold for $57,200. (*King Kong,* linen-backed poster, 81 x 41 inches, Christie's East, December 9, 1991, $57,200)

KRAUS, Gustaf Wilhelm
1804-1852
intaglio: (H) $1,392

KREIDOLF, Ernst
1863-1956
planographic: (H) $1,570

KRIEGHOFF, Cornelius
Canadian 1815-1872
planographic: (H) $388

KRIKHAAR, Herman
contemporary
planographic: (H) $634

KRIMS, Les
b. 1943
photo: (L) $200; (H) $275

KRIZ, Vilem
photo: (L) $248; (H) $825

KROJER, Tom
port/books: (H) $148

KROLL, Leon
American 1884-1974/75
planographic: (L) $165; (H) $385

KRONBERG, Louis
American 1872-1965
intaglio: (L) $55; (H) $275

KROYER, P.S.
intaglio: (H) $241

KRUGER, Barbara
American b. 1945
port/books: (H) $11,000
photo: (H) $17,600

KRUININGEN, Harrie van
intaglio: (H) $253
mixed-media: (H) $601

KRULL, Germaine
1897-1985
photo: (H) $1,290

KRUSCHNICK, Nicholas
American b. 1929
stencil: (H) $28

KRUSEMAN VAN ELTEN, Hendrik
Dirk
Dutch/American 1829-1904
intaglio: (L) $39; (H) $66

KRUSHENICK, Nicolas
stencil: (L) $83; (H) $215

KUBBOS, Eva
relief: (H) $157

KUBIN, Alfred
Austrian 1877-1959
planographic: (L) $142; (H) $888
port/books: (L) $390; (H) $1,403

KUBINYI, Kalman
American b. 1906
intaglio: (H) $44

KUBLER, Otto
American 20th cent.
intaglio: (L) $121; (H) $357

KUEHN, Heinrich
1866-1944
photo: (H) $4,400

KUHN, Walt
American 1877/80-1949
intaglio: (L) $88; (H) $303
planographic: (L) $522; (H) $605

KUKICH, D.R.
20th cent.
intaglio: (H) $110

KULLING, Ruedi and Atelier COHEN
posters: (H) $66

KUNICHIKA
relief: (H) $242

KUNICHIKA, (attrib.)
relief: (H) $250

KUNISADA
Japanese
relief: (L) $44; (H) $180

KUNISADA, Utagawa
Japanese 1786-1864
relief: (L) $88; (H) $523

KUNISADA, Utagawa (II)
relief: (H) $88

KUNISADA II, HIROSHIGE II
Japanese 19th cent.
relief: (H) $248

KUNITERU
Japanese
relief: (H) $248

KUNIYOSHI
relief: (L) $55; (H) $165

KUNIYOSHI, Utagawa
Japanese 1797-1861
relief: (L) $44; (H) $970

KUNIYOSHI, Yasuo
American 1893-1953
intaglio: (H) $2,000
planographic: (L) $880; (H) $16,500

KUNTZ, R. (after)
generic: (H) $825

KURELEK, William
1927-1977
planographic: (L) $415; (H) $2,115
photo-repro: (H) $460

KURELIK, William (after)
generic: (H) $11

KURODA, Aki
planographic: (H) $169

KURODA, Shigeki
intaglio: (L) $110; (H) $138

KURTZ
generic: (H) $110

KURZ, L.
planographic: (H) $193

KURZ and ALLISON, Publishers
c. 1880-1899
planographic: (L) $138; (H) $165

KURZWEIL, Maximilian
relief: (H) $935

KUSHNER, Robert
American b. 1949
intaglio: (L) $385; (H) $2,090

KVHITIA, Mikhail
Georgian 20th cent.
planographic: (H) $33

LA RUE, Warren de (Esq.)
1815-1889
port/books: (H) $2,090

LA VALLEY, Jonas Joseph
American 1858-1930
planographic: (H) $66

LAAGE, Wilhelm
1868-1930
relief: (H) $199

LAAR, van
port/books: (H) $1,650

LABORDE, Chas
intaglio: (H) $193

LABOUREUR, Jean Emile
French 1877-1943
intaglio: (L) $60; (H) $3,850
relief: (L) $321; (H) $5,292
planographic: (L) $374; (H) $4,693

Japan-born Yasuo Kuniyoshi was
an American painter and graphic
artist. His works from the 1930s
included still lifes and figure studies
of half-clad women. (Yasuo
Kuniyoshi, *Circus Performer Balanced
on a Ball*, 1930, lithograph on wove
paper, 14 x 10 ⅛ inches, Skinner,
September 6, 1991, $9,350)

LADELL, Edwin
planographic: (H) $215

LAHDE, G.L.
1765-1833
intaglio: (L) $284; (H) $359

LAIRESSE, Gerard de
Flemish 1641-1711
intaglio: (H) $574

LALIBERTE, Norman
planographic: (H) $194

LAM, Wifredo
Cuban 1902-1982
intaglio: (L) $248; (H) $4,950
planographic: (L) $283; (H) $2,860
port/books: (L)· $2,860; (H) $6,050

LAMBERT, Andre
French 20th cent.
intaglio: (H) $28

LAMBERT, Wifredo
relief: (H) $147

LAMY, John Peter
late 18/early 19th cent.
intaglio: (L) $133; (H) $273

LANCASTER, Percy
English 1878-1951
intaglio: (H) $111

LANCELEY, Colin
planographic: (L) $87; (H) $174

LANCES, Leo
1910-1981
photo: (H) $550

LANCRET, N. (after)
intaglio: (H) $238

LANCRET, Nicolas
French 1690-1743
port/books: (H) $2,203

LANDACRE, Paul
1893-1963
relief: (L) $220; (H) $1,650

LANDECK, Armin
b. 1905
intaglio: (L) $605; (H) $3,080

LANDSEER, Sir Edwin Henry (after)
intaglio: (L) $66; (H) $880

LANDSEER, Sir Edwin Henry
English 1802-1873
intaglio: (H) $183

LANDSEER, Thomas
British 1795-1880
intaglio: (H) $220

LANE, Fitz Hugh
American 1804-1865
planographic: (H) $2,310

LANE, Fitz Hugh, Lithographer
American 1805-1865
planographic: (H) $138

LANE, Lois
American contemporary
intaglio: (L) $330; (H) $385

LANGASKENS, Maurice
contemporary
intaglio: (H) $324

LANGE, Dorothea
American 1895-1965
photo: (L) $715; (H) $6,050

LANGE, Otto
1879-1944
relief: (L) $1,757; (H) $4,023
planographic: (H) $4,778

LANGMAID, Rowland
intaglio: (L) $116; (H) $381

LANSKOY, Andre
Russian/French 1902-1976
stencil: (H) $200
planographic: (L) $102; (H) $452
port/books: (H) $1,840

LANTELME
posters: (H) $132

LANYON, Peter
American 1918-1964
relief: (H) $66

LAPICQUE, Charles
French b. 1898
planographic: (L) $133; (H) $385

LAPINSKI, Tadeusz
Polish/American b. 1928
mixed-media: (L) $66; (H) $66

LAPORTE, G.H. (after)
intaglio: (H) $272

LARIONOV, Michel
Russian/American 1881-1964
stencil: (H) $143

LARRAZ, Julio
Cuban/American b. 1944
intaglio: (H) $2,200

LARSEN, Sally
port/books: (H) $4,400
photo: (L) $2,750; (H) $4,620

LARSSON, Carl
Swedish contemporary
intaglio: (H) $573
planographic: (L) $33; (H) $758

LARTIGUE, Jacques Henri
1894-1988
photo: (L) $330; (H) $2,371

LASANSKY, Mauricio L.
Argentinian/Amer. b. 1914
intaglio: (H) $165

LASINIO, Carlo
1759-1838
intaglio: (L) $2,386; (H) $2,386

LASSNIG, Maria
b. 1919
intaglio: (H) $395

LASZLO, Tarenski
intaglio: (H) $28

LATASTER, Ger
Dutch b. 1920
planographic: (H) $146

LATEGAN, Barry
b. 1935
photo: (H) $688

LATHROP, Dorothy P.
American b. 1891
planographic: (H) $83

LATHROP, William
intaglio: (H) $60

LAUBI
posters: (H) $1,045

LAUGHLIN, Clarence John
1905-1985
photo: (L) $550; (H) $1,980

LAUNAY, Nicolas de
b. 1792
intaglio: (H) $387

LAURENCIN, C.
intaglio: (H) $1,722

LAURENCIN, Marie
French 1883-1956
intaglio: (L) $121; (H) $8,265
stencil: (H) $248
planographic: (L) $605; (H) $9,900
port/books: (H) $3,850

LAURENCIN, Marie (after)
intaglio: (H) $3,137
planographic: (H) $427

LAURENS, Henri
French 1885-1954
intaglio: (H) $3,478
planographic: (H) $629

LAURINCE, N.
European 18th/19th cent.
intaglio: (H) $88

LAUTENSACK, Hanns
c. 1524-1565
intaglio: (L) $5,775; (H) $21,991

LAVATELLI, Carla
Italian 20th cent.
stencil: (H) $220

LAVENSON, Alma
photo: (L) $3,300; (H) $5,225

LAWRENCE, H.M.
posters: (H) $358

LAWRENCE, Jacob
American b. 1917
stencil: (H) $59
planographic: (H) $1,210

LAWRENCE, Jacob (after)
American b. 1917
stencil: (H) $770

LAWRENCE, Sir Tho.
intaglio: (H) $633

LAWSON, Robert
intaglio: (H) $192

LAWSON, Thomas W.
planographic: (H) $88

LAYORRE, G.
posters: (H) $110

LAYTIN, Peter
photo: (H) $160

LEHMAN, John
planographic: (H) $15

LEHMBRUCK, Wilhelm
German 1881-1919
intaglio: (H) $993
planographic: (L) $461; (H) $1,160

LEIBL, Wilhelm
German 1844-1900
intaglio: (L) $20; (H) $99

LEIBOWITZ, Freda
American 20th cent.
planographic: (H) $39

LEIGHTON, Alfred Crocker
1901-1965
planographic: (H) $312

LEIGHTON, Barbara (Barleigh)
1911-1986
relief: (L) $184; (H) $512

LEIGHTON, Clare Veronica Hope
Anglo/American 1901-1988
intaglio: (L) $99; (H) $504
relief: (L) $99; (H) $143

LEIGHTON, Frederic Lord (after)
intaglio: (H) $271
photo-repro: (H) $681

LEIRENS, Charles
Belgian 1888-1963
photo: (H) $2,150

LEISTIKOW, Walter
German 1865-1908
intaglio: (H) $55

LEIZEL, Balthasar Friedrich
late 18th cent.
intaglio: (H) $139

LELIEVRE, Philippe
intaglio: (H) $55

LEMERE, Bedford (and Co.)
(photographer)
port/books: (H) $593

LEMERICER, (after)
generic: (H) $1,100

LEMIEUX, Jean Paul
Canadian b. 1904
planographic: (H) $371

LEMMEL, Ch.
posters: (H) $220

LEMOS, Pedro J.
American 1882-1945
stencil: (H) $468

LENDVAI-DIRCKSEN, Erna
German 1883-1962
photo: (H) $573

LENNON, John
British 1940-1980
port/books: (H) $440

LEON, Edouard
French b. 1873
intaglio: (H) $33

LEON-DUFOUR, E.
planographic: (H) $110

LEONI, Ottavio
1574-1626
intaglio: (H) $1,268

LEPAPE, Georges
planographic: (H) $181

LEPERE, Auguste
intaglio: (L) $97; (H) $1,247
relief: (L) $165; (H) $665
port/books: (H) $1,320

LERFELDT, Hans Henrik
planographic: (H) $370

LERMITE, Schmid Jean Pierre (called)
1920-1977
stencil: (H) $199
planographic: (H) $455

LERNER, Nathan
American b. 1913
photo: (L) $480; (H) $550

LERSKI, Helmar
b. Germany 1871 d. 1956
photo: (L) $1,720; (H) $2,723

LESSER-URY
German 1861-1931
intaglio: (H) $3,688

LETENDRE, Rita
Canadian School b. 1929
stencil: (H) $97
planographic: (H) $49

LETI, Bruno
intaglio: (L) $52; (H) $87

LEUNIG, Michael
intaglio: (H) $209

LAZARS, Edinburgh, Publisher
intaglio: (L) $40; (H) $70

LAZI, Adolf
German 1884-1955
photo: (L) $502; (H) $1,290

LAZZELL, Blanche
American 1878-1956
planographic: (H) $3,520

LE BAS
French 18th cent.
port/books: (H) $275

LE BRETON, Louis (after)
South American d. 1866
intaglio: (H) $88

LE BRUN, Ch. (after)
intaglio: (H) $43

LE BRUN, Louise Elizabeth (after)
intaglio: (H) $202

LE CORBUSIER
Swiss/French 1887-1965
intaglio: (H) $2,200
stencil: (H) $1,204
planographic: (L) $413; (H) $3,533

LE GRAY, Gustave
French 1820-1882
photo: (L) $316; (H) $32,519

LE MONNIER, Henri
posters: (L) $165; (H) $275

LE PETIT, Alfred
posters: (H) $385

LEADER, Benjamin William (after)
intaglio: (H) $190

LEAR, Edward
English 1812-1888
planographic: (H) $220

LEBADANG
Vietnamese 20th cent.
intaglio: (H) $138
planographic: (H) $55

LEBAS, J.P.
intaglio: (H) $83

LEBEDEW, Wladimir
1891-1967
port/books: (H) $2,960

LECOMTE, Paul
1842-1920
posters: (H) $42

LECOMTE, Paul Emile
French b. 1877
intaglio: (H) $106

LEE, Bob
photo-repro: (H) $83

LEE, Doris
American b. 1905
planographic: (H) $400

LEE, Joe
port/books: (H) $523

LEE, Russell
photo: (L) $247; (H) $1,650

LEEUW, Willem van der
c. 1603-c. 1665
intaglio: (H) $533

LEFITTE, A.
intaglio: (H) $275

LEFORT, Henri
posters: (H) $125

LEFRANCQ, Marcel-G.
(photographer)
port/books: (H) $1,980

LEGER, Fernand
French 1881-1955
intaglio: (L) $1,053; (H) $2,643
stencil: (L) $275; (H) $4,620
planographic: (L) $187; (H) $13,557
port/books: (H) $4,374

LEGER, Fernand (after)
intaglio: (H) $647
stencil: (L) $121; (H) $605
planographic: (L) $110; (H) $1,882
photo-repro: (H) $303
port/books: (H) $11,015

LEGRAND, Louis
French 1863-1951
intaglio: (L) $180; (H) $1,247

LEGROS, Alphonse
French 1837-1911
intaglio: (L) $28; (H) $50

LEHEUTRE, G.
intaglio: (L) $70; (H) $280

LEUPIN, Herbert
Swiss b. 1916
posters: (H) $62

LEVAILLANT, Francois
port/books: (H) $1,315

LEVE, F.W.
French b. 1877
intaglio: (H) $73

LEVESON-MEARES, S.
stencil: (L) $43; (H) $139

LEVINE, Jack
American b. 1915
intaglio: (L) $110; (H) $935

LEVINE, Sherrie
American b. 1947
photo: (L) $2,860; (H) $7,150

LEVINE, Sherrie and Edward
WESTON
photo: (H) $3,300

LEVINSTEIN, Leon
1913-1988
photo: (H) $1,210

LEVINTHAL, David
photo: (H) $1,100

LEVITT, Helen
photo: (L) $1,540; (H) $1,980

LEVY, Leon (photographer)
port/books: (H) $495

LEWANDOWSKI, Edmund
b. 1914
stencil: (H) $242

LEWIS, Allen
relief: (H) $55

LEWIS, E.T.
intaglio: (H) $28

LEWIS, Martin
American 1883-1962
intaglio: (L) $660; (H) $19,800
planographic: (H) $4,400

LEWIS, Stanley
Canadian School b. 1930
relief: (H) $168

Roy Lichtenstein's early paintings were influenced by the Abstract Expressionists, but by the early 1960s he had developed his own style. His first one-man show was at the Leo Castelli Gallery in 1962. His series of large-scale comic-strip and comic-frame art emphasized primary colors and surface patterns. This lithograph of *Crying Girl* was published by the Leo Castelli Gallery in 1963. (Roy Lichtenstein, *Crying Girl, 1963*, offset lithograph in colors on wove paper, 18 $\frac{3}{16}$ x 24 $\frac{1}{8}$ inches, Christie-New York, May 11, 1992, $12,100)

Martin Lewis (1883-1962) was well known for his many prints of New York City street scenes. Night scenes were a favorite, allowing him to throw his forms into silhouette and show his proficiency at odd compositional effects. (Martin Lewis, *Subway Steps, 1930*, drypoint in brownish black on laid paper, 13 ¾ x 8 ⅞ inches, Christie-New York, November 4, 1991, $9,900)

LEWITT, Sol
American b. 1928
intaglio: (L) $263; (H) $1,786
stencil: (H) $3,740
planographic: (L) $220; (H) $275
port/books: (L) $2,310; (H) $26,400

LEYDEN, Lucas van
Dutch 1494-1533
intaglio: (L) $55; (H) $169,450
relief: (H) $113,883

LHOTE, Andre
French 1885-1962
planographic: (H) $357

LIANKO-ROBERTS, Marja
stencil: (H) $220

LIBERMANN, Max
German 1847-1935
intaglio: (H) $91

LICHTENSTEIN, Roy
American b. 1923
intaglio: (H) $3,080
stencil: (L) $550; (H) $5,280
relief: (L) $2,016; (H) $6,050
planographic: (L) $138; (H) $11,000
posters: (H) $935
mixed-media: (L) $1,210; (H) $37,400
photo-repro: (L) $148; (H) $12,100

port/books: (L) $9,941; (H) $19,800
others: (H) $1,760
generic: (L) $1,760; (H) $3,300

LIDSWELL, Quinton
intaglio: (H) $87

LIEBERMAN, Max
intaglio: (H) $22

LIEBERMAN, Sandy
American 20th cent.
planographic: (H) $110

LIEBERMANN, Max
German 1847-1935
intaglio: (L) $319; (H) $1,702
planographic: (L) $282; (H) $1,560
port/books: (H) $6,383

LIEBLING, Jerome
photo: (H) $320

LIEVENS, Jan
Dutch 1607-1672/74
intaglio: (L) $638; (H) $2,860

LIJN, Lillian
stencil: (H) $732

LINCOLN, Abraham
photo: (H) $825

LINCOLN, Edwin Hale
photo: (L) $100; (H) $160

LINDELL, Lage
stencil: (H) $810

LINDEN, Jean Jules
port/books: (L) $7,700; (H) $20,900

LINDENBERG
posters: (H) $412

LINDENMUTH, Tod
American 1885-1976
relief: (L) $165; (H) $770

LINDI
1904-1991
intaglio: (H) $139

LINDNER, Bernhard
relief: (H) $465

LINDNER, Ernest
1897-1988
planographic: (L) $195; (H) $244

LINDNER, Richard
German/American 1901-1978
stencil: (L) $465; (H) $1,322
planographic: (L) $165; (H) $2,982
mixed-media: (H) $649
photo-repro: (H) $418
port/books: (L) $2,475; (H) $6,383

LINDOE, Vivian
b. 1918
stencil: (H) $46

LINDSAY, Lionel Arthur
intaglio: (L) $209; (H) $870
relief: (L) $174; (H) $609
generic: (H) $70

LINDSAY, Norman Alfred
intaglio: (L) $1,044; (H) $1,392

LINDSAY, Sir Lionel Arthur
Austrian 1874-1961
intaglio: (H) $55

LINDSTROM, Bengt
Swedish b. 1935
intaglio: (H) $301
planographic: (H) $264
port/books: (H) $1,726

LINDT, John William
1845-1926
photo: (L) $122; (H) $261

LINK, O. Winston
b. 1914
photo: (L) $790; (H) $4,400

LINN, Kenneth A.
1903-1979
photo: (L) $660; (H) $1,430

LISMER, Arthur
Canadian 1885-1911
planographic: (H) $219

LISSITZKY, El
b. Poland 1890 d. Moscow 1941
planographic: (L) $4,620; (H) $110,000
photo: (L) $206; (H) $4,400

LIST, Herbert
1903-1975
photo: (L) $573; (H) $1,577

LITTLE, Phillip
American 1857-1942
intaglio: (H) $55

LITTLEFIELD, John Harrison (after)
American 1835-1902
intaglio: (H) $303

LITTON, Sidney
English 1887-1949
intaglio: (H) $50

LIVEMONT, Privat
1852-1936
planographic: (L) $303; (H) $2,750

LIVINGSTON, Beulah
photo: (H) $330

LIZARS, W.H., Publisher
intaglio: (L) $143; (H) $165

LJUNGGREN, Reinhold
planographic: (L) $405; (H) $675

LO SAVIO, Francesco
1935-1963
planographic: (H) $1,040

LOBDELL, Frank
intaglio: (H) $248

LOCHER, G.
intaglio: (H) $414

LOCHOM, Michiel van
Dutch 1601-1647
intaglio: (H) $110

LOCKE, Charles
planographic: (H) $138

LOCKE, Edwin
photo: (H) $358

LOCKE, Walter Ronald
American b. 1883
intaglio: (L) $55; (H) $66

LOCKER, Thomas
American 20th cent.
planographic: (H) $28

LODDIGES, Conrad (and Sons)
intaglio: (H) $275

LOEB, Dorothy
American b. 1887
planographic: (L) $275; (H) $523

LOEWENSBERG, Verena von
1912-1986
stencil: (H) $497
port/books: (H) $1,082

LOGAN, Robert Fulton
Canadian b. 1899
intaglio: (H) $83

LOHSE, Paul Richard
1902-1988
stencil: (H) $745

LOMBARD, Lambert (after)
intaglio: (H) $60

LOMBART, Pierre
intaglio: (H) $348

LONG, Sydney
intaglio: (H) $783

LONGABAUGH, Charles Oglesby
intaglio: (H) $88

LONGHI, Pietro (after)
1702-1785
port/books: (H) $17,431

LONGO, Robert
American b. 1953
planographic: (H) $11,015

LONGUEIL, J. de
intaglio: (H) $270

LORCH, Melchior
c. 1527-1583
intaglio: (H) $4,241
relief: (H) $928

LORD, Elyse Ashe
intaglio: (L) $192; (H) $743

LORENZ, Karl
b. 1888
port/books: (H) $3,560

LORING, John
American b. 1939
stencil: (H) $44

LORJOU, Bernard
French b. 1908
planographic: (H) $143

LORRAIN, Claude (Claude GELLEE)
French 1600-1682
intaglio: (L) $204; (H) $15,708
port/books: (H) $8,055

LORRAIN, Claude (Claude GELLEE)
(after)
intaglio: (L) $110; (H) $298

LORY, Gabriel
Swiss 1784-1846
intaglio: (L) $124; (H) $248

LORY, Gabriel (the younger)
Swiss 1784-1846
intaglio: (L) $787; (H) $2,733
port/books: (H) $23,014

LOSTUTTER, Robert
American contemp.
planographic: (L) $187; (H) $220

LOUTHERBOURG, P.J. de (after)
intaglio: (H) $267

LOUTTRE, Marc Antoine
relief: (L) $61; (H) $163

LOUYS, Jacob
Dutch 1595-after 1635
intaglio: (H) $110

LOVEJOY, Dr. Rupert S.
photo: (L) $412; (H) $1,100

LOVELL, J.L.
port/books: (H) $2,750

LOVING, Eugene E.
American 20th cent.
intaglio: (L) $55; (H) $120

LOWELL, Nate
intaglio: (H) $467

LOWENTHAL, Leupold von
German 19th cent.
planographic: (H) $165

LOWERY, Louis R.
1918-1988
photo: (H) $660

LOWRY, J.W.
English 1803-1879
planographic: (H) $77

LOWRY, Lawrence Stephen (after)
photo-repro: (L) $136; (H) $566

LOWRY, Lawrence Stephen
English 1887-1976
intaglio: (H) $384
generic: (H) $536

LOZOWICK, Louis
American 1892-1973
intaglio: (H) $1,100
planographic: (L) $271; (H) $15,950

LUBBERS, Adriaan
planographic: (H) $495

LUBECK, Gerald L.
planographic: (H) $60

LUCAS, Cornel
b. 1923
photo: (H) $230

LUCAS, David
English 1802-1881
intaglio: (L) $101; (H) $16,900

LUCAS, Jean
b. 1823
port/books: (H) $845

LUCASSEN, Reinier
planographic: (H) $152

LUCE, Maximilien
French 1858-1941
intaglio: (H) $790
planographic: (L) $90; (H) $3,994

LUCEBERT
Dutch b. 1924
intaglio: (L) $129; (H) $259
planographic: (L) $114; (H) $388
port/books: (H) $4,255

LUCINI, Antonio Francesco
1605-after 1640
intaglio: (H) $2,860

LUCIONI, Luigi
Italian/American 1900-1988?
intaglio: (L) $83; (H) $523

LUCY
20th cent.
planographic: (H) $348

LUGAR, Robert
port/books: (H) $2,420

LUGO, Amador
planographic: (H) $660

LUKE, Monte
photo: (H) $61

LUM, Bertha
American 1879-1954
relief: (L) $220; (H) $1,540

LUMSDEN, Ernest S.
British 1883-1948
intaglio: (H) $28

LUMSDEN, Ernest Stephen
1883-1948
intaglio: (H) $345

LUNDQVIST, Jan
contemporary
planographic: (L) $758; (H) $810

LUNDSTROM, Vilhelm
planographic: (H) $259

LUNTON, Thomas
intaglio: (H) $286

LUONGO, Aldo
stencil: (L) $468; (H) $935

LUPERTZ, Markus
German b. 1941
intaglio: (H) $355

LURCAT, Jean
French 1892-1966
relief: (H) $33
planographic: (L) $120; (H) $166

LUTHI, Urs
Swiss b. 1947
photo: (H) $135

LUTZ, E. (after)
planographic: (H) $132

LYCETT, Joseph
intaglio: (H) $435

LYNCH, James Henry (Samuel
Walters/Ackermann and Co.)
British ac. mid-19th cent.
planographic: (H) $358

LYNCH, Tom
American contemporary
photo-repro: (H) $22

LYNES, George Platt
photo: (L) $440; (H) $3,300

LYNN, George
intaglio: (H) $251

LYON, Danny
American b. 1942
photo: (L) $275; (H) $8,250

MAAR, Dora
photo: (H) $1,870

MACDONALD, Thoreau
relief: (H) $170

MACK, Heinz
b. 1931
stencil: (H) $269
planographic: (H) $433
mixed-media: (H) $577

MACKENZIE, James Hamilton and
Frank BENSON
intaglio: (H) $440

MACLEAN, William Lacy
American 1860-1940
intaglio: (H) $33

MACLEOD, William Douglas
intaglio: (H) $155

MACLISE, Daniel
Irish 1806/11-1870
intaglio: (H) $183

MACLISE, Daniel (after)
Irish 1806/11-1870
intaglio: (H) $271

MACNALLY, Matthew James
planographic: (H) $104

MACPHERSON, Robert
photo: (H) $440

MADRIGAL, August
planographic: (H) $6

MAEGHT EDITEUR, Publisher
port/books: (H) $2,203

MAESTRI, Michelangelo
Italian d.c. 1812
intaglio: (L) $1,540; (H) $2,640

MAGAFAN, Ethel
American b. 1916
intaglio: (H) $400

MAGEE, Alderson
planographic: (H) $132

MAGEE, John L.
planographic: (H) $175

MAGGIONI, Umberto
Swiss b. 1933
intaglio: (H) $78

MAGGIOTTO, Francesco (after)
Italian 1750-1805
port/books: (H) $25,916

MAGNELLI, Alberto
Italian 1888-1971
stencil: (H) $414

MAGRITTE, Rene (after)
intaglio: (L) $605; (H) $627
port/books: (L) $1,100; (H) $2,750

MAGRITTE, Rene
Belgian 1898-1967
intaglio: (L) $620; (H) $5,567
planographic: (L) $331; (H) $3,443
photo: (L) $183; (H) $287

MAHONY, Will
intaglio: (H) $130

MAIK
American contemporary
planographic: (H) $110

MAILLOL, Aristide
French 1861-1944
intaglio: (L) $55; (H) $520
relief: (H) $11,359
planographic: (L) $412; (H) $2,643
port/books: (L) $1,760; (H) $2,200

MAIMON
Israeli 20th cent.
planographic: (H) $143

MAISEL, David
photo: (H) $500

MAJOR and KNAPP, Lithographers
American begun 1867
planographic: (H) $715

MAJZNER, Victor
  intaglio: (L) $70; (H) $87

MAKIN, Jeffrey
  stencil: (L) $157; (H) $174

MAKUC, Vladimir
  European contemporary
  intaglio: (H) $28

MALAVAL, Robert
  planographic: (H) $82

MALBEST
  intaglio: (H) $11

MALINOVSKY, Lise
  port/books: (H) $259

MALLOL, Aristide
  planographic: (H) $462
  others: (H) $110

MAN, Felix
  b. 1893
  photo: (L) $605; (H) $1,100

MANDEL, C. Hull (after J.F. GOULD)
  port/books: (H) $440

MANE-KATZ
  French/Israeli 1894-1962
  port/books: (H) $440

MANESSIER, Alfred
  French b. 1941
  planographic: (L) $207; (H) $749

  During his lifetime Edouard Manet (1832-1883) scandalized the Parisian bourgeoisie. The French Academy sanctioned nudity only if it was in an allegorical form. In a remote time or place nudity was considered acceptable, but Manet shocked Parisian society by painting contemporary 19th-century nude women. Manet's lithograph *L'Execution de Maximilien, 1868,* similar to his painting of the same name, was supposedly a bid for acceptability. It was based on newspaper accounts of the Mexicans executing Maximilien, the French governor of Mexico. Manet depicted the firing squad as French soldiers, not Mexicans, and the French government repressed the paintings and lithographs. (Edouard Manet, *L'Execution de Maximilien, 1868,* lithograph on chine colle, 13 ⅛ x 17 ⅛ inches, Sotheby-New York, May 14, 1992, $14,300)

MANET
planographic: (H) $83

MANET, Edouard
French 1832-1883
intaglio: (L) $189; (H) $6,194
planographic: (L) $2,200; (H) $129,591
port/books: (H) $47,758

MANET, Edouard (after)
relief: (H) $193

MANFREID, Daniel de
relief: (H) $22

MANGOLD, Robert
American b. 1937
intaglio: (L) $1,045; (H) $3,300
stencil: (L) $496; (H) $880
relief: (L) $1,045; (H) $3,850
port/books: (H) $866

MANGUIN, H.C.
planographic: (H) $118

MANKES, Jan
intaglio: (H) $228

MANN, Sally
photo: (H) $950

MANNFELD, Bernhard
1848-1925
intaglio: (L) $223; (H) $742

MANOS, Constantine
photo: (H) $350

MANSEN, Matthias
b. 1958
relief: (L) $170; (H) $426

MANSHIP, Paul
American 1885-1966
planographic: (H) $935

MANTE AND GOLDSCHMIDT
photo: (L) $790; (H) $2,371

MANTEGNA, Andrea (after)
intaglio: (L) $1,036; (H) $1,790

MANTEGNA, Andrea (school of)
(Premier Engraver)
intaglio: (H) $22,550

MANTEGNA, Andrea
Italian 1431-1506
intaglio: (L) $5,742; (H) $29,903

MANTELLI, Girolamo
generic: (H) $3,080

MANTZ, Werner
b. Germany 1901 d. 1983
photo: (L) $717; (H) $990

MANUEL, Henri
photo: (H) $605

MANZU, Giacomo
Italian b. 1908
intaglio: (L) $465; (H) $14,093
planographic: (H) $1,417

MANZU, Giacomo and Cesare
BRANDI
Italian 1908-1991
port/books: (H) $605

MAPPENWERKE
generic: (H) $3,784

MAPPLETHORPE, Robert
American 1946-1989
photo-repro: (H) $3,300
photo: (L) $1,100; (H) $14,300

MARATTA, Carlo
Italian 1625-1713
port/books: (H) $1,045

MARC, Franz
German 1880-1916
relief: (L) $2,654; (H) $25,300

MARCA-RELLI, Conrad
American b. 1913
stencil: (H) $132
planographic: (H) $220
mixed-media: (H) $605

MARCH, Charlotte
photo: (H) $143

MARCKS, Gerhard
German b. 1889
relief: (H) $952
planographic: (H) $6,383

MARCOUSSIS, Louis
French 1883-1941
intaglio: (L) $1,591; (H) $60,642

MARDEN, Brice
American b. 1938
intaglio: (L) $1,320; (H) $2,750

MARESQUIER
posters: (H) $220

The 15th-century Italian artist Andrea Mantegna (1431-1506) drew upon the classical heritage of Northern Italy for much of his subject matter. This print of *Battle of the Sea God* is the left half of a two-plate composition. The missing right side is a continuation of the seagods on their water horses. In this print the emaciated woman holding up the tablet gives the theme of the piece "Invid" (envy). (Andrea Mantegna, *Battle of the Sea Gods: Left Half, 1470s,* engraving and drypoint in gray ink on paper, 11 ½ x 16 ⅝ inches, Sotheby-New York, May 14, 1992, $17,600)

MARGOLIES, Samuel L.
American b. 1897
intaglio: (L) $77; (H) $3,300

MARGULIES, Joseph
Austrian/American 1896-1984
intaglio: (L) $55; (H) $72
planographic: (H) $165

MARIANI, Carlo Maria
Italian contemporary
planographic: (H) $88

MARIESCHI, Michele
Italian 1696-1743
intaglio: (H) $3,579

MARIN, John
American 1870-1953
intaglio: (L) $522; (H) $1,430

MARINI, Marino
Italian 1901-1980
intaglio: (L) $220; (H) $6,373
stencil: (L) $1,100; (H) $1,796
planographic: (L) $72; (H) $4,921
port/books: (L) $5,508; (H) $17,600

MARISCH, Gustav
German 19th cent.
planographic: (H) $220

MARK, Mary Ellen
photo: (H) $605

MARKGRAF, Peter
generic: (H) $68

MARKHAM, Kyra
American b. 1891
planographic: (L) $357; (H) $2,420

MARKS, Gerald
American contemporary
stencil: (H) $28

MARRIOTT, F.
intaglio: (H) $102

MARS, Ethel
1876-c. 1956
relief: (H) $880

MARSH, Reginald
American 1898-1954
intaglio: (L) $138; (H) $6,600
planographic: (L) $495; (H) $1,980

MARSHALL, D. (after)
intaglio: (H) $381

MARTELLY, John Stockton de
American b. 1903
planographic: (H) $880

MARTENS, Friedrich
1809-1875
photo: (H) $765

MARTIN, Charles
port/books: (H) $3,300

MARTIN, Fletcher
American 1904-1979
stencil: (H) $110
planographic: (L) $77; (H) $330

MARTIN, J.F. (after)
planographic: (H) $755

MARTIN, Johan Fredrik
port/books: (H) $3,892

MARTIN, John
intaglio: (H) $3,967

MARTIN, Thomas Mower
Canadian 1838-1934
intaglio: (H) $97

MARTINET, Francois Nicolas
French b. 1760
intaglio: (H) $138

MARTINET, Francois Nicolas (after)
French ac. 1760
port/books: (H) $275

MARTINI, Alberto
planographic: (H) $752

MARVAL, Jacqueline
planographic: (H) $1,540

MARVY, Louis (after Rembrandt)
intaglio: (H) $22

MARYAN
planographic: (H) $111

MASANOBU
Japanese c. 1686-1764
relief: (H) $330

Robert Mapplethorpe's output of photographs consisted of classical themes of portraiture and still life as well as male homoeroticism and fetishism. *Calla Lily,* one of his series of flower portraits, is both serene and erotic, reminiscent of the paintings of Georgia O'Keeffe. (Robert Mapplethorpe, *Calla Lily,* printed 1988, gelatin silver print, 19 $\frac{1}{2}$ x 19 $\frac{1}{2}$ inches, Christie-New York, October 10, 1991, $12,100)

Animals were a central theme in Franz Marc's paintings and etchings. Using color systemically rather than naturally, he attempted to embody the spiritual nature of animals. The deer, representing gentleness and grace, was one of his favorite subjects. (Franz Marc, *Fabeltier, 1912*, woodcut with pochoir on laid Japan, 5 $\frac{9}{16}$ x 8 $\frac{7}{16}$ inches, Christie-New York, May 11, 1992, $25,300)

MASAREEL, Frans
European 1889-1972
relief: (L) $165; (H) $550

MASI, Oliverio
Italian b. 1949
planographic: (L) $33; (H) $55

MASON, Frank (after)
photo-repro: (H) $171

MASSANOGO
1686-1764
relief: (H) $180

MASSON, Andre
French b. 1896
intaglio: (L) $220; (H) $3,137
stencil: (H) $330
planographic: (L) $120; (H) $2,529
port/books: (L) $495; (H) $1,591
generic: (H) $495

MASSON, Antoine
1636-1700
intaglio: (H) $2,356

MASSON, Henri Leopold
Canadian b. 1907
stencil: (II) $390
planographic: (L) $93; (H) $511
port/books: (H) $928

MASTER B R MIT DEM ANKER
intaglio: (H) $32,987

MASTER DES HEILEGEN SEBASTIAN
ac. c. 1460-1480
intaglio: (H) $45,553

MASTER E.S.
ac. c. 1450-1467
intaglio: (L) $141,372; (H) $204,204
mixed-media: (H) $78,540

Everyday life of the city–crowded streets, burlesque halls, mobs at Coney Island–were the subject matter of Reginald Marsh's (1898-1954) many paintings and lithographs. The lines in Marsh's lithographs and drawings employ his background as an illustrator and cartoonist. (Reginald Marsh, *Striptease at New Gotham, 1935*, etching on Arches wove, 11 $\frac{7}{8}$ x 9 inches, Skinner, March 13, 1992, $4,950)

MASTER FP
ac. c. 1530
intaglio: (H) $803

MASTER IB
ac. 1523-1530
intaglio: (H) $439

MASTER LCZ
ac. c. 1480-1505
intaglio: (H) $82,467

MASTER MZ
ac. 1500
intaglio: (L) $527; (H) $29,845

MASTER OF THE DIE
ac. 1570
intaglio: (H) $592

MASTROIANNI, Umberto
intaglio: (H) $331

MATARE, Ewald
German 1887-1965
relief: (L) $2,387; (H) $2,580

MATEOS, Francisco
intaglio: (L) $268; (H) $409

MATHAM, Jacob
intaglio: (L) $601; (H) $1,224

MATHIEU, Georges
French b. 1921
stencil: (H) $577
mixed-media: (L) $712; (H) $1,080

MATIN, Samuel
American 20th cent.
relief: (H) $330

MATISSE, (after)
intaglio: (H) $55

MATISSE, Henri (after)
planographic: (H) $550

MATISSE, Henri
French 1869-1954
intaglio: (L) $1,760; (H) $60,642
stencil: (L) $550; (H) $4,971
planographic: (L) $248; (H) $38,500
mixed-media: (H) $523
port/books: (L) $1,673; (H) $30,800
others: (L) $1,210; (H) $14,300

MATSUBARA, Naoko
20th cent.
relief: (H) $28

MATTA, Roberto Echaurren
Chilean b. 1911
intaglio: (L) $198; (H) $1,569
relief: (H) $990
planographic: (L) $176; (H) $990
port/books: (L) $1,469; (H) $3,246

MATTA, Sebastian
intaglio: (L) $286; (H) $4,971
port/books: (L) $3,764; (H) $5,766

MATTER, Herbert
1907-1984
photo: (L) $825; (H) $1,045

MATULKA, Jan
Czechoslovakian/Am 1890-1972
planographic: (L) $2,860; (H) $25,300

MAUFRA, Maxime
French 1861/62-1918
planographic: (H) $3,994

MAUND
intaglio: (H) $440

MAURIN, Charles
intaglio: (L) $2,509; (II) $3,195

MAUTNER, Betti
photo: (H) $1,870

MAUVE, Anton
Dutch 1838-1888
intaglio: (H) $66

MAVIGNIER, Almir da Silva
b. 1925
stencil: (H) $213

MAX, Peter
German/American b. 1937
stencil: (L) $413; (H) $1,320
planographic: (L) $193; (H) $220
generic: (H) $1,200

MAXEY, Edward
photo: (L) $1,148; (H) $1,626

MAXWELL, M.
intaglio: (H) $35

MAYBERY, E.J.
intaglio: (L) $11; (H) $11

MAYER, A.
planographic: (H) $1,650

MAYER, Ferdinand, Lithographer/
Publisher
German/American b. c. 1817
planographic: (L) $660; (H) $825

MAYER, Luigi
port/books: (H) $1,650

MAYERHOFER-(PASSAU), Hermann
b. 1901
intaglio: (H) $155

MAYET, L.
planographic: (H) $275

MAYFIELD, William
photo: (H) $220

MAYNARD, Harold B.
intaglio: (H) $220

MAYNE, Roger
b. 1929
photo: (L) $478; (H) $1,722

MAYOREAK, Ashoona
b. 1946
planographic: (H) $156

MAYWALD, Wilhelm
German 1907-1985
photo: (L) $51; (H) $1,362

MAZELL, (after Paillou)
generic: (H) $55

MAZUR, Michael
American b. 1935
intaglio: (L) $303; (H) $990
planographic: (L) $1,210; (H) $4,950

MAZZA
posters: (H) $220

MAZZOLA, Francesco (Il
Parmigianino) (after)
intaglio: (H) $627
relief: (H) $9,941

MCARDELL, James
intaglio: (H) $193

MCBEAN, Angus
1904-1990
photo: (L) $435; (H) $1,284

MCBEY, James
English 1883-1959
intaglio: (L) $48; (H) $629

Henri Matisse's (1869-1954) first distinct style was as a Fauvist, an avant-garde school that used vivid non-naturalist colors. In 1916, Matisse found a retreat in Nice and spent much of his time there. His next fourteen years spent in this tranquil Mediterranean town were peaceful. This lithograph of a young woman in an organdy dress is representative of this period. (Henri Matisse, *La Robe d'Organdi, 1922*, lithograph on China paper, 16 $\frac{7}{8}$ x 11 inches, Butterfield, February 25, 1992, $19,250)

MCCLANE, Diane
generic: (H) $330

MCCRADY, John
American 1911-1968
planographic: (L) $286; (H) $715

MCCULLIN, Don
b. 1935
photo: (L) $497; (H) $593

MCDANIEL, Henry
generic: (H) $275

MCDARRAH, Fred W.
photo: (L) $440; (H) $550

MCDERMOTT, Messrs. David and Peter MCGOUGH
photo: (H) $3,300

MCELROY, (and another)
photo: (H) $316

MCIAN, Robert Ronald
port/books: (H) $484

MCINTYRE, Robert Finlay (after)
British ac. 1892-1897
planographic: (H) $165

MCKENNEY and HALL
planographic: (L) $248; (H) $605
port/books: (H) $2,640

MCKENNIE, Mariam
American 20th cent.
intaglio: (H) $6

MCKNIGHT, Thomas
American b. 1941
stencil: (L) $303; (H) $2,310

MCKNIGHT-SMITH, C.
generic: (H) $330

MCLAUGHLIN, Donald Shaw
American 1876-1938
intaglio: (H) $77

MCMICHAEL, A.G.
photo: (H) $3,025

MCMURTRY, Edward P.
photo: (H) $413

MCNULTY, William C.
intaglio: (H) $50

MCPHERSON, Craig
intaglio: (H) $28

MCWILLIAM, F.
planographic: (H) $61

MEADE, H.W., Publisher
posters: (H) $135

MECKENEM, Israhel van
German c. 1450-1503
intaglio: (L) $1,413; (H) $67,544

MECKSEPER, Friedrich
b. 1936
intaglio: (L) $331; (H) $780
port/books: (H) $4,421

MECRAY, John (after)
generic: (H) $330

MEDAILLE, F.
posters: (H) $385

MEDKOVA, Emila
photo: (H) $220

MEDLAND, Thomas (William
Alexander, Draughtsman)
British d. after 1822
intaglio: (H) $385

MEESON, Dora
intaglio: (L) $70; (H) $96

MEGARGEE, Edwin
19th/20th cent.
intaglio: (H) $385

MEID, Hans
1883-1957
port/books: (H) $2,482

MEIDNER, Ludwig
German 1884-1966
port/books: (H) $2,994

MEIER, Barton
American 1892-1963
relief: (L) $138; (H) $220

MEISSONIER, E. (after)
intaglio: (H) $6

MEISTERMANN, Georg
1911-1990
planographic: (L) $638; (H) $649

MELDOLLA, Andrea
d. 1563
intaglio: (H) $11,019

MELLAN, Claude
1601-1688
intaglio: (H) $5,498

MELROSE, Andrew
American 1836-1901
planographic: (H) $550

MELZER, Moritz
b. 1877
planographic: (H) $866

MEMPES, Mortimer
English 19th cent.
intaglio: (H) $165

MENDEZ, Leopoldo
b. Mexico 1902
relief: (L) $1,210; (H) $1,650

MENDJISKY, S.
planographic: (L) $140; (H) $198

MENPES, Mortimer
intaglio: (L) $55; (H) $440

MENSE, Carlo
planographic: (H) $69

MENTELLE, E. and P.G.
CHANLAIRE
intaglio: (H) $116

MENZEL, Adolf
German 1815-1905
intaglio: (H) $1,514
port/books: (H) $19,635

MERCIER, Jean A.
posters: (H) $550

MERIAN, (after)
intaglio: (H) $116

MERIAN, Matthaus
1593-1650
intaglio: (L) $166; (H) $773

MERIDA, Carlos
Guatemalan 1891-1984
port/books: (H) $1,540

Creditors of the Boston Trade Bank selected auctioneer Jim Bakker to sell the bank's collection of art and antiques. When a monotype triptych by Boston artist Michael Mazur realized $2,300 (retail price $4,000) it was one of the bargains of the day. (Michael Mazur, *Wakeby*, monotype triptych, 30 x 60 inches, Bakker, August 25, 1991, $2,300)

MERIGOT, James
port/books: (H) $3,850

MERYON
generic: (H) $2,200

MERYON, Charles
French 1821-1868
intaglio: (L) $25; (H) $3,968

MERYON, Charles and Edmund
BLAMPIED
intaglio: (H) $66

MERZ, Georg
German 18th cent.
port/books: (H) $495

MERZ, Mario
Italian b. 1925
intaglio: (H) $381

MESQUITA, Samuel Jesserun de
planographic: (H) $348

MESSAGIER, Jean
intaglio: (H) $68

MESSICK, Ben
American 1901-1981
planographic: (H) $138

MESSINGER, A.F. (attrib.)
photo: (H) $1,320

METLIKOVITZ
posters: (H) $330

METZ, C. (after)
intaglio: (H) $213

METZKER, Ray K.
b. 1931
photo: (L) $550; (H) $2,640

MEUNIER, Georges
French 1869-1934
planographic: (H) $198

MEUNIER, Henri
Belgian 1873-1922
posters: (H) $330

MEYER, C.H.
generic: (H) $40

MEYER, Henry (after)
intaglio: (H) $191

MEYER, Ouray
planographic: (L) $33; (H) $55

MEYER, Pedro
photo: (L) $413; (H) $468

MEYERINGH, Albert
Dutch 1645-1714
intaglio: (H) $69

MEYEROWITZ, Joel
photo: (L) $468; (H) $2,475

MICH
posters: (H) $385

MICHALS, Duane
photo: (L) $468; (H) $4,675

MICHAUX, Henri
Belgian b. 1899
intaglio: (H) $361
planographic: (H) $579

MICHELANGELO (after)
photo-repro: (H) $303

MICHELIN, Pneu
planographic: (H) $825

MIDDLETON, Janet (Holly)
b. 1922
stencil: (L) $138; (H) $253

MIDDLETON, Sallie
generic: (L) $40; (H) $100

MIDDLETON, WALLACE and CO.
planographic: (H) $55

MIELATZ, Charles F.W.
mixed-media: (H) $231

MIETH, Hansel
photo: (H) $1,320

MIGER, (after Marechal)
intaglio: (H) $880

MILBOURNE, C. (after W.J. Condit)
planographic: (H) $495

MILHSTEIN, Zvi
planographic: (H) $82

MILI, Gjon
photo: (H) $884

MILLBOURN, M. Vaughn
American b. 1893
generic: (H) $440

MILLEA, Tom
photo: (L) $400; (H) $495

MILLER, Frances St. Clair
English 20th cent.
intaglio: (H) $22

MILLER, John
1715-1790
intaglio: (H) $154

MILLER, Kenneth Hayes
American 1876-1952
intaglio: (L) $165; (H) $165

MILLET, Jean Francois
French 1814-1875
intaglio: (L) $1,100; (H) $25,133
planographic: (L) $9,744; (H) $9,900

MILLIERE, Maurice
French b. 1871
intaglio: (H) $715

MILNE, David
Canadian 1882-1953
intaglio: (H) $1,007
stencil: (H) $28

MILTON, Peter
American b. 1930
intaglio: (II) $231

MILTON, Peter
intaglio: (L) $550; (H) $1,815
mixed-media: (H) $330

MIMPO, H.
contemporary
planographic: (H) $275

MINAUX, Andre
French b. 1923
planographic: (L) $28; (H) $110

MIND, Gottfried
intaglio: (H) $1,569
port/books: (L) $1,239; (H) $5,797

MIND, Gottfried (attrib.)
intaglio: (H) $1,404

MINDLEFF, Cosmos
photo: (H) $11

MINKKINEN, Arno Rafael
photo: (H) $450

MINNE, J.
1887-1988
planographic: (H) $265

MINNS, Benjamin Edward
intaglio: (H) $70

MINOT, R.
American 19th cent.
intaglio: (H) $55

MIOTTE, Jean
planographic: (H) $169

MIRO, Joan
Spanish 1893-1983
intaglio: (L) $770; (H) $44,000
stencil: (L) $110; (H) $165
planographic: (L) $99; (H) $59,158
posters: (L) $50; (H) $5,815
mixed-media: (L) $2,860; (H) $7,011
port/books: (L) $248; (H) $16,500

MIRO, Joan (after)
intaglio: (H) $3,575
planographic: (L) $1,796; (H) $2,860
port/books: (H) $1,789

MISRACH, Richard
port/books: (H) $1,045
photo: (L) $350; (H) $2,310

MITCHELL, Joan
American b. 1926
planographic: (H) $770

MITCHELL, L.C.
posters: (H) $880

MITCHELL, S. Augustus, Publisher
American 19th cent.
intaglio: (H) $154

MITRA, Dan
American 20th cent.
planographic: (H) $193

MLITZIN, Wasile
intaglio: (H) $6

MODEL, Lisette
1901-1983
port/books: (H) $6,600
photo: (L) $1,320; (H) $1,870

MODERSOHN-BECKER, Paula
1876-1907
intaglio: (L) $2,553; (H) $13,829

MODIGLIANI, Amedeo (after)
Italian 1884-1920
generic: (H) $275

MODIGLIANI, Amedeo
Italian 1884-1920
intaglio: (H) $468

MODOTTI, Tina
Italian 1896-1942
port/books: (H) $3,300
photo: (L) $1,760; (H) $49,500

MOEGLE, Willi
German b. 1897
photo: (H) $287

MOHLITZ, Ph.
intaglio: (H) $521

MOHOLY, Lucia
Czech 1899-1989
photo: (L) $430; (H) $1,650

MOHOLY-NAGY, L. and E.
PISCATOR
port/books: (H) $381

MOHOLY-NAGY, Laszlo
Hungarian 1895-1946
planographic: (L) $17,894; (H) $32,065
photo: (L) $466; (H) $18,700

MOI VER, (Moshe Raviv-Vorobeichic)
b. Lithuania b. 1904
photo: (H) $3,440

MOLE and THOMAS
photo: (H) $220

MOLINIER, Piere
German b. 1900
photo: (L) $717; (H) $860

MOLL, Carl
Austrian 1861-1945
relief: (L) $722; (H) $888

MONDRIAN, (after)
generic: (H) $17

MONKS, John Austin Sands
American 1850-1917
intaglio: (H) $110

MONOGRAMMIST AZ
ac. 1530
intaglio: (H) $716

MONOGRAMMIST SK
ac. c. 1520
intaglio: (H) $3,691

MONORY
photo-repro: (H) $55

MONSEN, Frederick
photo: (L) $385; (H) $1,760

MONTAGNA, Benedetto
ac. 1510
intaglio: (L) $587; (H) $904

MONTAUL, E.
planographic: (H) $193

MONTAUT, E.
planographic: (H) $605

MONTAUT, M.M.
port/books: (H) $1,210

MONTIJN, Jan
contemporary
intaglio: (L) $202; (H) $311

MONTPEZAT, Henri de (after)
French 1817-1859
intaglio: (H) $880

MOON, Carl
American 1879-1948
photo: (L) $385; (H) $1,100

MOON, Carl (attrib.)
American 1879-1948
photo: (H) $880

MOON, Sarah
photo: (H) $600

MOORE, Benson B.
intaglio: (H) $33

MOORE, Bruce
posters: (H) $220

MOORE, Henry
English 1898-1986
intaglio:	(L)	$388;	(H)	$3,764
relief:	(L)	$839;	(H)	$8,800
planographic:	(L)	$578;	(H)	$10,999
port/books:	(L)	$1,193;	(H)	$15,846
photo:			(H)	$1,320
others:	(L)	$6,600;	(H)	$10,450

MOORE, J., Publisher
intaglio: (H) $20

MOORE, Raymond
1920-1987
photo: (H) $889

MOOS, Max von
1903-1979
planographic: (H) $155

MORA, Joseph Jacinto
Urug./American 1876-1947
planographic: (H) $132

MORAL, Jean (photographer)
port/books: (H) $3,575

MORALES, Armando
Nicaraguan/Amer. b. 1927
planographic: (L) $3,410; (H) $3,630

MORAN, Peter
American 1841-1914
intaglio: (L) $39; (H) $550

MORAN, Thomas
American 1837-1926
intaglio: (L) $110; (H) $1,980
planographic: (L) $66; (H) $1,320

MORAN, Thomas (after)
planographic: (L) $660; (H) $1,100

MORANDI, Giorgio
Italian 1890-1964
intaglio: (L) $5,667; (H) $86,968

MOREAU, J. von
intaglio: (L) $2,749; (H) $4,398

MOREAU, J.M. (le jeune) (after)
intaglio: (H) $240

MOREAU, Luc Albert
intaglio: (H) $100

MORELAND, George (after)
British 1763-1804
intaglio: (H) $77

MORELETT, Francois
contemporary
port/books: (H) $402

MORELLI, Francesco (after)
port/books: (H) $1,231

MORETTI, Lucien Philippe
planographic: (H) $21

MORGAN, Barbara
b. 1900
photo: (L) $467; (H) $1,980

MORGAN, W.
intaglio: (H) $43

MORGAN, W.J.
posters: (H) $825

MORGHEN, Filippo
1730-1870
intaglio: (H) $1,743

MORGNER, Michael
b. 1942
generic: (H) $2,601

MORI, Yoshitoshi
Japanese b. 1898
stencil: (H) $55

Italian artist Giorgio Morandi (1890-1964) is best known for his paintings of still-lifes and landscapes. During the war years in Italy he was equally well known for his etchings. Over half of his prints were executed between 1927 and 1933. Morandi drew directly on the plate without a preliminary image and seldom printed more than one plate. (Giorgio Morandi, *Grande Natura Morta con la Lampada a Petrolio, 1930*, etching, 12 x 14 ¼ inches, Finarte S.A., October 12, 1991, SF 115,000, $85,350)

MORISOT, Berthe
French 1841-1895
intaglio: (H) $1,210

MORITZ, Friedrich Wilhelm
1783-1855
planographic: (H) $107

MORITZ, Moritz von
1804-1871
planographic: (H) $19,635

MORLAND, George
intaglio: (H) $69

MORLAND, George (after)
intaglio: (L) $132; (H) $890

MORLAND, George
English 1763-1804
intaglio: (L) $124; (H) $580

MORLEY, Harry
intaglio: (H) $136

MORLEY, Lewis
photo: (L) $943; (H) $5,501

MORLEY, Malcolm
American b. 1931
intaglio: (L) $495; (H) $2,750
planographic: (H) $770

MORLON
planographic: (H) $302

MORRIS
American 20th cent.
intaglio: (H) $275

MORRIS, Rev. F.O.
1810-1893
intaglio: (L) $120; (H) $149
relief: (H) $120
port/books: (L) $165; (H) $990
others: (H) $248

MORRIS, Robert
American b. 1931
port/books: (H) $1,980

MORRIS, Wright
photo: (L) $605; (H) $715

MORRISROE, Mark
photo: (H) $800

MORRISSEAU, Norval
b. 1930
stencil: (L) $110; (H) $230

MORRRIS, Francis Orpen
1810-1893
intaglio: (H) $44

MORTENSEN, Richard
stencil: (L) $148; (H) $188
planographic: (L) $113; (H) $241

MORTENSEN, William
1897-1965
photo: (H) $3,080

MORTON, Cavendish and Concord
b. 1911
relief: (H) $92

MOSER, Carl
relief: (H) $442

MOSES, Henry
port/books: (H) $1,100

MOSES, Stefan
German b. 1928
photo: (L) $179; (H) $466

MOSKOWITZ, Ira
Polish/American b. 1912
intaglio: (H) $110
planographic: (H) $33

MOSKOWITZ, Robert
American b. 1935
mixed-media: (H) $1,210

MOTHERWELL, Robert
American 1915-1991
intaglio: (L) $358; (H) $18,150
stencil: (L) $770; (H) $14,300
planographic: (L) $605; (H) $14,300
mixed-media: (L) $2,750; (H) $50,600
photo-repro: (H) $1,210
port/books: (L) $550; (H) $14,300
others: (H) $3,575

MOTI, Kaiko
Indian b. 1921
intaglio: (H) $151
planographic: (H) $220

MOTTER, Francis Douglas
b. 1913
intaglio: (H) $46

MOTTRAM, C. (after John William Hill)
intaglio: (L) $440; (H) $545

MOTTRAN, (after HILL)
generic: (H) $660

MOUNT, William S.
American 1807-1868
planographic: (H) $138

MOURGUE and SALA
posters: (H) $275

MOURLOT, Fernand (pub.)
French 20th cent.
port/books: (H) $1,210

MOY, Seong
b. 1921
relief: (L) $253; (H) $358

MUCHA, Alphonse
Czechoslovakian 1860-1939
intaglio: (H) $4,400
planographic: (L) $1,045; (H) $21,490
posters: (L) $550; (H) $14,300
photo: (H) $502
generic: (H) $2,200

MUELLER, Hans
German 1888-1962
relief: (L) $66; (H) $99

MUELLER, Otto
German 1874-1930
relief: (L) $2,624; (H) $5,198
planographic: (L) $8,364; (H) $74,467

Alphonse Mucha (1860-1939) was one of the leading exponents of the Art Nouveau style. His numerous posters popularized flowers on slender, twining stems and bizarre undulations of flowing hair. Mucha also designed theater sets and costumes. His soft images sell well in Japan. *Le Fruit et la Fleur,* a pair of lithographs printed in 1897, was estimated at 3.2 million yen. The lot realized 2.86 million yen. (Alphonse Mucha, *Le Fruit et la Fleur,* two colored lithographs, each 23 ½ x 14 ¼ inches, Sotheby-Japan, April 14, 1992, 2.860,000 yen, $21,490)

MUHL, Roger
French b. 1929
planographic: (H) $83

MULAS, Ugo
Italian 1928-1973
photo: (H) $605

MULDER, L.
19th cent.
intaglio: (H) $334

MULINARI, Stefano
Italian 1670-1751
intaglio: (H) $66

MULLER
posters: (L) $275; (H) $330

MULLER, Alfredo
Italian/French b. 1869
intaglio: (H) $358
planographic: (L) $138; (H) $1,506

MULLER, Hans Alexander
relief: (H) $148

MULLER, Jan
Dutch 1571-1628
intaglio: (L) $257; (H) $17,942

MULLER, Otto
German 1874-1930
planographic: (L) $1,404; (H) $7,269

MULLER, Richard
1874-1954
intaglio: (L) $74; (H) $134

MULLER-BERNBURG, Ernst
20th cent.
generic: (H) $211

MULLER-BROCKMANN, Josef
Swiss b. 1914
posters: (H) $66

MULLINGHAM, Terence
intaglio: (H) $87

MULOCK, Ben R.
photo: (H) $880

MUMFORD, Ethel
posters: (H) $138

MUMMINGS, Sir Alfred (after)
British 1878-1959
planographic: (H) $99

MUMPRECHT, Rudolf
b. 1918
intaglio: (H) $213

MUNAKATA, Shiko
Japanese b. 1903
relief: (L) $2,356; (H) $23,143

MUNCH, Edvard
Norwegian 1863-1944
intaglio: (L) $679; (H) $26,267
relief: (L) $23,810; (H) $187,000
planographic: (L) $94; (H) $254,707

MUNNINGS, Sir Alfred J. (after)
English 1878-1959
planographic: (H) $413
photo-repro: (L) $55; (H) $413
generic: (H) $1,210

MUNNINGS, Sir Alfred J.
English 1878-1959
generic: (H) $389

MUNOZ, Lucio
Spanish b. 1929
planographic: (H) $341

MUNROE, Olivia
intaglio: (H) $17

MUNZER, Adolf
1870-1952
planographic: (H) $246

MURPHY, Alice Harold
American 20th cent.
port/books: (H) $55

MURPHY, Gladys Wilkins
American b. 1907
relief: (L) $110; (H) $440

MURPHY, Herman Dudley
American 1867-1945
intaglio: (H) $220

MURPHY, John J. A.
intaglio: (H) $1,760

MURRAY, Dr. John
photo: (L) $747; (H) $4,322

Different types of measurements are given for prints. Image, sheet, and platemark are all various ways of measuring. Margins are important and indicate if a print has been trimmed. If a contemporary print has been trimmed, it will affect the value more than that for an older print where both rarity and margin size affect the prices. Shiko Munakata (b. 1903) is a contemporary Japanese print designer; his form and line reflect the folk art of Japan. (Shiko Munakata, *Woman In Mirror*, woodcut with hand-coloring on tissue-thin Japan paper, sheet size 15 $\frac{5}{8}$ x 11 $\frac{3}{4}$ inches, image size 11 $\frac{3}{4}$ x 8 inches, Butterfield, February 25, 1992, $18,700)

During his years in Berlin, the Norwegian painter Edvard Munch (1863-1944) developed an interest in prints. He exploited the possibilities of the medium, using rich contrasts of black and white, comparing thick lines with webbed lines, and exploring the use of color. This woodcut of *The Bridge* was printed in 1920 after his return to Norway. The impression is a variant composition printed from a woodblock and lithographic plates; it has blue, yellow, orange red, dark blue, and green colors. Only two prints are known to exist with these colors. Other prints of this image are printed only in blue and green. (Edvard Munch, *Mädchen aud der Brücke*, woodcut with lithographic plates, 19 ⅝ x 17 inches, Sotheby-New York, October 31, 1991, $187,000)

MURRAY, Elizabeth
American b. 1940
stencil: (H) $660
planographic: (L) $4,950; (H) $8,250

MURRAY, J.G.
mixed-media: (H) $121

MUSI, Agostino de (called Veneziano)
Italian 1490-1540
intaglio: (H) $10,996

MUSIC, Zoran Antonio
Italian 1909-1952
intaglio: (L) $414; (H) $1,133
planographic: (L) $968; (H) $1,846

MUYBRIDGE, Eadweard (attrib.)
English 1830-1904
photo: (L) $660; (H) $20,900

MUYBRIDGE, Eadweard
1830-1904
photo-repro: (L) $605; (H) $700
port/books: (L) $825; (H) $14,300
photo: (L) $1,980; (H) $1,980

MYERS, Jerome
American 1867-1940/41
intaglio: (H) $138

NADELMAN, Elie
American, b.Poland 1882-1946
intaglio: (H) $3,300

NAGAI, Kiyosiri
planographic: (H) $33

NAGATANI, Patrick
photo: (L) $400; (H) $500

NAGATANI, Patrick and Andree
TRACEY
photo: (H) $605

NAGEL and WEINGARTNER
planographic: (H) $3,850

NAKAYAMA, Tadashi
Japanese b. 1927
relief: (H) $550

NAKIAN, Reuben
American b. 1897
intaglio: (H) $522

NANG, He
stencil: (H) $770

NANKIVELL, Frank A.
posters: (H) $275

NANOGAK, Agnes
b. 1925
stencil: (H) $55
relief: (H) $138

NANTEUIL, C. (after Appian)
planographic: (H) $50

NASH, John and Edward Wedlake
BRAYLEY
19th cent.
port/books: (H) $16,500

NASH, Paul
English 1889-1946
planographic: (L) $1,036; (H) $1,591

NASH, Willard
planographic: (H) $550

NASON, Gertrude
American 1890-1968
relief: (H) $220

NASON, Thomas W.
relief: (H) $220

NATKIN, Robert
American b. 1930
planographic: (L) $220; (H) $413

NAUMAN, Bruce
American b. 1941
intaglio: (H) $2,200
planographic: (L) $1,320; (H) $9,350
mixed-media: (H) $2,420

NAY, Ernst Wilhelm
German 1902-1968
intaglio: (L) $505; (H) $2,563
relief: (H) $1,370
planographic: (L) $1,898; (H) $6,383

NAYA, C.
intaglio: (H) $116

NEAL, David (Dalhoff) (after)
American 1838-1915
planographic: (H) $275

NEALE, William Henry (attrib.)
d. 1939
photo: (H) $790

NEESON, John
intaglio: (H) $70

NEGRE, Charles
photo: (H) $3,080

NEILL, William
photo: (H) $650

NEIMAN, Leroy
American b. 1927
stencil: (L) $165; (H) $1,705
planographic: (L) $330; (H) $660

NEIMANAS, Joyce
photo: (H) $500

NELSON, Lusha
photo: (H) $605

NEMES, Endre
contemporary
planographic: (L) $554; (H) $665

NEPVEU, V. le
French 19th cent.
planographic: (H) $110

NESBITT, Jackson Lee
American b. 1913
intaglio: (L) $248; (H) $303
planographic: (H) $110

NESBITT, Lowell
American b. 1933
stencil: (L) $55; (H) $275

NESCH, Rolf
1893-1975
relief: (H) $1,097
mixed-media: (H) $1,084
generic: (H) $4,964

NESENSOHN, Carl
1898-1970
photo: (H) $605

NETHERFIELD, Stafford C.
posters: (H) $176

NEUKOMM, Emil Alfred
Swiss 20th cent.
posters: (H) $66

NEULEBEN, (after)
intaglio: (H) $193

NEUMANN, Hans
Austrian b. 1888
relief: (H) $303

NEUQUELMAN, Lucien
French b. 1909
planographic: (H) $647

NEUVILLE, Alphonse de
French 1835-1885
intaglio: (H) $110
photo-repro: (H) $88

NEVELSON, Louise
Russian/American 1900-1988
intaglio: (H) $935
planographic: (L) $880; (H) $880
mixed-media: (L) $517; (H) $1,980
others: (H) $3,300

NEVILLE, A.W. (after)
intaglio: (H) $2,993

NEVILLE, A.W.
intaglio: (H) $400

NEVINSON, Christopher Richard
Wynne
1889-1946
intaglio: (L) $146; (H) $2,072
planographic: (H) $3,764

NEWBERRY, Clare Turley
planographic: (H) $390

NEWBOLD, George, Publisher
planographic: (H) $140

NEWELL, J.P., Lithographer
American ac. 1858-1870
planographic: (H) $825

NEWHALL, Beaumont
photo: (L) $134; (H) $605

NEWHOUSE, C.B. (after)
intaglio: (H) $151

NEWMAN, Arnold
b. 1918
photo: (L) $918; (H) $2,869

NEWMAN, Barnett
American 1905-1970
planographic: (L) $28,600; (H) $49,500

NEWTON, Alison Houston
Canadian b. 1890
relief: (L) $138; (H) $331

NEWTON, Helmut
German b. 1920
photo: (L) $770; (H) $20,900

NIBLOCK, Harry
American 20th cent.
port/books: (H) $55

NIBLOCK, Marguy
American 20th cent.
relief: (H) $28

NICHOL, George
port/books: (H) $3,080

NICHOLS, Dale
American b. 1904
planographic: (H) $193

NICHOLS, Jack
planographic: (H) $194

NICHOLSON, (after)
intaglio: (H) $99

NICHOLSON, Ben
British 1894-1982
intaglio: (L) $2,568; (H) $5,567

NICHOLSON, Sir William
English 1872-1949
relief: (L) $275; (H) $4,971
planographic: (L) $88; (H) $248
port/books: (H) $275

NICHOLSON, Sir William (after)
planographic: (H) $138

NICOLL, James Craig
American 1846-1918
intaglio: (L) $66; (H) $138

NICOLL, Marion Florence
1909-1985
relief: (H) $439
others: (L) $341; (H) $483

NICOLSON, John
intaglio: (H) $131

NIGHTINGALE, Basil
generic: (H) $222

NILSON, Johannes Esaias
1721-1788
intaglio: (H) $105

NISBETT, Robert Hogg
American 1879-1961
intaglio: (H) $99

NITSCH, Hermann
b. 1938
mixed-media: (H) $1,702

NITSCHE, Erik
Swiss b. 1908
posters: (H) $58

NITTIS, G. De
intaglio: (H) $963

NIXON, J.
planographic: (H) $17

NIXON, Nicholas
photo: (L) $880; (H) $935

NOBLE, John
1874-1935
planographic: (H) $165

NOCKOLDS, Roy
posters: (H) $715

NODA, Massaki
stencil: (L) $165; (H) $440

NODDER
intaglio: (L) $132; (H) $770

NOEH, Anna T.
Canadian School b. 1926
stencil: (H) $93

NOIR, M. le (attrib.)
relief: (H) $44

NOLAN, Sidney Robert
Australian b. 1917
stencil: (L) $157; (H) $174
planographic: (L) $87; (H) $378

NOLDE, Emil
German 1867-1956
intaglio: (L) $2,779; (H) $7,801
relief: (L) $2,698; (H) $23,015
planographic: (L) $6,473; (H) $98,175

NOOMS, Reinier (called ZEEMAN)
c. 1623-1664
port/books: (H) $13,352

NORDEN, Ronaldo
intaglio: (H) $44

NORDFELDT, Bror Julius Olsson
Swedish/American 1878-1955
intaglio: (H) $303
relief: (H) $15,400
others: (L) $3,300; (H) $7,700

NORDWALL, Raymond
planographic: (L) $66; (H) $99

NORFLEET, Barbara
photo: (H) $400

NORGAARD, Bjorn
planographic: (H) $56

NORTHCOTE, James (after)
intaglio: (L) $108; (H) $619

NORTON, M.E.
posters: (H) $110

NOSKOWIAK, Sonya
photo: (L) $2,420; (H) $4,400

NOVAK, Lorie
photo: (H) $450

NOVELLI, Gastone
intaglio: (L) $425; (H) $472
planographic: (H) $803

NOYER, Denis Paul
French b. 1940
planographic: (L) $77; (H) $165

NUGENT, G.
planographic: (H) $91

NUTTER, William
intaglio: (H) $81

NUTTING, Wallace
American b. 1861
planographic: (H) $99
photo-repro: (H) $165
photo: (H) $88
generic: (H) $77

NUYTTENS, Josef Pierre
American 1885-1960
intaglio: (H) $330

O'CONNER, Thom
American 20th cent.
planographic: (H) $55

O'HIGGINS, Pablo
Mexican b. 1904
relief: (H) $880
planographic: (H) $61

O'NEIL, Elaine
photo: (H) $300

O'SULLIVAN, Timothy
photo: (L) $440; (H) $660

OBERHARDT, William
American 1882-1958
planographic: (H) $17

OBERHAUSER, E. (after)
photo-repro: (H) $425

OBREGON, Alejandro
Spanish/Colombian b. 1920
intaglio: (H) $660

ODJIG, Daphne
b. 1928
stencil: (H) $184
planographic: (H) $215

OEHLEN, Albert
b. 1954
mixed-media: (H) $156

OERREES, T. Paul
posters: (L) $770; (H) $880

OESTERELEIN, Sharon
Russian contemporary
planographic: (H) $110

OGBORNE, John
intaglio: (H) $870

OGUISS, J.
planographic: (H) $2,318

OHARA, Frederick James
American b. 1904
relief: (H) $110

OHARA, Shoson
Japanese 20th cent.
planographic: (H) $66

OHOVILOK
20th cent.
generic: (H) $83

OKAMOTO, Taro
b. 1912
planographic: (H) $815

OKU
stencil: (H) $83

OLDENBURG, Claes
Swedish/American b. 1929
intaglio: (L) $385; (H) $2,200
stencil: (H) $909
planographic: (L) $198; (H) $5,225
posters: (L) $213; (H) $3,025
photo-repro: (L) $715; (H) $3,025
port/books: (H) $4,620

OLIVEIRA, Nathan
American b. 1928
planographic: (L) $385; (H) $3,850
port/books: (H) $2,200

OLSEN, John
port/books: (H) $2,610

OLSEN, Wiliam Skotte
port/books: (H) $296

OLSSON-HAGALUND, Olle
planographic: (L) $868; (H) $1,146

ONLEY, Toni
b. 1928
intaglio: (H) $137
stencil: (L) $93; (H) $253

OORTHUYS, Cas
photo: (H) $468

OPIE, James (after)
intaglio: (H) $101

OPPENHEIM, Louis
posters: (H) $3,850

OPPENHEIM, Meret
Swiss 1913-1985
relief: (L) $241; (H) $497
planographic: (H) $745

ORAZI, Manuel
planographic: (H) $495

ORKIN, Ruth
1921-1985
photo: (L) $1,210; (H) $7,700

ORLEANS, Princesse Marie
planographic: (H) $100

ORLIK, Emil
German 1870-1932
intaglio: (L) $97; (H) $290
port/books: (H) $5,291

ORLOWSKI, Alexander
planographic: (H) $483

OROZCO, Jose Clemente
Mexican 1883-1949
planographic: (L) $358; (H) $4,950

ORR, Alfred Everitt
posters: (H) $121

ORTEGA, Al
American 20th cent.
planographic: (H) $143

ORTIZ, Manuel Angeles
intaglio: (H) $287

OS, Pim Van
photo: (H) $1,320

OSTADE, Adriaen van
Dutch 1610-1685
intaglio: (L) $242; (H) $45,553

OSTENDORFER, Michael
relief: (H) $5,390

OSTERLUND, Allan
intaglio: (H) $290

OSTHAUS, Edmund H.
German/American 1858-1928
intaglio: (L) $138; (H) $275

OSWALD, Wenzel
German 19th cent.
planographic: (L) $303; (H) $358

OTTOCHIE
intaglio: (H) $224

OUBORG, Piet
planographic: (H) $329

OUDOT, R.
planographic: (H) $161

OUDRY, J.B. (after)
intaglio: (H) $240

OURY, Louis
French 19th/20th cent.
posters: (H) $220

OUTERBRIDGE, Paul (Jr.)
American 1896-1958
photo: (L) $2,420; (H) $24,200

OVEREND, William Heysmann
British 1851-1898
planographic: (H) $138

OXMAN, Katja
intaglio: (L) $440; (H) $770

OYSTON, George
British exhib. 1891-1897
planographic: (H) $209

OZANNE, N.
intaglio: (L) $101; (H) $111

PAFFGEN, C. O.
German b. 1930
photo: (H) $573

PAGE, John
intaglio: (H) $83

PAL
French 19th cent.
posters: (L) $495; (H) $800

PALADINO, Mimmo
Italian b. 1948
intaglio: (H) $1,034
relief: (H) $2,919
planographic: (H) $577
mixed-media: (H) $1,205
port/books: (H) $2,091

PALAZUELO, Pablo
planographic: (H) $514

PALENSKE, Reinhold H.
American 1884-1954
intaglio: (L) $88; (H) $275
planographic: (H) $165
generic: (H) $248

PALERMO, Blinky
German? 1943-1977
stencil: (L) $1,370; (H) $2,128
relief: (H) $1,803
photo-repro: (H) $1,010
port/books: (L) $10,638; (H) $17,730
others: (H) $2,128
generic: (H) $2,128

PALEY, Stanley
photo: (H) $220

PALLADIO, Andrea
port/books: (H) $3,850

PALLMALL, G. and W. NICOL and
W. MILLER
19th cent.
planographic: (H) $385

PALMER, Ethleen
stencil: (H) $244

This print by Dutch genre artist Adriaen van Ostade (1610-1685) has a foolscap watermark. The term foolscap is used interchangeably both as a watermark and as a paper size. The use of the term as a watermark dates back to 1479. Of the several variants of the watermark, all have the head of a court jester with a cap and a pointy collar. Later the term was used more generically and came to mean a paper size of about 13 ½ x 17 inches. (Adriaen van Ostade, *The Breakfast*, etching, 8 ½ x 10 ¼ inches, Sotheby-New York, May 15, 1992, $3,850)

PALMER, Samuel
1805-1881
intaglio: (L) $88; (H) $5,567

PALMORE, Tom
American b. 1945
planographic: (L) $275; (H) $440

PANKOK, Otto
1893-1966
intaglio: (L) $818; (H) $1,299
relief: (L) $496; (H) $2,246
planographic: (H) $1,553

PANLE, Hart
relief: (H) $88

PAOLOZZI, Eduardo
British b. 1924
stencil: (L) $175; (H) $213

PAONE, Peter
American b. 1936
port/books: (H) $187

PAPART, Max
French b. 1911
planographic: (L) $41; (H) $220
mixed-media: (H) $617

PAPERK, Josie
b. 1918
relief: (H) $98

PAPPRILL, Henry
intaglio: (H) $990

PAPWORTH, John Buonarotti
port/books: (H) $1,980

PAREDES, Vicenzo de (after)
planographic: (H) $220

PARKER, Olivia
photo: (L) $500; (H) $1,210

PARKINSON, Norman
1913-1990
photo: (H) $3,025

PARRILLA
Spanish 20th cent.
posters: (H) $1,100

PARRISH, Maxfield
American 1870-1966
planographic: (L) $220; (H) $1,100
generic: (L) $143; (H) $1,210

PARRISH, Maxfield (after)
generic: (H) $138

PARRISH, Stephen
American 1846-1938
intaglio: (L) $88; (H) $330

PARROCEL, Ch. (after)
intaglio: (H) $158

PARRY, Roger
photo: (H) $1,650

PARSONS, C.
planographic: (H) $121

PARSONS, Charles, Lithographer
American
planographic: (H) $5,060

PARTENHEIMER, Jurgen
b. 1947
intaglio: (H) $234

PARTOS, Paul
planographic: (H) $122

PARTRIDGE, Roi
American 1888-1984
intaglio: (L) $165; (H) $523

PASCHKE, Ed
American b. 1939
planographic: (L) $330; (H) $660

PASCIN, Jules
French/American 1885-1930
intaglio: (L) $413; (H) $578
planographic: (L) $181; (H) $330
port/books: (L) $9,544; (H) $9,918

PASMORE, Victor
English b. 1908
intaglio: (L) $317; (H) $1,234
planographic: (H) $175
mixed-media: (H) $1,049

PASTORINI
intaglio: (H) $110

PATER, Jean Baptiste Joseph (after)
French 1695-1736
photo-repro: (H) $364

PATON, Frank
English 1856-1909
intaglio: (H) $100

PATON, Frank and Joseph Bishop
PRATT
English 19th cent.
intaglio: (H) $165

PATRY, Pierre
Canadian School b. 1956
stencil: (H) $93

PATT, Rudolph
American 20th cent.
relief: (H) $55

PATTERSON, Margaret Jordan
American 1867-1950
relief: (L) $99; (H) $1,100

PAUL, John Dean (after)
port/books: (H) $1,980

PAUL, Rena George Hermann
French 19th cent.
intaglio: (H) $110

PAULE, Hans
Austrian School 1879-1951
intaglio: (H) $189
relief: (L) $189; (H) $233

PAULL, Grace
American b. 1898
planographic: (H) $204

PAXTON, Joseph
intaglio: (L) $275; (H) $2,090
port/books: (L) $880; (H) $1,870

PEAN, Rene
French
planographic: (H) $110

PEARLSTEIN, Philip
American b. 1924
intaglio: (L) $825; (H) $2,090
planographic: (L) $275; (H) $495

PEART, John
intaglio: (L) $43; (H) $157

PEARY, Admiral Robert E.
photo: (L) $467; (H) $1,650

PECHAUBES, Eugene
French 1890-1967
planographic: (L) $110; (H) $275

PECHE, Dagobert
1887-1923
planographic: (H) $1,443

PECHSTEIN, Max
German 1881-1955
intaglio: (L) $702; (H) $6,395
relief: (L) $1,925; (H) $28,571
planographic: (L) $660; (H) $10,665
port/books: (L) $2,128; (H) $35,460

PECK, Leonard
intaglio: (H) $70

PEDERSEN, Carl Henning
Danish b. 1913
planographic: (L) $226; (H) $414

PEET, Michael
planographic: (H) $22

PEHRSON, Karl Axel
planographic: (H) $598

PELIGRINI, Giovanni Antonio (after)
intaglio: (H) $165

PELLAN, Alfred
Canadian b. 1906
intaglio: (L) $167; (H) $873
stencil: (L) $234; (H) $421

PELLERIN
intaglio: (H) $138

PENA, Amado Maurilio (Jr.)
b. 1943
planographic: (L) $33; (H) $88

PENCK, A.R.
German b. 1939
stencil: (L) $770; (H) $3,575
relief: (H) $329
planographic: (L) $377; (H) $1,976
port/books: (H) $1,606

PENCZ, Georg
c. 1500-c.1550
intaglio: (L) $275; (H) $1,882

PENFIELD, Edward
American 1866-1925
posters: (L) $110; (H) $1,760

PENN, Irving
American b. 1917
photo: (L) $1,375; (H) $24,200

PENNANT, Thomas
intaglio: (L) $193; (H) $1,199

PENNELL, Joseph
American 1860-1926
intaglio: (L) $22; (H) $4,620
planographic: (L) $138; (H) $330
posters: (H) $330
port/books: (H) $303

PENNELL, M.
intaglio: (H) $110

PERCIER, Charles and Pierre Francois
Leonard FONTAINE
port/books: (H) $4,180

PERESS, Gilles
photo: (H) $500

PERGOLISI, (after BARTOLOZZI)
intaglio: (H) $138

PERLMUTTER, Jack
American b. 1920
planographic: (H) $44

PERNET
posters: (H) $495

PERRENOT, (after)
intaglio: (H) $59

PERRIER, F.
intaglio: (H) $128

PESCHERET, Leon R.
intaglio: (H) $138

PETERS, Rev'd Mathew William
(after)
intaglio: (L) $81; (H) $263

PETERS-EHBECKE
20th cent.
intaglio: (H) $105

PETERSEN, Martin
intaglio: (H) $165

Irving Penn's (b. 1917) portraits of celebrities are notable for their simple distinct poses. The backgrounds are plain, almost clinical, with neutral illumination from a north light. This portrait of Picasso was taken in 1957. This print, an edition of 47, was printed in 1985 on Rives paper hand-coated with platinum. Penn uses platinum prints and dye-transfer color prints, two of the most archivally stable printing processes. (Irving Penn, *Picasso, Cannes*, platinum print on Rives with aluminum backing, 18 ⅝ x 18 ⅝ inches, Christie-New York, April 15, 1992, $15,400)

PETERSON
planographic: (H) $6

PETERSON, Roland
intaglio: (H) $220

PETHER, William
1731-1795
intaglio: (H) $4,241

PETICOV, Antonio
Brazilian b. 1946
stencil: (H) $110
planographic: (H) $28

PETIT, Gaston
Canadian School b. 1930
planographic: (H) $111

PEYRE, Marie Joseph
port/books: (H) $990

PFAHL, John
photo: (L) $330; (H) $1,980

PFENNIGER, Matthias
1739-1813
intaglio: (H) $3,147

PHILI
posters: (H) $880

PHILLIPS, Matt
planographic: (H) $275

PHILLIPS, Peter
stencil: (H) $1,322

PHILLIPS, Walter Joseph
Canadian 1884-1963
intaglio: (H) $317
relief: (L) $137; (H) $5,748
port/books: (H) $874

PHLASH, Philin
photo: (L) $160; (H) $300

PHOTOGRAPHS - ANONYMOUS
photo: (L) $66; (H) $18,771

PIAUBERT, Jean
planographic: (L) $38; (H) $66

PIAZ, Teddy
posters: (H) $1,210

PIAZZETTA, Giovanni Battista (after)
Italian 1862-1754
intaglio: (H) $329
port/books: (H) $4,784

PIAZZETTA, Giovanni Battista (after)
intaglio: (L) $1,695; (H) $2,193

PIAZZETTA, J.B. (after)
intaglio: (H) $2,178

PICABIA, Francis
French 1878-1953
stencil: (H) $204
generic: (H) $682

PICASSO, Pablo
b. Spain 1881 d. France 1973
intaglio: (L) $385; (H) $724,324
stencil: (H) $578
relief: (L) $880; (H) $113,026
planographic: (L) $66; (H) $74,820
posters: (L) $303; (H) $5,815
mixed-media: (L) $3,555; (H) $6,600
photo-repro: (H) $1,650
port/books: (L) $1,988; (H) $35,200
others: (H) $4,745
generic: (L) $495; (H) $11,766

PICASSO, Pablo (after)
intaglio: (L) $138; (H) $2,200
stencil: (L) $220; (H) $6,600
relief: (H) $1,650
planographic: (L) $66; (H) $2,821
mixed-media: (H) $336
photo-repro: (L) $1,045; (H) $2,300
generic: (L) $523; (H) $4,557

PICASSO, Pablo and Lemagny
intaglio: (H) $2,007

PICHET, Roland
b. 1936
stencil: (H) $146

PICHET, Roland
Canadian School b. 1936
intaglio: (H) $47
planographic: (H) $56

PICHLER, Johann Peter
1765-1807
intaglio: (H) $2,051

PICK, Anton (after)
Austrian b. 1840
planographic: (H) $105

PICOT, V.M.
intaglio: (H) $155

PIECK, Anton
1895-1987
intaglio: (L) $417; (H) $534
relief: (H) $501

PIECK, Henri
b. 1895
intaglio: (H) $551

PIENE, Otto
German/American b. 1928
stencil: (H) $269

PIERTERSZ, Claes
Dutch 1620-1683
intaglio: (H) $132

PIETRI, Alberto de
planographic: (H) $66

PIGAL
mixed-media: (H) $162

PIGEOT
intaglio: (H) $165

PIGNON, Edourad
planographic: (H) $61

PIJUAN, Joan Hernandez
planographic: (H) $251

PILLEMENT, J. (after)
intaglio: (H) $1,584

PILLSBURY PICTURES
photo: (H) $935

PIMLOTT, Philip
American 1871-1960
port/books: (H) $110

PINET, Charles F.
French 1867-1932
intaglio: (H) $88

PINKAS, Julius (called PASCIN)
intaglio: (H) $2,287

PINTO, Angelo
American 20th cent.
relief: (H) $275

PIPER, John
English b. 1903
stencil: (H) $533
planographic: (L) $55; (H) $812

PIPER, John (after)
photo-repro: (L) $263; (H) $609

PIRANDELLO, Fausto
1899-1975
planographic: (H) $945

PIRANESE, J.B.
intaglio: (L) $620; (H) $1,027

PIRANESI, (after)
intaglio: (H) $275

PIRANESI, Francesco (after)
intaglio: (H) $110

PIRANESI, Francesco
Italian 1758-1810
intaglio: (L) $825; (H) $1,100

PIRANESI, Francesco, Publisher
Italian 1758-1810
intaglio: (L) $6,362; (H) $6,362

PIRANESI, G.B.
intaglio: (L) $1,003; (H) $1,751

PIRANESI, Giovanni Battista
Italian 1720-1778
intaglio: (L) $110; (H) $34,558
port/books: (L) $770; (H) $83,728

PIROU, Eugene
photo: (H) $357

PISSARRO, Camille
French 1830-1903
intaglio: (L) $281; (H) $103,475
relief: (H) $30,971
planographic: (L) $770; (H) $35,750

PISSARRO, Georges Manzana
stencil: (L) $541; (H) $580

PISSARRO, Orovida
French 1893-1968
intaglio: (H) $297

PISTOLETTO, Michelangelo
Italian b. 1933
stencil: (L) $4,400; (H) $4,534

PITALOOSIE, Saila
b. 1942
planographic: (H) $92

PITSEOLAK, Peter
mixed-media: (H) $293

PIZA, Arthur Luiz
French b. 1928
intaglio: (H) $116

PLANSON, Andre
planographic: (H) $351

PLATT, Charles
intaglio: (H) $110

PLATT LYNES, George
photo: (H) $935

PLEISSNER, Ogden
American 1905-1983
intaglio: (H) $1,100
planographic: (L) $110; (H) $440
generic: (L) $193; (H) $440

PLOSSU, Bernard
photo: (H) $770

POIGNANT, Axel
photo: (H) $70

POKRASSO, Ron
contemporary
planographic: (H) $550

POLCZER, Lojos
intaglio: (H) $50

POLIAKOFF, Serge
French 1900-1969
intaglio: (H) $3,300
stencil: (H) $1,464
planographic: (L) $1,049; (H) $5,394

POLIAKOFF, Serge (after)
planographic: (H) $2,217

POLKE, Sigmar
German b. 1941
photo-repro: (L) $649; (H) $938
photo: (H) $1,147

POLLACK, Max
Austrian b. 1886
intaglio: (H) $55

POLLARD, J. (after)
intaglio: (H) $22

POLLARD, James
English 1797-1859/67
intaglio: (H) $348

POLLARD, James (after)
intaglio: (H) $357
port/books: (L) $440; (H) $1,299

POLLARD, R. and Sons, Publishers
others: (H) $165

POLLARD, R., Publisher
intaglio: (H) $101

POLLOCK, Jack Henry
planographic: (L) $92; (H) $137

POLLOCK, Jackson
American 1912-1956
stencil: (L) $8,800; (H) $9,900

POMODORA, Arnaldo
intaglio: (H) $1,700

POMOLOGICAL POMONA
planographic: (H) $1,210

PONTING, Herbert
1871-1935
photo: (L) $383; (H) $12,844

POOLE, Horatio Nelson
American 1885-1934
intaglio: (H) $11

POONS, Larry
American b. 1937
stencil: (L) $88; (H) $330
planographic: (H) $385

POPE, A. (Jr.)
planographic: (H) $88

POPE, Alexander (after)
American 1849-1924
planographic: (H) $99

POPKINS, Samuel K.
American 20th cent.
intaglio: (H) $22

PORCELLA, Phil
photo: (H) $140

PORTER, Eliot
port/books: (L) $1,650; (H) $6,600
photo: (L) $495; (H) $1,210

PORTER, Fairfield
American 1907-1975
planographic: (H) $770

PORTER, Katherine
American b. 1941
stencil: (H) $33

PORTERFIELD, Wilbur
photo: (H) $522

PORTMANN, H.
Swiss 20th cent.
posters: (L) $41; (H) $62

POSADA, Jose Guadalupe
Mexican 1851-1913
relief: (H) $248

POST, William B.
photo: (L) $880; (H) $1,320

POSTERS
posters: (L) $121; (H) $7,150

POSTERS-MOVIE
posters: (L) $110; (H) $57,200

POTTER, Louis McClellan
American 1873-1912
generic: (H) $28

POTTHAST, Edward
American 1857-1927
posters: (H) $275
generic: (H) $1,100

POUGHEON, Eugene Robert
French b. 1886
intaglio: (H) $5,225

POULBOT, Francisque
French School 1879-1946
planographic: (L) $111; (H) $168

POUWELSZOON, Claes
intaglio: (H) $1,988

POWER, Cyril
1872-1951
intaglio: (L) $230; (H) $391
relief: (L) $942; (H) $2,779

POYNTER, F.J. (after)
photo-repro: (H) $220

PRADES, A.F. de (after)
British ac. 1860-1879
intaglio: (H) $330

PRANG, L.
19th cent.
planographic: (H) $220

PRANG and CO., (after Julian O.
Davidson)
American 19th cent.
planographic: (H) $605

PRANG and MAYER, Publishers
19th cent.
planographic: (H) $660

PRATT, Christopher
stencil: (H) $1,261

PREISLER, J.M.
intaglio: (H) $2,300

PREUSS, J.A. (publishers)
photo: (H) $198

PREVOST, Antoine
Canadian School b. 1930
port/books: (H) $166

PREVOST, J.L.
generic: (H) $15

PRIETO, Gregorio
planographic: (H) $251

PRINCE, Douglas
photo: (H) $150

PRINCE, Len
photo: (H) $770

PRINCE, Richard
American b. 1925
photo: (L) $4,400; (H) $18,700

PRIVAT-LIVEMONT
planographic: (H) $182

PROCACCINI, Camillo
Italian 1546/51-1629
intaglio: (L) $1,882; (H) $19,635

PROCH, Don
b. 1944
planographic: (H) $293

PROCHASKA, J.
American 20th cent.
port/books: (H) $413

PRODHOMME, F. (after)
planographic: (H) $440

PRUD'HON, (after)
French 1758-1823
planographic: (H) $121

PRZYREMBEL, Hans
photo: (H) $251

PUGH, Clifton Ernest
intaglio: (L) $261; (H) $435

PURCELL, Charles Roy
American b. 1946
intaglio: (H) $11

PURCELL, Rosamund
photo: (L) $280; (H) $400

PURCELLS, M.
intaglio: (H) $87

PURRMANN, Hans
German 1880-1966
planographic: (H) $1,257

PURSELL, Weimer
posters: (H) $176

PUSHMAN, Hovsep
American 1877-1966
planographic: (L) $143; (H) $176

PUYDT, Paul Emile de
port/books: (H) $418

PUYO, Emile Constant Joachim
1857-1933
photo: (H) $956

PYBUS, Henry (attrib.)
photo: (H) $5,335

PYK, Madeleine
contemporary
planographic: (H) $462

PYNE, William Henry
English 1769-1843
port/books: (H) $7,150

QUAD, Matthias
1557-1609
intaglio: (H) $25,133

QUIGLEY, Edward W.
1898-1977
photo: (L) $935; (H) $2,860

RAALTE, Henri van
intaglio: (L) $261; (H) $609

RABEL, Fanny
American 20th cent.
planographic: (H) $11

RABENDING, E., J. MAGILL,
J. MOFFAT and others
photo: (H) $1,284

RAEBURN, H. Macbeth
Continental 20th cent.
intaglio: (H) $39

RAEDERSCHEIDT, Anton
1892-1970
mixed-media: (H) $2,114

RAETZ, Markus
contemporary
intaglio: (L) $321; (H) $362
stencil: (H) $241

This lithograph is numbered 195/200. This could mean that it was the 195th impression pulled through the press or merely that it was the 195th impression signed by the artist. (Robert Rauschenburg, *Artist's Rights Today*, lithograph printed in colors with embossing, 39 ½ x 27 inches, Weschler, December 14, 1991, $1,100)

RAFAELLI, J.F.
intaglio: (H) $83

RAFFAEL, Joseph
American b. 1933
intaglio: (H) $550
planographic: (L) $770; (H) $1,870

RAFFAELLI, Jean Francois
French 1850-1924
intaglio: (L) $96; (H) $4,754

RAFFRAY
intaglio: (H) $46

RAGLESS, Max
intaglio: (H) $209

RAIMONDI, Marcantonio
c. 1480-1527
intaglio: (L) $143; (H) $1,601

RAINER, Arnulf
German b. 1929
intaglio: (L) $388; (H) $1,184
stencil: (H) $361
planographic: (H) $704
mixed-media: (L) $1,251; (H) $10,854
port/books: (L) $1,082; (H) $4,610
photo: (H) $573

RAMBERG, J.H.
intaglio: (H) $535

RAMOS, Mel
American b. 1935
stencil: (L) $562; (H) $1,221
planographic: (H) $605
mixed-media: (H) $550
photo-repro: (H) $642
generic: (H) $145

RANDALL, A.J.
photo: (H) $143

RANFT, Richard
Swiss 1862-1931
intaglio: (H) $1,446
posters: (H) $165

RANKIN, David
stencil: (L) $70; (H) $174

RANKIN, Myra Warner
relief: (H) $220

RANTOUL, Neal
photo: (H) $250

RAPHAEL, (after)
Italian 1482-1520
photo-repro: (H) $77

RAPHAEL, Joseph
American 1869/72-1950
intaglio: (H) $303

RASKIN, Joseph
American 1897-1981
port/books: (H) $132

RASKIN, Saul
Russian/American b. 1878
intaglio: (L) $165; (H) $248

RATTNER, Abraham
American 1895-1978
planographic: (H) $165
port/books: (L) $825; (H) $825

RAUSCHENBERG, Robert
American b. 1925
intaglio: (L) $7,150; (H) $10,450
stencil: (L) $110; (H) $3,850
planographic: (L) $715; (H) $11,000
posters: (L) $41; (H) $511
mixed-media: (L) $550; (H) $47,300
photo-repro: (L) $220; (H) $2,928
port/books: (L) $880; (H) $15,400
photo: (L) $2,161; (H) $2,161

RAUTERT, Timm
German b. 1941
photo: (H) $573

RAVANESI, Bill
photo: (L) $130; (H) $160

RAVO, Rene
posters: (H) $495

RAY, Man
American 1890-1976
intaglio: (L) $204; (H) $1,464
stencil: (L) $880; (H) $7,700
planographic: (L) $82; (H) $2,750
photo-repro: (L) $671; (H) $1,100
port/books: (L) $418; (H) $23,100
photo: (L) $670; (H) $66,000

RAY-JONES, Tony (photographer)
port/books: (H) $589

RAZZIA
posters: (H) $440

READ, S.
intaglio: (H) $139

Man Ray (1890-1976) was a painter, sculptor, photographer, and filmmaker. Always experimenting and interested in avant-garde movements, he became a Surrealist, one of a group of artists who explored the imagery of dreams and the unconscious. (Man Ray, *Head of a Woman, 1946*, solarized gelatin silver print, 8 x 6 ¼ inches, Butterfield, December 10, 1991, $2,750)

READ, W.
generic: (H) $44

REASE, W.H.
planographic: (H) $248

REBOUR, Francisque
European 19th/20th cent.
intaglio: (H) $55

RED STAR, Kevin
planographic: (L) $132; (H) $220

REDON, Georges
French 1869-1943
intaglio: (L) $22; (H) $88
posters: (L) $165; (H) $715
generic: (H) $22

REDON, Odilon
French 1840-1916
intaglio: (L) $161; (H) $5,965
planographic: (L) $330; (H) $74,565
generic: (L) $33; (H) $302

REDONDELA, Agustin
intaglio: (H) $764

REDOUTE, Pierre Joseph
French 1759-1840
intaglio: (H) $660
port/books: (H) $1,320

REDOUTE, Pierre Joseph (after)
intaglio: (L) $209; (H) $825
generic: (H) $545

REED, Doel
American 20th cent.
intaglio: (L) $715; (H) $990

REED, Ethel
posters: (H) $132

REED, Roland
photo: (H) $358
generic: (H) $176

REES, Frederic Lloyd
planographic: (L) $739; (H) $1,044

REEVE, R.G. (after F.G. Turner)
planographic: (H) $1,210

REEVE, R.G.
intaglio: (L) $348; (H) $425

REEVES, Richard Stone
20th cent.
generic: (H) $99

REICH-MUNSTERBERG, Eugene
German b. 1866
intaglio: (H) $55

REICHERT, Josua
planographic: (H) $223

REID, Bill
stencil: (L) $585; (H) $3,317

REINA
planographic: (H) $33

REINAGLE, Phillip (after)
intaglio: (H) $387

REINEERMAN, F. and LAFON (after)
intaglio: (H) $580

REINHARDT, Ad
American 1913-1967
stencil: (H) $660
port/books: (L) $2,475; (H) $5,500

REINHARDT, Joseph
1749-1829
intaglio: (L) $116; (H) $331

REINHART, Johann Christian
1761-1847
intaglio: (H) $2,891

REISS, Lionel S.
port/books: (H) $385

REJLANDER, Oscar Gustav
photo: (L) $904; (H) $1,670

REMBRANDT
Dutch 1606-1669
intaglio: (L) $55; (H) $956,894
generic: (L) $358; (H) $1,018

REMBRANDT, (and pupil)
intaglio: (L) $1,296; (H) $2,392

REMBRANDT, (after)
intaglio: (L) $88; (H) $99

REMBRANDT, (pupil of)
intaglio: (L) $533; (H) $2,791

REMON, Georges
port/books: (H) $130

RENART
French 20th cent.
planographic: (H) $55

RENAU
20th cent.
posters: (H) $165

Each season numerous lots by Rembrandt are offered at auction. Five lots of *The Three Trees* were offered during the 1991-1992 auction season. The price range was from $248 to $95,075. The low end was for a light struck copy of a late edition; the high end was a vintage Rembrandt print with a distinct burr mark, watermark, and platemark and in good condition. Many of Rembrandt's plates were reworked and reprinted well into the 19th century. (Rembrandt, *The Three Trees, 1643*, etching with drypoint and engraving, 8 $\frac{7}{16}$ x 11 inches, Christie-London, July 2, 1992, $95,075)

RENESON, Chet
 planographic: (H) $182

RENESSE, Constantijn Daniel van
 1626-1680
 intaglio: (H) $6,562

RENGER-PATZSCH, Albert
 American 1897-1966
 photo: (L) $394; (H) $2,200

RENI, Guido
 Italian 1575-1642
 intaglio: (H) $3,190

RENOIR, (after)
 intaglio: (H) $385
 stencil: (H) $116

RENOIR, Pierre Auguste
 French 1841-1919
 intaglio: (L) $165; (H) $9,941
 planographic: (L) $396; (H) $83,644

REPTON, Humphrey
 English 1752-1818
 port/books: (L) $3,520; (H) $7,700

REPTON, Humphrey and John Adey
 REPTON
 port/books: (H) $6,600

RET, Etienne
 American b. France 1900
 intaglio: (H) $55
 planographic: (L) $17; (H) $22

REUTER, John
photo: (H) $400

REVERE, Paul
American 1735-1818
intaglio: (H) $48,400

REVES-BIRO, Emery P.
photo: (L) $935; (H) $1,650

REY, Jim
posters: (H) $17

REYNI, Ingalvur av
planographic: (H) $148

REYNOLDS, S.W. (after Mme Vigee
Le Brun)
intaglio: (H) $218

REYNOLDS, Sir Joshua (after)
intaglio: (L) $39; (H) $581

REYNOLDS, Sir Joshua
English 1723-1792
generic: (H) $14

RHEAD, Louis
American 1857-1926
posters: (L) $220; (H) $825
generic: (H) $468

RIAB
French 19th/20th cent.
planographic: (H) $28

RIBERA, Jusepe de
Spanish 1588/91-1652/56
intaglio: (L) $964; (H) $13,592

RIBOUD, Marc
b. 1923
photo: (L) $2,090; (H) $2,420

RICCI, Marco
Italian 1676-1729
intaglio: (H) $2,585

RICE, Daniel and James G. CLARK
generic: (H) $44

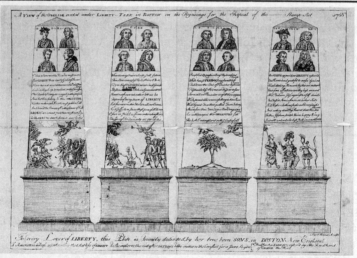

Prints of the American Revolution are another specialized form of collecting. Prints by Paul Revere (1735-1818) are very rare. This print of *The Obelisk*, one of only three known copies, was discovered in a closet by an appraiser from Skinner Galleries. The print, in good condition, was estimated at $15,000-$25,000 and sold for $48,400, a record price for any print by Revere. (Paul Revere, *A View of the Obelisk Erected Under Liberty-Tree in Boston on the Rejoicing for the Repeal of the Stamp Act 1766*, engraving, plate size 10 x 13 ⅜ inches, Skinner, March 21, 1992, $48,400)

RICE, Leland
photo: (H) $330

RICE, William S.
American 1873-1963
relief: (L) $330; (H) $880

RICH, James Bartlett
photo: (H) $100

RICHARDS, Ceri
British b. 1903
planographic: (L) $100; (H) $174

RICHARDS, Eugene
photo: (L) $150; (H) $500

RICHE, De Lobel
intaglio: (H) $11

RICHER, Hans
photo: (H) $605

RICHERT, Charles
American b. 1880
relief: (H) $440

RICHERT, Charles Henry
American b. 1880
relief: (H) $413

RICHFIELD, Robert
photo: (H) $300

RICHTER, Gerhard
American b. 1928
stencil: (L) $836; (H) $922
mixed-media: (H) $426
photo-repro: (L) $505; (H) $3,901
port/books: (L) $2,340; (H) $11,540
photo: (L) $2,867; (H) $10,392

RICHTER, Hans
German ac. 1597
photo: (L) $412; (H) $4,950

RICHTER, Henry (after)
intaglio: (H) $120

RICHTERICH, Marco
b. 1929
planographic: (H) $139

RIDINGER, Johan Elias
German 1698-1767
intaglio: (L) $124; (H) $445

RIEBESEHL, Heinrich
German b. 1938
photo: (H) $502

RIEBICKE, G.
photo: (H) $790

RIEKMAN
photo: (H) $1,210

RIESENBERG, Sidney
American b. 1885
posters: (H) $247

RIGER, Robert
American b. 1924
planographic: (H) $220

RIGGS, Robert
American 1896-1970
planographic: (L) $1,045; (H) **$2,750**

RILEY, Bridget
British b. 1931
stencil: (H) $88

RIMMER, William Henry
American 1816-1879
port/books: (H) $220

RINEHART, F.A.
1861-1928
photo: (L) $247; (H) $3,080

RINKE, Klaus
German b. 1939
photo: (H) $860

RIOPELLE, Jean Paul
Canadian b. 1922/23
intaglio: (L) $462; (H) **$647**
stencil: (H) **$1,419**
relief: (H) **$291**
planographic: (L) $92; (H) **$1,041**

RIPART, G.
posters: (H) $121

RIPLEY, Aiden Lassell
American 1896-1969
intaglio: (L) $110; (H) $165

RITCHIE, A.H.
American 1882-1895
intaglio: (L) $330; (H) **$440**

RITTASE, William M.
photo: (H) $440

RITTS, Herb
American
photo: (L) $593; (H) $7,700

RIVERA, Diego
Mexican 1886-1957
relief: (H) $1,100
planographic: (L) $1,210; (H) $14,300
port/books: (H) $5,060

RIVERS, Larry
American b. 1923
intaglio: (H) $1,100
stencil: (L) $770; (H) $4,400
planographic: (L) $880; (H) $8,800
mixed-media: (L) $1,210; (H) $4,400
photo-repro: (H) $550
others: (H) $3,520
generic: (L) $121; (H) $3,575

RIVIERE, Henri
French 1864-1951
relief: (L) $450; (H) $1,371
planographic: (L) $221; (H) $715

ROBAUDY
posters: (H) $275

ROBBE, Manuel (after)
French 1872-1936
intaglio: (L) $550; (H) $715

ROBBE, Manuel
French 1872-1936
intaglio: (L) $99; (H) $2,750

ROBBENNOLT, Linda Murphy
photo: (H) $495

ROBERT, Nicolas (attrib.)
French 1614-1685
intaglio: (H) $248

ROBERTS, David
b.Scotland,British 1796-1864
planographic: (L) $110; (H) $825

ROBERTS, Hazel
posters: (H) $275

ROBERTS, Holly
photo: (H) $700

ROBERTS, Kathleen
intaglio: (H) $51

ROBERTS, Linda (after)
American contemporary
planographic: (L) $83; (H) $99
generic: (H) $248

ROBERTSON, George and John
BOYDELL
intaglio: (H) $165

ROBERTSON, Grace
b. 1930
photo: (H) $115

ROBERTSON, James
photo: (L) $121; (H) $550

ROBINS, Thomas Sewell (after)
intaglio: (H) $90

ROBINSON, David
photo: (L) $160; (H) $180

ROBINSON, James
American b. 1944
photo: (H) $287

ROBINSON, John
stencil: (L) $52; (H) $87

ROCHE, Pierre
relief: (L) $482; (H) $723

ROCHETTE, G.
posters: (H) $247

ROCKMORE, Noel
American b. 1928
generic: (H) $66

ROCKWELL, Norman
American 1894-1978
intaglio: (H) $1,100
planographic: (L) $412; (H) $1,375
posters: (L) $33; (H) $495
photo-repro: (H) $220

RODCHENKO, Alexander
Russian 1891-1956
photo: (L) $1,100; (H) $5,928

RODE, Bernhard
1725-1797
intaglio: (H) $56

RODHE, Lennart
contemporary
stencil: (H) $636
planographic: (H) $628

RODIN, (after)
intaglio: (H) $28

RODIN, Auguste
French 1840-1917
intaglio: (L) $1,018; (H) $13,745

RODO BOULANGER, Graciela
b. Bolivia 1935
intaglio: (L) $193; (H) $495
planographic: (L) $6;(H) $550

ROETHLISBERGER, William
1862-1943
planographic: (H) $107

ROGALSKI, Walter
American
intaglio: (H) $121

ROH, Franz
German 1890-1965
photo: (L) $786; (H) $1,863

ROHDE, Werner
German 1906-1990
photo: (L) $502; (H) $1,100

ROHLFS, Christian
German 1849-1938
relief: (L) $1,882; (H) $3,176
planographic: (H) $605

ROLFE, Henry L.
planographic: (H) $220

ROLING, Mark
planographic: (L) $66; (H) $220

ROLING, Marthe
stencil: (H) $108

ROLLINS, Tim and K.O.S.
American 20th cent.
mixed-media: (H) $385

ROMNEY, (after)
generic: (H) $17

RONDELKEK, J.W.
American(?) 20th cent.
photo: (H) $303

ROOSKENS, Anton
Dutch 1906-1976
stencil: (H) $695

ROPS, Felicien
Belgian 1833-1898
intaglio: (L) $204; (H) $321
posters: (H) $1,045
port/books: (H) $321

ROSA, Salvator
Italian 1615-1673
intaglio: (H) $3,927

ROSASPINA, Francesco, Publisher
port/books: (H) $404

ROSE, Ruth Starr
American 20th cent.
planographic: (L) $121; (H) $132

ROSENBERG, Louis
American b. 1890
intaglio: (H) $33
port/books: (H) $220

ROSENQUIST, James
American 1933-1991
intaglio: (L) $275; (H) $1,650
stencil: (L) $413; (H) $2,833
planographic: (L) $55; (H) $5,500
photo-repro: (L) $56; (H) $165

ROSENTHAL, Joseph
photo: (H) $13,200

ROSENTHAL, Steve
photo: (H) $350

ROSETTI, J.
posters: (H) $357

ROSS, Alan
photo: (L) $165; (H) $385

ROSS, Gordon
planographic: (H) $138

ROSS, Horatio
photo: (L) $982; (H) $5,108

ROSS, James
American 20th cent.
planographic: (H) $55

ROSSING, Karl
1897-1987
relief: (H) $142

ROSSINI
intaglio: (H) $275

ROSSINI, Luigi
Italian 1790-1857
intaglio: (H) $66
port/books: (L) $8,800; (H) $18,700

ROSSLER, Jaroslav
Czech 1902-1990
photo: (L) $358; (H) $3,740

ROST, Ernest C.
intaglio: (H) $110

ROTELLA, Mimmo
Italian b. 1918
planographic: (L) $186; (H) $186

ROTH, Dieter
German b. 1930
intaglio:	(H)	$369
stencil:	(H)	$1,135
planographic:	(L) $55; (H)	$358
mixed-media:	(H)	$2,269
photo-repro:	(L) $241; (H)	$319
port/books:	(L) $922; (H)	$8,865

ROTH, Ernest David
American 1879-1964
intaglio: (L) $55; (H) $110

ROTHE, G.H.
German b. 1935
intaglio: (L) $33; (H) $880

ROTHENBERG, Susan
American b. 1945
intaglio:	(L) $1,870; (H)	$4,180
relief:	(L) $1,320; (H)	$5,500
planographic:	(H)	$1,870

ROTHENSTEIN, Michael
English b. 1908
stencil:	(H)	$483
planographic:	(H)	$220

ROTHSTEIN, Arthur
photo: (L) $330; (H) $2,860

ROUAULT, Georges
French 1871-1958
intaglio:	(L) $33; (H)	$26,400
relief:	(L) $165; (H)	$176
planographic:	(L) $193; (H)	$7,937
photo-repro:	(H)	$891
port/books:	(L) $5,567; (H)	$77,000

ROUAX, J.
intaglio: (H) $11

ROUS, Floren
intaglio: (H) $232

ROUSSEAU, Henri (called Le
Douanier)
French 1844-1910
planographic: (H) $3,850

ROUSSEL, K.X.
planographic: (H) $3,079

ROVAGLIA, A.
posters: (H) $192

ROVNER, Michal
photo: (H) $850

ROWLANDSON, (after)
intaglio: (H) $121

ROWLANDSON, Thomas
English 1756-1827
intaglio: (H) $1,335
port/books: (H) $171

ROWLANDSON, Thomas (after)
British 1756-1827
intaglio: (H) $99

ROWLEY, Frank
photo: (H) $825

RUBEN, Ernestine
photo: (L) $380; (H) $700

RUBENS, Sir Peter Paul
Flemish 1577-1640
intaglio: (L) $12,174; (H) $15,950

RUBIN, Reuven
Israeli 1893-1974
intaglio: (H) $3,960

RUBINSTEIN, Eva
photo: (H) $500

RUBLE, Gary Aro
photo: (H) $193

RUBLE, Ronald
American b. 1935
intaglio: (L) $28; (H) $55

RUCKER, Colby
intaglio: (H) $77

RUDBERG, Gustav
planographic: (H) $636

RUDGE, M.M.
intaglio: (H) $92

RUDISILL, A.J.
generic: (H) $100

RUEGG, Ernst Georg
1883-1948
intaglio: (H) $155

RUELAS, Julio
Mexican 1870-1907
intaglio: (H) $825

RUETZ, Michael
German b. 1940
photo: (L) $645; (H) $1,218

RUFF, Thomas
German b. 1958
photo: (L) $8,250; (H) $13,200

RUMMELL, Richard (after)
American 1848-1924
mixed-media: (H) $50

RUNCIMAN, Alexander
intaglio: (H) $6,959

RUNCIMAN, John and Alexander
intaglio: (H) $1,789

RUNGIUS, Carl
American 1869-1959
intaglio: (L) $715; (H) $2,860

RUNNELS, Vic
generic: (H) $11

RUPERT OF THE RHINE, (Prince)
1619-1682
intaglio: (L) $5,493; (H) $42,412

RUSCHA, Ed
American b. 1937
intaglio: (H) $1,100
stencil: (L) $468; (H) $7,150
planographic: (L) $1,430; (H) $15,400
port/books: (H) $2,475

RUSCHA, Edward and Jim GANZER
contemporary
intaglio: (H) $990

RUSHBURY, Henry
intaglio: (H) $114

RUSHBURY, Sir Henry
intaglio: (H) $127

RUSSELL, A.J.
photo: (H) $275

RUSSELL, Benjamin (after)
American 1804-1885
planographic: (H) $1,045

RUSSELL, Gyrth
Canadian 1892-1970
intaglio: (H) $97

RUSSOLO, Luigi
Italian 1885-1947
intaglio: (L) $520; (H) $3,967

RUTH, G.
intaglio: (H) $61

RUTHERFORD, Mark
posters: (H) $358

RUTING, Lance
photo: (L) $32; (H) $168

RUZICKA, Dr. Drahomir Joseph
1870-1960
photo: (L) $412; (H) $2,860

RUZICKA, Rudolph
American b. 1883
relief: (H) $248

RYAN, Lewis Carleton
American 1894-1987
relief: (H) $330

RYDER, Chauncey Foster
American 1868-1949
intaglio: (L) $55; (H) $83

RYERSON, Margery
American b. 1886
planographic: (L) $77; (H) $83

RYSSEL, Paul van
French 1828-1909
intaglio: (L) $331; (H) $414

RYSSELBERGHE, Theo van
Belgian 1862-1926
intaglio: (L) $364; (H) $994

SABOGAL, Jose
Peruvian 1888-1956
relief: (L) $198; (H) $220

SADELER, J.
intaglio: (L) $77; (H) $841

SADLER, Walter Dendy
English 1854-1923
intaglio: (L) $99; (H) $248

SADLER, Walter Dendy (after)
British 1854-1923
photo-repro: (H) $66

SAENREDAM, Jan
Dutch 1600-1682
port/books: (H) $8,247

SAENREDAM, Jan
Dutch
intaglio: (L) $260; (H) $2,310

SAENREDAM, Jan
Dutch 1565-1607
intaglio: (H) $2,860

SAFTLEVEN, Cornelis
Dutch 1607-1681
intaglio: (H) $2,199

SAGE, Phillip
American 20th cent.
intaglio: (H) $132

SAINT PHALLE, Niki de
French b. 1930
stencil: (L) $755; (H) $1,365
planographic: (L) $794; (H) $1,452

SAINT-AUBIN, Augustin de
French 1736-1807
intaglio: (L) $3,927; (H) $5,027

SAINT-MEMIN, Charles Balthazar
Julien Fevret de
French/American 1770-1852
intaglio: (L) $75; (H) $440

SAINT-NON, Jean Claude Richard de
1727-1771
intaglio: (L) $369; (H) $1,538

SAITO
intaglio: (H) $22

SAITO, Kiyoshi
Japanese b. 1907
relief: (L) $50; (H) $660

SALAMANCA, Antonio
Italian 1500-1562
intaglio: (H) $50

SALFTLEVEN, Herman
c. 1609-1685
intaglio: (H) $12,958

SALGADO, Sebastiao
b. 1944
photo: (L) $880; (H) $2,200

SALINGER, Adrienne
photo: (H) $160

SALLBERG, Harald
intaglio: (H) $598

SALLE, David
American b. 1952
intaglio: (L) $1,100; (H) $1,650
mixed-media: (H) $2,860
port/books: (H) $3,080

SALLIETH, M. de
intaglio: (H) $401

SALMON, William
port/books: (H) $605

SALT, Henry (after)
intaglio: (H) $533

SALVADOR CARMONA, Juan
Antonio
generic: (H) $1,136

SALVIATI, Giuseppe (after)
ac. c. 1540-70
relief: (H) $1,538

SALVO, Dana
photo: (L) $180; (H) $200

SALZMANN, Auguste (photographer)
1824-1872
port/books: (H) $8,800

SAMARAS, Lucas
Greek/American b. 1936
stencil: (H) $660

SAMPLE, Paul S.
American 1896-1974
planographic: (H) $99

**SAMUEL BOURNE, SHEPHERD and
ROBERTSON**
photo: (H) $56,973

SANCHEZ, Emilio
Cuban b. 1921
planographic: (H) $22

SANDBACK, Fred
American b. 1943
relief: (L) $567; (H) $638
port/books: (H) $482

SANDBERG, Sean
relief: (H) $3,300

SANDBY, Paul (after)
port/books: (H) $4,922

SANDER, August
German 1876-1964
photo: (L) $323; (H) $4,950

SANDER, Henry Frederick Conrad
German
port/books: (H) $35,200

SANDZEN, Birger
American 1871-1954
relief: (L) $330; (H) $468

SANGER, Isaac
American b. 1899
relief: (H) $66

SANSON, Antoine
b. 1660/70
intaglio: (H) $417

SANT, James (after)
planographic: (H) $92

SANTOMASO, Giuseppe
Italian b. 1907
intaglio: (L) $357; (H) $698
planographic: (L) $357; (H) $721

SANZIO, Raffaelo (after)
Italian 1483-1520
intaglio: (H) $105

SARGENT, John Singer
American 1856-1925
planographic: (L) $5,500; (H) $10,450

SARONY, Napoleon
photo: (H) $467

SARONY and CO., NY
generic: (H) $935

SARONY and MAJOR, Lithographers
American
planographic: (L) $115; (H) $770

SARONY, MAJOR and KNAPP
planographic: (H) $15,950

SARTAIN, William
American 1843-1924
intaglio: (H) $44

SASSONE
stencil: (H) $660
planographic: (H) $660

SAUDEK, Jan
Czech b. 1935
photo: (L) $430; (H) $1,650

SAURA, Antonio
Spanish b. 1930
stencil: (H) $397
planographic: (L) $204; (H) $568
port/books: (H) $649

SAURET, Andre
planographic: (H) $55

SAURET, Andre, Publisher
planographic: (H) $629

SAUVAIRE, Henri
photo: (H) $660

SAVAGE, Charles Roscoe
photo: (H) $770

SAVIGNAC, Reymond
20th cent.
posters: (L) $107; (H) $275

SAVIN, Maurice
French 1894-1973
intaglio: (H) $110

SAVINIO, Alberto
1891-1952
intaglio: (H) $1,106

SAVIO, Francesco Lo
1935-1963
planographic: (H) $1,503

SAVOIE, Robert
Canadian School b. 1939
intaglio: (L) $93; (H) $278

SAVORELLI and Petro CAMPORESI,
(after)
port/books: (H) $2,224

SAWAII, Noboru
b. 1931
intaglio: (L) $110; (H) $390

SAWREY, Hugh David
planographic: (H) $61

SAYER, Robert
18th cent.
intaglio: (H) $209
generic: (H) $251

SAYRE, F. Grayson
American 1879-1938/39
stencil: (L) $50; (H) $248

SCACHERI, Mario
photo: (H) $825

SCAVULLO, Francesco
photo: (H) $1,430

SCHAAF, Albert E.
1866-1955
photo: (H) $825

SCHAD, Christian
German 1894-1982
photo: (H) $430

SCHALDACH, William J.
intaglio: (L) $55; (H) $110

SCHALL, F. (after)
intaglio: (H) $75

SCHANTZ, Philip von
contemporary
planographic: (L) $573; (H) $961

SCHARFF, William
planographic: (H) $56

SCHARL, Josef
German 1896-1958
intaglio: (H) $165

SCHATT, Roy
photo: (L) $550; (H) $2,200

SCHAUFFELEIN, Hans Leonard
port/books: (H) $2,356

SCHELFHOUT, Lodewijk
contemporary
intaglio: (L) $194; (H) $605

SCHELLENBERG, Johann Ulrich
1709-1795
intaglio: (H) $100

SCHERFIG, Hans
planographic: (L) $148; (H) $565

SCHETKY, J.C., Esq. (after)
1778-1874
planographic: (H) $5,170

SCHIAVONE, Andrea
intaglio: (H) $6,050

SCHIELE, Egon
German 1890-1918
intaglio: (H) $17,357
planographic: (L) $8,800; (H) $18,700

SCHIESTL, Matthaus
1869-1939
planographic: (H) $70

SCHIESTL, Rudolf
1878-1931
planographic: (H) $351

SCHILE, H.R., Publisher
planographic: (H) $220

SCHILLE, H.
generic: (H) $225

SCHILLER, Lawrence
photo: (H) $1,540

SCHIOLER, Inge
stencil: (H) $771

SCHLEMMER, Oskar
German 1888-1943
intaglio: (H) $15,823
planographic: (L) $6,978; (H) $12,480

SCHMIDT, F.
German
generic: (H) $50

SCHMIDT, Joost
photo: (L) $3,575; (H) $3,850

SCHMIDT-ROTTLUFF, Karl
German 1884-1976
intaglio: (H) $3,209
relief: (L) $550; (H) $12,946
planographic: (H) $1,870

SCHMIEDEBERG-BLUME, Else von
planographic: (H) $121

SCHNABEL, Julian
American b. 1951
mixed-media: (L) $2,750; (H) $3,575
port/books: (H) $4,400

SCHNEIDER, Gary
photo: (H) $450

SCHNEIDER, Gerard
French 1896-1948
intaglio: (H) $129

SCHNEIDER, Otto
American 1875-1946
intaglio: (H) $220

SCHOLDER, Fritz
American b. 1937
planographic: (L) $110; (H) $467

SCHOLTE, Rob
contemporary
stencil: (L) $1,941; (H) $2,718
planographic: (H) $1,553

SCHONBERG, Eva
intaglio: (H) $66

SCHONEN, Kurt
American 20th cent.
intaglio: (H) $165

SCHONGAUER, Martin
German c. 1450-1491
intaglio: (L) $440; (H) $44,000

SCHOONHOVEN, Jan
stencil: (H) $971
planographic: (H) $164

SCHRAG, Karl
American b. Germany 1912
intaglio: (L) $220; (H) $330

SCHRANTZ, Joseph (after)
German b. 1803
planographic: (H) $248

SCHREIBER, Georges
Belgian/American 1904-1977
planographic: (L) $83; (H) $165

SCHREYER, Lothar
German 1886-1966
planographic: (H) $83

SCHRODER, Arnold
photo: (H) $3,300

SCHROEDER-SONNENSTERN, Emil
Friedrich
planographic: (H) $102

SCHUBERT, Otto
1892-1970
port/books: (H) $112

SCHULTHEISS, Carl Max
American b. 1885
intaglio: (H) $55

SCHULTZE, Bernard
German b. 1915
intaglio: (L) $255; (H) $721

SCHUMACHER, Emil
German b. 1912
intaglio: (L) $866; (H) $2,269

SCHURR, Jerome
American b. 1940
stencil: (H) $110

SCHUTTE, Thomas
contemporary
relief: (H) $241
planographic: (H) $201

SCHUTZ, Anton
20th cent.
intaglio: (H) $28

SCHWARTZ, Elliot
photo: (H) $150

SCHWARTZ, William S.
Russian/American 1896-after 1934,
d. 1977
planographic: (H) $55

SCHWEIZER, Helmut
German b. 1946
photo: (H) $143

SCHWITTERS, Kurt and Theo van
DOESBURG
photo-repro: (H) $7,946

SCOTT, Janet Laura
American 20th cent.
relief: (H) $165

SCOTT, Leighton
American 1847-1898
planographic: (H) $110

SCOTT, Nigel
b. 1951
photo: (H) $990

SCOTT, Peter (after)
photo-repro: (H) $381

SCOTT, Septimus E.
British 20th cent.
posters: (H) $550

SCOTT, William
b. 1913
stencil: (H) $545
planographic: (L) $123; (H) $587

SCULLY, Sean
Irish b. 1945
intaglio: (L) $2,750; (H) $4,950
relief: (L) $3,471; (H) $3,850
planographic: (H) $13,200

SEARS, Olga
American 1906-1990
relief: (H) $110

SEBAH, P.
photo: (H) $1,052

SEBASTIAN, Robert
stencil: (H) $98

SEBEK, J.
posters: (H) $385

SECUNDA, Arthur
American 20th cent.
planographic: (H) $28

SEEKS, A.S.
planographic: (H) $110

SEELEY, George H.
1880-1955
photo: (L) $550; (H) $1,650

SEELIG, Heinz
mixed-media: (H) $990

SEGAL, Georges
French b. 1924
planographic: (H) $497

SEGALL, Lasar
Brazilian 1890-1957
relief: (H) $660

SEGUI, Antonio
Argentinian b. 1934
planographic: (H) $102

SEGUIN, Armand and Paul GAUGIN
intaglio: (H) $990

SEIDEMANN, Bob
photo: (L) $880; (H) $1,320

SEIDENSTUCKER, Friedrich
German 1882-1966
photo: (L) $430; (H) $502

SEIWERT, Franz Wilhelm
1894-1933
relief: (H) $682

SEKINO, Junichiro
Japanese 1914-1988
stencil: (H) $358
relief: (H) $77

SELIGMANN, Kurt
Swiss 1900-1962
intaglio: (L) $715; (H) $880
port/books: (H) $3,973

SELMA, Fernando
intaglio: (H) $411

SEMOHAM, Daphine
planographic: (H) $11

SEMPERE, Eusebio
planographic: (H) $514

SERLIO, Sebastiano
Italian 1475-1554
port/books: (H) $5,280

SERRA, Richard
American b. 1939
stencil: (L) $4,180; (H) $6,050
planographic: (H) $1,650
mixed-media: (H) $10,638

SERRANO, Andres
photo: (H) $3,850

SERUSIER, Paul
French 1863-1927
planographic: (H) $624

SERZ, John
American
intaglio: (H) $1,210

SEUPHOR, Michel
contemporary
stencil: (H) $582

SEUTTER, Matthaus
German 1678-1757
intaglio: (L) $275; (H) $453

SEVERINI, Gino
Italian 1883-1966
stencil: (L) $1,485; (H) $1,795
planographic: (L) $1,002; (H) $4,444
posters: (H) $138

SEYMOUR, Samuel (after Thomas
BIRCH)
American
intaglio: (H) $2,200

SHAFER, L.A.
posters: (H) $165

SHAGIN, Ivan
photo: (H) $3,575

SHAHN, Ben
American 1898-1969
stencil: (L) $110; (H) $2,640
planographic: (L) $66; (H) $660
posters: (L) $825; (H) $1,650
port/books: (H) $440
generic: (H) $1,320

SHANAHAN
intaglio: (H) $33

SHANKER, Louis
relief: (H) $165

SHAPIRO, Joel
American b. 1941
relief: (H) $1,100

SHARAKU, Toshusai (attrib.)
Japanese
relief: (H) $259

SHARE, H. Pruett
19th cent.
intaglio: (H) $28

SHARP, William
planographic: (H) $55

SHARPE, Charles William
British 1818-1899
intaglio: (H) $880

SHAW, G. Gayfield
intaglio: (L) $43; (H) $52

SHAW, George Bernard
1856-1950
photo: (H) $918

SHAW, Mark
photo: (H) $1,143

SHAW, Robert
intaglio: (H) $138

SHAYER, William (after)
intaglio: (L) $22; (H) $516

SHAYKHET, Arkadi
photo: (H) $1,210

SHEARMAN and HART,
Lithographers
American 19th cent.
planographic: (H) $605

SHEELER, Charles
American 1883-1965
planographic: (H) $13,200

SHEETS, Millard
American 1907-1989
stencil: (H) $303
planographic: (H) $248

SHEIKH, Fazal
photo: (L) $160; (H) $380

SHELTON, Margaret D.
1915-1984
relief: (L) $176; (H) $536

SHEPHERD, David (after)
photo-repro: (L) $165; (H) $688

SHEPPARD, Warren (after)
generic: (H) $44

SHERATON, Thomas
port/books: (H) $880

SHERE, Samuel
photo: (H) $308

SHERMAN, Cindy
American b. 1954
photo: (L) $2,310; (H) $18,150

SHERMAN, Russell
planographic: (H) $77

SHERWOOD
intaglio: (H) $11

SHIELDS, Henry and James MEIKLE
port/books: (H) $2,877

SHINN, Everett
American 1876-1953
port/books: (H) $412

SHINODA, Toko
planographic: (H) $4,070

SHORE, Henrietta
American d. 1963
planographic: (L) $303; (H) $825

SHORRE, Harriet
b. 1939
intaglio: (H) $33

SHORT, Sir Frank
English 1857-1945
intaglio: (H) $116
planographic: (H) $77

SHOTTER, Thomas (Boys)
planographic: (H) $1,934

SHOULBERG, Harry
American b. 1903
stencil: (H) $220

SHOYEN, Aagd
intaglio: (H) $29

SHRIER, Joan Asquith
planographic: (H) $385

SHUHO, Yamakawa
relief: (H) $303

SHUNKO
Japanese late 18th/19th cent.
relief: (H) $165

SICHEM, Christoffel van
1546-1624
relief: (H) $6,283

SICKERT, Walter Richard
English 1860-1942
intaglio: (L) $545; (H) $4,573

SIEFF, Jeanloup
b. 1933
photo: (L) $660; (H) $825

SIEGEN, Ludwig von
1609-1680
intaglio: (H) $31,416

SIEMIANOWSKI, Roman
b. 1915
photo: (L) $357; (H) $990

SIERHUIS, Jan
planographic: (H) $114

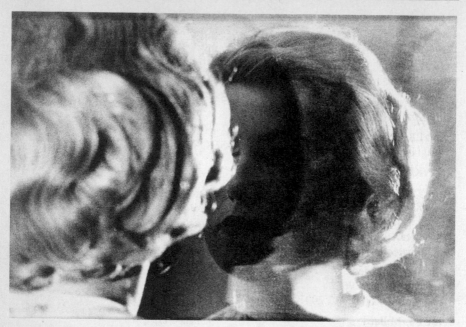

The boundary between photography and contemporary art has become increasingly blurred. Most often, photographer Cindy Sherman's works are offered in mixed sales of contemporary art alongside oils, watercolors, lithographs, acrylics, mobiles, and installations. (Cindy Sherman, *Untitled Self Portrait with Mirror, 1980*, gelatin silver print, 6 ⅝ x 9 ½ inches, Christie-New York, October 13, 1992, $8,250)

SIGLER, Hollis
  American b. 1948
  planographic: (H) $330

SIGNAC, Paul
  French 1863-1935
  planographic: (L) $1,046; (H) $11,000

SIGNORINI, Telemaco
  Italian 1835-1901
  intaglio: (L) $957; (H) $2,488

SILVER, Michael
  photo: (H) $1,000

SILVERMAN
  generic: (L) $220; (H) $330

SILVERTHORNE, Jeffrey
  photo: (H) $160

SILVESTER, R. (after)
  intaglio: (H) $387

SILVESTRE, Israel (the younger)
  French 1621-1691
  intaglio: (H) $248
  port/books: (H) $6,977

SIMBARI, Nicola
  Italian b. 1927
  stencil: (H) $990
  planographic: (H) $110

SIMEON, Dwayne
  stencil: (H) $146

SIMMONS, Laurie
  b. 1949
  photo: (L) $1,320; (H) $8,250

SIMON, Stella F.
  1877-1972
  photo: (L) $247; (H) $1,100

SIMON, T. Frantisek
Czech 1877-1942
intaglio: (L) $110; (H) $660
planographic: (L) $193; (H) $330

SIMONIN, Francine
Canadian School b. 1936
planographic: (H) $234

SIMONS, Montgomery P. (attrib.)
photo: (H) $2,750

SIMONTON and MILLARD
photo: (H) $612

SIMPSON, Jackson
intaglio: (L) $22; (H) $83

SIMPSON, William (after)
Scottish 1823-1899
port/books: (H) $303

SIMSON, Don
planographic: (H) $11

SINGIER, Gustave
French 1909-1984
planographic: (L) $183; (H) $303

SINGLETON, Henry (after)
intaglio: (L) $99; (H) $174

SINSABAUGH, Art
photo: (L) $3,025; (H) $3,300

SIPPRELL, Clara
photo: (H) $165

SIQUEIROS, David Alfaro
Mexican 1896/98-1974
relief: (H) $357
planographic: (L) $303; (H) $1,870
port/books: (H) $1,100

SIRKS, J.
1885-1938
intaglio: (H) $119

SISKIND, Aaron
1903-1991
port/books: (H) $7,700
photo: (L) $450; (H) $4,400

SKEEN and CO., (photographer)
port/books: (H) $790

**SKEEN and CO., PLATE and CO.
and C.H. KERR**
photo: (H) $553

SKIPPE, John
British 1742-1811
relief: (H) $523
port/books: (H) $1,980

SKOGLUND, Sandy
photo: (L) $3,025; (H) $5,500

SLAVIN, Neal
photo: (H) $300

SLEVOGT, Max
German 1868-1932
port/books: (L) $70; (H) $4,400

SLOAN, J. Blanding
American b. 1886
intaglio: (L) $110; (H) $138
relief: (L) $220; (H) $220

SLOAN, John
American 1871-1951
intaglio: (L) $132; (H) $11,000
posters: (H) $935

SLOANE, Thomas O'Conor (Jr.)
photo: (H) $605

SLOCOMBE, Charles Philip
English 1832-1895
port/books: (H) $28

SLUYS, Leslie van der
relief: (L) $139; (H) $157

SMILLIE, James (after Thomas COLE)
port/books: (H) $660

SMILLIE, James David
American 1833-1909
intaglio: (H) $110
port/books: (H) $44

SMITH, Bill
generic: (H) $193

SMITH, Charles
relief: (H) $2,090

SMITH, David
American 1906-1965
planographic: (H) $8,800

SMITH, Edward C.
intaglio: (H) $125

SMITH, Edwin Dalton
English b. 1800
port/books: (H) $121

John Sloan was a member of The Eight, also called the Ash Can School. This group, reacting to the sweetness of the Impressionists and the bland subject matter of the academic schools, painted realistic scenes of everyday city life. The eight were Robert Henri, John Sloan, William Glackens, Everett Shinn, George Luks, Ernest Lawson, Arthur B. Davies, and Maurice Prendergast. John Sloan's background as an artist reporter for the *Philadelphia Press* had demanded a quick eye, rapid pencil, and good memory. This etching of *Connoisseurs of Prints* was executed in 1905 shortly before the Ash Can School was informally founded. (John Sloan, *Connoisseurs of Prints*, etching, $4 \frac{7}{8} \times 6 \frac{7}{8}$ inches, Sotheby-New York, February 14, 1992, $3,300)

SMITH, G.
  French 20th cent.
  planographic: (H) $220

SMITH, George
  English 1802-1838
  port/books: (H) $5,280

SMITH, Gordon Appelbe
  planographic: (H) $170

SMITH, Jack Wilkinson
  American 1873-1949
  planographic: (H) $55

SMITH, John
  port/books: (H) $1,980

SMITH, John Raphael
  1752-1812
  intaglio: (L) $942; (H) $942

SMITH, Kimber
  American b. 1922
  planographic: (L) $182; (H) $265

SMITH, Lawrence Beall
  American b. 1909
  planographic: (L) $66; (H) $143
  port/books: (L) $99; (H) $143

SMITH, Richard
  planographic: (H) $523

SMITH, Rupert Jasen
stencil: (L) $675; (H) $1,980

SMITH, Sydney Ure
intaglio: (L) $157; (H) $209

SMITH, W. (after C. Burton)
planographic: (H) $275

SMITH, W. Eugene
1918-1978
photo: (L) $495; (H) $8,800

SMITH, W. Morris and Alexander
GARDNER
photo: (H) $302

SMITH, Wuanita
American 1866-1959
intaglio: (H) $66

SMITH, Xanthus (after)
planographic: (H) $220

SMOTZER, Teresa
American 20th cent.
intaglio: (H) $11

SMYTH
intaglio: (H) $196

SNOW, John
b. 1911
planographic: (L) $171; (H) $317

SNYDER, Laurie Sieverts
photo: (H) $100

SODERBERG, Yngve
1896-1971
intaglio: (L) $83; (H) $110

SOFER, Gregory
intaglio: (H) $17

SOFFICI, Ardengo
planographic: (H) $756

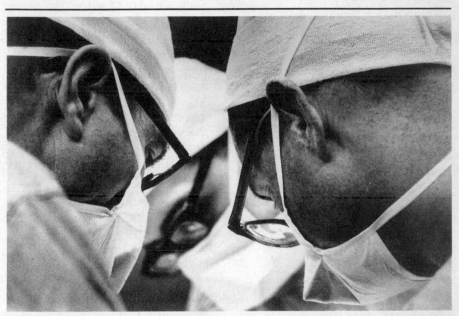

W. Eugene Smith is renowned for his powerful photo-essays, a form he helped develop while on the staff at *Life Magazine* during the 1940s and early 1950s. Some of his best known essays were on the *Country Doctor, Nurse Midwife,* and *Minamata.* Smith developed his own prints which they have a distinct tonality: the prints are usually dark and the white highlights are often bleached. Smith signed his prints with a stylus. (W. Eugene Smith, *Doctors, c. 1950*, gelatin silver print, 13 ⅛ x 19 ¼ inches, Butterfield, December 10, 1991, $550)

SOGNO
posters: (H) $220

SOHIER, Sage
photo: (L) $100; (H) $300

SOKOSH, David
mixed-media: (H) $300

SOLANA, Jose Gutierrez
Spanish 1886-1945
intaglio: (H) $515
port/books: (L) $1,826; (H) $5,137

SOLIS, Virgil
German 1514-1562
intaglio: (H) $660
relief: (H) $55

SOLOMBRE
intaglio: (H) $35

SOLOMON, Rosalind
photo: (L) $200; (H) $400

SOMERSET, Geraldine and The
Grand Duchess Olga
ALEXANDROVNA (attrib.)
(photographers)
port/books: (H) $5,533

SOMMER, Frederick
photo: (L) $4,950; (H) $6,050

SOMOV, Andrej
port/books: (H) $98

SONDERBORG, Kurt R.H. (Rudolf
Hoffman)
b. 1923
stencil: (H) $426

SOPER, Eileen A.
English 20th cent.
intaglio: (H) $110

SOPER, George
English b. 1890
intaglio: (H) $66

SORENSON, Arne Haugen
port/books: (H) $222

SORLIER, Charles
planographic: (L) $1,818; (H) $4,133

SORLIER, Charles (after Marc
Chagall)
20th cent.
planographic: (L) $210; (H) $11,930
posters: (H) $1,988

SORMAN, Steven
b. 1948
planographic: (H) $990
mixed-media: (L) $1,320; (H) $2,090

SOULAGES, Pierre
French b. 1919
intaglio: (L) $1,082; (H) $3,064
planographic: (L) $638; (H) $1,690

SOULAS, Louis Joseph
intaglio: (H) $161

SOUTHWORTH and HAWES,
(attrib.)
photo: (H) $1,284

SOWERBY, James
English c. 1740-c. 1803
port/books: (L) $150; (H) $715

SOWERBY, James de Carle and
Edward LEAR
port/books: (H) $2,860

SOYER, Moses
Russian/American 1899-1974
planographic: (L) $99; (H) $900

SOYER, Raphael
Russian/American 1899-1987
intaglio: (L) $77; (H) $440
stencil: (H) $660
planographic: (L) $77; (H) $16,500
port/books: (L) $83; (H) $8,250

SPANISH SCHOOL, 19TH CENTURY
intaglio: (H) $68

SPANO, Michael
b. 1949
photo: (H) $1,760

SPARE, Austin Osman
English b. 1888
port/books: (H) $495

SPEEDE, John
generic: (H) $481

SPENDER, Humphrey
b. 1910
photo: (H) $96

SPERLI, Johann Jakob
1770-1841
intaglio: (H) $232

SPINA, Phillip
intaglio: (H) $77

Raphael Soyer's favorite themes were urban views, interiors, and quiet moments in the lives of people. A Social Realist, he made many lithographs during the 1930s and 1940s that were gently suggestive of the lives of the underprivileged. (Raphael Soyer, *Waiting*, etching, 7 ½ x 9 ¼ inches, Freeman/Fine Arts, February 21, 1992, $440)

SPITZBERG, Carl
German 1808-1885
planographic: (H) $275

SPOERRI, Daniel
European b. 1930
generic: (H) $171

SPRINGER, Ferdinand
German b. 1907
intaglio: (L) $85; (H) $163
mixed-media: (H) $62

SPRINGKLEE, Hans
German b. 1540
relief: (H) $77

SPRONCKEN, Arthur
intaglio: (L) $114; (H) $126

SPROSSE, Carl
1819-1874
intaglio: (H) $211

SPRUANCE, Benton
American 1904-1967
planographic: (L) $88; (H) $8,400
port/books: (H) $143

SPRUANCE, Penelope
American
planographic: (H) $55

SQUIRRELL, Leonard R.
intaglio: (H) $136

STAATS, Greg
photo: (H) $495

STACKPOLE, Peter
photo: (L) $550; (H) $825

STACY
photo: (H) $275

STAEL, Nicholas de
French 1914-1955
intaglio: (H) $1,320
planographic: (H) $7,395

STAFFORD, George
intaglio: (H) $130

STAHL/WAHNSCHAFFE
photo: (L) $440; (H) $605

STALL
posters: (H) $357

STANCZAK, Julian
American b. 1928
stencil: (H) $55

STANKOWSKI, Anton
(photographer)
German b. 1906
port/books: (H) $573

STANLEY, Bob
American b. 1932
stencil: (L) $178; (H) $263

STANLEY, John Mix
American 1814-1872
port/books: (H) $44

STANLEY, John Mix (after)
planographic: (H) $1,100

STAPLES, Owen
1866-1949
intaglio: (H) $49

STAR, Kevin Red
planographic: (H) $138

STARN TWINS
American b. 1961
photo: (H) $1,320

STAUFFER-BERN, Karl
Swiss 1857-1891
intaglio: (L) $58; (H) $101

STEARNS, Stanley
generic: (H) $190

STEELE, Juliette
planographic: (H) $330

STEELE, T.S.
generic: (H) $198

STEFFEN, Bernard
stencil: (H) $500

STEGEMEYER, Elfriede
mixed-media: (H) $7,150

STEICHEN, Edward
American 1879-1973
photo: (L) $715; (H) $60,500

STEINBERG, Saul
Rumanian/American b. 1914
planographic: (L) $302; (H) $2,090
posters: (H) $467
port/books: (L) $4,950; (H) $7,700

STEINER, Ralph
1899-1986
photo: (L) $550; (H) $3,080

STEINERT, Otto
1915-1978
photo: (L) $1,320; (H) $1,650

STEINITZ, Kate
b. German 1889 d. 1975
photo: (H) $323

STEINLEN, Theophile Alexandre
Swiss/French 1859-1923
intaglio: (L) $166; (H) $1,425
planographic: (L) $54; (H) $4,709
posters: (L) $275; (H) $3,147
port/books: (L) $231; (H) $7,700

STEINLEN, Theophile Alexandre
(attrib.)
Swiss/French 1859-1923
intaglio: (H) $385

STEIR, Pat
American b. 1938
intaglio: (H) $2,310
relief: (L) $660; (H) $1,320
mixed-media: (H) $3,300

STELLA, Frank
American b. 1936
intaglio: (L) $5,161; (H) $28,929
stencil: (L) $1,760; (H) $15,291
relief: (H) $29,700
planographic: (L) $660; (H) $7,700
mixed-media: (L) $3,300; (H) $20,900
photo-repro: (H) $1,882
port/books: (L) $6,050; (H) $82,500
others: (H) $4,950
generic: (L) $358; (H) $468

STERN, Bert
port/books: (H) $4,070
photo: (L) $385; (H) $4,950

STERNBERG, Harry
American b. 1904
intaglio: (L) $413; (H) $440
planographic: (H) $413

STERNER, Albert
American 1863-1946
intaglio: (H) $165
planographic: (H) $440

STERNFELD, Joel
photo: (H) $275

STETTNER, Louis
photo: (L) $440; (H) $715

STEVENS, Dorothy Austin
intaglio: (H) $115

STEVENS, W.
planographic: (H) $1,980

STEWART, John
photo: (H) $3,080

STIEGLITZ, (after)
port/books: (H) $385

STIEGLITZ, Alfred
American 1864-1946
photo: (L) $935; (H) $46,200

STIEGLITZ, Alfred (Editor)
port/books: (L) $1,210; (H) $9,350

STIEGLITZ, Alfred and Edward
STEICHEN
photo: (H) $1,210

STIMPSON, J. (and another)
photo: (H) $553

STINSON, George
planographic: (H) $55

STIRLING, Glen
American 20th cent.
relief: (H) $275

STOCK, G.R. (after E.A.S. Douglas)
port/books: (H) $248

STOCKLIN, Niklaus
Swiss 1896-1982
posters: (L) $91; (H) $182

STOCKWELL, John
stencil: (L) $550; (H) $715

STODART, E. Jackson
intaglio: (H) $425

STOHRER, Walter
contemporary
intaglio: (H) $426
port/books: (H) $201

STOKES CO., Frederick A., Publisher
(after R.F. Zogbaum)
port/books: (H) $138

STOLTENBERG, Donald
port/books: (H) $523

STOLZ, Albert
posters: (H) $440

STORHARD, F. (after)
port/books: (H) $165

STORRS, John
American 1885-1956
relief: (L) $605; (H) $1,650

STORY-MASKELYNE, Nevil
photo: (H) $589

STOTHARD, Thomas (after)
intaglio: (H) $348
port/books: (H) $243

STOTZ, C.C. (photographer)
port/books: (H) $193

STOUMEN, Lou
photo: (L) $1,045; (H) $2,475

STOWE, Laura
intaglio: (H) $11

STRAND, Paul
American 1890-1976
photo: (L) $600; (H) $55,000

STRANG, Ian
British b. 1886
intaglio: (H) $132

STRANG, William
Scottish 1859-1921
intaglio: (H) $80

STRAUD, Virginia
stencil: (H) $88

STRINGER, John
relief: (H) $35

STRUCK, Hermann
intaglio: (L) $66; (H) $220

STRUSS, Karl
1886-1980
port/books: (H) $522
photo: (L) $1,320; (H) $2,640

STRUTH, Thomas
b. 1954
photo: (H) $3,300

STRUTT, J.G. (after)
generic: (H) $193

STRUYCKEN, Peter
port/books: (H) $1,265

STUART, James and Nicholas
REVETT
port/books: (H) $8,250

STUBBS, George
intaglio: (L) $329; (H) $1,257

STUBBS, George (after)
intaglio: (H) $715

STUCK, Franz von (after)
port/books: (H) $825

STUCK, Franz von
German 1863-1928
intaglio: (L) $267; (H) $267

STURGES, Jock
photo: (L) $468; (H) $1,650

STURGESS, John (after)
intaglio: (H) $275
port/books: (H) $1,039

SUBIRACHS, Jose Maria
planographic: (L) $137; (H) $365

SUDEK, Josef
Czech 1896-1976
port/books: (L) $1,540; (H) $4,675
photo: (L) $573; (H) $8,800

SUDRE, Jean Pierre
photo: (H) $432

SUGAI, Kumi
Japanese b. 1919
intaglio: (H) $471
stencil: (H) $266
planographic: (L) $385; (H) $2,928
port/books: (L) $3,137; (H) $4,077

SUHSER, Franz
German 19th cent.
planographic: (H) $165

SULMAN, T.
intaglio: (L) $139; (H) $565

SULTAN, Donald
American b. 1951
intaglio: (L) $1,320; (H) $7,700
stencil: (L) $1,650; (H) $3,300
planographic: (L) $990; (H) $1,100
mixed-media: (L) $1,100; (H) $1,760
port/books: (L) $2,200; (H) $11,000

SUMMERS, Carol
American b. 1925
stencil: (H) $220
relief: (L) $165; (H) $523
planographic: (L) $165; (H) $440
port/books: (H) $1,100

SUMMERS, Ivan
intaglio: (H) $11

SUMMERS, Robert
American b. 1940
planographic: (H) $87

SUNAMI, Soichi
photo: (H) $1,045

SURENDORF, Charles
American b. 1906
port/books: (L) $165; (H) $220

SURREY, Phillip Henry Howard
Canadian School 1910-1990
planographic: (H) $141

SURVAGE, Leopold
French 1879-1968
relief: (L) $261; (H) $321
port/books: (H) $497

SUTCLIFFE, Frank Meadow
1853-1941
photo: (L) $306; (H) $1,530

SUTHERLAND, Graham
English b. 1903
intaglio: (L) $660; (H) $1,292
planographic: (L) $309; (H) $945
port/books: (L) $1,050; (H) $4,226

SUTHERLAND, Patrick
photo: (H) $153

SUTHERLAND, T.
port/books: (H) $44

SUTHERLAND, Thomas
intaglio: (H) $275

SUZAN
intaglio: (H) $22

SVENSSON, Roland
planographic: (L) $926; (H) $2,530

SVETLOV, Valerien
port/books: (H) $715

SWAN, James
American 1847-1910
intaglio: (H) $44

SWANDALE, George (after)
intaglio: (H) $186

SWANELL, John
b. 1946
photo: (H) $803

SWANN, Dan
intaglio: (H) $150

SWANN, James
American b. 1905
intaglio: (L) $33; (H) $523

SWANSON, Gary R.
port/books: (H) $413

SWEET, R.
port/books: (L) $440; (H) $990

SWETT, Moses (Pendletons and Co., Printers)
American ac. 1826-1837
planographic: (H) $303

SWIFT, Dick
intaglio: (H) $165

SZASZ, Endre
Hungarian b. 1926
planographic: (H) $44

SZKOLA, Alex
planographic: (L) $55; (H) $110

SZWEDZICKI, C. Publisher
port/books: (H) $3,025

TABARD, Maurice
1897-1984
photo: (H) $4,620

TABOR and CO., (attrib.)
port/books: (H) $770

TACCANI, Silvia
photo: (H) $300

TAIT, Edith
photo: (H) $880

TAJIMA, Hiroyushi
planographic: (H) $28

TAKAHASHI, Rikio
Japanese b. 1917
relief: (H) $55

TALBOT, J.
intaglio: (H) $550

TALBOT, William Henry Fox
English 1800-1877
photo: (L) $314; (H) $3,850

TALBOT, William Henry Fox (attrib.)
English 1800-1877
photo: (L) $589; (H) $5,697

TALLER, E.L.
planographic: (H) $110

TAMAYO, Rufino
Mexican b. 1899
intaglio: (L) $1,430; (H) $4,125
relief: (L) $193; (H) $715
planographic: (L) $141; (H) $4,400
mixed-media: (L) $1,430; (H) $4,125
port/books: (L) $2,260; (H) $7,150
others: (L) $1,430; (H) $5,500

TANGUY, Yves
French/American 1900-1955
intaglio: (L) $550; (H) $4,182

TANNER, Benjamin
generic: (H) $500

TANNING, Dorothea
American b. 1912
intaglio: (L) $220; (H) $393
planographic: (L) $110; (H) $215
port/books: (H) $467

TAPIES, Antoni
Spanish b. 1923
intaglio: (L) $660; (H) $5,290
planographic: (L) $284; (H) $2,482
mixed-media: (L) $866; (H) $11,540
port/books: (L) $2,454; (H) $21,276

TAPPAN and BRADFORD,
Publisher, (after Samuel Worcester Rowse)
American 19th cent.
planographic: (H) $440

TAPPERT, Georg
German 1880-1957
port/books: (H) $4,207

TARKAY
Israeli b. 1935
planographic: (L) $358; (H) $523

TARSIN, Jan
stencil: (H) $138

TATAFIORE, Ernesto
b. 1943
others: (H) $213

TAUBERT, Bertholdo
French 20th cent.
planographic: (H) $61

TAUBES, Frederick
American 1900-1981
intaglio: (H) $44
planographic: (H) $83

TAYLOR, George
intaglio: (H) $306

TAYLOR, I. and J.
port/books: (L) $2,860; (H) $5,775

TAYLOR, John
19th cent.
generic: (H) $50

TAYLOR, Prentiss
American b. 1907
port/books: (L) $88; (H) $143

TAYLOR, Stephanie
intaglio: (H) $130

TAYLOR, W.
posters: (H) $220

TAYLOR, W.L. (after)
generic: (H) $77

TEICHEL
planographic: (H) $282

TELLANDER, H. (after)
generic: (H) $83

TENIERS, David (after)
port/books: (H) $127

TENNESON, Joyce
photo: (H) $1,500

TENNIEL, John
English 1820-1914
port/books: (H) $44,000

TERECHKOVITCH, Constantin
(Kostia)
Russian/French 1902-1978
planographic: (L) $110; (H) $358

TESCHNER, Richard
1870-1948
intaglio: (H) $154
port/books: (H) $493

TESKE, Edmund
photo: (L) $275; (H) $495

TESTA, Pietro
1617-1650
intaglio: (H) $1,885

TEUNN, (Nijkamp)
contemporary
planographic: (H) $220

TEYLER, Johan
1648-after 1699
intaglio: (H) $7,854

THAKE, Eric
relief: (L) $157; (H) $391

THALEMANN, Else
German
photo: (L) $394; (H) $717

THAULOW, Frits
Norwegian 1847-1906
intaglio: (L) $1,217; (H) $2,210

THAULOW, Frits (after)
intaglio: (H) $495

THIEBAUD, Wayne
American b. 1920
intaglio: (L) $1,100; (H) $6,600
stencil: (H) $7,150
relief: (L) $3,025; (H) $13,200
planographic: (L) $1,210; (H) $13,200
port/books: (H) $25,300

THIELER, Fred
b. 1916
intaglio: (H) $213
stencil: (H) $1,154

THIEME, Anthony
Dutch/American 1888-1954
port/books: (H) $88

THOMA, Hans
1839-1924
intaglio: (H) $224
generic: (L) $155; (H) $2,616

THOMAS, F.
port/books: (H) $39

THOMAS, G.
intaglio: (H) $304

THOMAS, John
planographic: (H) $6

THOMKINS, Andre
contemporary
relief: (H) $241

THOMPSON, Art
stencil: (L) $44; (H) $49

Wayne Thiebaud (b. 1920) has printed a number of simple, uncluttered compositions of cakes, soups, ice cream cones, and candy apples. (Wayne Thiebaud, *Candy Apples, 1987*, woodcut in colors on Tosa Kozo paper, 15 ¼ x 16 ½ inches, Butterfield, October 23, 1991, $9,900)

THOMPSON, Elizabeth (after)
intaglio: (H) $233

THOMPSON, Mildred
planographic: (H) $66

THOMPSON, Nathan
photo: (H) $412

THOMSON, John
1837-1921
port/books: (H) $2,104

THOMSON, William
intaglio: (H) $27
planographic: (H) $27

THORBURN, Archibald
Scottish 1860-1935
photo-repro: (H) $271

THORNE-THOMSEN, Ruth
photo: (L) $280; (H) $605

THORNTON, Dr. Robert John
British 1768-1837
intaglio: (L) $468; (H) $2,750
port/books: (H) $72

THORPE, John Hall
relief: (H) $251

THORPE, Lesbia
relief: (H) $174

THORTON
late 18th cent.
intaglio: (H) $97

THURAH, Laurids Lauridsen de
port/books: (H) $7,150

TICE, George
b. 1938
port/books: (H) $3,300
photo: (L) $550; (H) $660

TIDD, Marshall M., Lithographer
Anglo/American ac. 1853-1870
planographic: (H) $605

TIE-FENG, Jiang
Chinese b. 1938
stencil: (L) $715; (H) $1,100

TIEDEMAN, Cylia Von
photo: (H) $1,320

TIEPOLO, Giovanni Battista
Italian 1696-1770
intaglio: (L) $1,760; (H) $3,169
port/books: (H) $29,445

TIEPOLO, Giovanni Domenico
Italian 1727-1804
intaglio: (L) $302; (H) $5,558
port/books: (L) $7,737; (H) $52,622

TIEPOLO, Lorenzo
1736-1776
intaglio: (L) $1,389; (H) $15,708

TILSON, Joe
English b. 1928
planographic: (H) $129
mixed-media: (H) $567
port/books: (H) $922

TILY, Euguene James
English b. 1870
port/books: (H) $110

TING, Walasse
American b. 1929
planographic: (L) $165; (H) $1,424

TINGUELY, Jean
Swiss 1925-1991
intaglio: (L) $1,360; (H) $2,983
stencil: (H) $793
planographic: (L) $550; (H) $2,259
posters: (L) $133; (H) $3,066
mixed-media: (L) $642; (H) $8,030
photo-repro: (L) $362; (H) $2,087

TISCHBEIN, Johann Heinrich Wilhelm
mixed-media: (H) $1,980

TISSOT, James Jacques Joseph
French 1836-1902
intaglio: (L) $221; (H) $15,906
port/books: (H) $5,955

TITEUX, Eugene (after)
French d. 1904
port/books: (H) $121

TITTLE, Walter Ernest
American 1880/83-1960
intaglio: (H) $303

TOBEY, Mark
American 1890-1976
intaglio: (H) $523
planographic: (L) $284; (H) $826
port/books: (L) $1,100; (H) $3,300

TOBIASSE, Theo
Israeli/French b. 1927
stencil: (H) $385
planographic: (L) $165; (H) $858

TODD, Milan
stencil: (H) $174

TOGASHI, M.
intaglio: (H) $25

TOLEDO, Francisco
Mexican b. 1940
intaglio: (L) $248; (H) $2,750
planographic: (H) $990

TOMKINS, Charles and P.W.
intaglio: (H) $116

TOOKER, George
American b. 1920
planographic: (H) $2,200

TORII, Kiyomitsu (I)
1735-85
relief: (H) $242

TORLAKSON, James
American b. 1951
intaglio: (L) $110; (H) $605

TORNERO, Sergio Gonzalez
Chilean b. 1927
intaglio: (H) $50

TORRES-GARCIA, Joaquin
Uruguayan 1874-1949
relief: (H) $2,530
port/books: (H) $2,420

TOTOYA, Hokkei
1780-1850
relief: (H) $176
port/books: (H) $477

TOULOUSE-LAUTREC, Henri de (after)
intaglio: (H) $165
planographic: (L) $132; (H) $176
port/books: (H) $28
generic: (H) $715

TOULOUSE-LAUTREC, Henri de
French 1864-1901
intaglio: (L) $154; (H) $550
planographic: (L) $176; (H) $416,840
posters: (L) $7,700; (H) $19,048
port/books: (L) $1,941; (H) $49,500

Despite his decadent lifestyle and death at an early age, Henri Toulouse-Lautrec (1864-1901) produced some 735 paintings, 275 watercolors, 350 graphic works, and 5,000 drawings and sculptures. His posters extolled Jane Avril, Aristide Bruant, and other stars of the cafe-concert stage of Montmarte. The posters' simplified forms and bold flat areas of brilliant color owe much to the Japanese woodblock prints fashionable at the time. (Henri Toulouse-Lautrec, *Jane Avril*, lithograph printed in colors and Japan backed, first state of three, 48 ¾ x 35 ¾ inches, Butterfield, June 10, 1992,$49,500)

TOULOUSE-LAUTREC, Henri de and Henri Gabriel IBELS
1864-1901
port/books: (H) $3,169

TOULOUSE-LAUTREC CIRCLE,
Publisher
port/books: (H) $681

TOUSSAINT, Fernand
posters: (H) $165

TOWN, Harold Barling
planographic: (H) $484
posters: (H) $122
mixed-media: (H) $1,164

TOYOKUNI
relief: (L) $72; (H) $121

TOYOKUNI, (III)
Japanese 1786-1864
relief: (L) $66; (H) $132
generic: (H) $203

TOYOKUNI, (I)
Japanese
relief: (L) $88; (H) $495

TOYOKUNI, Kochoro
relief: (H) $88

TOYOKUNI, Nidai
relief: (H) $66

TOYOKUNI, Utagawa
Japanese 1769-1825
relief: (L) $73; (H) $776

TRACY, John M.
American 1844-1893
planographic: (H) $495

TRAGER, Philip
photo: (H) $320

TRAILL, Jessie Constance Alicia
intaglio: (H) $957

TRAMPEDACH, Kurt
planographic: (H) $132

TRAVIS, Dave Lee
photo: (H) $134

TRAVIS, Paul Bough
American b. 1891
planographic: (L) $110; (H) $220

TREMOIS, P.Y.
French b. 1921
intaglio: (L) $139; (H) $363

TRENTO, Antonio da
relief: (L) $1,150; (H) $2,750

TRETCHIKOFF, (after)
generic: (H) $22

TREU, Martin
ac. 1540-1543
intaglio: (H) $231
port/books: (H) $174

TREVELYAN, Julian
intaglio: (L) $328; (H) $357

TREW, Christoph Jakob
port/books: (H) $22,000

TRIER, Hann
German b. 1915
planographic: (H) $355
mixed-media: (H) $577

TRIPE, Capt. Linnaeus
1822-1902
photo: (H) $765

TRIPLEX, Werbeserv.
posters: (H) $41

TRIPP, Jan Peter
German b. 1945
intaglio: (L) $66; (H) $176

TRISTAN, Tzara
port/books: (H) $14,300

TROEDEL, Charles
planographic: (L) $609; (H) $1,740

TROEDEL and CO., Charles
planographic: (H) $174

TROVA, Ernest
American b. 1927
stencil: (L) $92; (H) $143
planographic: (H) $121

TRUE, David
American b. 1942
intaglio: (L) $660; (H) $1,650

TRUMBELL, (after)
intaglio: (H) $22

TRUSLEW, N.
intaglio: (H) $390

TSCHACBASOV, Nahum
American b. 1899
port/books: (H) $1,210

TSCHUDI, Lili
b. 1901
relief: (L) $522; (H) $2,779

TUCKERMAN, Jane
photo: (H) $350

TUNNICLIFFE, Charles Frederick
English b. 1901
intaglio: (L) $166; (H) $520

TUPKE-GRANDE, Helene
German 19/20th cent.
relief: (H) $413

TURNBULL
intaglio: (H) $28

TURNER, A.D.
planographic: (H) $198

TURNER, F.C. (after Richard Gilson
Reeves)
British 19th cent.
port/books: (H) $550

TURNER, Francis Calcraft (after)
intaglio: (L) $193; (H) $639

TURNER, J.M.W. (after)
intaglio: (H) $333
port/books: (L) $259; (H) $309

TURNER, Pete
photo: (H) $400

TURPIN, Pierre Jean Francois (after)
French 1775-1840
port/books: (H) $187

TURRELL, James
b. 1943
intaglio: (H) $1,980
port/books: (H) $5,500

TWACHTMAN, John Henry
American 1853-1902
intaglio: (H) $385

TWOMBLY, Cy
American b. 1929
planographic: (L) $1,100; (H) $3,025
posters: (H) $284
mixed-media: (H) $2,200
port/books: (L) $5,500; (H) $10,456

TYSON, Dorsey Potter
intaglio: (H) $241

TYTGAT, Edgard
Flemish 1879-1957
port/books: (H) $2,020

U.S. ARMY SIGNAL CORPS
photo: (H) $3,850

UBAC, Raoul
Belgian b. 1910
planographic: (L) $139; (H) $199
port/books: (H) $1,193

UBEDA, Augustin
French b. 1925
planographic: (H) $55

UECKER, Gunter
b. 1930
planographic: (H) $269

UELSMANN, Jerry
American b. 1934
photo: (L) $1,100; (H) $1,500

UGHI, Ludovico
ac. c. 1750
intaglio: (L) $2,256; (H) $13,945

UHL, Joseph
port/books: (H) $1,100

UHLENHUTH, Professor E.
port/books: (H) $1,179

ULMANN, Doris
1882-1934
photo: (L) $1,100; (H) $1,210

ULRICHS, Timm
German b. 1940
stencil: (H) $496

UMBDENSTOCK, G.
posters: (H) $1,430

UMBO
German 1902-1980
photo: (L) $358; (H) $2,750

UNDERHILL, Irving
photo: (H) $302

UNDERWOOD, Leon
port/books: (L) $503; (H) $580

UNDERWOOD and UNDERWOOD
port/books: (H) $825

URAY, Ch.
posters: (H) $357

URSULA, (Schultze-Bluhm)
b. 1921
intaglio: (H) $156

URUSHIBARA, Yoshijuro
Japanese 1880-1953
relief: (L) $77; (H) $460

UTAGAWA, Kunisato
Japanese School 1786-1964
relief: (H) $234

UTAMARO
relief: (H) $83

UTAMARO, Kitagawa
1753-1806
relief: (H) $1,543

UTRILLO, Maurice
French 1883-1955
planographic: (L) $83; (H) $6,600

UZILEVSKY, Marcus
b. 1937
stencil: (H) $83

VACHON, John
photo: (H) $247

VAILLANT, Wallerant
1623-1677
intaglio: (H) $1,649

VALADON, Suzanne
French 1865-1938
intaglio: (L) $1,100; (H) $2,200

VALENTE, Alfredo
1899-1973
photo: (L) $1,650; (H) $1,760

VALENTI, Italo
b. 1912
intaglio: (H) $381
planographic: (H) $662

VALENTINE, D.T.
port/books: (L) $275; (H) $275

VALLARDI, Antonio
Italy
intaglio: (H) $994

VALLEE, Armand
b. 1921
stencil: (H) $92

VALLET, Louis (after)
French b. 1856
port/books: (H) $99

VALLOTTON, Felix
Swiss 1865-1925
relief: (L) $1,048; (H) $7,540
port/books: (L) $1,650; (H) $5,159

VALTAT, Louis
French 1869-1952
planographic: (H) $161

VAN DER LAAN, Kees
posters: (H) $660

VAN DER ZEE, James
1886-1983
photo: (L) $385; (H) $1,540

VAN DYKE, (after)
19th cent.
intaglio: (H) $61

VAN DYKE, Willard
photo: (L) $1,100; (H) $1,210

VAN LOO, C. (after)
intaglio: (H) $240

VAN RIEL, Frons
photo: (H) $440

VAN SWART, Jan
relief: (H) $367

VAN VECHTEN, Carl
photo: (L) $247; (H) $825

VANDERBILT, Gloria
American 20th cent.
planographic: (H) $110
generic: (H) $250

VANDROUS, John C.
American b. 1884
intaglio: (H) $39

VANNI, Francesco
Italian 1563-1610
relief: (H) $7,109

VARIAN, George
posters: (H) $110

VARIN, Ràoul
French 20th cent.
intaglio: (L) $121; (H) $935

VASARELY, Victor
French b. Hungary 1908
stencil: (L) $110; (H) $1,320
planographic: (L) $165; (H) $3,308
posters: (H) $41
port/books: (L) $165; (H) $7,092

VASI, Giuseppe
1710-1782
port/books: (L) $1,193; (H) $9,649

VEBER, Jean
planographic: (L) $20; (H) $64

VECHTEN, Carl van
1880-1964
photo: (L) $550; (H) $1,045

VEDOVA, Emilio
planographic: (L) $378; (H) $756

VELDE, Bram van
Dutch 1895-after 1980
planographic: (L) $95; (H) $1,035
posters: (H) $204

VELDE, Jan van de (II)
1593-1641
intaglio: (H) $199
port/books: (L) $1,128; (H) $8,639

VELDHOEN, Aad
port/books: (H) $474

VELONIS, Anthony
stencil: (H) $358

VENET, Bernar
planographic: (H) $613

VENEZIANO, Agostino
1490-1536
intaglio: (H) $19,906

VENTOUILLAC, Guy
posters: (H) $220

VENTURINI, Giovanni F.
1650-1710
intaglio: (H) $194

VERFIEUX, E.
relief: (H) $660

VERICO, Antonio
Italian b.c. 1775
intaglio: (H) $248

VERKOLJE, Nicholas
1673-1746
intaglio: (H) $754

VERNER, Elizabeth O'Neil
intaglio: (H) $220

VERNET, Antoine Charles Horace
(called Carle)
French 1758-1836
intaglio: (L) $154; (H) $207
planographic: (H) $100

VERNET, C. (after)
intaglio: (H) $825
planographic: (H) $193

VERNET, Claude Joseph (after)
port/books: (H) $17,431

VERNET, J. (after)
intaglio: (L) $139; (H) $182

VERNEUIL, M.P.
port/books: (H) $318

VERNIER, Ch. (after)
planographic: (H) $363

VERNIER, Edmond
posters: (H) $220

VERONESI, Luigi
photo: (L) $982; (H) $1,670

VERTES, Marcel
French 1895-1961
planographic: (L) $33; (H) $131
port/books: (L) $550; (H) $770

VERWEY, Kees
stencil: (H) $228
planographic: (H) $379

VESPIGNANI, Renzo
Italian contemporary
intaglio: (L) $423; (H) $567
planographic: (H) $426

VIC
posters: (H) $330

VICENTE, Eduardo
port/books: (L) $913; (H) $1,141

VICKREY, Robert
American b. 1926
stencil: (L) $440; (H) $935
planographic: (H) $55

VICTORUS, Paul B.
port/books: (H) $176

VIDA
photo: (H) $400

VIDAL, Pierre
planographic: (H) $402

VIEIRA DA SILVA, Maria Helena
French b. 1988
intaglio: (H) $409
planographic: (L) $139; (H) $248

VILLEMOT, Bernard
posters: (L) $275; (H) $550

VILLERET, Francois Etienne
French 1800-1866
planographic: (H) $275

VILLON, J. (after)
intaglio: (L) $160; (H) $299
port/books: (L) $132; (H) $550

VILLON, Jacques
French 1875-1963
intaglio: (L) $80; (H) $52,250
planographic: (L) $174; (H) $1,124
port/books: (L) $941; (H) $4,125

VILLOT, C.
posters: (H) $357

VINCENT, Rene
French 1879-1936
planographic: (H) $385
port/books: (H) $385

VINCKEBOONS, David
Dutch 1576-1629
intaglio: (L) $364; (H) $994

VINCKEBOONS, David (after)
intaglio: (H) $635

VINEA, F.
intaglio: (H) $165

VISAT, Georges (after Marc Chagall)
intaglio: (H) $3,566

VISHNIAC, Roman
photo: (L) $825; (H) $3,025

VISSCHER, Cornelis de
intaglio: (L) $849; (H) $2,893
planographic: (H) $1,446

VISSER, Carel
relief: (H) $177

VLAMINCK, Maurice de
French 1876-1958
intaglio: (L) $90; (H) $715
relief: (L) $1,882; (H) $6,349
planographic: (L) $165; (H) $2,640
port/books: (H) $3,357

VLEUGHELS, N. (after)
1669-1737
port/books: (H) $245

VLIET, Jan Georg van
ac. 1630-1640
intaglio: (L) $492; (H) $5,742

The painter Jacques Villon (1875-1963) was an accomplished graphic artist. As a young man he earned a living making posters and lithographs. By 1903 he had exhibited at the Salon and was able to devote himself to noncommercial art forms. In 1911 he adopted an analytical form of Cubism, demonstrated in this 1913 drypoint of a young woman. (Jacques Villon, *Portrait de Jeune Femme*, drypoint, 21 ⅝ x 16 ⅜ inches, Sotheby-New York, May 14, 1992, $52,250)

VOBECKY, Frantisek
photo: (H) $550

VOET, Alexandre (the younger) (after P.P. Rubens)
intaglio: (H) $378

VOGELER, Heinrich
1872-1942
intaglio: (L) $1,251; (H) $3,198
port/books: (H) $30,043

VOISARD
intaglio: (H) $20

VOLCKAMER, Johann Christoph
17th/18th cent.
port/books: (H) $176

VOLCKAMER, Johann Christoph (after)
port/books: (H) $935

VOLKMANN, Hans Richard von
German 1860-1927
intaglio: (H) $138
planographic: (H) $99

VOLKMAR, Charles
American 1841-1914
intaglio: (H) $303

VOLPATO, Giovanni
1733-1803
intaglio: (L) $913; (H) $1,740
mixed-media: (H) $1,927

VON DEM BUSSCHE, Wolf
port/books: (H) $1,980

VON GLOEDON, Baron Wilhelm
photo: (H) $935

VOSS, Jan
planographic: (H) $296
port/books: (L) $481; (H) $621

VROMAN, Adam Clark
photo: (H) $2,860

VUILLARD, Edouard
French 1868-1940
intaglio: (L) $187; (H) $294
planographic: (L) $653; (H) $18,018

WACHTEL, Marion Kavanagh
American 1876-1954
others: (H) $138

WAGHENAER, Lucas Jansz
intaglio: (H) $538

WAGNER, Catherine
photo: (H) $550

WAGNER, J.
1706-1780
intaglio: (H) $868

WAIN, Louis (after)
planographic: (L) $137; (H) $234
photo-repro: (H) $59

WAKEMAN, David Rice
20th cent.
intaglio: (H) $22

WALCOT, William
English 1874-1943
intaglio: (L) $87; (H) $127
port/books: (H) $132

WALD, Carol
intaglio: (H) $55

WALKER, Ann
intaglio: (H) $11

WALKER, Clay
relief: (H) $66

WALKER, George
port/books: (H) $11,891

WALKER, James
planographic: (H) $248

WALKER, Jeff
mixed-media: (H) $660

WALKER, Lewis Emory (attrib.)
photo: (H) $2,475

WALKER, W.B., Publisher
intaglio: (H) $890

WALKOWITZ, Abraham
American 1880-1965
planographic: (L) $385; (H) $550

WALSH, T.N.H (after)
English 19th cent.
intaglio: (H) $330

WALSON, J.
planographic: (H) $55

WALTER, A.B.
intaglio: (H) $99

WALTHER, Franz Erhard
German b. 1939
planographic: (H) $199
photo: (H) $1,218

WALTNER, (after BURNE-JONES)
generic: (H) $550

WALTON, W.L. (after)
planographic: (H) $2,200

WARD, Charles
intaglio: (H) $5
planographic: (H) $35

WARD, James
intaglio: (H) $2,321
planographic: (H) $1,721

WARD, Lem
generic: (H) $248

WARD, Lem and Steve WARD
generic: (H) $110

WARD, Lyno Kendall
American 20th cent.
relief: (L) $88; (H) $248

WARD, William
1766-1826
intaglio: (H) $1,649

WARE, Issac
port/books: (L) $605; (H) $1,045

WARE, Issac and William KENT
port/books: (H) $660

WARHOL, Andy
American 1928-1987
intaglio: (H) $1,210
stencil: (L) $13; (H) $35,729
relief: (L) $880; (H) $1,375
planographic: (L) $330; (H) $2,248
posters: (L) $461; (H) $682
mixed-media: (H) $1,210
photo-repro: (L) $241; (H) $7,150
port/books: (L) $1,210; (H) $55,000
photo: (H) $4,125
others: (H) $1,045
generic: (L) $495; (H) $1,511

WARHOL, Andy (after)
port/books: (H) $3,776

WARING, J.
port/books: (H) $1,100

WARNECKE, Harry
photo: (H) $1,100

WARNER, Edward
intaglio: (H) $52

WARNER, Robert and Benjamin S.
WILLIAMS
  English 19th/20th cent.
  port/books: (L) $9,900; (H) $13,200

WARNERS
  relief: (H) $130

WARTHEN, Ferol S.
  relief: (H) $1,100

WASHBURN, Brad
  photo: (L) $320; (H) $600

WATERLOO, Anthonie
  Dutch 1609/10-1690
  intaglio: (L) $260; (H) $297
  planographic: (H) $11,501

WATKINS, Carleton E.
  American 1825-1916
  port/books: (H) $605
  photo: (L) $220; (H) $12,100

WATKINS, Francis
  generic: (L) $66; (H) $154

WATSON, Albert
  b. 1942
  photo: (H) $383

WATSON, Charles
  intaglio: (H) $83

WATSON, James
  1740-1790
  intaglio: (L) $1,885; (H) $2,199

WATTEAU, (attrib.)
  intaglio: (H) $35

WATTEAU, A. (after)
  intaglio: (L) $214; (H) $321

WATTEAU, Antoine
  French 1684-1721
  intaglio: (H) $1,178

WATTEAU, Jean Antoine (after)
  French 1684-1721
  intaglio: (H) $248

WATTS, George Frederick (after)
  intaglio: (H) $954

WATTS, L. (after Miss Drake)
  generic: (H) $550

WAWRZONEK, John
  photo: (L) $330; (H) $1,200

WEARY, Allen M.
  intaglio: (H) $165

One of the earliest photographers, Carleton Watkins spent most of his life in California recording spectacular images of Yosemite. He became famous for his technical mastery and his artistry. After he was forced into bankruptcy in 1874, his creditors sold his negatives to his competitor I. Taber. This view of Yosemite, photographed in the 1870s, was printed in 1890 by Taber & Co. A vintage print by Watkins would be more valuable than a later printing by Taber. (Carleton Watkins, *The Yosemite Falls, 2550 Feet, California*, mammoth plate albumen print, Butterfield, May 13, 1992, $495)

WEBB, John Cothe
generic: (H) $66

WEBB, Joseph
intaglio: (H) $358

WEBB, Todd
b. 1905
photo: (L) $275; (H) $935

WEBBER, Wesley
American 1839/41-1914
planographic: (H) $440

WEBER
20th cent.
posters: (H) $74

WEBER, Andreas Paul
German 1893-1980
planographic: (L) $116; (H) $147

WEBER, Bruce
b. 1946
photo: (L) $2,358; (H) $3,929

WEBER, George
b. 1907
stencil: (H) $64

WEBER, Max
American 1881-1961
relief: (L) $330; (H) $2,420

WEBER, Sybilla Wittel
intaglio: (H) $44

WEBSTER, Thomas (after)
intaglio: (H) $194

WEBSTER, Thomas (after)
English 1800-1886
intaglio: (H) $143

WEEGEE
English 1899-1968
photo: (L) $394; (H) $9,350

WEGMAN, William
American b. 1943
photo: (L) $1,430; (H) $16,500

WEIBEL, Jakob Samuel
1771-1846
intaglio: (H) $1,077

WEIDENAAR, Reynold H.
American 1915-1985
intaglio: (L) $121; (H) $350

WEIDENAAR, Reynolds
intaglio: (H) $660

WEIDITZ, Hans (the younger)
relief: (H) $275

WEIGALL, C.H. (after)
port/books: (H) $192

WEIL, Mathilde
photo: (H) $302

WEILER, Milton
generic: (H) $440

WEILUC
posters: (H) $440

WEIROTTER, Franz Edmund
intaglio: (L) $165; (H) $1,292

WEIRTRATTER, F.E.
intaglio: (H) $28

WEISBUCH, Claude
French b. 1928
intaglio: (L) $297; (H) $319
planographic: (L) $347; (H) $501

WELF, Edmund
20th cent.
posters: (H) $66

WELLER, M. Dell
intaglio: (H) $22

WELLING, James
b. 1951
port/books: (H) $3,300

WELLS, Hewitt
port/books: (H) $154

WELLS, W.
intaglio: (H) $66

WELLSTOOD, W. (after J.W. HILL)
American
intaglio: (H) $1,760

WEMAERE, Pierre
planographic: (L) $139; (H) $518

WENCKI, Paul
intaglio: (H) $22

WENGENROTH, Stow
American 1906-1976
planographic: (L) $165; (H) $8,800

WERKMAN, Hendrik Nicolaas
Dutch 1882-1945
mixed-media: (H) $569
others: (H) $12,013

WERNER, Gosta
port/books: (H) $4,670

WESSEL, Henry
photo: (H) $358

WESSELMANN, Tom
American b. 1931
stencil: (L) $1,193; (H) $4,950
mixed-media: (H) $3,025
others: (L) $4,400; (H) $20,900

WEST, Benjamin (after)
intaglio: (L) $83; (H) $209

WEST, Levon
American 1900-1968
intaglio: (L) $44; (H) $522

WESTALL, Richard (after)
intaglio: (H) $610

WESTALL, William (after)
intaglio: (H) $397

WESTERHOUT, Arnold
Flemish 1651-1725
intaglio: (H) $413

WESTON, Brett
b. 1911
photo: (L) $770; (H) $8,800

WESTON, Edward
American 1886-1958
photo: (L) $358; (H) $88,000

WESTON, Edward and Cole
WESTON
photo: (L) $770; (H) $1,540

WESTON, Edward and Brett
WESTON
photo: (L) $1,100; (H) $22,000

WETHERILL, Elisha Kent Kane
American 1874-1929
intaglio: (H) $65

WETLI, Hugo
1916-1972
planographic: (H) $205

WETZEL, T.T. (after)
generic: (H) $44

Omnipresent Weegee (a nickname derived from the Ouija board) was the moniker of street photographer Arthur Fellig. Murders, botched holdups, gangland executions, and society dames were his subjects. (Weegee, *Jazz Club, c. 1950,* silver print, 6 ½ x 8 ½ inches, Swann, October 8, 1991, $1,210)

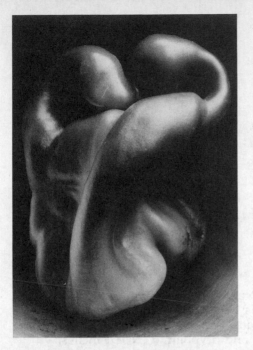

High prices for photographs are only a recent phenomenon. Edward Weston's (1886-1958) best-selling image was *Pepper No. 30, 1930,* but when they were offered in 1932 for two dollars, only twelve copies were sold. *Pepper No. 30, 1930* was one of a series where Weston photographed single objects, both organic forms and artifacts, removed from their ordinary context. The sensuous form of the pepper is evocative of the more than 100 nude studies that Weston produced between 1918 and 1945. In the 1940s, Weston was stricken with Parkinson's disease and depended on his son Brett, a respected photographer, to do his printing. This later printing of *Pepper No. 30, 1930* was done by Brett Weston in 1955. (Edward Weston with Brett Weston, *Pepper No. 30, 1930,* gelatin silver print, 9 ⅜ x 7 ½ inches, Christie-New York, April 15, 1992, $3,300)

WHEATLEY, Francis (after)
intaglio: (L) $83; (H) $545
generic: (L) $88; (H) $121

WHISTLER, (after)
intaglio: (H) $28

WHISTLER, James Abbott McNeill
American 1834-1903
intaglio: (L) $220; (H) $30,800
planographic: (L) $468; (H) $4,950

WHITCOMB, Thomas (after)
intaglio: (H) $221

WHITE, Clarence
photo: (H) $1,980

WHITE, Clarence H. and Alfred STIEGLITZ
American 19th/20th cent.
photo: (H) $55,000

WHITE, Henry
1819-1896
photo: (L) $765; (H) $2,554

WHITE, Minor
American 1908-1976
photo: (L) $880; (H) $27,500

WHITE, Styaken
generic: (H) $80

WHITEFIELD, Edwin
1816-1892
planographic: (H) $220

WHITEFIELD, Edwin (after)
Anglo/American 1816-1892
planographic: (H) $770

WHITEHEAD, Buell
19th/20th cent.
planographic: (H) $55

America-born James Abbott McNeill Whistler spent most of his life working and studying abroad. This 1879 print of an English harbor is marked with his butterfly monogram. (James Abbott McNeill Whistler, *The Adam and Eve, Chelsea*, etching and drypoint, 6 ⅞ x 11 ⅞ inches, Sloan, May 21, 1992, $1,100)

WHITELEY, Brett
intaglio: (H) $435
stencil: (H) $283

WHITESELL, Pop
American 1876-1958
photo: (L) $275; (H) $303

WHITFIELD, Edwin (Charles W. Burton, Lithographer)
Anglo/American 1816-1892
planographic: (H) $715

WHITLEY, Pete
intaglio: (H) $22

WHITTEMORE, Amy
photo: (H) $330

WIDICK, Patti Anne
20th cent.
planographic: (H) $138

WIERIX, Hieronymus
intaglio: (H) $348

WIERIX, Jan
Netherlandish c. 1549-after 1615
intaglio: (H) $61

WIERTZ, Jupp
posters: (H) $132

WILCOX, L.A.
posters: (H) $880

WILD, J.
Swiss 20th cent.
posters: (H) $79

WILDING, Dorothy
1893-1976
photo: (L) $191; (H) $1,817

WILEY, William T.
American b. 1937
planographic: (L) $193; (H) $770

WILHELM, Gottleib Tobias
intaglio: (H) $90

WILIMOVSKY, Charles A.
American b. 1885
relief: (H) $11

WILKE, Ulfert
contemporary
port/books: (H) $1,540

WILKEY, Harry
intaglio: (H) $11

WILKIE, Sir David (after)
intaglio: (H) $147

WILKINS, Gladys Murphy
American b. 1907
relief: (H) $220

WILKINSON, Charles A.
Franco/British b. 1830
relief: (H) $110

WILKINSON, D.
intaglio: (L) $220; (H) $248

WILKINSON, Henry
intaglio: (L) $93; (H) $205

WILLEBRANT, James
stencil: (H) $139

WILLETTE, Adolphe
French 1857-1926
posters: (L) $232; (H) $455

WILLIAMS, Fred
planographic: (L) $174; (H) $414

WILLIAMS, Frederick Ronald
intaglio: (H) $696
planographic: (H) $370

WILLIAMS, Hugh William (after)
intaglio: (H) $64

WILLIAMS, John Scott
American 1897-1976
intaglio: (H) $193

WILLIAMS, T.R.
1825-1871
photo: (L) $306; (H) $3,161

**WILLIAMS and STEVENS and
ACKERMAN and CO.,** Publishers
planographic: (H) $3,520

WILLINGER, Laszlo
photo: (H) $154

WILSON, Alexander
American 1766-1813
intaglio: (L) $55; (H) $385

WILSON, Alexander and Alexander
LAWSON
American 18th/19th cent.
intaglio: (H) $22

WILSON, Charles Banks
American b. 1918
planographic: (L) $55; (H) $248

WILSON, Charles J.A.
Scottish/American 1880-1965
intaglio: (H) $73

WILSON, Robert
contemporary
planographic: (L) $88; (H) $110

WILSON, Ronald York
planographic: (H) $122

WILSON, Sidney E.
British b. 1869
intaglio: (H) $143

WILSON, Sol
Polish/American 1894/96-1974
stencil: (H) $83

WINCHELL, Paul
American 20th cent.
intaglio: (L) $33; (H) $39
planographic: (L) $11; (H) $165

WINKLER, Johann Benedikt (after
David Tennier)
c. 1727-1797
intaglio: (H) $56

WINKLER, John
intaglio: (H) $248

WINKLER, John W.
American 1890-1979
intaglio: (H) $275

WINKLER, John W.
American 20th cent.
intaglio: (H) $110

WINOGRAND, Garry
1928-1984
photo: (L) $1,320; (H) $5,500

WINTERS, Terry
American b. 1949
intaglio: (L) $1,540; (H) $2,750
planographic: (L) $330; (H) $8,25(
port/books: (L) $13,200; (H) $25,3(

WIRSCHING, Otto
1889-1919
port/books: (H) $246

WIRSUM, Karl
American b. 1939
photo-repro: (H) $77

Daguerreotypes are fragile and were usually framed in a case. Although the photographer and sitter may be unknown, many portraits are very appealing to collectors. (Anonymous, *Portrait of Mulatto Woman, 1850s*, sixth-plate daguerreotype, Swann, April 13, 1992, $467)

WIRZ/WYDLER
Swiss 20th cent.
posters: (H) $133

WISCHURA, Gerhard
photo: (H) $430

WITHERILL, Huntington
photo: (L) $330; (H) $468

WITHERSTINE, Donald
relief: (H) $220

WITKIN, Joel Peter
photo: (L) $1,300; (H) $17,600

WITSEN, W.A.
1860-1923
intaglio: (L) $434; (H) $701

WITTE, Karin
intaglio: (H) $667

ʾITTIG, Werner
ᵉlief: (H) $1,694
ᵗt/books: (H) $1,412

ᴄOTT, Marion Post
ᵢcan 1910-1990
ᴸL) $275; (H) $1,210

WOLF, Sylvia
photo: (H) $150

WOLF and RICHTER
planographic: (H) $440

WOLFSON, William
American b. 1894
intaglio: (H) $275
planographic: (L) $165; (H) $1,870

WOLIN, Jeffrey
photo: (H) $300

WOLVECAMP, Theo
stencil: (L) $168; (H) $841

WOOD, C. Haigh (after)
planographic: (H) $48

WOOD, Grant
American 1891-1942
planographic: (L) $660; (H) $6,050

WOOD, John
British 1801-1870
photo: (H) $160

Images of cult figures sell–posters, photographs, memorabilia. Marilyn Monroe, James Dean, Elvis Presley, The Beatles. Hundreds of photographs of Marilyn Monroe are offered for sale each year. Some are informal shots, others are stills from her many movies. This famous 1954 shot of Marilyn Monroe by Garry Winogrand (1928-1984) was a publicity still for the movie *The Seven Year Itch*. (Garry Winogrand, *Marilyn Monroe, The Seven Year Itch*, printed 1980s, gelatin silver print, 15 $\frac{3}{4}$ x 10 $\frac{1}{2}$ inches, Christie-New York, October 13, 1992, $2,420)

WOOD, Robert and James DAWKINS
  port/books: (H) $2,090

WOOD, Thomas Waterman
  American 1823-1903
  intaglio: (L) $66; (H) $193

WOOD, William John
  intaglio: (H) $549

WOODALL, Ronald
  generic: (H) $98

WOODBURY, Charles H.
  American 1864-1940
  intaglio: (L) $28; (H) $358

WOODBURY, Walter Bentley
  1834-1885
  photo: (H) $2,295

WOODHOUSE, Frederick (Jr.)
  planographic: (L) $783; (H) $783

WOODS, J.G.
  posters: (H) $165

WOODVILLE, William
  1752-1805
  intaglio: (H) $33

WOOLCOCK, Marjorie
  relief: (L) $122; (H) $157

WOOLF, Paul J.
  photo: (H) $660

WOOLF, Samuel J.
  American 1880-1948
  planographic: (H) $66

WOOLLETT, William (after Benjamin WEST)
  intaglio: (H) $440

WOOLWARD, Florence H.
  port/books: (H) $10,450

WORLEN, Georg Philipp
  1886-1954
  port/books: (H) $614

WORN, Walter
  1901-1963
  relief: (H) $1,144

WORSEL, Troels
  intaglio: (H) $93
  planographic: (H) $167

Associated American Artists was a New York City gallery and early publisher of prints. The prints were always issued in editions of 250. *Approaching Storm*, printed in 1940, was an AAA print that typified Wood's meticulous, sharply detailed manner. (Grant Wood, *Approaching Storm*, lithograph, 11 7/8 x 8 7/8 inches, Arthur A. James, April 23, 1992, $2,750)

WORTH, Don
b. 1924
photo: (L) $330; (H) $1,210

WORTH, Thomas
planographic: (L) $165; (H) $220

WORTMAN
intaglio: (H) $6

WOTRUBA, Fritz
German 1907-1975
planographic: (H) $171

WOUTERS, Gomar
intaglio: (H) $803

WRIGHT, Orville
photo: (H) $5,280

WRIGHT, Wilbur and John T. DANIELS
photo: (H) $18,700

WUNDERLICH, Paul (Fritz J. Raddat)
planographic: (H) $944

WUNDERLICH, Paul
German b. 1927
planographic: (L) $91; (H) $3,922
photo-repro: (H) $284

WYCK, Thomas
Dutch 1616-1677
intaglio: (H) $82

WYCKAERT, Maurice
planographic: (H) $93

WYETH, Andrew
American b. 1917
planographic: (H) $578
generic: (H) $875

WYETH, N.C.
American 1882-1945
posters: (H) $330

WYLLIE, William Lionel
intaglio: (L) $149; (H) $735
photo-repro: (H) $61

WYSS, Franz Anatol
b. 1940
intaglio: (H) $233

XANTI
posters: (H) $825

YAMAGATA, Hiro
Japanese b. 1932
stencil: (L) $2,200; (H) $2,640

YAMAGUCHI, Jen
intaglio: (H) $688

YAMAWAKI, Iwao
1898-1987
photo: (L) $2,750; (H) $4,620

YARBOROUGH, Rick
intaglio: (H) $275

YATO, Tamotsu (attrib.)
photo: (H) $2,475

YAU, Adrian
intaglio: (L) $880; (H) $880

YAVNO, Max
1921-1985
photo: (L) $440; (H) $4,400

YEVONDE, Madame
1893-1975
photo: (L) $553; (H) $948

YOKOI, Tomoe
Japanese b. 1943
intaglio: (L) $110; (H) $275

YOSHIDA, Hiroshi
Japanese 1876-1950
intaglio: (H) $186
relief: (L) $110; (H) $550

Many collections are built on different themes: the White Mountains, strawberries, WPA prints, the beach, dogs, etc. The Uwe Scheid Collection, "Dogs in Focus," consisted of over 90 dog photographs of every type: big dogs, little dogs, dogs with celebrities, daguerreotypes of dogs, pornographic pictures of dogs with women, and dog protraits by celebrated photographers such as Richard Avedon and William Wegman. When the Uwe Scheid Collection was sold at Christie's in London, it realized 21,186 British pounds ($37,711). (Anonymous, *Portrait of an Alert St. Bernard, 1860s,* halfplate tintype, 5 x 7 inches, Christie-London, May 7, 1992, $316)

YOSHITOSHI
Japanese 19th cent.
relief: (H) $605

YOSHITOSHI
1839-1892
relief: (H) $242

YOUNG, Charles Morris
American b. 1869
intaglio: (H) $83

YOUNG, Jac
intaglio: (H) $413

YRISARRY, Mario
Philippine-Amer. b. 1933
stencil: (H) $33

YUNKERS, Adja
American 20th cent.
intaglio: (H) $165
planographic: (L) $55; (H) $495

ZACK, Leon
French 1892-1980
port/books: (H) $911

ZADAC, Z.A.
Canadian
stencil: (H) $46

ZADKINE, Ossip
Russian/French 1890-1967
intaglio: (H) $130
planographic: (H) $447

ZALCE, Alfredo
planographic: (L) $2,310; (H) $3,300

ZANOTTO, Francesco
port/books: (H) $3,960

ZAO-WOU-KI
Chinese/French b. 1921
intaglio: (L) $41; (H) $1,464
planographic: (L) $182; (H) $1,150

ZBINDEN, Emil
b. 1908
relief: (H) $388

ZELMA, Georgi
photo: (H) $3,300

ZENIUK, Jerry
b. 1954
intaglio: (H) $567

ZETTERBERG, Nils
contemporary
planographic: (H) $795

ZHEHR
American 20th cent.
planographic: (H) $77

ZIEGLER, Johann Christian
c. 1750-1812
intaglio: (L) $422; (H) $774

ZILLE, Heinrich
German 1858/64-1929
planographic: (L) $510; (H) $983
port/books: (H) $1,648

ZILSER, G.
planographic: (H) $165

ZIMBEROFF, Tom
photo: (H) $220

ZOCCHI, Giuseppe (after)
intaglio: (L) $273; (H) $3,555

ZOFFANY, Johann (after)
intaglio: (L) $369; (H) $410

ZORACH, Marguerite Thompson
1888-1968
relief: (H) $2,750

ZORACH, William
Lithuanian/Am. 1887-1966
relief: (L) $605; (H) $2,750

ZORN, Anders
Swedish 1860-1920
intaglio: (L) $55; (H) $6,050

ZSISSLY, (Malvin Marr Albright)
b. 1897
planographic: (H) $88

ZUCCARELLI, Francesco (after)
1702-1788
intaglio: (H) $11,279

ZULOAGA Y ZABALET, Ignacio
(after)
Spanish 1870-1945
intaglio: (H) $55

ZUNIGA, Francisco
Mexican b. Costa Rica 1913
intaglio: (H) $2,090
planographic: (L) $358; (H) $4,950

ZWART, Piet
1885-1977
photo: (L) $275; (H) $1,320

APPENDICES

Appendix A: Museums*

ALABAMA

Birmingham
Birmingham Museum of Art (F)

Huntsville
Huntsville Museum of Art

Montgomery
Montgomery Museum of Fine Arts (F)

Tuscaloosa
University of Alabama, University Art Gallery (F)

ALASKA

Anchorage
Anchorage Museum of History and Art (F)

Fairbanks
Elmer E. Rasmuson Library (F)

Juneau
Alaska State Museum
Alaska State Library (F)

ARIZONA

Phoenix
Heard Art Museum
Phoenix Art Museum (PO) (F)

Tempe
University Art Centers, Arizona State University (F)

Tucson
Center for Creative Photography (F)
Tucson Museum of Art
University of Arizona Museum of Art (F)

ARKANSAS

Little Rock
Arkansas Arts Center (F)

CALIFORNIA

Berkeley
University Art Museum, University of California, Berkeley (F)

Beverly Hills
Academy of Motion Picture Arts and Sciences Library (PO)

La Jolla
La Jolla Museum of Contemporary Art (F)

Long Beach
California State University State Collections (F)

Los Angeles
Los Angeles County Museum of Art (P)
Southwest Museum (F)
U.C.L.A. Grunwald Center for the Graphic Arts (F)
U.C.L.A. University Research Library (F)

Malibu
J. Paul Getty Museum (P)

Monterey
Monterey Peninsula Museum of Art (F)

Oakland
Oakland Museum (F)

Pasadena
Norton Simon Museum of Art (P)
Pasadena Public Library (F)

Sacramento
Crocker Art Museum (P)
California State Library (F)

San Diego
San Diego Museum of Art
Timken Art Gallery

San Francisco
M.H. de Young Memorial Museum
California Palace of the Legion of Honor (P)
San Francisco Museum of Modern Art

San Marino
Huntington Library, Art Collection and Botanical Gardens (P)

---

*Museums or libraries with significant print, poster, or photography collections have been marked with a P (prints), PO (posters), or F (photographs).

Santa Barbara
Santa Barbara Museum of Art (PO)
(F) (P)

Stanford
Stanford University (F)

Stockton
The Haggin Museum

COLORADO

Colorado Springs
Colorado Springs Fine Art Center

Denver
Denver Art Museum
Museum of Western Art

CONNECTICUT

Bridgeport
Housatonic Museum of Art
Bridgeport Public Library Historical
Collections (PO)

Farmington
Hill-Stead Museum

Hartford
Stowe-Day Foundation (F)
Wadsworth Atheneum

Mystic
Mystic Seaport Museum

New Britain
New Britain Museum of American
Art

New Haven
Yale University Art Gallery (F) (P)
Yale Center for British Art (P)

New London
Lyman Allyn Museum

Ridgefield
Aldrich Museum of Contemporary
Art

Stamford
Whitney Museum of American Arts

Storrs
William Benton Museum of Art,
University of Connecticut

DELAWARE

Wilmington
Delaware Art Museum (F)

Winterthur
Winterthur Museum and Gardens

DISTRICT OF COLUMBIA

Washington
Corcoran Gallery of Art (F)
Georgetown University Special
Collections (F)
Hirshhorn Museum and Sculpture
Garden (F)
Library of Congress Prints and
Photograph Division (P0) (F)
National Museum of American Art,
The Smithsonian (P)
National Gallery of Art (P)
National Portrait Gallery (P)
The Phillips Collection
The Smithsonian (F)

FLORIDA

Coral Gables
Lowe Art Museum, University of
Miami
Metropolitan Museum and Art
Centers

Fort Lauderdale
Museum of Art

Jacksonville
Cummer Gallery of Art

Miami Beach
Bass Museum of Art

Orlando
Orlando Museum of Art

St. Petersburg
Museum of Fine Arts

Sarasota
The John and Mable Ringling
Museum of Art (F)

West Palm Beach
Norton Gallery and School of Art

GEORGIA

Albany
Museum of Art

Athens
Georgia Museum of Art, University of Georgia (P)

Atlanta
High Museum of Art (F) (P)

Columbus
Columbus Museum of Arts and Crafts (F)

Savannah
Telfair Academy of Arts and Sciences, Inc.

HAWAII

Honolulu
Contemporary Museum
Honolulu Academy of Arts

IDAHO

Boise
Boise Gallery of Art

ILLINOIS

Champaign
Krannert Art Museum, University of Illinois

Chicago
Art Institute of Chicago (F) (PO) (P)
Exchange National Bank (F)
Museum of Contemporary Art (F)
Terra Art Museum
University of Chicago (F)

INDIANA

Bloomington
Indiana University Art Museum (F) (P)

Evansville
Evansville Museum of Arts and Science

Indianapolis
Indianapolis Museum of Art

Notre Dame
Smite Museum of Art, University of Notre Dame (F)

Terre Haute
Sheldon Swope Art Gallery

IOWA

Cedar Falls
Gallery of Art, University of Northern Iowa

Cedar Rapids
Cedar Rapids Museum of Art (P)

Davenport
Davenport Museum of Art

Des Moines
Des Moines Art Center

Fort Dodge
Blanden Memorial Art Museum

Iowa City
University of Iowa Museum of Art

Mason City
Charles H. MacNider Museum

KANSAS

Lawrence
Spencer Museum of Art, University of Kansas (F) (P)

Topeka
Kansas State Historical Society

Wichita
Edwin A. Ulrich Museum of Art, Wichita State University
Wichita Art Museum

KENTUCKY

Lexington
University of Kentucky Art Museum
University Library (F)

Louisville
J.B. Speed Art Museum

Owensboro
Owensboro Museum of Fine Art

LOUISIANA

Jennings
Zigler Museum

New Orleans
New Orleans Museum of Art (F)

Shreveport
R.W. Norton Art Gallery

MAINE

Brunswick
Bowdoin College Museum of Art
(F)

Orono
University of Maine Art Gallery (F)

Portland
Portland Museum of Art (F)

Rockland
William A. Farnsworth Library and
Art Museum

Waterville
Colby College Museum of Art (F)

MARYLAND

Annapolis
U.S. Naval Academy Museum (P)

Baltimore
Baltimore County Library (F)
Baltimore Museum of Art (F) (PO)
(P)
Walters Art Gallery

MASSACHUSETTS

Andover
Addison Gallery of American Art
(F) (P)

Boston
Boston Athenaeum (F)
Boston Public Library (F) (P)
Boston University Photographic
Resource Center (F)
The Institute of Contemporary Art
Museum of Fine Arts (F) (P)

Science Museum (F)
Isabella Stewart Gardner Museum

Brockton
Brockton Art Museum

Cambridge
Arthur M. Sackler Art Museum
Busch-Reisinger Museum
Fogg Art Museum (F) (P)
Massachusetts Institute of
Technology - Hayden Gallery (F)

Framingham
Danforth Museum

Northhampton
Smith College Museum of Art (F)
(P)

Salem
Peabody Museum of Salem (PO)

Springfield
Museum of Fine Arts

Waltham
Rose Art Museum, Brandeis
University (F)

Wellesley
Wellesley College Museum, Jewett
Art Center (F) (P)

Williamstown
Sterling and Francine Clark Art
Institute (P)

Worcester
Worcester Art Museum (P)
Worcester Antiquarian Society (F)
(P)

MICHIGAN

Ann Arbor
Michigan Historical Collection (F)
University of Michigan Museum of
Art

Detroit
Detroit Institute of Arts (F)

Flint
Flint Institute of Arts (F)

Grand Rapids
Grand Rapids Art Museum

Kalamazoo
Kalamazoo Institute of Arts (F)

MINNESOTA

Duluth
Tweed Museum of Art, University of Minnesota

Minneapolis
Minneapolis Institute of Arts (F) (P)
University Gallery, University of Minnesota (P)
Walker Art Center (F) (PO) (P)

Moorhead
Plains Art Museum

St. Paul
Minnesota Museum of Art

MISSISSIPPI

Laurel
Lauren Rogers Museum of Art

MISSOURI

Kansas City
Nelson-Atkins Museum of Art (F) (P)

St. Louis
Missouri Historical Society (F)
St. Louis Art Museum (F) (P)

Springfield
Springfield Art Museum (F)

MONTANA

Billings
Yellowstone Art Center

Great Falls
C.M. Russell Museum

NEBRASKA

Lincoln
Sheldon Memorial Art Gallery, University of Nebraska Art Gallery (F)

Omaha
Joslyn Art Museum (F) (P)

NEVADA

Las Vegas
Las Vegas Art Museum

NEW HAMPSHIRE

Hanover
Hood Museum of Art, Dartmouth College (PO) (F) (P)

Manchester
Currier Gallery of Art

NEW JERSEY

New Brunswick
Jane Zimmerle Art Museum, Rutgers University (PO) (P)

Newark
Newark Museum (F) (P)
Newark Public Library (P)

Princeton
The Art Museum, Princeton University (F)

Trenton
New Jersey State Museum (F)

NEW MEXICO

Albuquerque
Albuquerque Museum
Jonson Gallery, University of New Mexico (F) (P)

Santa Fe
Museum of Fine Arts, Museum of New Mexico (F)

NEW YORK

Brooklyn
Brooklyn Museum (P)

Buffalo
Albright-Knox Art Gallery (F) (P)

Canajoharie
Canajoharie Library and Art Gallery

Corning
The Rockwell Museum

Elmira
Arnot Art Museum

Glens Falls
Hyde Collection

Huntington
Heckscher Museum

Ithaca
Herbert F. Johnson Museum of Art,
  Cornell University (F) (P)

New York City
The Bronx Museum of the Arts
Cooper-Hewitt Museum (PO) (P)
The Frick Collection (P)
Solomon R. Guggenheim Museum
International Center of
  Photography (F)
Jewish Museum (F)
Life Picture Collection, Time Inc. (F)
Metropolitan Museum of Art (F) (P)
Museum of American Folk Art
Museum of the City of New York
  (PO) (F)
Museum of Modern Art (PO) (F) (P)
New Museum of Contemporary Art
New York Historical Society (F) (P)
New York Public Library (PO) (F)
  (P)
Pierpont Morgan Library (F) (P)
Whitney Museum of American Art
  (F)

Poughkeepsie
Vassar College Art Gallery (F) (P)

Rochester
International Museum of
  Photography at George Eastman
  House (F)
Memorial Art Gallery of the
  University of Rochester

Syracuse
Everson Museum of Art of Syracuse
  and Onondaga County (F)

Utica
Munson-Williams-Proctor Institute,
  Museum of Art (P)

West Point
West Point Museum (PO)

NORTH CAROLINA

Charlotte
Mint Museum of Art (F) (P)

Durham
Duke University Art Museum (F)

Greensboro
Weatherspoon Art Gallery

Raleigh
North Carolina Museum of Art

OHIO

Akron
Akron Art Museum (F)

Cincinnati
Cincinnati Art Museum (F) (P)
Taft Museum

Cleveland
Cleveland Center for
  Contemporary Art
Cleveland Museum of Art (F) (P)

Columbus
Columbus Museum of Art (F)
Wexner Center for the Visual Arts,
  Ohio State University

Dayton
Dayton Art Institute (F)

Oberlin
Allen Memorial Art Museum,
  Oberlin College (F)

Oxford
Miami University Art Museum

Toledo
Toledo Museum of Art (P)

OKLAHOMA

Norman
Museum of Art, University of
  Oklahoma

Oklahoma City
National Cowboy Hall of Fame and
  Western Heritage Center,
  Oklahoma Museum of Art
Oklahoma City Art Museum

Tulsa
Philbrook Museum of Art
Thomas Gilcrease Institute of
American History and Art

OREGON

Eugene
Museum of Art, University of
Oregon (F)

Portland
Oregon Historical Society (F)
Portland Art Museum (F)

PENNSYLVANIA

Bethlehem
Lehigh University Art Galleries

Chadds Ford
Brandywine River Museum

Philadelphia
Barnes Foundation
Institute of Contemporary Art,
University of Pennsylvania
Free Library of Philadelphia (F)
Pennsylvania Academy of the Fine
Arts (P)
Philadelphia Museum of Art (F) (P)

Pittsburgh
Museum of Art, Carnegie Institute
(F) (P)

RHODE ISLAND

Providence
Museum of Art, Rhode Island
School of Design (F) (P)

SOUTH CAROLINA

Charleston
Gibbes Art Gallery

Greenville
Greenville County Museum of Art

Murrells Inlet
Brookgreen Gardens

SOUTH DAKOTA

Brookings
South Dakota Art Museum

TENNESSEE

Chattanooga
Hunter Museum of Art

Knoxville
The Tennessee Valley Authority
Graphics Department

Memphis
Brooks Memorial Art Gallery (P)
Dixon Gallery and Gardens

Nashville
Tennessee Botanical Gardens and
Fine Arts Center, Inc.
Carl Van Vechten Gallery of Fine
Arts, Fisk University (F)
Vanderbilt Art Gallery

TEXAS

Austin
Archer M. Huntington Art Gallery,
University of Texas (P)
Harry Ransom Humanities
Research Center (PO) (F)

Dallas
Dallas Museum of Art

El Paso
El Paso Museum of Art

Fort Worth
Amon Carter Museum (F) (P)
Kimbell Art Museum (P)
Modern Art Museum of Fort Worth

Houston
Contemporary Art Museum
Museum of Fine Arts, Houston (F)

San Antonio
Witte Memorial Museum (F)

UTAH

Provo
B.F. Larsen Gallery
Brigham Young University Art
Museum

Salt Lake City
Utah Museum of Fine Arts,
University of Utah
Utah State Historical Society

Springville
Springville Museum of Art

VERMONT

Bennington
Bennington Museum

Middlebury
Christian A. Johnson Gallery,
   Middlebury College

Shelburne
Shelburne Museum, Inc.

VIRGINIA

Charlottesville
University of Virginia Art Museum

Newport News
Mariners Museum
War Memorial Museum of Virginia
   (PO)

Norfolk
Chrysler Museum

Richmond
Valentine Museum
Virginia Museum of Fine Arts

Williamsburg
Abby Aldrich Rockefeller Folk Art
   Center

WASHINGTON

Pullman
Museum of Art, Washington State
   University

Seattle
Seattle Art Museum (F) (P)
Henry Art Gallery, University of
   Washington

Tacoma
Tacoma Art Museum

WEST VIRGINIA

Huntington
Huntington Museum of Art

WISCONSIN

Madison
Elvehjem Museum of Art,
   University of Wisconsin-Madison
   (F)

Milwaukee
Milwaukee Art Museum

WYOMING

Cody
Buffalo Bill Historical Center, The
   Whitney Gallery of Western
   Art

Laramie
Art Museum, University of
   Wyoming

Rock Springs
Community Fine Arts
Center

Appendix B: Publications*

AMERICAN ARTIST (M)
1515 Broadway
New York, NY 10036

**AMERICAN COLLECTORS
JOURNAL (T)**
P.O. Box 407
Kewanee, IL 61443

AMERICANA (M)
29 West 38th Street
New York, NY 10018

THE ANTIQUE GAZETTE (T)
6949 Charlotte Pike
Suite #106
Nashville, TN 37205

**ANTIQUE MARKET REPORT
(M)**
650 Westdale Drive
Suite #100
Wichita, KS 67209

ANTIQUE MONTHLY (M)
1305 Greensboro Avenue
P.O. Drawer 2
Tuscaloosa, AL 35402

ANTIQUE PRESS (T)
12403 N. Florida Avenue
Tampa, FL 33612

THE ANTIQUE REVIEW
P. O. Box 538
12 E. Stafford Avenue
Worthington, OH 43085

**THE ANTIQUE TRADER
WEEKLY (T)**
P.O. Box 1050
Dubuque, IA 52001

ANTIQUE WEEK (T)
27 N. Jefferson
P.O. Box 90
Knightstown, IN 46168

**ANTIQUES (THE MAGAZINE
ANTIQUES) (M)**
575 Broadway
New York, NY 10012

**ANTIQUES & COLLECTING
HOBBIES(M)**
1006 South Michigan Avenue
Chicago, IL 60605

**ANTIQUES AND THE
ARTS WEEKLY/
THE NEWTOWN BEE (T)**
5 Church Hill Road
Newtown, CT 06470

APERTURE (M)
20 East 23rd Street
New York , NY 10010

ART & ANTIQUES (M)
633 3rd Avenue
New York, NY 10107

ART & AUCTION (M)
250 West 57th Street, Room 215
New York, NY 10017

**THE ART/ANTIQUES
INVESTMENT REPORT (N)**
99 Wall Street
New York, NY 10005

ART IN AMERICA (M)
575 Broadway
New York, NY 10012

ARTFORUM
65 Bleecker Street
New York, NY 10012

ARTNEWS (N)
5 West 37th Street
New York, NY 10018

---

*Key: (J)–Journal; (M)–Magazine; (N)–Newsletter; (T)–Tabloid.

THE ARTNEWSLETTER (N)
5 West 37th Street
New York, NY 10018

ART TODAY (M)
650 Westdale Drive
Wichita, KS 67209

ARTWEEK (T)
12 South First Street
Suite 520
San Jose, CA 95113

COLLECTOR (T)
436 West 4th Street, Ste. 222
Pomona, CA 91768

THE COLLECTOR (T)
Box 158
105 South Buchanan
Heyworth, IL 61745

COLLECTORS JOURNAL (T)
421 First Avenue, Box 601
Vinton, IA 52349

COLLECTOR'S NEWS & THE ANTIQUE REPORTER (T)
P.O. Box 156
506 Second Street
Grundy Center, IA 50638

FINE ART AND AUCTION REVIEW (T)
1683 Chestnut Street
Vancouver, B.C. V6J 4M6
Canada

JOEL SATER'S ANTIQUES AND AUCTION NEWS (T)
P.O. Box 500
Mount Joy, PA 17552

JOURNAL OF NEW ENGLAND PHOTOGRAPHY (T)
Photographic Resource Center
602 Commonwealth Avenue
Boston, MA 02215

JOURNAL OF THE PRINT WORLD (T)
1000 Winona Road
Meredith, N.H. 03253

KOVELS ON ANTIQUES AND COLLECTIBLES (N)
P.O. Box 22200
Beachwood, OH 44122

LEONARD'S ANNUAL PRICE INDEX OF PRINTS, POSTERS AND PHOTOGRAPHS (J)
30 Valentine Park
Newton, MA 02165

LIGHT WORK (M)
316 Waverly Avenue
Syracuse, New York 13244

MAINE ANTIQUE DIGEST (M.A.D.) (T)
P.O. Box 645
71 Main Street
Waldoboro, ME 04572

MASS BAY ANTIQUES (T)
133 Main St.
North Andover, MA 01845

MIDATLANTIC ANTIQUES MAGAZINE (T)
P.O. Box 908
Henderson, NC 27536

NEW ENGLAND ANTIQUES JOURNAL (T)
4 Church Street
Ware, MA 01082

NEW ENGLAND JOURNAL (J)
The Photographic Historical Society
of New England
P.O. Box 189
West Newton, MA 02165

THE NEW YORK ALMANAC (T)
P.O. Box 335
Lawrence, NY 11559

NEW YORK-PENNSYLVANIA COLLECTOR (T)
P. O. Box C
Fishers, NY 14453

THE PHOTOGRAPHIST (J)
Western Photographic Collector's
  Association
P.O. Box 4294
Whittier, CA 90602

THE PRINT COLLECTOR'S NEWSLETTER (N)
119 East 79th Street
New York, NY 10021

PRINT QUARTERLY
80 Carlton Hill
London NW8 OER
England

RENNINGER'S ANTIQUE GUIDE (T)
P.O. Box 495
Lafayette Hill, PA 19444

SOUTHWEST ART (M)
5444 Westheimer, Ste. 1440
Houston, TX 77056

WEST ART (T)
P.O. Box 6868
Auburn, CA 95604

WEST COAST PEDDLER (T)
P.O. Box 5134
Whittier, CA 90607

Appendix C: Auction Houses

AB STOCKHOLM AUKTIONSVERT
Gallerian/T-Baneplanet
Kungstradgarden
Box 16256, 103 25 Stockholm
Sweden

ADER TAJAN
12 rue Favart
75002 Paris
France

ALDERFER AUCTION COMPANY
501 Fairgrounds Road
Hatfield, PA 19440

AUKTIONSHAUS ARNOLD
Bleichstrasse 42
6000 Frankfurt am Main 1
Germany

JAMES R. BAKKER
370 Broadway
Cambridge, MA 02139

BARRIDOFF GALLERIES
Post Office Box 9715
Portland, ME 04101

GALERIE GERDA BASSENGE
Erdenerstrasse 5a
D-1000 Berlin 33
Germany

BONHAM'S
Montpelior Street
Knightsbridge
London SW7 1HH
England

BONHAMS'S CHELSEA
65-69 Lots Road
London SW10 0RN
England

FRANK H. BOOS GALLERY, INC.
420 Enterprise Court
Bloomfield Hills, MI 48302

RICHARD A. BOURNE CO., INC.
Corporation Road-Hyannis, MA
02601
Mail: P.O. Box 141
Hyannis Port, MA 02647

JEFFREY BURCHARD
2528 30th Avenue North
St. Petersburg, FL 33713

BUTTERFIELD & BUTTERFIELD
220 San Bruno Avenue
San Francisco, CA 94103

CAMDEN HOUSE AUCTIONEERS, INC.
427 N. Canon Drive
Beverly Hills, CA 90210

CHRISTIE'S
502 Park Avenue
New York, NY 10022

CHRISTIE'S-AUSTRALIA
298 New South Head Road
Doublebay, Sydney N.S.W. 2028
Australia

CHRISTIE'S EAST
219 East 67th Street
New York, NY 10021

CHRISTIE, MANSON & WOODS LTD.
8 King Street, St. James's
London SW1Y 6QT
England

CHRISTIE'S ROME
114 Piazza Navona
00186 Rome
Italy

CHRISTIE'S SCOTLAND
164-166 Bath Street
Glasgow G2 4TG
Scotland

CLEARING HOUSE AUCTION GALLERIES, INC.
207 Church Street
Wethersfield, CT 06109

GEORGE W. COLE AUCTIONS
187 East Market Street
Rhinebeck, NY 12572

JAMES COX GALLERY
26 Elwyn Lane
Woodstock, NY 12498

EUGENE C. DAYMUDE AUCTIONS
1330 St. Charles Avenue
2nd Floor
New Orleans, LA 70130

DOBIASCHOFSKY AUKTIONEN AG
Monbijoustrasse 30
CH-3001 Berne
Switzerland

DOROTHEUM KUNSTABTEILUNG
Dorotheergasse 17
1010 Vienna-Wein
Austria

DOUGLAS AUCTIONEERS
Route 5
South Deerfield, MA 01373

WILLIAM DOYLE GALLERIES
175 East 87th Street
New York, NY 10128

DU MOUCHELLE ART GALLERIES
409 East Jefferson Avenue
Detroit, MI 48226

PATRICK DUMOUSSET-PATRICK DEBRAUX
105, rue de la Pompe
75116 Paris
France

DUNNING'S AUCTION SERVICE, INC.
P.O. Box 866
755 Church Road
Elgin, IL 60123

FERNANDO DURAN
Substa De Arte
Conde de Aranda, 23
(Semiesquina a Velazquez)
28001 Madrid
Spain

EBERHART AUCTIONEN
Seestrasse 13
8702 Zollikon 2-Zurich
Switzerland

ROBERT C. ELDRED CO., INC.
1483 Route 6A, Box 796
East Dennis, MA 02641

FINARTE CASA D'ASTE S.P.A.
Piazetta Bossi, 4
20121 Milan
Italy

FINARTE S.A.
via Pasteur, 1
6830 Chiasso
Italy

FINARTE CASA D'ASTE
via Margutta 54
Rome 00187
Italy

GALERIE FISCHER LUZERN
6006 Luzern
Haldenstrasse 19
Switzerland

FREEMAN/FINE ARTS CO.
1808 Chestnut Street
Philadelphia, PA 19103

PIERRE-YVES GABUS
Galerie et Administration
rue de la Fontaine 6
CH-2022 Bevaix
Switzerland

GARTH'S AUCTIONS, INC.
2690 Stratford Road, P.O. Box 369
Delaware, OH 43105

GERMANN AUKTIONSHAUS
Zeltweg 67
83032 Zurich
Switzerland

MORTON M. GOLDBERG AUCTION GALLERIES, INC.
547 Baronne Street
New Orleans, LA 70113

GRANIER AUKTIONSHAUS
Welle 9
4800 Bielefeld 1
Postfach 1640
Germany

GROGAN & COMPANY
890 Commonwealth Avenue
Boston, MA 02215

CHARLES E. GUARINO AUCTIONEER
P.O. Box 49, Berry Road
Denmark, ME 04022

HANZEL GALLERIES
1120 South Michigan Avenue
Chicago, IL 60605

HARTUNG & HARTUNG
Karolinenplatz 5a
8000 Munich 2
Germany

HAUSWEDELL & NOLTE
Poesldorfer Weg I
2000 Hamburg 13
Germany

LESLIE HINDMAN AUCTIONEERS
215 West Ohio Street
Chicago, IL 60610

HODGINS ART AUCTIONS LTD.
#100, 437-36th Avenue S.E.
Calgary, Alberta
T2G 1W5 Canada

HOTEL DES ENCANS DE MONTREAL
2825 Bates
Montreal, Quebec
H3S 1B3 Canada

ARTHUR JAMES GALLERY
615 East Atlantic Avenue
Del Ray Beach, FL 33483

LEONARD JOEL
1195 High Street
Armadale, Victoria 3143
Australia

JOYNER FINE ARTS
222 Gerrard Street
Toronto, M5A 2E8
Canada

JAMES D. JULIA
Route 201
Fairfield, ME 04937

KARL & FABER
Amiraplatz 3
8000 Munich 2
Germany

G.A. KEY FINE ART AUCTIONEERS
8 Market Place Aylsham
Norwich, Norfolk NR11 6EH
England

GALERIE KOLLER
Hardturmstrasse 102
8031 Zurich
Switzerland

GALERIE KORNFELD-BERN
Laupenstrasse 41
Postfach 6265
3001 Bern
Switzerland

KUNSTHALLEN KUNSTAAUKTIONER
Gothersgade 9
1123 Kobenhavn K
Copenhagen
Denmark

KUNSTHAUS AM MUSEUM
Carola van Ham
Drususgasse 1-5
Postfach 10 10 64
5000 Koln 1
Germany

BUBB KUYPER
Jansweg 39
2011 KM Haarlem
Netherlands

LAURIN-GUILLOUX-BUFFETAND-TAILLEUR
12, rue Drouot
75009 Paris
France

KUNSTHAUS LEMPERTZ
Neumarkt 3
D 5000 Koln 1
Germany

LITCHFIELD AUCTION GALLERY
P.O. Box 1337
425 Phantom Road
Litchfield, CT 06759

GUY LOUDMER
45, rue Lafayette
75009 Paris
France

LOUISIANA AUCTION EXCHANGE, INC.
2031 Government Street
Baton Rouge, LA 70806

RUDOLF MANGISCH
Muhle Tiefenbrunnen
Seefeldstrasse, 233
8008 Zurich
Switzerland

MAYNARD'S ANTIQUES & FINE ARTS
415 West 2nd Avenue
Vancouver, B.C.
V5Y 1E3 Canada

JOHN MORAN AUCTIONEERS
3202 East Foothill Blvd.
Pasadena, CA 91107

MYERS, ANTIQUES & AUCTION GALLERY
1600 4th Street North
St. Petersburg, FL 33704

MYSTIC FINE ARTS
47 Holmes Street
Mystic, CT 06355-2623

NEAL AUCTION COMPANY
4139 Magazine Street
New Orleans, LA 70115

NORTHEAST AUCTIONS
Ronald Bourgeault Auctioneer
694 Lafayette Road
Hampton, NH 03842

NOSTALGIA GALLERIES, LTD.
657 Meachem Avenue
Elmont, NY 11003

AUCTION PHILA SRL
Corso di Porta Romana, 132
20122 Milan
Italy

PHILLIPS, SON AND NEALE
11 New Bond Street
London W1Y 0AS
England

PHOTOGRAPHIC RESOURCE CENTER
602 Commonwealth Avenue
Boston, MA 02215

JEAN-LOUIS PICARD
5, rue Drouot
75009 Paris
France

BRUUN RASMUSSEN KUNSTAUKTIONER
Bredgade 33
1260 Copenhagen K
Denmark

BRIAN RIBA
Riba Auctions, Inc.
P.O. Box 53
Main Street
S. Glastonbury, CT 06073

D & J RITCHIE INC.
Auctioneers and Appraisers
288 King Street East
Toronto, Ontario
M5A 1K4 Canada

HUGO RUEF
Gabelsbergerstrasse 28
D-8000 Munich 2
Germany

C.M. RUSSELL MUSEUM & AUCTION
400 13th Street North
Great Falls, MT 59401

SAVIOA'S AUCTIONS
Route 23
South Cairo, NY 12482

KUNSTAUKTIONSHAUS SCHLOSS AHLDEN
3031 Ahlden/Aller
Germany

SCHOPPMANN & PARTNER
Benrather Strasse 11
4000 Dusseldorf 1
Germany

SELKIRK GALLERIES
4166 Olive Street
St. Louis, MO 63108

SKINNER, INC., AUCTIONEERS
357 Main Street
Bolton, MA 01740

C.G. SLOAN & COMPANY, INC.
4920 Wyaconda Road
North Bethesda, MD 20852

SOTHEBY'S
1334 York Avenue
New York, NY 10021

SOTHEBY'S ARCADE AUCTIONS
1334 York Avenue
New York, NY 10021

SOTHEBY'S AMSTERDAM
Rokin 102
1012 K2 Amsterdam
Netherlands

SOTHEBY'S JAPAN
1334 York Avenue
New York, NY 10021

SOTHEBY'S LONDON
34-35 New Bond Street
London W1A 2AA
England

SOTHEBY'S MONACO
Adresse Postale: B.P. 45
98001 Monaco CEDEX

SOUTH BAY
485 Main Street
East Moriches, Long Island
NY 11940

SWANN GALLERIES
104 East 25th Street
New York, NY 10010

KENNETH VAN BLARCOM
63 Eliot Street
S. Natick, MA 01760

VENATOR & HANSTEIN
Caecilienstrasse 48
5000 Koln 1
Germany

**VILLA GRISEBACH
AUKTIONEN**
Fasanenstrasse 25
D-1000 Berlin 15
Germany

DE VUYST
Kerkstraat 22 54
9160 Lokeren Belgie
Belgium

WAVERLY AUCTIONS INC.
4931 Cordell Avenue
Suite AA
Bethesda, MD 20814

WESCHLER'S
909 East Street, N.W.
Washington, D.C. 20004

WINTER ASSOCIATES
21 Cooke Street
Box 823
Plainville, CT 06062

ARNO WINTERBERG
6900 Heidelbergl
Blumenstrasse 15
Postfach 105927
Germany

**WOLF'S AUCTIONEERS AND
APPRAISERS**
1239 West 6th Street
Cleveland, OH 44113

**YOUNG FINE ARTS GALLERY
INC.**
P.O. Box 313
North Berwick, ME 03906

**SAMUEL YUDKIN &
ASSOCIATES**
2109 Popkin Lane
Alexandria, VA 22307

**AUKTIONSHAUS MICHAEL
ZELLER**
D-8990 Lindau (B)
Bindergasse 7
Postfach 1867
Germany

Appendix D: Indexing Guidelines ─────────────

Guidelines for Listing Artists' Last Names

These fundamental rules are based on the *Anglo-American Cataloguing Rules* revised in 1979 and published by the American Library Association.*

Try to ascertain how the artist signed his name, or the most common listing of the name, before turning to the general rules.

Ex. The famous American cartoonist Al Capp is listed "CAPP, Al," and not by his given name, Alfred Gerald Caplin.

English — Names are listed under the prefix.
Ex. DECAMP, Joseph Rodefer

Dutch — The listing is under the part of the name that follows the prefix unless the prefix is ``ver.''
Ex. GOGH, Vincent van

French — Look under the prefix if it is an article (le, la, les) or a contraction of an article and a preposition (du, des, de le, del).
Ex. LE SIDANER, Henri
If the article and preposition are separate words, look under the part of the name following the preposition.
Ex. LA PAGE, Raymond de

German — If the prefix is an article or a contraction of an article and a preposition, look under the prefix (Am, Aus'm, Vom, Zum, Zur). Otherwise, look under the name following the prefix.
Ex. SCHWIND, Moritz Ludwig von

Italian — Modern names are catalogued under the prefix.
Ex. DEL LUNGO, Isidoro
Medieval names are listed under the name that follows the prefix.
Ex. ROBBIA, Luca della

Spanish — If the prefix is an article only, look under the article.
Ex. LAS HERAS, Manual Antonio
Look for other Spanish names under the part following the prefix (de, del, de las).

Exceptions — There are exceptions to every rule. If you can't find a name where you think it should be, look under the variants.
Ex. MEYER VON BREMEN, George

─────────
*Indexes of names in books published prior to 1979 may not conform to these rules.

Appendix E: Classification Index

For the purpose of this price guide it was necessary to divide all works of art into one of eleven categories. There is some overlap; posters may be lithographs or photomechanical reproductions and for classification purposes refers to size and original use. "Others" is a term we have employed as a catch-all, and "generic" is a term used when the auction house catalog classifies the image as a print.

I—INTAGLIO

aquatint
carborundum
drypoint
electric tooling
engraving
etching
mezzotint
roulette
simultaneous color printing
softground
stipple engraving
sugarlift
zinograph

P—PLANOGRAPHIC

chromolithograph
lithograph
lithotint
monoprint

M—PHOTO-MECHANCAL REPRODUCTION

cliche verre
collotype
heliogravure
photoengraving
photogravure
photolitho
offset lithograph
offset photograph
offset printing

R—RELIEF

cliche verre
collograph
linocut
letter press
metal cut
metal relief
nature print
stipple wood engraving
stone cut
woodcut
wood engraving

PO—POSTERS

lithoposter

PO—PORTFOLIOS/BOOKS

book
sets (more than one)

O—OTHERS

blind print
brochure
embossed
fax
laser print
mixograph
office copier
volchrome

S—STENCIL

screen print
serigraph
silk screen
pochoir

MM—MIXED MEDIA

any mixture of print processes

PH—PHOTOGRAPHS

albumen print
ambrotype
bromoil print
calotype
carbon print
carbro print
cyanotype
daguerreotype
dye transfer
gelatin silver print
photogravure
platinum print
silver bromide print

G—GENERIC

Appendix F: List of Illustrations

Permissions

The author would like to acknowledge the following for use of photographs (works are listed in the order in which they appear in the book):

E & J Ale Paper Sign, courtesy James D. Julia; *Nord Express*, courtesy Fusco & Four Associates; *Rotterdamsche Lloyd, 1930*, courtesy Fusco & Four Associates; *Old Glory Goes Up on Mount Suribachi, Iwo Jima*, courtesy Christie's; *Migrant Mother*, courtesy Swann Galleries; *The Shooting of Lee Harvey Oswald*, courtesy Swann Galleries; *At Lynchburg, Virginia*, courtesy Rona Schneider Collection; *'Tween the Gloamin' and the Mirk, When the Kye Come Hame, 1883*, courtesy Rona Schneider Collection; *The Olive Trees of the Riviera, 1884*, courtesy Rona Schneider Collection; *Rodney's Victory Off Cape St. Vincent, 1780*, courtesy Beverley R. Robinson Collection, U.S. Naval Academy Museum; *Capture of the ``Resistance'' and ``Constance'' by British frigates ``San Florenzo'' and ``La Nymphe,''* courtesy Beverley R. Robinson Collection, U.S. Naval Academy Museum; *Snowy Heron or White Egret*, courtesy William Doyle Galleries; *Raven*, courtesy Christie's; *Cool Forest, 1953*, courtesy Reba and Dave Williams Collection; *Mother and Son*, courtesy Reba and Dave Williams Collection; *Le Suite Vollard*, courtesy Christie's London; *Face à Face*, courtesy Barridoff Galleries; *American Filigree*, courtesy Wolf's Auctioneers and Appraisers; *Three Studies for a Self-Portrait*, courtesy Butterfield and Butterfield; *Cincinnati Street Scene*, courtesy Swann Galleries; *The Train, 1975*, courtesy Weschler's; *Les Jeux de la Poupee (The Doll's Game)*, courtesy Swann Galleries; *The County Election*, courtesy Dunning's Auction Service; *Der Blaue Engel (The Blue Angel)*, courtesy Sotheby–New York; *Sikovsky S-42*, courtesy Butterfield and Butterfield; *Robert E. Lee, 1865*, courtesy Christie's New York; *Y.M.C.A. Locker Rooom*, courtesy Grogan and Company; *American Winter Scenes, Morning*, courtesy Sotheby–New York; *The North American Indian, A Series of 20 Volumes*, courtesy Christie's New York; *Five Paintbrushes 1973*, courtesy Christie's New York; *Adam and Eve*, courtesy Christie's London; *D Train, 1988*, courtesy Christie's New York; *Portrait of Aubrey Beardsley*, courtesy Swann Galleries; *U.S. Grant*, courtesy Swann Galleries; *Church Tower, Portsmouth*, courtesy Young Fine Arts Gallery; *Bildnis E.H. 1917*, courtesy Christie's London; *Young Woman Wearing a Black Hat*, courtesy Frank H. Boos Gallery; *Moon Bridge at Kameido*, courtesy Skinner, Inc., Auctioneers; *Miss America*, courtesy Morton M. Goldberg Auction Galleries; *Jailhouse Rock*, courtesy Camden House; *Chez Mondrian*, courtesy Christie's New York; *King Kong*, courtesy Christie's East; *Circus Performer Balanced on a Ball*, courtesy Skinner, Inc., Auctioneers; *Crying Girl*, courtesy Christie's New York; *Subway Steps, 1930*, courtesy Christie's New York; *L'Execution de Maximilien, 1868*, courtesy Sotheby–New York; *Battle of the Sea Gods: Left Half, 1470s*, courtesy Sotheby–New York; *Calla Lily*, courtesy Christie's New York; *Fabeltier, 1912*, courtesy Christie's New York; *Striptease at New Gotham, 1935*, courtesy Skinner, Inc., Auctioneers; *La Robe d'Organdi, 1922*, courtesy Butterfield and Butterfield; *Wakeby*, courtesy James R. Bakker Galleries; *Grande Natura Morta con la Lampada a Petrolio, 1930*, courtesy Finarte S.A.; *Le Fruit et la Fleur*, courtesy Sotheby–Japan; *Woman in Mirror*, courtesy Butterfield and Butterfield; *Mädchen aud der Brücke*, courtesy Sotheby–New York; *The Breakfast*, courtesy Sotheby–New York; *Picasso, Cannes*, courtesy Christie's New York: *Artist's Rights Today*, courtesy Weschler's; *Head of a Woman, 1946*, courtesy Butterfield and Butterfield; *The Three Trees, 1643*, courtesy Christie's London; *A View of the Obelisk Erected Under Liberty-Tree in Boston on the Rejoicing for the Repeal of the Stamp Act 1766*, courtesy Skinner, Inc., Auctioneers; *Untitled Self Portrait with Mirror, 1980*, courtesy Christie's New York; *Connoisseurs of Prints*, courtesy Sotheby–New York; *Doctors, c. 1950*, courtesy Butterfield and Butterfield; *Waiting*, courtesy Freeman/Fine Arts Co.; *Candy Apples 1987*, courtesy Butterfield and Butterfield; *Jane Avril*, courtesy Butterfield and Butterfield; *Portrait de Jeune Femme*, courtesy Sotheby–New York; *The Yosemite Falls, 2550 Feet, California*, courtesy Butterfield and Butterfield; *Jazz Club, c. 1950*, courtesy Swann Galleries; *Pepper No. 30, 1930*, courtesy Christie's New York; *The Adam and Eve, Chelsea*, courtesy C. G. Sloan & Company, Inc.; *Portrait of Mulatto Woman, 1850s,* courtesy Swann Galleries; *Marilyn Monroe, The Seven Year Itch,* courtesy Christie's New York; *Approaching Storm,* courtesy Arthur A. James Gallery; *Portrait of an Alert St. Bernard, 1860s,* courtesy Christie's London.